Oct 2023 - New ed.

P9-DWH-557

Library
Justice Institute of BC
715 McBride Boulevard
New Westminster, BC V3L 5T4

the

LANGUAGE
of
EMOTIONS

the
LANGUAGE
of
EMOTIONS

Karla McLaren

SOUNDS TRUE
Boulder, Colorado

Sounds True, Inc., Boulder, CO 80306

© 2010 Karla McLaren

SOUNDS TRUE is a trademark of Sounds True, Inc.
All rights reserved. No part of this book may be used or reproduced
in any manner without written permission from the author and publisher.

Cover and book design by Rachael Pierce Murray

Published 2010

Printed in Canada

McLaren, Karla.
    The language of emotions : what your feelings are trying to tell you /
Karla McLaren.
        p. cm.
    Includes bibliographical references and index.
    ISBN 978-1-59179-769-2 (pbk.)

    1. Emotions. 2. Emotions--Psychological aspects. I. Title.
    BF531.M357 2010
    152.4--dc22

                                2009053634

14 13 12 11

Poems ("Beyond") on page 1, ("Wild Girl") on page 9, and ("All Right!") on page 230 by Karla
McLaren © 1997.

Poem ("The Guest House") on page 159 from *The Essential Rumi* by Coleman Barks © 1995
HarperSanFrancisco. Used by permission.

Contents

PART II
Embracing Your Emotions

Preface

ON THE MORNING OF Friday, July 3, 2009, three days before I was due to turn in my first draft of this book, my friend Esmé called to tell me that she couldn't awaken my mother. It was a shock, but I knew what it meant because Mom had been on and off hospice with end-stage renal failure for five years. I told Esmé that I'd be right over, and I grabbed my son, Eli, just in case we had to lift Mom or, I don't know . . . something.

As we drove over to Mom's apartment, I was calm but focused—thinking ahead about whom to call; going through Mom's meds in my mind; seeking possible drug interactions; letting Eli know what we might see; and preparing myself. When we arrived at Mom's twenty minutes later, and I saw my mother's body, gray and motionless in her bed, my own body began to sob—*boom*, as quickly as that. My mind was considering possibilities and ideas, but my body knew what was going on. I dropped immediately into full-on grief, but because I was immersed in this book you're holding, I didn't fight my grief or try to appear pulled together. I trusted my body and my emotions to do what was necessary, and I didn't interfere.

We called doctors, the hospice, and family; we organized food and learned (clumsily) how to care for Mom's comatose body, and I cried throughout the days and nights that followed. I didn't cry ceaselessly, because that's not how grief works; I cried in a kind of responsive rhythm, in waves. I was able to function and cry, sleep, eat, cry, order meds and report to hospice, talk on the phone, cry, organize things, cry, welcome visitors, go home and shower, and cry.

On Saturday night (about twenty hours into her coma), after everyone had watched Fourth of July fireworks from the balcony at Mom's, I was alone with her. I set up some cushions on the floor next to her bed so that I could hear if she needed anything, and I tried to sleep. But I couldn't. I was completely exhausted, but all I could do was cry about the despair and losses in Mom's life, the pileup of estrangements that haunted her, the continually missed opportunities for her to be honest and vulnerable with others. And suddenly, I realized that I couldn't stop crying because I was feeling my mom's grief instead of my own. I couldn't relax, I couldn't stop obsessing about her losses, and I couldn't sleep—which told me that this wasn't *my* grief, because my grief doesn't torment me like that.

So I got up on one elbow and said out loud, "Mom, I've done enough. I'm not going to feel all the grief you refused to feel. You know I love you, but you screwed up! I can't fix it for you, and I need some sleep." My body relaxed, I lay back down, and I rolled over and went to sleep. Not for long, because comatose bodies need a lot of care, but I did sleep. That miserable and alien form of grief never returned, but my own comforting grief did, and I cried and grieved in healthy ways throughout the rest of the long weekend.

Mom died on Monday morning, July 6, and with the help of my sister-in-law Janelle, Mom's hospice nurse, Carmen, and Esmé, we washed and dressed Mom's body. I did Mom's makeup because she came from an age when women didn't go out without their "face" on, and as we waited for the van from the crematorium to arrive, I felt . . . fine. Complete. I didn't need to cry anymore. And this surprised me. I had prepared for her death in my mind for years, and I always saw myself grief-stricken, angry, exhausted, and wanting to be completely alone for weeks or months on end. But I was wrong. My emotions jumped in and totally took care of me.

After a few days of sleeping, I got right back to this book, and I turned it in just two weeks late. I think people were expecting me to fall apart, but I didn't—because I did the falling apart while Mom was dying. I don't have to do it for the rest of my life. That's the astonishing secret that lives inside the emotional realm: If you trust and attend to your emotions, they'll take care of you. If you don't, your life will be pretty miserable, and you'll leave a mess for others to clean up.

Emotions kept me company and protected me on one of the hardest weekends of my life. I am grateful to them and I love them; they're astonishing, powerful, healing, and humorous, and I'm honored to be able to translate their language into something that I hope will help you as much as it helps me. Welcome.

A note before you begin: The work I do occurs in a sacred and private space that does not lend itself to the presentation of case studies or composite histories. In this book, I rely instead upon storytelling, analogies, and personal experiences in order to create a similar kind of sacred space with you.

You are the expert of your own experience—no book, system, ideology, or person should ever be allowed to supplant your own wisdom. If the ideas and practices in this book make sense to you, use them with my blessing. If they don't make sense, ignore them with my blessing. If you're struggling with repetitive anxieties, depressions, panics, rages, or any other emotional state that isn't working for you, it's important to get yourself checked out by your doctor or therapist. There's help for all of us now, and it's good help; therefore, if your chemistry, your heredity, or your past history have created imbalances in your brain or your emotional realm, then by all means, get thee to the doctor. There will definitely be work for you to do with all of your emotions—questions to ask, things to consider— whether you're on medications or not. The important thing is to make sure you're safe, comfortable, and well cared for before you begin. Honor your individuality and your unique emotional makeup, make changes at your own pace (or not at all), and approach this work with due caution and a deep dedication to your own integrity.

Blessings and Peace,
Karla McLaren
December 18, 2009

PART I

Restoring Your Native Language

Beyond sculptures and symphonies,
beyond great works and masterpieces
is the greater, finer art of creating a conscious life.
Genius appears everywhere,
but never so magnificently
as in a life well lived.

1

Introduction

Creating a Conscious Life

How would it feel to set strong boundaries for yourself while simultaneously building close and healthy relationships? Or to have full-time intuitive knowledge about yourself and your surroundings? What could you accomplish if you had an internal compass that unerringly brought you back to your truest path and your deepest self? Or if you had free access to a constant source of energy, rejuvenation, and certainty?

Each of these abilities lives within you right now; they live within your emotions. With the help of your emotions, you can become self-aware and immensely resourceful in your relationships. If you can learn to focus and work honorably with the incredible information inside each of your feeling states, you can become intimately connected to the source of your intelligence, you can hear the deepest parts of yourself, and you can heal your most profound wounds. If you can learn to see your emotions as tools of your deepest awareness, you'll be able to move forward as a whole and functional person. This should be wonderful news, but our culture's deeply conflicted attitudes about emotions make this rather difficult to accept.

Our current understanding of emotion lags far behind our understanding of nearly every other aspect of life. We can chart the universe and split the atom, but we can't seem to understand or manage our natural emotional reactions to provoking situations. We work with nutrition and exercise to increase our energy, but we ignore the richest source of energy we possess—our emotions. We are intellectually brilliant, physically resourceful, spiritually imaginative, but emotionally underdeveloped. This is a shame because emotions contain indispensable vitality that can be channeled toward self-knowledge, interpersonal awareness, and profound healing. Unfortunately, we don't treat them as such. Instead, emotions are categorized, celebrated, vilified, repressed, manipulated, humiliated, adored, and ignored. Rarely, if ever, are they *honored*. Rarely, if ever, are they seen as distinct healing forces.

I am an empath, which means that I'm able to read and understand emotions. You're an empath too—we all are—but I'm aware of this skill, and since early childhood I've learned to see and feel emotions as distinct entities, each with its own voice, character, purpose, and use. The emotions are as real and as distinct to me as colors and shades are to a painter.

Empathic skills aren't unusual; they are normal human attributes present in each of us: they are our nonverbal communication skills. Through empathy, we can hear the meaning behind words, decipher the postures people unconsciously adopt, and understand the emotional states of others. The ability to empathize is now thought to reside in special brain cells called mirror neurons. Mirror neurons were first found in the premotor cortex of macaque monkeys in the 1990s, but they were soon discovered in humans as well. Mirror neurons have become an exciting area of research because they help scientists understand how socializing information is transmitted between primates.[1]

Empathy makes us sensitive and intuitive, but it is a double-edged sword. Empaths can get right to the center of any issue (they often feel what other people refuse to acknowledge), but in a culture that can't figure out what emotions *are*, let alone how to deal with them, strong empathy is a difficult skill to possess. Empaths certainly feel the emotions that are all around us, but awareness of the healing capacities inside those emotions is rare. This is unfortunate, because it is our emotional sensitivity and agility—our empathy—that helps us move forward, understand deeply, and connect with ourselves, other people, our vision, and our purpose. In fact, research by neurologist Antonio Damasio (see his book *Descartes' Error*) has shown that when the emotional brain centers are disconnected from the rational processing centers (through surgery or brain damage), patients are unable to make decisions and, in some cases, are unable to understand other people. Verbal skills and pure rationality may be what make us so smart, but it is our emotions and our empathy that make us brilliant, decisive, and compassionate human beings.

Though empathy is a normal human ability, most of us learn to shut it off or dampen it as we acquire verbal language. Most of us learn, by the age of four or five, to hide, squelch, or camouflage our emotions in social situations. We catch on very quickly to the fact that most people are inauthentic with one another—that they lie about their feelings, leave important words unsaid, and trample unheedingly over each other's obvious emotional cues. Learning to speak is often a process of learning *not* to speak the truth and attaining an uncanny level of pretense in most relationships. Every culture and subculture has a different set of unspoken rules about emotions, but all of them require that specific emotions be camouflaged, overused, or ignored. Most children—empaths one and all—eventually learn to shut down their empathic abilities in order to pilot their way through the social world.

In my life, a serious trauma occurred at the age of three that interfered with my ability to shut down my empathic abilities. I was repeatedly molested at that age, and along with myriad other insults to my psyche, I missed the transition into speech as a central communication device. I separated myself from human culture to the extent that I could, and as a result, I did not join in with the emotional socialization that my peers received. Those of us who don't shut down our empathic skills remain awake (often painfully so) to the undercurrents of emotion all around us. This has been my experience.

My search for emotional understanding has been guided and pushed by my position as an empath. Throughout my life I've searched for information about emotions as specific entities and precise messengers from the instinctual self, but what I've found is that emotions are given very little respect. Much of the information we have about emotions tells us to stop the natural flow of the emotions, or place them into simplistic categories (these emotions are good, and those emotions are bad), all of which mirror that early socialization we receive on which emotions are right, wrong, acceptable, and unacceptable. I searched diligently, but there didn't seem to be an approach to emotions that explained them in enlightened or useful ways.

In my teens, my search led me toward spirituality, metaphysics, and energetic healing. In these ideologies, I found some useful tools to help me manage my empathic skills, but still no functional understanding of the emotions. In many spiritualist or metaphysical belief systems, the body and its ills, the world and its upheavals, the mind and its opinions, and the emotions and their pointed needs are treated as stumbling blocks to be overcome, or as interruptions to be transcended. There is a sad rejection of the richness inherent in all of our faculties and all of our aspects, and I've noticed a fragmentation in most metaphysical teachings. I took what assistance I could from those teachings, but in regard to the emotions, there was very little I could use.

For example, healthy anger acts as the honorable sentry or boundary-holder of the psyche, but most information about anger focuses on the unhealthy expressive states of rage and fury, or the repressive states of resentment, apathy, and depression. Sadness offers life-giving fluidity and rejuvenation, but very few people *welcome* sadness. Most people barely tolerate it. Furthermore, depression isn't a single emotion, but a strangely ingenious constellation of factors that erect a vital stop sign in the psyche. Healthy and properly focused fear is our intuition, without which we would be endangered at all times, but this goes directly against accepted beliefs about fear.

I also see quite clearly that happiness and joy can become dangerous if they are trumpeted as the emotions of choice—as the only emotions any of us should ever feel. I've seen so many people whose lives imploded after they disallowed the protection of anger, the intuition of fear, the rejuvenation of sadness, and the ingenuity of depression in order to feel only joy. In short, throughout my life I've found that what we're taught about emotions is not only wrong, it's often dead wrong.

Because I missed that important early passage of turning off my preverbal empathic skills in deference to the verbal skills of emotional subterfuge, I could not afford to listen to those dangerous ideas. I was surrounded by currents of emotion in every moment, and as such, I knew that our accepted beliefs about emotions were nonsensical. I used my anger to separate myself from the cultural conditioning we all receive about emotions because I knew I couldn't survive or flourish within those conditions. I knew I'd have to find my own way. I also knew I couldn't simply study the emotions intellectually, historically, or psychologically, but that a full-bodied level of research—from the heart, mind, body, and soul—had to be brought to bear on a topic as full-bodied as the emotions. I knew I'd have to become a genius—not at math or physics or anything normally associated with genius, but an *emotional* genius—if I was going to survive as an empath in our mostly nonempathic culture.

This book is the result of my lifelong search for a deep and functional understanding of emotions. Its information and skill set comes not from any particular culture or teaching, but directly from the realm of the emotions themselves. Certainly, I've studied everything I could get my hands on, but I also did something unusual: instead of forcing my language upon the emotions, I listened closely to the emotions and engaged them in an empathic dialogue.

This form of dialogue is not difficult; it's just unusual. Empathic skills allow us to see the world as alive with knowledge and meaning. They help us listen to the meaning underneath words, to understand living things and nature, and to connect emotively with the world around us. Listening to an instrumental piece of music and letting it tell you a story—that's an empathic dialogue. We all know how to do it. I just do it with unusual things like the emotions themselves.

Dialoguing with emotions is not a process in which you name emotions as if they were street signs or manage them as if they were symptoms of disease. This dialogue allows you to dive into all of your emotions in order to understand them at their own deep and primal level; it helps you remove the perceived disability of *having* emotions while it allows you to see your emotions in new and meaningful ways. In short, if you can empathically communicate with your emotions as the specific and brilliant messengers they are, you'll have all the energy and information you need to create a meaningful and conscious life.

Though we've all been trained to categorize and deny our emotions and ignore our empathy, they don't ever go away; they're always available to us. I've found that if we can just pay attention, each of us can access our own empathic skills and access the brilliant information inside each emotion.

HOW TO READ THIS BOOK

This book is laid out in an empathic way, which means that we begin with an exploration of trouble and difficulty—always knowing that the emotions will help us find our way out of the trouble. When we look at things empathically, we drop down underneath the obvious, behind the merely rational, and beneath the surface of what *seems* to be going on. As we learn to listen to our emotions, this empathic approach is absolutely vital because we've all been socialized to use our emotions in ways that make *other* people feel comfortable. However, we haven't learned to use emotions in ways that work.

The chapters in Part I drop us down, step-by-step, into the trouble we've created by treating the emotions as problems. In these early chapters, we work as healthy emotions do: we name the problem, we drop down to its foundation, we find the brilliance in the problem, and then we come back up to the everyday world with more information, more depth, and more skill.

In Part II, each emotion has its own chapter, message, and practice, but you'll see that Part II continually refers you back to the information in Part I—to chapters on proper judgment, the five elements and the seven intelligences, distractions and addictions, and how trauma affects our ability to interpret our emotions skillfully. The language and the wisdom of the emotions live inside you, but there's a little bit of empathic work to do before you can get underneath the socialization that has separated you from them.

2

My Empathic Journey

The Difficult Beginnings of Empathy

WILD GIRL

While I was up in the trees listening to the wind
I heard your mother wish she were childless.
While I was under the hedge listening to the cat
I heard my father long for someone, not his wife.
While I was flat-out on the lawn listening to the clouds
I heard the neighbors lose their hope.
Then, when I was racing on my bike, listening to my ears
I heard the church lie about all of it.
And you thought I wasn't paying attention.
Why is it that outsiders always have insight
But insiders rarely have outsight?

I GREW UP AMONG geniuses and artists in the 1960s. My father was a writer and an amateur inventor, my mother and sister Kimberly were amazingly skilled visual artists, my brothers, Michael and Matthew, were musical composers and trivia kings, my brother Matthew was a math and language prodigy, and my sister Jennifer was a genius at training animals. At that time, society saw genius as a merely intellectual quality, but in the oasis of our home, intellectual, linguistic, musical, mathematical, and artistic genius had equal value. My brothers and sisters and I grew up immersed in art and wordplay, in math and painting, in trivia and logic, and in movies, music, and comedy. Our family always had a comfortable relationship with the idea of "genius." Most of us were intellectual geniuses (as measured by the Standford-Binet IQ test), but through my mother's influence, we also worked toward artistic genius, musical genius, genius with animals, genius with cooking—you name it. We commandeered the idea of genius and used it wherever and however we liked.

We laughed about my dad's snoring genius, my mom's forgetfulness genius, and Jennifer's genius at making up bizarre new punch lines to jokes we all thought we knew. My brothers invented a silly phrase— "emotional genius"—and it always made us laugh. None of us could envision an emotional person—a sloppy, weeping, raging, fearful person—as a genius. The two words seemed to fight each other in the most ridiculous way, which is why I came back to them throughout my life. Was it possible, I wondered, for people to be as brilliant in their emotional lives as they were in their intellectual and artistic lives? Could people ever learn to move beyond the polarized modes of repression or expression of emotion and into a life-expanding understanding of the function of emotion itself? Questions like these have always fascinated me.

In the third year of my life, everything changed. Along with my younger sister and many of the girls in our neighborhood, I was repeatedly molested by the father of the family that lived across the street. That experience threw me headlong into categories of genius my family would never have wanted to consider and certainly would never have wished upon their toddler daughters. That experience also threw me headlong into the tumultuous realm of fierce emotions and uncontrolled empathy.

(A note for sensitive people: empathy makes me deeply aware of the way words and images affect us. Though I will recount dark moments and I will describe fierce emotions, I won't relate graphic accounts of the traumas I or others have experienced. I will be very careful with your sensibilities, because there is no reason—there is no excuse—to traumatize you with stories of horror. I will maintain my privacy and respect your dignity by telling my stories in a gentle and nonspecific manner.)

At the time when most children are beginning to back away from their empathic skills in deference to the more accepted (and safer) realm of spoken language, I was brought into full-body contact with human evil. Instead of moving further away from my nonverbal skills as children normally do, I moved further into them in response to the assaults. The path of my development shifted in startling ways; language (along with many other things) became very troublesome for me. I developed a stutter, forgot simple words, and became mildly dyslexic and very hyperactive. I began to rely on empathy when words failed or when I couldn't understand people, but this reliance created terrible upheavals around and inside me.

Through my empathic ability, I was able to feel what others were feeling, whether they wanted me to or not. I knew when my family members were fighting or lying, even when no one else could tell. I knew when other kids didn't like me, and why. I knew when teachers didn't know their subject matter and when principals didn't like children. I also knew when my molester was on the prowl: I was able to steer clear of him or choose to enter his house so the younger girls wouldn't be attacked that day. I picked up far too much information, but I had no coherent or acceptable way to bring it out into the open. Most people can hardly bear hearing the truth from a close adult friend; almost no one wants to hear the truth from a child. I learned that the hard way. I could sense the real feelings underneath the social masks and react to the truth of whatever situation I witnessed. I would blurt out the true (but unwanted) words, point to the actual situation under the social banter, find the absurdity beneath the seeming normality— in short, I stirred up everything and everyone around me.

Though my family didn't discover the molestation for two long years, they did protect me in some ways. They treated my unusual skills and deficits as valid parts of my individual nature. Though tests and medications were urged, my family shielded me from the further indignities of pharmaceutical and psychological typecasting. (Unlike the present day, when there is tremendous help for abused, learning disabled, and hyperactive children, the 1960s were a wasteland.) With my family's support, I was able to grow as an iconoclastic and unusual child in a family full of outsiders. There, in that realm of art and genius, I was surrounded by music and culture, comedy and drama, and plenty of love. I was able to channel many of my feelings into art or music, I was able to let my imagination soar, and I was able to talk in some measure about the things I saw and felt.

I did try to fit in with the gang of kids in my neighborhood, but I wasn't very skilled at dealing with people. I was too honest and too strange. I always talked about things no one wanted to discuss (like why their parents pretended not to hate each other, or why they lied to our teacher about their homework, or why they wouldn't admit they were crushed when someone insulted them), I had serious control issues, and I had a hair-trigger temper. I ended up spending much of my early childhood with animals because they were easier to be with. I didn't have to hide my empathic skills—I didn't have to pretend not to see or understand my furry friends. Domesticated animals love to be seen and understood, and they love to be in close relationships with people. Most important, animals don't lie about their feelings, so they didn't require me to lie about my own. I didn't need to be in control of my animal friends because they were in control of their own behavior. It was a tremendous relief. I had found my people; it didn't matter that they were clothed in cat or dog suits. I even found a guardian angel.

During the turbulent years of the molestations, my mother would send me out each morning—stuttering and agitated—to play in the front yard, but she didn't yet know that our yard was in direct line of sight to my molester's house. I took to watering the lawn with the fear and nausea I felt when I was in our front yard. I'd grasp the hose tightly, stick out my tongue, bug out my eyes a little, and shake all over as the water poured out and nearly drowned the lawn. My family and other kids would laugh (in fairness, I did look ridiculous), which isolated me even more. After a few days of this, a long-haired tangerine tabby cat named Tommy Tiger poked his nose through our hedge. To the great relief of our lawn, my morning watering ended, and my relationship with Tommy began.

Tommy was an absolute original—wise and self-assured, but willing to be silly; fierce and protective, but infinitely patient and gentle with me. I've known many excellent cats since then, but never anyone like Tommy. He was my protector, my teacher, and my closest friend. He made everything safe; he chased away bad dogs and eased bad memories. Tommy and I curled up on the lawn each morning, and I'd whisper all my secrets—all of them—into his silky orange fur, and because I spent so much time with him, I began to see the world through his eyes. I could feel his full-body experience of lounging on a soft lawn in a puddle of sunshine, I learned exactly where to pet him for the best purrs, and I understood the angry growl that came from the pit of his stomach when he had to guard his territory against the numbskull neighborhood dogs who had no manners. I don't remember when I stopped whispering to Tommy, but soon I was happy just to lie there with him in a silence that was filled with honest emotions. Communicating with him in this way was a massive improvement on (ugh) spoken language.

When I was with Tommy, I had the security and quiet I needed to think about humans and their bizarre behaviors. I'd think about people being terrible, and then an emotional picture would come into my mind to warn me about the danger of not trusting anyone. I'd think about my parents' and siblings' constant, noisy busyness—no one had time for me—and then I'd see fleeting images of their fatigue and despair and anxiety. Lying there with Tommy, I began to learn how to empathize with humans once again. With Tommy's help, I was able to survive that time. Those years were wrenchingly painful and often terrifying, yet I have come to regard them as a profound blessing. My wounding took me out of the normal world and gave me the opportunity to view humankind and human interactions in a unique way.

INITIATION

The author and mythologist Michael Meade has said in lectures that sexual assault is an initiation—done at the wrong time, in the wrong way, by the wrong person, with the wrong intent—but nevertheless, it is an initiation; it's a separation from the regular world, and a wounding that changes the initiate forever. My childhood ended in a split second, and I aged a thousand years in one afternoon. I learned by the age of three about brutality and weakness, about love and horror, about anger and forgiveness, and about the kinds of monsters people create out of their own unlived emotions. I saw the ugliest parts of human nature, but I had Tommy and my other animals, my art and music, my family, and my empathic skills to rely upon during all of it. My initiation into the heart of human evil did not end, as so many similar stories do, in drug addiction, insanity, illness, imprisonment, or suicide. No, my initiation dropped me into the underbelly of the human soul, where I learned to understand desperate torment—and strangely enough, heartbreaking beauty—firsthand. My empathic skills, instead of driving me crazy, helped me pilot my way through my childhood.

Though I've learned to work with them, let me state emphatically that my empathic skills weren't any kind of gift at first. Had I been given a choice, I would have asked to be *far* less sensitive, *far* less empathic. However, I didn't have a choice, because those repeated assaults removed any functional boundaries or sense of safety that I had. I lost my sense of self; I lost the "skin" most people have around their psyches. I lost many normal skills, and I was dangerously open to the commotion and clamor of the world, which is why the protection of anger was so necessary for me. The tantrums I had throughout childhood were not only a signal that something damaging had occurred, they were also a stopgap way to create an emergency boundary around my dangerously exposed little self.

In short, my empathic aptitude was an ingenious survival response. I see now that my empathy came forward protectively in response to the trauma, but before I learned to work with my empathic skills, they were not protective at all. I endured full-blown, full-body contact with others that made me see and feel their emotions as if they were real, physical things. My own and other people's emotions would often knock me down. You may have experienced something like this yourself.

Certainly, your own emotions have enveloped you, startled you, embarrassed you, strengthened you, or hit you like a ton of bricks. If you're sensitive to nonverbal cues and body language, other people's emotions, even hidden ones, may have affected you in the same way. We all know what it's like to be near an angry parent, a depressed friend, an excited child, or a frightened animal—the feelings of others *can* travel. Of course, much of the effect other people's emotions have on us comes from our ability to act out other people's pain or joy because we've experienced it ourselves. That's a perfectly logical explanation, but many of us have picked up the emotions of others even when no facial or social cues have been present. We see and feel the emotions as if they're our own.

There was no help for me. Emotional imbalances such as the ones I exhibited were called hyperactivity, brain damage, or whatever else, none of which were curable or explainable. No one thought to ask why I had so many emo-tions flying through me so much of the time. One neurologist saw that I had no social or sensory filters, but couldn't offer any advice beyond suggesting that I spend time alone in darkened rooms. Of course, Ritalin was urged, but my mother said a strong "No!" to that. Her sense was that if I had that much energy, I must *need* that much energy, and instead of drugging it away, I should learn to deal with and marshal it. She was probably right in the long run, but being hyper made my school years (and most of my childhood) a sort of waking nightmare. I saw so much, I heard so much, and I felt so many people's feelings—I was just on fire most of the time. I tried to process all the emotional content, but I worked almost completely in the dark because I didn't know how to explain my perceptions to others. I didn't know how to tell people that their unlived and dishonored emotions were affecting *me*. In that time, as in this one, emotions were not seen as real things.

But emotions *are* real. Emotions carry distinct and diverse messages that can be distinguished with absolute certainty—I knew that beyond doubt. The emotions were completely distinct and obvious to me—yet I found support nowhere, I found information nowhere, and I was com-pletely alone (with humans, anyway) in my perceptions. I realized early on that my relationship with emotions could not be solved in the everyday world. My solutions would have to come from another place altogether.

AN UNUSUAL DEFENSE MECHANISM

During my years as a molestation victim, I learned how to dissociate—to leave my body and take my awareness away from the abuses that were vis-ited upon me. I learned to send my imagination and attention away from what was occurring in the room. Many accident or trauma victims report a similar sense of dissociation during their ordeals, perhaps a floating feeling or a sense of being numbed or removed from the ordeal in some way. It's a very natural thing—a protective neural response—to dissociate in response to overwhelming stimuli, but when the overwhelming stimulus is repeated, dissociation can become a repetitive act that ensures survival. Dissociation, which is often a child's only defense, therefore becomes a dependable and comforting escape route. Many repeatedly traumatized children become masters of dissociation and imaginative travel.

In many cases, survivors of repeated trauma learn to use dissociation not just as a survival skill, but as a life skill, as a powerful stress reliever in many situations. For me, dissociation wasn't just an emergency survival tool; it was a great reliever and moderator of my empathic skills. I learned to simply disconnect when too many unlived emotions were oozing from the people around me. When I could no longer function in social situations, I created a form of privacy by leaving my body and my life far behind. In fact, I remember almost none of my childhood. Even into my high school years and beyond, I have only sketchy and incomplete memories. I really wasn't there.

I don't want you to think that dissociation is some special or frightening skill. It's not at all. We all jump in and out of our focused awareness every day. Daydreaming is a common dissociative experience, and repetitive tasks like driving can send you into dissociation, too. Have you ever gotten home, or arrived at work, with no memory of making turns or changing lanes? Your body skillfully drove the car and shifted gears, but your attention was someplace else. That's what it's like to be dissociated and out of your body. Dissociation is perfectly mundane. It's simply a condition where your bodily instincts take over, and your mind goes off on a tangent for a while—it's no big deal. However, for many traumatized people, the tangent goes on and on. There's very little connection to life in the everyday world. Dissociated people live in the future, in the past, and in fantasy. They have a hard time getting down to earth. They may be functional and brilliant, they may run corporations (they're not helpless), but major portions of their selves remain untouchable and impervious to the world around them.

When I dissociated, I could leave this world of suffering. Nothing could hurt me, and no one could find me, because I was gone. In those blissful times, I felt a sense of lightness and peace, and I met angels and guides who lived in an alternate, deeply meaningful spiritual world just beside this one. Many trauma survivors feel nothing but blankness in their dissociative episodes, but I had a definite sense of stepping into a real and separate place. Perhaps my empathic abilities, which helped me to see under the surface of regular life, also helped me create another reality in the altered state of dissociation. Through my empathic and dissociative abilities, I learned to live with a foot in both worlds: the world of my everyday in-body life—family, school, eating, and all that—and the world of my floating, energetic, visionary, out-of-body life. While I still related somewhat to the oasis of my family, the repeated assaults—and the fact that no one rescued me—taught me that human beings were pretty much a waste of oxygen. I stayed out of my life and out of this world a great deal of the time. I became an observer of human beings. I wasn't one of them.

ANIMAL GIRL

Though most of the kids in the neighborhood didn't understand me, they did find a way for me to fit in, bless their hearts. I became known as the animal girl—the one who could go up to fierce dogs and pet them. By the age of seven, I had learned to use my empathic skills to calm and comfort injured animals, so I became a kind of neighborhood triage veterinarian. The kids would bring disoriented birds, mauled cats, or sick puppies to me, and I'd try to figure out what was wrong. Often, when I'd touch traumatized animals, I got the sense that their emotional selves were faint and faraway; there would be a whisper of a feeling, but that was all. My sense was that their selves weren't really near their injured bodies. I knew about that!

With the help of these animals, I began to learn what the dissociative out-of-body state was all about—for them and for me. In that atmosphere of being needed, I was able to reassociate and stay focused in my body, and I was able to create an atmosphere of calm and quiet for the animal. I'd take the fierce, hyperactive energy that was always available to me, and turn it into heat and stillness. I'd emanate heat from my hands or from my torso and sort of envelop the animal's body in that heat. I'd create a container for the animal's severed self, a quiet, warm, and welcoming place to return to.

At first, many of the injured animals just took a deep, slow breath and died. I thought I'd killed them, but my mom pointed out that they were dying already, and that I'd created a safe and peaceful place for them to do so. I learned to be quieter and more still and to let the living or the dying happen on its own. I learned that the only thing up to me was the creation of the atmosphere. If the animals were going to come back,

LIBRARY

17

they would often startle into consciousness and then shake, tremble, kick, and jerk back to life. It didn't take very long for them to return, but the process of coming back from trauma to a fully in-body life was always dramatic and emotive. I learned to be calm and patient and to wait until the animals came back before I did anything about their injuries. When the animals had reassociated, I could dress their wounds or create a sickbed and begin the convalescence. I watched the process at that age—I understood it at that age—but I couldn't yet translate it into my own dissociated state and my own traumatic injuries. That would come later.

THE METAPHYSICAL PORTION OF THE JOURNEY

When I was ten years old, my mother became quite ill with arthritic symptoms and was headed for a wheelchair. Conventional medicine of the day could do nothing but chart her symptoms and offer ineffectual drugs, so she refocused her search elsewhere. She found yoga and changed her thoughts, her diet, her attitudes, and her health—all for the better. Our family followed along with her studies; we learned about spirituality, alternative health care, meditation, and healing modalities of all kinds. Mom got so healthy that she taught yoga for many years. I'd go to her classes and notice that, like me, many of the people doing yoga were not fully in their bodies either. There was something about the yoga that seemed to ask (or make it easy for) people to dissociate, and I liked finding a place where my own dissociated state was seen as a sign of spiritual attainment! While other people had to struggle to reach altered states, my dissociative skills allowed me to jump back and forth between states at will. I spent quite a few years in the branch of spirituality that celebrates out-of-body states, because I wasn't a broken or damaged person in that world. My dissociative abilities made me an advanced being and a member of a human "in" crowd for the first time. I liked that very much.

At the time, I thought it bizarre to find so many dissociated people in one place—nice for me, but bizarre. In the ensuing decades, I've seen that many forms of spiritualism and metaphysics exert a strong pull on dissociated trauma survivors, who form a significant part of our population. Dissociative, out-of-body spiritual practices can be very attractive to trauma survivors (whose in-body experiences were miserable). Also, many of the psychological markers typical in trauma survivors—their overbearing sense of responsibility combined with many kinds of magical thinking, their extreme sensitivity to emotional undercurrents, and their dissociative abilities—are supported and even encouraged in some spiritual groups. Many metaphysical and spiritual groups actually seem to preferentially select for trauma survivors. In many cases, these groups offer the only sense of community, belonging, or healing that trauma survivors can find.

The problem is this: Many of these groups don't understand their positions as *de facto* critical-care facilities for often dissociated trauma survivors, many of whom are empaths. This lack of awareness and sensitivity leads to a great deal of unnecessary turmoil and retraumatization for people who can least afford it. Other examples of dissociative teachings are astral travel, energy work, channeling, and some forms of meditation and breath work. In these teachings, the body is often considered an imprisoning vessel for a spirit that wants its freedom. As I piloted my way through these kinds of spiritual practices, I saw that some trauma survivors, when taught to leave their bodies in these ways, would often be destabilized to the point of being thrown into dissociation so severe that it looked like a nervous breakdown—because when already dissociated people move their attention further from their everyday lives, they often can't find their way back home again.

I learned by the age of sixteen how to help people get reassociated into their bodies, and that became the focus of my healing practice. I knew what to do; it wasn't any different from the work I did with traumatized cats, dogs, and birds. I'd create a safe, warm, quiet atmosphere—a secure place to come back to—and I'd stay with people until they were reintegrated. These breakdowns always seemed to surprise people in spiritual groups, but they were common. There's no surprise at all if you think about it. If you train people to dissociate—which is an emergency survival tool in the psyche—you can trigger psychiatric emergencies. Dissociation is a powerful tool; therefore, it has powerful effects.

As my understanding of human dissociation grew, I began to see that people needed focused awareness and strong grounding in order to stay integrated. They needed to *become* safe containers, and they needed to develop their own skills. I learned, and soon taught, how to create boundaries and how to support people in reintegrating themselves. Eventually,

I was also able to bring in the information I learned in my work with animals. I was able to recall that the emotions are not bad and scary things, but signs that the psyche is trying to heal itself. I learned to see emotions as necessary expressions of what were perhaps unspeakable inner truths, but it took a while because my view of emotions had become very skewed indeed.

My early metaphysical training, along with my childhood trauma, taught me to view emotions of any kind as signs of imbalance, of incorrect thinking patterns, of insufficient detachment, and of improper spiritual development. The idea of emotions *as* imbalance made perfect sense because I knew people whose emotions had twisted them into pathetic fiends. I came to believe that emotions were the root of all evil.

In order to be more spiritual, I struggled and strained to be emotionless and nonjudgmental—to have only joy in my heart—but I wasn't very good at it. My emotional state became very unbalanced, and I experienced constant dissociative episodes. Luckily, my healing career let me see firsthand that other metaphysical students (even those with less complicated childhoods) weren't doing any better in their emotionless states than I was; everyone was losing this battle with emotions. I began to understand that emotions were unavoidable, so I tried to live with them. I pretended to be peppy and happy, but I secretly let my emotions (especially anger) run through me when they needed to—it was all I could think to do. I had no role models or mentors to show me any other methods.

As I struggled with my own powerful emotions, I continued to learn about healing. My healing practice brought me into contact with many trauma survivors. I helped these people rebuild the outer boundaries of their personal space and connect themselves to the earth with a process called *grounding*. As I worked, though, I saw a pattern that frightened me. Once these survivors were reassociated, they'd often be overtaken by anger, anxiety, or depression. I completely stopped healing—obviously, I was hurting people, right? "Spiritual" meant emotionless, so I was making people worse, right?

Wrong. A series of events and visions led me to see a little bit of what such strong emotions were for: they provided protection, deep cleansing, and strengthening of the psyche, and they increased people's ability to stay focused in their own bodies. I soon discovered the special relationship between anger and the successful healing of personal boundaries (there is a specific boundary-building ability inside anger) and the absolute necessity of fear in a healthy psyche (fear in its flowing state is intuition). I also saw a connection between strong emotions and reintegration in dissociated people. Though I was still brainwashed against the emotions, that animal-girl knowledge was coming back to me. I began to see the upwelling of powerful emotions as the human version of the kicking, trembling, and struggling animals do when they come back to their bodies after a trauma. Gingerly, I began to include the furies, depressions, griefs, and exhilarations in my work, and I watched in awe as people became whole again. The emotions taught me more than anyone or anything else ever has or could.

I learned that emotions help us protect and heal ourselves at all times— including before, during, and especially after trauma—and that they create vital, connecting links throughout the psyche. They help people reassociate, certainly, but they also help people think more deeply and more clearly and become physically secure and aware. I learned that emotions exist to help us survive and navigate our way through life. Emotions are fluid, ever-changing, and extremely versatile. Emotions *move,* and they carry massive amounts of information with them. They're often deeply perceptive (if sometimes painfully so) and profoundly healing, as long as we approach them correctly, interpret them honorably, and treat them with respect.

When I learned to combine the messages of the emotions with the useful techniques I learned in my metaphysical studies, I was able to begin to heal myself (and to teach others to heal themselves). Over two decades, I worked with emotions in my healing practice, and from 1997 to 2003, I produced a series of books and tapes on down-to-earth, emotionally intelligent spiritual healing. I specialized in healing dissociative trauma, and I found safe and coherent ways to use meditative skills without disturbing people's ability to remain grounded in their own bodies and their own lives.

Most important, I learned to manage my own empathic skills and dissociative abilities so that I'm no longer tormented by them. I've learned to keep my attention focused in my body, even during difficulties and trauma. I've also learned to regulate my empathy; I've learned to give people and animals their privacy, and to pay deep attention to others only when necessary.

MOVING ONWARD

In 2003, I left my healing career, partially because I could no longer watch people get so hurt and confused by all the irresponsible information, and partially in response to the attacks of September 11, 2001, where so many people, Americans included, used their spiritual beliefs and resulting emotions in horrific and wholly unacceptable ways. I needed to get completely out of the spiritual community in order to question everything I had ever done or thought about spirituality, about emotions, about social movements, about true believers, about alternative healing, about judgment and the intellect, about religion—about everything. I returned to school to study human society and social structures in the exquisite field of sociology. I studied cults, lethal violence, the sociology of emotions, the sociology of religion, neurology, cognitive and social psychology, criminology, the social construction of murder, and the inner workings of cliques in elite academic communities. I also taught art and singing in maximum-security prisons, edited academic books, performed sociological studies, and evaluated the canon of the skeptical community, who vociferously deny the existence of the soul, the aura, the chakras, psychic abilities, and almost everything else I ever believed in.[2]

Leaving my career was a painful but extremely valuable experience because it helped me continue to heal a psyche that had been split apart in childhood. I had worked in my early life to integrate my body and my awareness, I had delved deeply into the world of spirituality, I had studied each of the emotions, but I had not yet focused on my intellect with the same intensity. Now I have, and I can come back to this work—to *my* work—with new information, new awareness, and new focus. I am no longer working in the metaphysical realm, and I have let go of most of my magical thinking, but I have returned to my work with the emotions because their language is still completely foreign to so many of us.

However, my work is not just about the emotions because each of us is a physical being, an intellectual being, an intuitive being, *and* an emotional being; therefore, we must bring all parts of ourselves to this process, or indeed to any important process. When we can stand balanced and upright at the center of our lives—at the center of our well-considered thoughts, our well-cared-for bodies, our honored emotions, and our far-reaching vision—we won't be merely intelligent about emotions, and we won't simply bring balance to our psyches. We will be ingenious, inquiring explorers who can bring new awareness to our deepest issues, new commitment to each of our relationships, and new dedication to a waiting world.

3

Troubled Waters

How We Got So Confused

WHAT *are* EMOTIONS? THIS seems to be a very simple question, and yet psychologists, behaviorists, neurologists, evolutionary biologists, and sociologists cannot yet agree on a clear definition. Is an emotion a mood, a feeling, an impulse, a neurochemical event, or all of these? Do emotions come from thoughts or instincts, or do thoughts and instincts arise from emotions? Can we call one emotion primary and another secondary? Do primates and other mammals share all of our emotions or just some of them?

These questions are extremely important for researchers, and tremendous advances in psychosocial and neurobiological knowledge have occurred over the last half-century. However, while categorization and classification systems are essential to science, they can have little connection to life as it is lived in the everyday world. These studies are fascinating, but they can drag us off the point, which is that you and I want to understand our emotions right now and work with them in our everyday lives.

I have concerns about classification systems anyway. Classification systems used in everyday life tend to lead people toward rigidity. I've heard people decree that, for instance, anger is negative and happiness is positive; or that anger is a secondary emotion (actually, it's considered in most classification systems to be a primary or universal emotion), and you're *really* feeling something else, and so on. But that advice doesn't really help you or me in real life. Sometimes, it will make us struggle to repress our honest "negative" emotions and feign the "positive" ones (not a good idea if you want to understand *all* of your emotions). Even if we classify emotions down to a hairbreadth of accuracy, our understanding of *what to do* with emotions tends to remain pretty unsophisticated.

The socially accepted view is that there are good emotions and bad emotions. These categories have a bit of interplay, but basically, good emotions are the ones that make us easy to be around, while bad emotions are the ones that shake things up. The good emotional states are happiness, pleasantness, joy, and some forms of sadness (*if* an appropriately saddening situation has occurred, and *if* it has occurred within a recent time frame). Anger dips a little toe into the good category when it's a response to injustice, but the acceptable time frame for anger is a lot shorter than that allowed for sadness. Notice how people will let you be sad about a senseless death for a lot longer than they'll let you be angry about it.

The bad emotions category is very large indeed. Sadness that lasts too long (or deepens into despair or grief) is definitely bad. Depression is bad, but suicidal urges are emergency-room bad. Anger is bad, as are peevishness, righteous indignation, and wrath. Rage and fury, then, are extra-strength bad. Hatred, we won't even go into. Jealousy is bad, bad, bad. Fear is so bad, we've got bumper stickers that shout to others that we, at least, haven't got any fear—not a drop! So all the fear-based emotions are bad, too. Anxiety, worry, and trepidation are bad, and panic is call-the-hospital bad. Shame and guilt—they're so bad that we don't even know what they mean anymore! We're persistently trained and implored to express or, more often, repress our emotions so that other people feel comfortable.

We've neatly sewn up the emotions, and in so doing, we've sewn ourselves right into a straitjacket. Anyone who feels anything other than the light, fresh-scented emotions is, by association, bad. This simplistic good/bad system imprisons so many of us: we who are angry, we who are grieving, we who are fearful, we who feel shame—many of us with legitimate emotional issues are pushed out of the way to make room for the perky and the superficial. Most emotional people languish on the fringe, because even though we've categorized the heck out of emotions, we still don't treat emotions—or the people who feel them—intelligently.

I've had the blessing of being forced to look at emotions in unusual ways. Aside from my influences in childhood, my empathic healing practice consisted of people who weren't finding help in conventional places. In many cases, people who finally ended up at my door had been through every modality they could afford; people don't go to empathic healers first! Many had run the gamut of psychotherapy and conventional medicine; they'd been through religious pursuits and numerous spiritual disciplines; and they'd been through physical and dietary regimens to heal their traumas and quiet their minds and hearts. With these people, I couldn't fall back on any of the accepted *or* fringe treatments for emotional imbalance because all of those treatments had already failed to bring relief.

I also couldn't fall back on accepted beliefs about the emotions because those didn't work either. For instance, many of my clients thought that joy and happiness were the only healthy emotions, which is nonsense. Real joy and real happiness can only exist in relation to *all* of the emotions; they're a boxed set. We can't just pick and choose our emotions. That would be like picking and choosing certain glands and organs (I want only my heart and brain—none of those gooey digestive organs), or deciding to walk using only the two most attractive toes on each foot. Joy and happiness are lovely in their place, but they're not by any stretch of the imagination better than fear, anger, grief, or sadness. Each emotion has its own valid place in our lives. Joy and happiness are just two states in a rich and brilliant continuum of emotions.

Many of the people I worked with had already tried to magically "transform" negative emotions into positive ones, to turn anger into joy, or whatever, but that didn't work. Anger *isn't* joy, just as joy isn't contentment, and sadness isn't grief. Each of our emotions has its own individual message, its own wants and needs, and its own purpose in the psyche; our emotions can't change into something else just because we'd like them to.

"Transforming" an emotion usually means repressing the life out of the real-but-unwanted one and then fabricating a better one out of thin air or affecting it as if it were a party hat. That kind of transformation looks good at first, but it eventually makes people confused and emotionally incoherent. I saw that the people who came to me for help were filled with ideas *about* their emotions—with shoulds and oughts and have-tos— but they had no feeling at all *for* their emotions. They were disconnected from their feelings and from their innate intelligence.

My approach with each person was to clear away all the suggestions and routines, all the categories and systems, and all the fixes and crutches. We got back to the original situation, which was always that the person saw, felt, or experienced life in an unusual but valid way, considering the situation. When we got down to the truth of who they were, we created a secure atmosphere and looked at their emotions empathically. When we brought empathy into the situation, we became more intelligent about emotions.

YOU'RE SO EMOTIONAL!

I laugh when people call each other "emotional." I want to ask: "Which emotion—because there are, like, two dozen of them! Do you even know which aspect of *emotional* you're talking about?"

Let's bring in *Merriam-Webster's Collegiate Dictionary* and *Roget's Thesaurus:* both references give us synonyms for "emotional" along with the definition, and there are some very pleasant ones. If we're emotional, Webster and Roget say that we're also conscious, perceptive, passionate, responsive, sensitive, and sensible. Those are very nice things to be! However, both references go on to call us susceptible, vehement, dramatic, hysterical, histrionic, and perturbed. That's not so nice. Yet look at emotion's antonyms, its opposites: indifference, unconcern, apathy, dispassion, calm, repose, at peace, and stillness—those are all synonyms for social disconnection. Three of them are even synonyms for death! To be emotionless is to be disconnected, indifferent, and basically unavailable for relationships. The state of being emotionless is not something to celebrate.

Emotions are necessary—even when they're uncomfortable or socially inappropriate—because they are a part of your psyche, a part of your neural network, a part of your socialization, and a part of your humanity. Emotions aren't the enemy, but they have come to be vilified because empathic awareness is so unusual. In a culture that swings from trampling the emotions one moment to glorifying them the next, it's savvy to turn down our empathic skills—the whole subject is rife with peril and confusion. It's easier to make fun of a crying man or shame an angry woman than it is to support their socially unacceptable emotions. It's also easier to pretend that we didn't get hurt by someone's insensitivity; it's easier to hide our honest emotions and shun them in other people. The only problem is that we truly need our emotions. We can't live functional lives without them. Without our emotions, we can't make decisions; we can't decipher our dreams and visions; we can't set proper boundaries or behave skillfully in relationships; we can't identify our hopes or support the hopes of others; and we can't connect to, or even find, our dearest loves.

Without access to our emotional selves, we grow in this culture like trees in the wrong soil, becoming tall but not strong, and old but not mature. Our emotional awareness goes underground in childhood, and we turn toward every other kind of development—physical, scholastic, artistic, financial, intellectual, religious, or athletic. We become knowledgeable and functional in every area but one. Because we turn away from our emotions by the time we're five or so, our understanding of them tends to stay at that level of development. We don't grow up as emotive people; we grow up as people who learn *not* to emote. We have a retroactive learning curve; as our intellectual skills come forward, our emotions move backward.

Many current therapies, meditation systems, books, and teachers are trying to remedy this glaring inequity, and much good work is being accomplished (Daniel Goleman's seminal work *Emotional Intelligence* is a must-read). The emotions are being brought into a better light, and self-awareness is becoming more fashionable. Some of us are learning to listen to one another more carefully, to reflect one another's emotions properly, and to support each other skillfully—but in most cases, the emotions are still being alternately demonized and exalted. The emotions are not being treated as important and distinct forces with which we can change our lives. The emotions are not being honored as the brilliant messengers they are.

Before we go any further, I want you to understand that I'm not advocating an ungrounded descent into the emotions—an emotional orgy for emotion's sake. That's not what empathic work is about. When people think about emotions, they often freeze up and don't process information properly. When I talk of honoring the emotions, I don't mean for us to prostrate ourselves in front of their temple; we don't want to swing from vilifying the emotions to glorifying them, because both positions are inappropriate. Both positions objectify the emotions as unconnected good or bad things that happen *to* us, rather than as tools of our greatest humanity and evolution.

Empathic work teaches us to find the middle ground between vilification and glorification of the emotions, and between expressing and repressing them. When we can see *all* of our emotions as vital tools, we can invite all of them into a conscious and supportive dialogue. When we can treat our emotions as essential aspects of ourselves—as our native language—we'll begin to understand that there is an honorable way to work with our emotions, and an honorable way to think about them. When we approach the emotions honorably, we won't banish certain emotions to the underworld; we will instead seek a middle ground where all emotions can exist and work properly.

EXPRESSION, REPRESSION, AND THE MIDDLE GROUND

When we express our emotions, we hand them over to the outside world, where we hope they'll be noticed, honored, and transformed. Emotional expression relies on the outer world to decipher our emotions. While this expression of true feelings can be healthy at times, it isn't always the best way to work with our emotions. Emotional expression can make us dependent upon external action, books, friends and family, or therapists for emotional relief. If these external supports are not available to us, we might not be able to process our feelings because our emotional skills will depend on things or people outside of ourselves. Many of us have encountered this difficulty when we're overtaken by, say, anger or depression, and have no one to talk to. If we don't have internal emotional skills, we can feel trapped in our emotional states, unable to moderate or even understand our moods unless someone or something outside of us is available.

The other choice in this either/or system of emotional management is to repress our emotions. When we repress our emotions, we hand them off to the inner world, where we hope they'll disappear, transform themselves, or maybe come up again at a better time (whenever *that* might be). Repression is the only internal emotional management skill most of us have. If we can't express emotions safely or masterfully, we'll stuff them down into our psyches. Emotional repression relies on the unconscious, interior world (and often on our bodies) to accept and *do something* with our emotions. When we repress a very unwelcome emotion (like sadness or rage), we press it inward—we count to ten, think happy thoughts, or repeat a cherished phrase. We don't know what to do with the inconvenient, embarrassing, or dangerous feeling. We just want to wipe the slate clean and go on with our day. The problem with repression is that the inner world is where emotions come *from*. Shoving the emotions back where they came from—without consciously processing them—creates an unpleasant short circuit in the psyche.

Emotions are messages from our instinctive selves. They can be important carriers of absolute (and often unwanted) truth. Although many emotions aren't welcome in most psyches, each of them has an indispensable function and something meaningful and precise to say. If we ignore and repress an emotion, we won't erase its message—we'll just shoot the messenger and interfere with an important natural process. The unconscious then has two choices: to increase the intensity of the emotion and present it to us one more time (this is how unresolving moods or escalating emotional suffering may be activated), or to give up on us and stuff the emotional energy deep into our psyches. Now, that instinct will no longer be readable as itself—as fear or anger or despair—but it will still contain all its original intensity and information. Usually, this squelched intensity mutates into something else, like tics, compulsions, psychosomatic illness, addictions, or neuroses. Repressing our emotions is a perilous way to manage them.

Expressing our emotions is somewhat better than repressing them. At the very least, it allows a flow of honesty in our lives. If we're out there crying or raging or whatever, at least we're letting our emotions flow. However, if our emotions are very strong, expressing them can create both interior and exterior turmoil. Exterior turmoil comes about when we pour our strong emotions all over some unfortunate soul and try to make him or her responsible for our moods. We'll say, "You *made* me angry, you *made* me cry!" and in so doing, we'll not only hurt that person, but we'll give him or her control over our emotional state. We won't be active, responsible individuals—we'll be powerless marionettes, jerking and dancing in reaction to the people and situations around us.

Interior turmoil arises when we realize that we may have hurt, degraded, or frightened someone with our many outbursts. We'll feel some sense of release with the expression of our strong emotions, but we'll be disappointed about our poor relating skills or ashamed about our lack of control. Expressing strong emotions at others can damage our ego structure and our sense of self-esteem. Then, our lowered self-esteem tends to make us less able to manage our emotions properly the next time, and we tend to slide into an almost uncontrollable habit of flinging our strong emotions all over the place. We become trapped in a cycle of attacks and retreats, enmeshment and isolation, and explosions and apologies. Our internal checks and balances seem to get broken, and we become emotionally volatile.

Current neurological and psychological research is also showing that constantly expressing strong emotions tends to wear a groove into your brain. If you let loose with rage or anxiety, your brain will begin to learn how to rage and be anxious; therefore, the next time you meet a possibly enraging or anxiety-producing situation, your brain may move to rage or anxiety simply because you taught it to. The plasticity of your brain doesn't just apply to learning new skills or new languages; it also applies to learning how to manage your emotions.

Both repression and expression can be helpful to us in certain situations, but they cannot between them address every emotional situation we encounter. Take repression, for instance. When we're infuriated at a baby, repressing the fury is a good idea—it's never right to express fury toward a baby. But once we've repressed the fury and made the baby safe, we need to be able to address that fury in private, or it will rear its head once again, perhaps with more energy the next time. Because here's the situation: emotions are always true—they always tell the truth about how we're actually feeling—but they may not always be *right* or appropriate in each situation. Therefore, we have to learn how to understand, interpret, and work with them, and we must find the middle path between repression and improper expression. We must learn to honor and attend to our emotions in a deeper, more mature, and more evolved way. We must learn not to work *against* the emotions with repression or *for* the emotions with incompetent expression. We must learn to work *with* our emotions.

There is a middle ground in the emotional landscape; there is a way to work with emotions in a respectful and honorable way. I call the process *channeling* the emotions, by which I don't mean to suggest some metaphysical idea of calling forth disembodied spirits. I'm referring to the actual meaning of the word "channel," which is to direct or convey something along a chosen pathway in a conscientious manner. If we can learn to properly channel our emotions, we can begin to work with them in vibrant and ingenious ways. We can interpret the messages our emotions carry and make use of the instincts our emotions contain.

The hand-off we do with emotional expression—that hand-off to the outer world—doesn't bestow any skills upon us. Likewise, the hand-off we do with repression, when we shove our emotions back into the inner world, makes us even less skilled. Neither approach works because neither one accepts emotions as important and useful messengers that help us learn and evolve. When we stop handing off our emotions, and instead learn to channel them honorably, we can take our emotions into our own hands. We can listen to them, feel them consciously, and express them in ways that will bolster our self-image and our relationships, rather than tearing them down.

When you can channel your emotions, you'll discover something most people don't know, which is that each of your emotions contains vital skills and abilities that help you survive and thrive. Your emotions don't disappear when you're not feeling them; instead, each of your emotions moves through you at all times, and each one endows you with specific gifts and abilities. Let me show you what I mean.

THREE EMPATHIC EXERCISES

I'd like you to have a tangible experience of the empathic work we'll be doing so that you can see how easy and comfortable it is to channel your emotions. Let's start with a simple flow-inducing exercise. You can be sitting, standing, or lying down.

Exercise 1

Please take a deep breath and fill up your chest and your belly so that you feel a little bit of tension—not too much, just a little. Hold your breath for a few seconds (count to three), and as you breathe out, make small, gentle spiraling movements with your hands, your arms, your feet, your legs, your neck, and your torso. Move your body in gentle, easy, relaxing ways.

33

Now, breathe in again, expand your chest and your belly until you feel a little bit of tension, hold for three seconds—and breathe out with a sigh as you spiral your arms and your legs and your neck. You can even hang your tongue out. Just let go. You're a ragdoll. Let it go.

Now breathe normally and check in with yourself. If you feel a bit softer and calmer, and maybe even a little bit tired, thank the emotion that helped you release some of your tension and restore some of your flow: thank your sadness.

That's what healthy, flowing sadness feels like, and that's what it does— it helps you let go, and it helps you bring some flow back to your system. Each of the emotions has this free-flowing state that brings you specific gifts and tools. We've learned to identify emotions only when they move to an obvious mood state, but that's not all they are. You don't have to cry to be sad; you can just let go. Sadness is about releasing things and relaxing into yourself.

Take a moment to notice how aware you are of your body. Sadness is an internal emotion that brings you back to yourself and makes you aware of your interior state. And that's why we tend to avoid sadness in our everyday lives. It's not the right emotion to walk around with all the time because it doesn't protect your boundaries, and it doesn't make you focused and ready for action. That's not its job—it's not supposed to do those things. Sadness brings flow back to you, it calms you, and it helps you release uncomfortable things you've been grasping on to—like muscle tension, fatigue, lost hopes, or disappointments. Sadness helps you let go of things that aren't working anyway. It's important to use the skills your sadness brings you because it's necessary to let go regularly—you know, *before* everything piles up into identifiable emotional distress, muscle pain, or misery. Maintaining your flow and letting go is an easy thing to do now that you know what sadness feels like.

Whenever you need to, you can consciously welcome your sadness and restore a sense of flow to your life by breathing in and gathering any tension, and then breathing out gently as you make spiraling movements with your body, shake yourself off, shimmy, yawn, or sigh (maybe when no one else is around). It's that simple. To channel your sadness, you just relax and let go.

Exercise 2

Now, let's try something different. Thank your sadness for helping you let go and relax, and sit up straight. Open your eyes a bit, and smile as if you're greeting a very good friend. You can even say, "Hi!" Stretch your arms out and stretch your torso, keep smiling and keep your eyes open, take a comfortable breath, and thank your happiness.

Happiness is a momentary emotion that helps you identify things that are fun and rewarding. It's a good little rest stop in your soul, and you can bring it forward by opening your eyes and smiling. Your facial expressions and your emotions are tied together, and you can bring an emotion forward just by making the face. So be careful about the faces you make; your brain may think that you're angry or sad or happy simply because your facial expressions say you are.

When you smile, you can bring your happiness forward and share it. Happiness is a very good emotion to share with others (if it's the right time to be happy). It's also an emotion that tends to arise naturally when you've done good work with some of your deeper emotions. For instance, when you've really cried yourself out, you'll often start laughing. Or if you've worked through an intense conflict with someone, you'll both tend to laugh and smile a lot when it's done. Happiness is an excellent little rest stop. However, you shouldn't trap happiness or try to keep it active at all times because it doesn't contain all the skills you need to live a whole and happy life. You need *all* of your emotions.

Exercise 3

Thank your happiness for bringing the fun, and let's try another empathic exercise. For this one, you'll need a quiet place where you can sit or stand comfortably.

When you've found your quiet place, lean your body forward a little bit, and try to hear the quietest sound in your area. Keep your shoulders down and away from your ears; good posture helps your hearing. You can also open your mouth a little (relaxing your jaw creates more space in your ears) and gently move your head around as you pinpoint the quietest sound and filter out the more obvious ones. Keep your eyes open, but rely on your ears for now.

When you've located this quiet sound, hold still for a moment. Stand up if you are sitting and try to locate the sound with your eyes; then move toward it, recalibrating as you near the sound. Time may seem to slow down somewhat, your skin may feel more sensitive (almost as if it's sensing the air around you), and your mind may clear itself of anything that isn't related to your quiet sound. When you pinpoint the sound, thank the emotion that helped you find it. Thank your fear.

Surprising, isn't it? Healthy and free-flowing fear is nothing more or less than your instincts and your intuition. When you need it to, your fear focuses you and all of your senses, it scans your environment and your stored memories, and it increases your ability to respond effectively to new or changing situations. When your fear flows nicely, you'll feel focused, centered, capable, and agile. Thank your fear.

Your free-flowing fear brings you instincts, intuition, and focus. If you can bring your fear forward when you're confused or upset, you can access the information you need to calmly figure out what's going on; you don't need to *feel* afraid to access the gifts your fear brings you. You can also access your fear when you're unsure about what you should do or when you're uncomfortable in your relationships. Fear helps you focus on your internal knowledge as it connects you to your surroundings. So it's different from sadness, which focuses you inside yourself and on what you need to release in order to relax and let go of things that don't serve you. With fear, your focus helps you stand upright in your body and lean forward a bit, to bring your instincts and your intuition to the moment. It's almost as if you're listening to the quietest sound inside yourself, to that voice that's having a hard time being heard. Unlike flowing sadness, flowing fear has a forward, listening, sensing capacity that helps you interact with your environment and other people. If you can rely on fear's calm, listening, sensing stance, it will help you read people and situations empathically. It's a wonderful emotion, but all of them are! They're an amazing tool kit, full of magic, which is why it's so absurd that we've been taught to distrust our emotions.

Learning to trust and honorably channel our emotions—to hear them, to feel them, to attend to them, and to converse with them—is the central skill of our empathic practice. But in order to achieve this level of emotional agility, we've got to be able to understand emotions in their flowing states, in their mood states, and in what I call their "raging rapids" states. To do this, we need some tools and some ground beneath us. As we're going through our daily lives—arguing with family members, being slowed down at work or school by interpersonal conflicts, seeking to deepen our relationships, learning to support our loved ones emotionally, discovering our true selves and finding our true paths—we need some tangible emotional tools. We need a way to identify our emotions, to understand them, and to begin to learn their language so that we can communicate with them empathically instead of being at their mercy or treating them cruelly. Therefore, we've got to look deeply into accepted wisdom about the emotions, and we've got to clear away the nonsense that threatens to stupefy us all. In order to do that, we've got to bring in unusual, empathic information. This is where the fun begins.

4

It Takes a Village

Surrounding Your Emotions with Support

WHEN PEOPLE EXPERIENCE EMOTIONS in their flowing states, they're often astonished that their emotions don't feel dangerous, time-consuming, or embarrassing. The emotions are so gentle in their flowing states that it's hard to identify them at first. The emotions have been shoved so far into the shadows that we often aren't aware of what's going on inside us. Our natural and innate empathic intelligence is simply not welcomed, exercised, or honored.

But empathy is a normal human skill, and from the animals I've known, I'd say it's a skill in most animals as well. The skill of empathy allows us to read the interior state, the intentions, the emotions, the desires, and the possible actions of other people or animals. If we're very good at reading emotions, our social intelligence and our emotional intelligence tend to be very high. We *get* people and animals and their needs in the way some intellectual geniuses *get* mathematics or physics, or in the way artistic geniuses *get* colors, shape, and perspective. Empathy is one of the multiple kinds of intelligence we have.

However, most of us grew up in a world where multiple intelligences were not yet understood. It was only in 1983 that Harvard psychologist Howard Gardner's work on multiple intelligences became known. Dr. Gardner identified more than just the *logical* intelligence that most people focused on at the time—the intelligence that allows us to do math and science, identify patterns, and use logic and deductive reasoning. Logical intelligence is the one that can be measured on an IQ test, and for decades, it was the only aptitude that was openly called intelligence.

Dr. Gardner saw intelligence differently, and he put a name to six other forms of intelligence that go along with logical intelligence. Four of these intelligences are *linguistic* intelligence, which allows us to write, communicate, and learn other languages skillfully; *musical* intelligence, which allows us to identify tone, pitch, and rhythm and to appreciate, compose, and perform musically; *bodily-kinesthetic* intelligence, which allows us to utilize our bodies and our musculature with great skill (think of dancers, athletes, and gymnasts); and *spatial* intelligence, or the ability to recognize patterns in space and to utilize space in novel ways. Architects, builders, people who are good at geometry, and most visual artists are in the spatial intelligence category.

The other two intelligences Dr. Gardner identified are *interpersonal* intelligence, which allows us to understand the intentions, motivations, and desires of others, and *intrapersonal* intelligence, which gives us the ability to understand *our own* motivations, intentions, and desires. These are incredibly important forms of intelligence that help us pilot through the social world.

To be an effective empath, it's important to focus on these interpersonal and intrapersonal areas of intelligence, though all of our other intelligences are important as well. Right now as you're reading, you're using your linguistic intelligence, and in the chapter where we learn our five empathic skills, you'll use your bodily-kinesthetic and spatial intelligences as well. None of our intelligences exists without the others, so it's not as if you have to turn any of them off. In fact, you use your logical intelligence all the time, and while your musical intelligence may not seem to be active right now, musical ability is connected to your ability to use and understand language, because language incorporates rhythm, pitch, phrasing, and listening. When you're reading, you're also relying upon your interpersonal intelligence to translate the words on the page and decide what I mean, what I intend, and what I want you to understand, and you're using your intrapersonal intelligence to respond, react, and feel your way through what you're reading.

With the ground of Dr. Gardner's work to stand on, we can refer to intelligence as a constellation of abilities, and not simply those skills you use on IQ tests. However, here's the problem for empaths: when most of us were growing up, the only kind of intelligences that mattered were the logical and spatial forms. Maybe our musical and artistic intelligences were accessed in school, and probably our bodily, sports-focused abilities were, too, but PE and art were probably not an equal focus of our school day. When I went to school, PE and art were not seen as essential to learning, and now, with all the budgetary problems and the testing-focus facing schools, PE and art are even less likely to take up a large part of the school day. Therefore, we don't tend to access all of our intelligences at school.

It is telling that our interpersonal and intrapersonal intelligences are not a part of our formal schooling at all. I think I took a class called Citizenship once, but I can't really remember it. What I do remember, in school and out of it, is that behavioral and social skills were often taught on the fly. We learned how to act by watching others or by being praised or yelled at, but there wasn't any actual instruction. We learned to be in relationships and to be siblings or friends through osmosis or by the seat of our pants. We didn't receive direct instruction about our relationships or our emotions unless we made some huge social mistake, such as openly displaying unwanted emotions like anger, jealousy, or envy in our mood states. We were taught math and logic, we were taught art and music, we were taught PE, and we were taught reading, writing, and languages. But in regard to our emotions, our interpersonal skills, and our intrapersonal skills, we were just supposed to have figured it out somehow.

We got demerits or gold stars for our behavior, but we didn't learn how to identify our emotions or work with them skillfully. If we acted out our anger, we'd probably be sent to the principal or the school counselor, or we'd have to go to detention or stay after school. The anger would take us out of the normal school day, out of the classroom, and out of the way. And the other kids would learn, "You don't do that. You don't express anger, or you'll be shamed." If we acted out our fear or our sadness, we might be seen as weaklings and maybe become targets for the other kids, or we might become the teacher's pet, which is often the same thing as being a target.

We certainly didn't learn that anger helps us set effective boundaries, that fear is our intuition, or that sadness helps us relax and let go of things we don't need anyway. What I also noticed at school, and it may have been different for you, is that acting out our compassion was also frowned upon. For instance, if a child was being isolated and identified as a geek or a target, you took your social survival into your own hands if you tried to befriend him or stick up for him (if you didn't have status, that is). Sometimes, I saw kids with status—you know, the cool kids, the pack leaders—reach out with compassion and essentially throw a cloak of protection over a social outcast, but it didn't happen as often as it needed to.

What I saw growing up, and what I still see, is that we're asked to grow to maturity while keeping two of our most important intelligences under wraps, in the shadows, out of the way, and off the radar. As adults, we tend to need therapists, counselors, and psychiatrists to help us access our emotions and our interpersonal and intrapersonal intelligences, even though these intelligences belong to us and are essential to pretty much everything we do. It's not surprising, then, that we don't know what emotions are, what they want, or what they do. It's also not surprising that we're left to create a ground under the emotions by ourselves. Dr. Gardner's multiple intelligences give us an excellent foundation, but I also want to add another model, which is the four-element or *quaternity* model.

IT'S ELEMENTAL, MY DEAR

In order to create more support for our transition into empathic awareness, I like to present the four-element or quaternity model, where earth is the physical world and your body, air is your mental and intellectual realm, water is your emotional and artistic realm, and fire is your visionary or spiritual realm. This model gives us a way to both deepen and clarify our understanding of concepts. If we can place people or situations into a quaternal model and observe their earthiness, their airy aspects, their watery movements, and their fiery natures, we can understand a little bit more about them.

The four-element theory is not a scientific one. We are not—nothing is—made up of only four elements. This elemental framework is mythological and poetic in origin, and it has been used for centuries and across cultures as a way to gain understanding of the world. As we're learning now, the fire element, with its dreams and visions that seem to come "out of nowhere," is turning out to be a function of an exquisitely attuned brain and nervous system. When we speak of the fire element, therefore, it's important to keep in mind that the entire realm of fire—dreams, spirituality, and vision—is very likely a function of neurological (and not paranormal) processes. However, this doesn't make our fiery aspects any less fascinating or useful.

In our modern world, we have grown in leaps and bounds toward an intellectual understanding of the universe, the earth, human and animal behavior, and the brain; however, we haven't grown as strongly in our ability to put our understanding into everyday practice. As we explore this concept of the quaternity, we're engaging not just our logical abilities, but also our intelligences that understand nuance, mythology, and dreams. In truth, we have to engage the older and more empathic parts of our brains to understand the deep and gorgeous realm of the emotions.

Even though the quaternity model is mythological, understanding our own four elements and their interactions brings unusual stability into our lives. When we can envision the emotions as our internal water element— as the part of us that embodies fluidity and flow—we can bring great clarity to our intrapersonal and interpersonal intelligences. With water as our model, we can understand the function of emotions, the properties of emotions, and the position emotions should take in our whole lives.

Water has many distinct properties, and it's valuable to study them in relation to the emotions. Water is soft and flowing, but it can wear down boulders and mountains. It's a great conductor of heat and energy, and it can carry things within itself through its ability to support weight and create buoyancy. It moves and flows around anything put in its path, and it usually finds its way to the deepest, most grounded places. Water can even travel upward; it moves constantly. If you put a lot of energy into it, water can change its form; it can shape-shift into vapor or form itself into a solid block of ice. Water moves back and forth between states in a constant flow, just as emotions move (or *should* move) between their free-flowing and obvious mood states in a constant flow. Water makes plant life possible, it quenches and bathes every living creature, and it regulates the temperature of our entire planet. The unusual properties and qualities of water make life on earth possible.

The unusual properties and qualities of your watery emotions can do the same for your living system—if you will let them. When you understand that water needs to flow, you can begin to behave properly when water rises in your own psyche. If you can simply allow your emotions to flow as water does, and if you can respond to them honorably, you can create balance within yourself. Movement and flow are the central properties of water, and of the emotions themselves. Mythologically and psychologically, water is the unconscious, the great container, the place from which all life and all impulses originate. The word "emotion" even has roots in the water. It comes from the Latin *emotus* or *emovere:* to move outward, to flow outward. Allowing your emotions to flow naturally is the foundation of the ability to channel emotions properly and skillfully. If you can simply let your emotions flow—if you can notice them, welcome them, and let them move freely through your life—you will begin to heal. You won't have to increase your emotional flow with overt expression (that often creates *too much* flow if your emotions are very fierce); rather, you can consciously welcome each of your emotions.

WELCOMING YOUR EMOTIONS: AN EXAMPLE

Here's an example of welcoming your emotions: Imagine you've just been cut off on the freeway. The emotions that arise are usually fear and anger. Fear in its mood state ramps up your instincts and your intuition to let you know you're endangered, and anger rushes forward to help you rebuild your disrupted boundaries. If you *express* these emotions, you might scream and swear, gesture rudely, or even chase the offensive driver, none of which would take you out of danger *or* rebuild your boundaries. If you *repress* your fear (your instincts) and your anger (your ability to set boundaries) and try to ignore the rudeness and keep driving, you'll most likely be less aware and less conscious for the next few moments or miles— again, you won't reduce your danger or rebuild your sense of safety. But if you welcome both emotions and allow them to flow through your system, you can use them to increase your awareness. You could use your fear to sharpen your senses. That's what properly flowing fear does—it increases your focus and awareness. Your fear could help you ask yourself where your attention was and why you were so startled. Your fear could also help you think about ways to prevent such inattentiveness in the future. You could also use your anger to make the proper corrections and get yourself away from the unsafe driver. Properly honored anger would enable you to quickly and consciously rebuild the "traffic boundaries" around your car; it would protect you from the recklessness of others and help you become a more skillful driver yourself. When you welcome and attend to your fear and anger consciously, neither one will endanger you or the other driver; rather, they'll simply help you increase your awareness and skill.

When you and your car are out of danger and your emotions have been attended to consciously, both your fear and your anger will then flow and move on—as they should. Neither emotion will need to stay active in its mood state, and you won't have to obsessively relive the incident or drive unconsciously for the rest of the day, because you'll have handled the situation, and the emotions, appropriately. If you can honor your emotions and welcome them as the life-giving water element they are, they will behave exactly as water does. They'll flow and change, shift their states, react and respond appropriately, and create the perfect ecosystem in which you can flourish. Allowing your emotions to flow freely inside your psyche brings life-affirming water and empathic awareness into your life.

LEARNING TO WORK EMPATHICALLY

Through the model of earth, air, water, and fire, we can see that our emotions are a great and flowing oceanic force, without which we could not live or grow. Yet still we try to live without—or in spite of—our emotions. We struggle to change or delete our emotions. We try to live without water in our souls and then wonder why our lives refuse to work, or why our world is filled with unrelieved emotional pain. If we can place the four-element model before us, we can see that none of the elements (and indeed, none of us) can exist without the watery emotions. We tell ourselves we can go beyond our minds, or transcend our bodies, or ignore our spiritual longings, or transform our emotions. That's all a load of hooey, but let's face it: each one of us tries to make that hooey work in one way or another.

With the help of the four-element model, we can enter the world of each element in a more functional and mature fashion. Consciously placing each of our elements in relation to the whole helps us envision balance and flow in all parts of ourselves. We begin to understand how our lives function, or malfunction, when any element is out of balance in our psyches. We begin to see that balance is necessary if we want to experience our emotions (or any part of our lives) in brilliant ways; we've got to have full and conscious access to our airy intellectual intelligences and capacities, our earthy physical perceptions and intelligences, our fiery visionary wisdom, and our watery emotional awareness and intelligences. If we're truly serious about healing and personal growth, we can't just pay attention to one or two parts of ourselves. If we want to be strong, aware, and emotionally agile, we've got to build a village inside of us and learn to honor our full quaternity of earth, air, water, and fire *and* all seven of our intelligences.

We need this village inside us when we enter a subject empathically, because we don't just study it dispassionately; instead, we drop down into the heart of troubling issues and work in the depths. What I have observed is that the emotions identify imbalance and then move from imbalance to understanding to resolution. Often, we try to ignore this emotional process; we try to jump to solutions first, but solutions that have no foundation in the understanding of the issues are not real solutions. They're just stopgap fixes that don't carry enough energy with them to do any real good. However, it's easy to understand why we avoid the emotional movements that drop us into trouble, because we've all been socialized to avoid trouble (and most emotions) at any cost. The good news is that if we agree to dive into trouble as our emotions ask us to, and if we allow them to flow naturally, they'll contribute the energy and intelligence we need to work our way back out of that trouble—quickly, and without any unnecessary drama.

For instance, sadness in its mood state slows us down and makes us stop pretending that everything is all right. If we mistakenly fight the sadness, our lives will soon come to a complete stop anyway. If we can instead move honorably into sadness, we'll find the rejuvenation and healing that lives at the very heart of sadness. Or consider that anger in its mood state riles us up and makes us stop pretending that we weren't hurt or offended. If we fight our anger, we'll miss the boat completely and probably get hurt *again* because we didn't speak up. If we can instead move honorably into our anger, we'll learn to rebuild what has been broken and protect ourselves and others with the fiery strength and certainty anger contains. The only real way out of any imbalance is to go through it consciously. If you can bring all parts of yourself to the imbalance and gain a complete picture of a problem, you can work toward a complete solution.

If you want to be able to rely on your physical skills when emotions arise, you've got to know how your emotions and your body interrelate. If you want to be able to think quickly and process your emotions intelligently, you've got to understand the ideas you have about your emotions and your intellect. Correspondingly, if you want to have access to visionary or spiritual knowledge about your emotions, you've got to know what relationship your fiery spirit has with your watery emotions. It's important not to move toward the emotions in unbalanced or facile ways, because in order to work with them properly, you need the deep knowledge that only a whole and resourced psyche possesses. The emotions are powerful, and you don't want to fool around with them; as we all know, they can be dangerous when they move into the raging rapids or when they're handled carelessly.

As we learn to invite our full village of elements and intelligences into our empathic process, it's important to stop for a moment and look at the unnecessary struggle that has been manufactured between our airy logical intelligences and our watery emotional intelligences. If we subscribe to the false idea that being emotional is the opposite of being rational, we'll set up an unfortunate fight inside of ourselves. The truth is that our emotions and our logic work together—or they should—in a healthy psyche.

The airy parts of our intelligence—our logical, spatial, and linguistic intelligences—are beautiful, worthy, and utterly necessary, but they're just part of the whole village inside us. They cannot be balanced or stable unless they're intimately and compatibly connected to each of the other intelligences and each of the elements in the quaternity. When we separate our air element from its brothers and sisters—from earth and water and fire—we dishonor it, we disable it, and we expose it to unnecessary danger. The problem absolutely isn't in the logical air element itself. The problem is in how our extremely unbalanced culture has trained us to treat the air element inside (and outside) of ourselves. We cannot bring our emotions out into the open until we understand how our intellects are both idolized and demonized, in much the same way our emotions are. And we certainly can't honor and channel our emotions skillfully until we know how to approach our intellect empathically, and how to approach our emotions intelligently. We need to bring our good judgment to the forefront.

IN DEFENSE OF JUDGMENT

By introducing the word *judgment*, I'm opening a big can of worms, because the ideas we have about judgment are just as befuddled as the ideas we have about emotions, if that is possible. When I refer to judgment, I refer to your capacity to react as an individual and use your discerning intelligence freely. If you have good judgment, you can disagree with others, go off on your own mental tangent, and strike out on your own path of discovery. This is an important set of skills; however, this solid, adult capacity to judge has gotten very bad press in the last few decades.

The theory is that judgment stops you from experiencing life completely, because you're too busy categorizing and thinking about things to be fully present in each unfolding moment. This no-judgment rule has had some positive effects, but it has also created a great deal of turmoil. This call for nonjudgmentalism comes from nearly every spiritual teacher we could name (including Jesus, Buddha, and Lao-tzu), but its application in the everyday world is exceedingly confused. This confusion isn't an unusual occurrence (think of the trouble humans have in deciphering any sacred text or injunction), but when people forbid themselves the faculty of judgment, they take the airy part of their wholeness and throw it out the window.

We need to rescue our much-wronged ability to judge from its forced exile and bring it back to a place of honor at the very center of our lives, because we need to be able to rely on our airy intelligences if we want to be wholly intelligent and intelligently empathic. We can ask ourselves: "Why do we forget that the word 'judgment' is a synonym for 'intelligence?'" When we say someone has poor judgment, that's not a compliment!

I understand, of course, that by referring incorrectly to judgmentalism, spiritual teachers intend to denigrate name-calling and the tendency to place people or experiences into simplistic "right" or "wrong" categories. I agree that name-calling is usually a bad thing, but because the idea of judgment has been so distorted, many people have become bewildered. They believe that all facets of real, adult judgment are forbidden to them, and unfortunately, this makes working with their emotions nearly impossible. Instead of moving gracefully away from the simplistic right/wrong thinking that can hinder their awakening, many people stop using *all* of their judgment, when in reality, only a partial suspension of certain aspects of judgment is ever necessary.

THE PROPER USE OF JUDGMENT

Judgment, in its truest sense, simply tells you what a thing is and whether it works for you or not. Healthy judgment is a combination of your airy intellect and your watery emotions coming together to form a considered opinion. Healthy, mature judgment isn't bad-tempered name-calling or simpleminded categorization of the world. It's just an internal decision-making process about what a thing is and whether it suits you or not. If you try to emote without thinking—without judging—you'll fly off the handle. But if you try to judge without feeling your way through your decision, you won't ever be able to decide. Thoughts and emotions are partners. They're not enemies.

Healthy judgment helps us define ourselves in the world, and it helps us separate the wheat from the chaff. This process of definition keeps us focused and centered. Healthy judgment helps us decide between this idea and that, between this option and that. Healthy judgment does not need to trash the path not chosen; it just needs to be free to make decisions and engage with its environment. Trying to squelch judgment is futile, because we're active, reactive, and responsive beings. We'll always have our own thoughts and feelings about events, and we'll always judge and process our environments independently—no matter how many rules we ingest or how authoritarian our teachers are. Healthy judgment is a natural process of making intelligent and competent decisions with our hearts and minds acting together, and with our logical intelligences and our intrapersonal intelligences respectfully communicating with each other. This is very different from bad-tempered name-calling or labeling.

Let's look at the difference between judging and name-calling by focusing on something simple. Let's imagine a rug that doesn't work in the room we're in. We can judge the rug and see that its pile is too high for the traffic it gets or that its color is so light that its shows more wear and dirt than it should. Let's agree that the rug isn't ideal for the room. Perhaps we feel sad that so much money was wasted, perhaps we think about putting runners over the traffic areas, but we freely process information about the rug and add that information to our skill set. That's judgment. It's not name-calling; it's a considered, decisive process. We have a problem with the rug, we have feelings about it, and we're definitely judging it, but we're not doing damage to our minds, our emotions, or our psyches. Therefore, we move forward with more knowledge about rugs and rug care and about purchases in general.

Now let's get into name-calling about the same rug: "Why would anyone buy this rug? What kind of moron puts a pale, fluffy rug in a public area? Look at the way those colors clash; it looks like someone ate a box of crayons and then threw up on the floor! How can anyone think that this wretched excuse for a carpet . . . " With name-calling, we get personally affronted and belligerent, which means it's not about the rug any longer; it's about the chip on our shoulder, our childhood issues, or our unlived emotions. With name-calling, we throw blame all over the place, and we don't internalize any useful information about the rug. In both of these examples, we don't like the rug. But with name-calling, we fly off the handle and make wild assumptions and accusations.

These sorts of attacks damage us. They damage our emotions by lobbing them all over the room; they damage our intellects when we use them against others; and they damage us as individuals because our behavior is embarrassing to us and everyone around us. This name-calling doesn't make us smarter, stronger, or more aware—it just pits us in futile opposition to a floor covering. When we judge appropriately, we restrict ourselves to the decisions we *can* make with the information we have, and we process our emotions coherently. Healthy judgment helps us choose what works in our lives. It helps us carefully evaluate situations and people with our minds and our emotions, and it helps us connect to our honest reactions and opinions.

Healthy judgment helps us become more intelligent, and it helps us identify and articulate each of our emotions in its free-flowing state, in its mood state, and in its raging rapids state (if it has one).

The intellect is exceedingly important and useful, but it was never meant to perform the Herculean tasks we've forced upon it in our airy, logical-intelligence-only society. Conversely, it was also never meant to be thrown out with the trash. The logical intellect has very specific functions and very specific properties, but most of us try to bend and mangle the poor intellect into something it's not and can never be. If we want to be intelligent about the intellect, we need to understand the interplay between the intellect and the other three elements in the quaternity.

RESTORING THE INTELLECT TO ITS RIGHTFUL POSITION

Let me give you some examples of how a functional quaternity operates: Our emotions convey messages between our unconscious and conscious minds, and they give us the skills and abilities we need to deal with each situation we encounter. We might have a gnawing, wordless sense of something that keeps us from finishing a project, a strange *something* that holds us back. If we can drop into our emotions, perhaps we can catch a fleeting glimpse of a large well of some emotional state—but that's all. If we don't have a functioning quaternity, we might give up on the emotion because we can't understand it immediately. However, when we're functional, we can invite our intellect into the situation and ask for its help. We can make equal room for the emotion *and* our thoughts about the emotion. We can trust our emotions and our minds to work together as we alternate between feeling the emotion and naming it in a back-and-forth rhythm, bringing our logical and linguistic intelligences to the task: "Is it fear?" No. "Is it anxiety?" That's closer. "Is it worry?" Yes. "What about . . . ?"

When our logical intelligences and our emotional intelligences can work together, we become able to feel *and* think about things consciously. When our emotional state is named and understood intellectually, we can work with it properly. This is how a balanced psyche behaves. In an unbalanced psyche, the intellect might take over and squash or devalue the unnamed emotion, but in a whole psyche, the intellect will act as an interpreter and contribute its skills toward greater emotional understanding.

In this next example, the emotions and the intellect support another element within the whole self. Many of us have had a vision of a different kind of life, of an opportunity off in the distance. This is an example of our fiery vision soaring beyond the present and into an alternate future. If we don't know how to rely on the village of elements and intelligences inside us, that vision might never come to fruition; it might be relegated to the scrap heap of fantasies. However, if we allow our full selves to work freely, we can move decisively toward that vision and make it real. Our emotions can translate the vision into urges and feelings that can move themselves into the sphere of the body in the form of dreams and desires. If we honor our dreams and desires, rather than squelching them because we're afraid or because they seem illogical, we can make day-to-day movements toward that vision. Our logical intelligences can help us gather data and plot a logical course for the journey. Our emotions can contribute the skills and impetus we need to stay on course. Our bodies can help us walk toward the vision and make it real in our everyday world. Our visionary spirits can remind us, when we get tired or confused, about the excitement just ahead of us.

In this example, our intuitive spirit sees and holds a vision, our emotions move the vision into our bodies, our bodies sense the vision and walk toward it, and our logical intelligence makes plans so that the vision can become a reality. In an unbalanced psyche, our logical intelligence might overthink and eventually crush our vision (it might squelch an idea it didn't initiate), or our dishonored emotions might overreact and scare us away from the vision. But in a whole psyche, our logic will fully support our fiery visions with its ability to translate, plot, and plan.

Each situation we encounter activates different strengths, but the function of each part of us is always the same. Our emotions move energy, abilities, and information from one place to another by reacting and feeling their way through life. Our minds translate, categorize, and store the content of any material presented to them. Our bodies feel and process any material viscerally; they bring it down to earth. Our visionary spirits supply the overview, the big picture of the whole situation in relation to all other situations. In a properly moderated psyche, our four elements and our seven intelligences are like dancers in an intricately choreographed ballet; each moves and performs in its own rhythm and in its own way. In a poorly moderated psyche or system (which is unfortunately the norm in our culture), the elements and intelligences don't dance; they smack into and trip over one another in confusion and gracelessness.

Most of us have poorly moderated psyches. This is nothing to be ashamed of; it's just how things are. It's how we've been trained and raised, and it's how we train and raise one another. We *can* learn to bring democracy to our inner lives (and we'll focus on that in the very next chapter), but we can only achieve true balance when we can understand the serious imbalance we've endured.

Most of us have been taught to value only our clearly "intellectual" intelligences and we've learned to sequester our four elements, and by that I mean our spiritual or visionary lives are very separate from our day-to-day lives, while our intellectual lives are separate from our emotional lives. We've all been trained to squelch our emotions and overemphasize our intellects. We don't seem to know how to feel deeply and think brilliantly at the same time, and we're nearly incapable of connecting our emotional flow to our intellectual processes. Most of us also maintain a separation between the spirit and the body because it's all we know how to do. We don't know how to incorporate meditation, daydreaming, or contemplation into the everyday world of driving, working, and paying the rent. In our imbalance, the realms of earth and fire can seem utterly disconnected from one another.

Whether our personal split lives in the territory of body and spirit or in the territory of mind and emotion, we all experience a split in some part of our souls. It's a fact of modern life. You see and feel this sort of split in an either/or personality. *Either* he can live in this world of money and competition, *or* he can go to a retreat and live like a Franciscan monk, but he can't do both, because his body and spirit don't communicate. *Either* she can study every available bit of information and be absolutely certain, *or* she can turn away from all thought and feel her way through every situation, but she can't possibly use her intellect and emotions together.

When we're split apart, there's no flowing movement between our body and spirit (or between our thoughts and emotions), and there's no understanding of the importance of each of our intelligences; instead, there's a wild pendulum-swing between seemingly opposite poles. Every element and intelligence is alternately glorified and then ignored. The body isn't allowed to walk the truth of the other elements, the spirit isn't allowed to bring its visions to each part of the psyche, the mind isn't allowed to translate for the other struggling elements, and the emotions aren't allowed to convey energy and information between the warring factions. The outcome of an imbalance like this, in a culture that relies almost exclusively on intellect, is that the sadly isolated mind has no choice but to escalate its skittery, airy process.

When the body and spirit are at odds, and the portaging abilities of the emotions are ignored by both, the intellect will often go into high gear. It has to, because there is a strangulation of every other element and a desperate lack of flow in the psyche. When stagnation is present, the logical, spatial, and linguistic intelligences nearly always step forward—not because they're better, or smarter, or quicker than any of our other aspects, but simply because they're the only intelligences that get much exercise or notice in our schooling and our culture.

When there is no communication between the elements, and the intellect is forced to take a forward position in our psyches, we'll think too much, often to the point of tormenting ourselves with all our misused and overburdened mental energy. Nothing will be accomplished, because our bodies won't be allowed to bring our thoughts into the world in visceral ways. Nothing will become clear, because our emotions won't be allowed to make decisions, feel the consequences of our thoughts, or bring emotive information to our intellects. No true brilliance will ensue, either, because our visionary spirits won't be allowed to help our minds observe the larger picture of where things come from and where they'll eventually go.

The psyche doesn't function properly when the intellect is in charge; instead, it spins and whirls into endless planning, scheming, "what-if-ing," and obsessing. This is the way most of us experience the intellect, but this is not a true or whole experience. An out-of-balance intellect does behave badly—it does create many problems—but it has no other options. You see, our airy, logical intelligences can't balance our system all by themselves. They can't do the job of our other elements or our other intelligences; they can only escalate their own process, which unbalances our system even further.

Here's an example: Imagine trying to make a decision between two jobs, one in your area offering less money and one in a faraway town offering more. If you use only your mind in making the decision, you'll center your attention on travel and finances—on whether moving or staying put would make more sense. Your decision will be very logical. But what if the move would eat up the extra money in the second job, bringing both to equal footing financially? If there were no advantage to either one, you might find yourself in an indecisive muddle. You'd go back and forth in your mind, from one job to the other. Which is better? Which should you choose? If your airy intellect was the only element working freely in your psyche, you might careen back and forth between the two jobs and choose one over the other without any real certainty. But even after you made the decision, you'd probably continue to second- and third-guess yourself, because logic alone has no power or grounded direction.

However, if you honored the entire village inside you, you would have more options. If you couldn't make a distinction between two equally logical choices, your emotional intelligences could provide their feeling sense of the emotive difference between the two jobs. How would staying put feel? How would moving on feel? What duties and responsibilities would come with each job, and how would you feel about them and about the people you'd have to work with? If you could get a *feeling* for each job, you'd have a clearer sense of which one made more sense for you. Your emotions could help you feel the difference between the two jobs and the two towns, and this would help your body feel the visceral differences in each of your choices—perhaps one is in a wetter climate or nearer to mountains. You could get a physical sense for staying put or moving on, because your bodily-kinesthetic intelligence would bring visceral energy and information into the situation. If you would allow your body and your emotions into the decisive process, your mind could calm down and take its proper position in your psyche. It could even relax enough to allow a visionary perspective to emerge. When your mind was grounded and centered properly, you'd have the peace and quiet you needed to ask yourself where your life is going in the grand scheme of things and if either job would help you get there. When you can rely on all parts of yourself, your judgment will not be merely intellectual; it will be emotively grounded, life-affirming, visionary, and wholly intelligent.

However, if you rely too heavily on your logical intellect, you won't be able to make clear or whole judgments because your intellect can only work with the flat facts of the material presented to it. It can't dive down into the feelings and nuances under the facts—not without your watery emotions it can't. It also can't soar above all the facts without your fiery vision, and it can't make the facts useful and tangible without the help of your earthy body. When your logical intellect is isolated from the whole of your quaternity, it is less intelligent, less functional, and less wise. An intellect working alone will always have poor judgment, because it won't have access to the whole picture. What your airy intellect can do all alone is think incessantly, create fantasies and battle plans, revisit issues hundreds of times, and torment your body and your spirit, not to mention itself. However, when you can give it its rightful place in your balanced village of elements and intelligences, your intellect becomes brilliant.

When you can surround your emotions with a village of skills and abilities, your logical intelligences and your emotional intelligences will be able to work together. When you can allow your emotions to flow, you'll free your beleaguered intellect from the impossible task of ruling your entire life without support. Then your intellect will be as free as the air itself, able to translate information masterfully because it won't be expected to actually ferry information from one place to another. Transporting information, skills, and energy—that's the emotions' job. The logical intellect has its own job; it translates, organizes, stores, and retrieves information. When the two can work together in your balanced psyche, you'll become intelligent in deep and meaningful ways.

Many of us have fallen into the trap of thinking that spirit and science, or logic and emotion, or physical life and spiritual life, are at odds with one another, but this is preposterous. None of our intelligences are at odds with one another, and none of the four elements are at odds with each other in the natural world. They're only at odds in lopsided and confused human psyches. Mysteries and beauties abound in all parts of us, and true genius dances in the places where those parts intertwine.

5

Reviving Your Essential Nature

Making Room for Your Central Self

IF YOU WANT TO work with your emotions empathically, you've got to bring all parts of yourself into the process and into balance. Bringing balance to your system means welcoming each of your elements and intelligences into the whole of your psyche. Your movements into wholeness start from where you are, from your strengths and from your comfort zone. You'll always have a quadrant or a set of intelligences you rely upon most strongly—you'll always be your unique self—but when you have free and conscious access to the entire village of your psyche, you'll have a bigger, brighter, and more functional self to rely on. If you can enter this balancing practice with the understanding that you've already got one or two well-exercised elements to start with, you'll feel more comfortable. If you can say, "Okay, I've got the earthy body down pat" or "I'm already a very intellectual person," you can work from a position of strength. You can then add intuition and vision, emotional flow, artistic and linguistic skills, intellectual awareness, or physical competence into your mix and move forward into wholeness. Imbalance is a dependable fact of modern life, but it isn't a life sentence. If you can stand upright and look for your lost elements, you'll find them. When you find them, you can reanimate them.

BALANCING YOUR ELEMENTS

Understanding the function of each of your elements helps you self-diagnose your personal imbalances. For instance, if you can't get things done, if you dream or wish for things you can never make happen in this world, then you'll know your earth element is being neglected. If you just can't figure things out and nothing makes sense, you'll know your air element isn't being allowed to take its proper place—there's no translating going on, and you're probably not using your best judgment. If you can't feel or experience life fully—if things don't flow or connect for you, and you don't know how you feel—then you'll know your water element isn't welcome in your life. If you don't have any sense of distance or perspective—if you can't rise above your situation and dream of other lives or outcomes, or if you can't believe in or trust intuition or vision—then you'll know your fire element is not operating in your psyche. Balancing your village of elements and intelligences is a lifelong practice, but it's fairly simple once you realize you *have* a village inside you. Regaining access to lost quadrants, supporting and nurturing overworked intelligences, and balancing yourself is a simple process of entering each element consciously. Conscious practices in the realm of each element bring that element back into balance in your whole self, and that helps you create a ground under yourself so that you can interpret the language of emotions.

Balancing Earth

If your earth element is out of sorts—if you've ignored *or* overworked your body and your bodily-kinesthetic abilities—you should move into conscious physical activity, nutrition, and rest. Restoring balance to your earth element means bringing your physical life into consciousness, not only by allowing your body to build, feel, explore, and create, but by taking excellent and respectful care of yourself. Dance, exercise, gardening, rock climbing, martial arts, or any sort of movement that brings you into contact with your body and the world around you helps bring your earthy intelligences into balance. If you're primarily logical, you can design a brilliant exercise or dietary regimen for yourself, as long as you let your body tell you when the perfectly logical things you suggest don't feel right. If you're primarily emotional, you can work in tactile art-forms like ceramics (or whatever you like best), or bring emotive dance like salsa, samba, or African dance into your life, as long as you let your body rest or do more purely physical exercises when it needs to. If you're primarily spiritual, you can choose spiritual movement practices like yoga, tai chi, or qigong, as long as you let your body play, rest, fool around, and wrestle with the world when it needs to. If you're primarily earthy, and you're trying to balance your physicality with your other elements, you can use movement practices such as salsa, tai chi, or complex dance to bring emotive, visionary, or intellectual awareness into your physical life.

Balancing Air

If your logical air element is gusting like crazy (or is as still as death), you should move into conscious mental activity. Study, read, learn a language, or research things that interest you. If you don't like to read and research, you can do puzzles, play games, or crunch numbers. Anything that gives your mind specific, well-defined tasks will help it focus with clear intent. Make plans and bring logic to your process—whatever that may be. If you're primarily physical, you can bring intellectual study and planning into your physical life, into your diet and exercise or into your home and work environments, as long as you sit still and let your thoughts do all the moving every now and then. If you're primarily emotional, you can make a deep study of art, psychology, mythology, sociology, or cultural anthropology (or anything that centers on artistic expression, relationships, cultures, or human development), as long as you let your mind ponder freely without connecting its thoughts when it needs to. If you're primarily spiritual, you can study comparative religion or make a deep and historical study of the beliefs you hold; you can become more intelligent about spiritual beliefs, as long as you let your mind explore things logically (without any faith-based rules) when it so desires. If you're primarily intellectual and you'd like to bring more balance to your air element, you can use your mind to help support your physical experiences, your emotional knowledge, and your visionary awareness.

Balancing Water

If your water element is overflowing (or dried up), you should move into conscious expressive activity. Anything that releases feelings through your body or your mind will help bring your water element back into balance. Restoring balance to your water element means learning the language of the emotions and bringing their wisdom into your life consciously. Dance and expressive movement, music and art of all kinds, writing (especially poetry), and any nature pursuit is deeply healing for your emotive self. Your emotions need to flow freely and feel the connections between all things, and they need to be able to express their knowledge through art or action. If you're primarily earthy, you can learn to move your body in sensual and sensitive ways. You can learn to slow down and feel the textures of foods, of your own body, and of the world around you with dance, sculpture, water play, and healthy sensuality. You can learn to balance your physical strength and stability with unstructured, flowing movements. If you're primarily mental, you can make a study of the emotions, as you're doing right now. Or you can express yourself emotively through writing, music, and poetry, as long as you give your emotions the freedom to scatter words and ideas without form or reason when they so desire. If you're primarily spiritual, you can express yourself through flowing (not static) meditative movements like tai chi or qigong, as long as you give your emotions the freedom to flow without structure as well. You can also meditate in nature or spend quiet time by bodies of water to remind your visionary spirit of the necessity of flow in the world. If you're primarily watery and emotional, and you'd like to bring more balance to the village inside you, you can bring your interpersonal and intrapersonal awareness to your intellectual pursuits (watch how people relate to each other), your physical experiences (become aware of how you feel inside), and your spiritual visions (explore how they relate to your everyday life).

Balancing Fire

If your fire element is raging or dampened, you should move into conscious spiritual or contemplative activity and make room for dreams, intuitions, and visions in your everyday life. Religious observance and meditation can be healing for some, but you'll also find spiritual healing in nature walks; in time spent with animals, children, and elders; and in any time spent by a body of water. The visionary part of you needs its space (and plenty of contact with living things) in order to be at its best. If you're primarily physical, you can move into a physical meditative practice such as yoga, tai chi, or qigong, as long as you let yourself wander into

visionary flights of fancy every now and then. If you're primarily intellectual, you can bring spiritual texts and ideas into your thought process and
study the great dreamers and visionaries, as long as you also let yourself
know the truth without a study guide. If you're primarily emotive, you
can bring a visionary overview to your emotive process; you can look at
emotions from above—in culture, across cultures, within your family, and
within your psyche. If you're primarily visionary, and you'd like to balance
your psyche, you can bring your eagle-eyed vision to your physical life,
your intellectual processes, and your emotional awareness.

BRINGING IT ALL TOGETHER

When you can bring your emotional aspects, your intellectual gifts, your
bodily skills and strengths, and your visionary spirit into respectful peer
relationships, you'll be able to dance in the realm of brilliance. Your body,
if you bring it to a place of balance, will be able to act upon, live out, and
walk the talk of your emotional truths, your intellectual information, and
your visionary certainty. Your logical mind, if you give it its freedom, will
be able to translate between your quadrants and provide facts and knowledge to support your body's sensations, your emotional realities, and your
visionary ideas. Your emotions, if you allow them to move freely from one
place to another, will be able to convey energy and information between
your visionary spirit, your body, and your mind. Your spirited vision, if
you give it its honorable place, will be able to soar and climb and bring its
timeless wisdom to your physical, emotional, and intellectual lives.

When you perform this balancing act, though, an unusual thing happens. When you can get all parts of yourself working together, you'll
suddenly realize that you're not any one of your elements or any one
of your intelligences. It can be startling (even disorienting) to suddenly
realize that you're not *just* your body or your emotions or your intellect
or your artistic abilities or your vision. It can feel disconcerting—almost
as if your feet have left the ground. You *have* each of your elements and
intelligences, but you aren't any one of them. When you move away
from imbalance and diminishment (where you saw yourself as primarily intellectual or spiritual or emotional or physical), an entirely new
world opens up. When the village of elements and intelligences is in

balance inside you, a fifth element or a meta-intelligence—your intelligence *about* your intelligence—arises at the center of your psyche. This
new element is called *nature, wood,* or *ether* in various wisdom traditions. Though none of your quadrants could exist without it, this central
nature only truly flourishes when your four outer quadrants are in
proper relationship with one another. This nature element becomes the
new center of your self, soul, ego, or personality, which is no longer
based upon one or two elements or intelligences alone. When this true
nature arises, you'll have free and equal access to each part of yourself.
Consequently, you'll be able to live and breathe as a whole and agile
person. However, this true and essential nature won't flourish (and won't
even be apparent to you) until the whole village inside you is recognized
and honored.

This idea of a new being or a new element arising out of balance and
wholeness appears in many traditions and many cultures. Chinese Taoist
practices work with the five-phases model of earth, metal, water, fire, and
wood. In that system, metal is the intellectual air element, and the wood
element is the one that arises when all the elements are balanced. Wood
in the Chinese five phases isn't a plank of dead wood—it's a living tree or
the realm of plant life that arises when earth, metal, water, and fire are balanced. The Taoists also work with an interesting dietary five-phases model
of sweet, sour, salty, bitter, and hot. When a dish can incorporate all five
tastes, the hypothesis goes, it heals the body and balances all the organs
and bodily systems.

Many Native American and African cosmologies speak of the four
directions or the four seasons as the outer aspects of the sacred wheel—or
the mystic spiral—of life. In these cosmologies, however, there is always a
central focal point from which the directions or the seasons flow. North,
south, east, and west only exist in relation to center, and the four seasons
only exist in relation to the spiral of life or to the great Earth Mother at
the center of time. In the Christian tradition, where the Trinitarian system
of the Father, the Son, and the Holy Ghost prevails, many people sense
a lack of balance and wholeness. In some parts of the Christian church,
people are trying to create a holy quaternity by adding Mary and the
whole concept of the feminine into the Trinity. Many people believe that

the Christian church would be revitalized and reborn if the trinity were squared and balanced by the inclusion of Mary. Again, you have this idea of a new life arising out of wholeness and balance among the elements.

The same sort of life arises when the four elements are balanced within your own personality. A fifth-element self—an evolved and integrated new self—suddenly awakens and begins to look at the world in new ways as your meta-intelligence arises and increases your capacities and your options. You no longer swing wildly between being too mental or not smart enough, too physical or too ungrounded, too emotional or too frozen, or too spiritual or too coarse. When you're standing upright in the center of your four elements, you're something and someone new.

A NEW VISION OF SELF

When a meta-intelligent, fifth-element personality appears at the center of the self, the belief that the body is coarse and imprisoning fades away as the body's earthy reality creates a strong foundation for the quaternity. The idea that the mind is irksome and untrustworthy (or smarter than anything else) fades away as the mind brings its airy brilliance to a fully functioning psyche. The idea that the emotions are erratic and dangerous fades away as the emotions infuse the psyche with life-giving fluidity, just as the belief that the spirit is illusory or disconnected from life fades away as the spirit brings it fiery vision to the whole. The mistaken belief about the trouble with judgment also fades away, because when we honor earth, air, water, and fire equally, we can make whole judgments that are nothing like the name-calling that passes for judgment in an unbalanced psyche. In essence, the presence of balance in the quaternity makes almost everything we know about the personality and the ego fade into obscurity, to be replaced by a vibrant new picture of what it is to be fully human.

When I hear people from one-element, two-element, or even three-element systems talking authoritatively about how the personality functions, I shake my head, because all that can be seen from outside the quaternity is shadows and specters and broken shards of self. When something as complex as the psyche is viewed from an unbalanced position, the conclusions based on that view will be unbalanced as well. It is simply impossible to understand or even describe the central self when you don't possess one yourself. So listen carefully when people denigrate the ego or suggest that we be selfless. What imbalances prompt them to attack the center of the soul?

When people attack the central self or any of the elements in the quaternity, ask yourself: "Are they speaking from full knowledge?" You can't truly comprehend the personality until you've seen a healthy and resourced one—just as you can't truly comprehend any of the four elements until you understand the quaternity. You can't get a full and complete description of the ego, the personality, or the self until it arises at the very center of a balanced and resourced psyche. That broken and desperate *thing* that arises in an unbalanced system is just a shadow of true self, true personality, or true ego. When you choose to be partially conscious, nothing useful can stand upright at the center of your soul; you'll be lucky to be able to walk and chew gum at the same time!

When you live in an unbalanced quaternity, you'll consistently forget to act or think or feel or dream. Instead of becoming fuller and deeper with each day, you and your psyche will just become more lopsided. Your personality will be alternately flat or spiky, your ego will swing between utter dejection and utter inflation, and your self-esteem will career wildly between ungrounded highs and unrealistic lows. But when you can access the grounding and balancing properties of each of your elements and each of your intelligences, you'll have a stable foundation and a home. You'll be able to work miracles in your life because you'll have full and conscious access to all of the tools nature and evolution gave you to survive life on this planet.

This balancing act is simple in theory; you just include your physical life, your emotions, your intellectual processes, and your spiritual knowledge in your everyday life. You can review the balancing practices on pages 58–60 every day, or you can create your own practices to balance your quaternity, but the reality is that you'll have to work at it every day at first. It's not an easy thing to maintain balance in a culture that doesn't support or understand it. As you move through your day, you'll notice how difficult it is to share your emotional or visionary perceptions with certain people, while others won't want to hear anything but your intellectual input. Moving into the full village of your psyche is an exciting and heady experience, but there is discomfort involved. I won't mince words—it can be a painfully lonely time at first. You'll gain immeasurable freedom when you break away from systems and mindsets that keep you blindfolded and hobbled, but you'll leave a lot of friends and acquaintances behind you. Full-on intelligence and five-element people are unusual, and there's not a lot of support for wholeness in our culture.

Some people can even become defensive if you suggest that the body is wise, the mind is stable, the emotions are healing, or fiery vision can free them; therefore, for your own growth and happiness, it's best not to shake up everyone around you. Instead, find a way to work through these balancing practices with the support of a close friend. If you can't find a partner, though, don't worry. I can assure you that the loneliness is only temporary. *All* personal growth requires that you leave some people behind, but such growth also brings new people and new experiences into your life. Soon you'll have the support you need to maintain your changes. Even before support appears, though, there is an interesting benefit. Once they get the hang of it, five-element people who welcome their multiple intelligences love their own company and rarely feel lonely. When you can stand upright in the village of your whole self, there is so much to see and experience that the idea of loneliness soon fades into the mist.

I have a warning, though. If you try, as I once did, to change the unbalanced systems or groups around you, you may halt your forward progress. Unbalanced systems require lots of scapegoats, fans, flunkies, and cronies in order to keep themselves going—they seem to have a magnetic force around them that will drag you in before you even know it. So watch yourself, because staying engaged with unbalanced people or systems can delay your own movement into wholeness. Here are some clear signs of imbalance: the presence of segregation (of people, elements, or intelligences); the inability to tolerate mystery (and the need to explain things from one-sided perspectives); the repudiation of whole elements or intelligences; and the absence of humor. These are warning signs I never ignore. My best advice for you, if you want to live in harmony with your four elements, is to be rather quiet and circumspect about the changes you're making. It's best to just bless the heck out of unbalanced people and systems, take yourself out of their sphere of influence, and focus on your

THE LANGUAGE OF EMOTIONS

own inner work and your own emotions. Certainly, study the unbalanced people and systems around you—they're always fascinating—but protect yourself from their grasp by keeping your inner work private and sacred.

There is rich magnificence at the center of your resourced psyche, and there is deep connection to the world when you have a whole self from which to view it. At the beginning of the journey, though, you will experience loss—of relationships, of cherished but unworkable mindsets, and of your old sense of self. Understand that this loss has a purpose; it helps you realize that change is certainly occurring. If you can flow with the river of change, rather than try to grasp at your old moorings, you can turn this time of loss into a period of exquisite personal growth. However, let's be clear that learning the language of emotions is not a normal or accepted transition in much of our culture. The emotions live in an element we don't value and in intelligences we don't exercise consciously. Therefore, entering the realm of the emotions means moving away from the status quo.

If you need support in letting go of old ways of being, repeat the free-flowing sadness exercise on pages 33–34 or skip forward to the chapter on sadness (page 295), where you'll learn that properly honored loss always leads to rejuvenation and rebirth. When you fight loss or refuse to release that which no longer serves you, you won't be able to live or breathe freely. Your sadness will help you understand that it is only by moving consciously into loss that you can live again.

EXAMPLES OF FULLY RESOURCED PERSONALITIES

I'd like to give you some full-bodied examples of what it looks and feels like to work at the center of your village of intelligences and elements. It's hard to find stellar examples—that I'll grant you—but it's easier when you know what to look for. I found an excellent example of fully resourced behavior in a *Hana Hou!* magazine story about Nainoa Thompson, a Hawai'ian man who is the lead navigator for the Polynesian Voyaging Society's oceangoing canoe, the *Hokule'a*. Thompson was trained in the ancient art of "wayfinding," which is the Polynesian form of non-instrument navigation. If you consider that early Tahitians set sail in their canoes and eventually found (and populated) Hawai'i after watching seabirds coming from the general direction of the Hawai'ian archipelago, you'll understand that wayfinding is quite an art and quite a science.

Wayfinding requires strong logical knowledge of tides and star positions and the ability to fully plot the voyage, but it also relies on earthy strength and competence in canoeing and sailing, the bodily-kinesthetic ability to sense subtle changes in the sea and the air, and a deep intrapersonal ability to listen to emotional reactions in oneself and the interpersonal ability to be aware of the emotional tenor of the crew. Beyond that, wayfinding requires a sincere connection to the traditions, beliefs, and dreams of the Polynesian tribes for whom wayfinding was and is a spiritual practice. Only a person with strong fiery awareness and deep grounding in tribal knowledge can understand the messages of the sea gods and goddesses. Wayfinding also requires a fifth-element ego that can make whole decisions based on the flows of information from all of the directions (and can fill in when important information is not available).

During his first long voyage as lead navigator in 1980, Thompson and his crew sailed *Hokule'a* (without instruments) from Hawai'i to Tahiti. Midway through the voyage, *Hokule'a* was trapped in the doldrums, a frustrating and dangerous zone of dead winds punctuated by furious, sky-obscuring squalls. Thompson barely slept for days on end as the squalls pushed *Hokule'a* in one direction, then another, then another. In the dead of night, the canoe was making good speed under a fierce squall, but in what direction? There was no way of knowing, as the night sky was completely obscured by clouds and rain. Thompson was exhausted and deeply confused; his mind and body could not orient themselves. He backed up against the rail, and suddenly a calm came over him and he had a vision of the moon—even though he could not see it with his eyes. For a moment, his intellect fought the vision, but Thompson felt a strong sense of knowing emanating from the vision, so he turned the canoe. As soon as he did, he felt a physical and emotional sense of rightness, which was followed by a tiny break in the cloud cover, revealing the moon in the exact position his vision had foretold. Thompson cannot explain the experience with his rational mind alone—and he doesn't even try. His central self knows that there is much more to navigating than merely being a good logician and sailor.

There's an insightful Latin saying, *Adaequatio rei et intellectus,* which means that the understanding of the knower must be adequate to the thing to be known. Nainoa Thompson, with his years of sailing and canoeing, his physical strength and abilities, his trust in the visionary process, his emotional skills and ability to calm himself in the presence of fear and exhaustion, and his sense of being connected to the ancestors, provides a wonderful example of this saying, because he was certainly adequate to the task set before him. With nothing external to rely on, he went inside and found the answer within the village of himself.

When we attempt great or new things, we require great resources inside ourselves—and strong checks and balances in our psyches, so we don't become confused in the presence of flow. When we can rely equally on all of our elements and intelligences, we'll have full and conscious access to everything we need to make whole decisions and strong movements. However, along with that powerful level of access, there will also be a central being who is separate from each of the elements and intelligences, and who can moderate the flows of each one (as Thompson was able to do when the seemingly illogical vision of the moon appeared to him). This central self can say, "My logical mind cannot understand this fiery vision, but that doesn't mean the vision is untrue." When there is a central self functioning, each of the elements can work in balance with—and in relation to—its brother and sister elements.

For another take on the five elements, it's fun to look at groups of people who create a fifth-element entity at the center of their relationships. In the 1960s, two such groups of four men appeared on different stages and created popular art forms that endure to this day. The first group of four was the Beatles, who encompassed the four elements (though each man was and is a whole person and not simply an example of one quadrant). Ringo Starr held the earth element, or the grounded beat and foundation; George Harrison held the air element, or the intellectual aspect; John Lennon held the water element, or the emotive and sometimes explosive aspect; and Paul McCartney held the fiery position as the visionary or leader of the group (though he and Lennon often traded, and argued about, their water and fire duties). At the center was the fifth element that arose in response to this balanced quaternity of men: the music of the Beatles, which captivated, challenged, and enthralled millions (and could not be replicated by any of the men once their quartet had disbanded). Even today, people write endlessly about the mystique of the Beatles without touching on the underlying aspect of elemental wholeness that made their music so memorable and delightful.

The second group of four men lived and worked in the fictional realm of the *Star Trek* television series. In that quaternity (though each man was also a whole being and not just a one-element character), Mr. Scott held the earth element and was responsible for the efficient running of all things mechanical; Spock held the air element and the intellectual expertise; Dr. McCoy held the water element and the emotional awareness (and healing duties); and Captain Kirk held the fiery, visionary leadership role. Though other recurring characters (such as Lieutenant Uhura, who held both air and water in her position as communications officer and musician) added important elemental balance to the mix, these four men personified clear-cut elemental qualities. At the center of their quaternity lived the ship (and the mission) from which their lives and stories flowed: the *Enterprise,* which had a presence and a story all its own. And just as it is with the Beatles, reams and reams of paper are dedicated to the astounding cultural phenomenon of *Star Trek,* while the central theme of wholeness and quaternal balance that makes the show so unforgettable is overlooked.

Although we don't consciously honor all of our intelligences in our daily lives and haven't been trained to look for five-element people or behaviors, the quaternity and the healing central nature element seem to find a way to make themselves known—through art, fiction, symbolism, or in any way possible. This is helpful, because having models of fully resourced and five-element behaviors is important if you want to become adept in the oceanic realm of the emotions. When you're asking big questions or attempting big things, you need a big, strong, and balanced center from which to process all the information you gather. You can't learn new skills and you can't dive into profound mysteries if you don't bring all of your resources into play.

Remember this: the understanding of the knower must be *adequate* to the thing to be known. As you move into the powerful realm of the emotions, especially in a world where the emotions have been relegated to the deep shadow, you'll need to be physically stable, mentally centered, emotionally agile, and spiritually aware. You'll also need to have a fully resourced self at the center of your psyche who can say, "Oh my, that's intense rage, but I don't have to blast someone, I can ask my vision and my logic to lead me into an understanding of it," or "This is powerful sadness, but I don't have to run from it. I can ask what needs to be released and what needs to be rejuvenated," or "This is panic; it's a freezing reaction. I can ask my body how I can begin to move again, and I can ask my spirit to help me come back from shock and near-death into life." Your fully resourced central nature holds the key, not just to emotional brilliance, but to brilliance in your entire life, and it can only arise consciously when you consciously welcome all of your elements and intelligences. The tasks on pages 58–60 will help you create the foundation you need to revive your wholeness and restore your unique central nature.

RESTORATION AND DISTRACTION: UNDERSTANDING THE DIFFERENCE

By now, you most likely know where your elements and your intelligences fit into your psyche (or where they don't). Your task is to bring the lost parts of yourself back into your awareness so that you can restore your wholeness. The balancing tasks for each of your elements are fairly simple in and of themselves (you just become conscious of that element and its way of working in the world), but the process of restoring your psyche to wholeness can be somewhat of a hurdle. Because we don't have any practice at balancing or integrating ourselves, we can take the balancing tasks a little too far. We can spiral into distractions with those tasks; we can trick ourselves into using them in place of the skills and abilities they represent. Keep an eye out for this distracting tendency in your own psyche.

Watch yourself as you meditate or move or do your art or your research. Make sure that you're not relying on these tasks to the exclusion of everything else. It is surprisingly easy to throw yourself into the balancing practices while ignoring the element or the intelligence you're supposed to be balancing—to assiduously meditate instead of simply letting yourself float and dream; to read and research instead of allowing free thought; to exercise intently rather than letting your body move sensually through the world; or to do your art or music when you become upset, rather than sitting with your feelings as they are. Be aware of this tendency.

Make sure that you can work with your emotions as well as you work with artistic media; that you work planning and logic into your daily life, rather than spending long hours reading, surfing online, or playing solitaire when life scatters you; that you work intuitive vision into your everyday life, rather than sequestering yourself with an isolating meditative practice; and that you work the physical world and your body's needs into your daily deliberations, rather than relying on exercise or movement as after-the-fact stress-relieving tools. Each part of you has its healing processes and balancing activities, but be careful how you use them, because you can begin to rely on the processes and activities so heavily that you won't develop any internal skills. The purpose of gathering your village of elements and intelligences is to help your psyche become more functional, to give your central self more resources so that you can work with your emotions skillfully and honorably. If your practices isolate or distract you from the world or your own life, your central self won't be fully resourced.

This resourcing process isn't about becoming perfect. It's about becoming whole. A whole psyche reacts to and engages with the world because it has many resources and abilities available to it. A whole psyche is adequate to the task of partnering with the emotions, while a perfectionist psyche can only operate within a narrow corridor of rigid preconceptions and strict control. If you find yourself focusing on your inner balancing work with grim determination and perfectionism, understand this: the flow inside you has evaporated. Welcome water back into your psyche, not in the form of scheduled practices, but in the form of the emotions themselves. Allow yourself to feel whatever you're feeling, and your psyche will be able to flow once again. If any of your balancing tasks begin to loom over you, step back and reassess what you're doing, refocus yourself, and get back on track. You'll get the hang of it.

Remember that balance is a goal—it's not a fact. There will be moments, days, and even months when one or two of your elements or intelligences will be in the background for one reason or another (for instance, in a work environment where visionary awareness isn't at the forefront, in a scholastic environment where emotional awareness isn't valued, and so on). There are many situations in which only parts of you are activated, just as there are many places on earth where all the elements of earth, air, water, and fire aren't equally represented. Think of the cold, dark, deep ocean, or granite rock-faces where nothing grows, or the searing center of the desert. There are many natural environments where certain elements aren't in evidence, yet because our planet is an integrated system, nature continues to flourish, even in harsh environments.

That's an important thing to remember. Your village of elements and intelligences will create an integrated system that will help you thrive in harsh environments. When your psyche is unbalanced, you often create drama simply because you don't have access to your whole self. However, when you honor all of your elements and intelligences, the resourcefulness you embody can help you avoid unnecessary drama. For instance, if you create an arid desert of the soul by hiding in your intellect and your dreamy vision, you'll be endangered by your own dismissal of your physical and emotional realities. However, if you *enter* some situation (like a spiritual practice) that requires an airy-fiery, desertlike soul—and you have access to *all* of your resources—you can build irrigation systems of physicality and emotion inside yourself to create a restful oasis.

Or if you're struggling miserably in the deep water of your squashed and dishonored emotions, you may drown, but if you *choose* to enter the deep water of your strong emotions as a whole person, you'll be able to swim and survive. You might choose to follow your air bubbles to the surface (as divers do) and let your thoughts lead you up and out of the depths of emotion so you can catch your breath. You could also create an island of earth through some physical practice, so you'll have a place to rest between dives. Or you might allow your fiery eagle nature to soar above the river of your emotions so that you can remember where things came from and where they'll eventually go.

In short, your fully resourced personality can help you remain whole even when trouble is present. When you're whole, you can weather the hard times and the harsh places—just as the earth itself does—because you'll have a functional and multifaceted nature self at the very center of your psyche. When you're whole, you won't require everything around you to be unmoving and controllable, as perfectionists do, and you won't be happy only when conditions meet your exacting standards. When you're whole, you'll have real and varied emotions, real physical triumphs and difficulties, real intellectual joys and struggles, and real visionary awakenings and confusions; you'll have a whole and full life. Sometimes you'll stand up, and sometimes you'll fall down, but you'll be a full-fledged participant in the flows of life, and you'll experience true equilibrium. You'll be able to navigate your flows of earth, air, water, and fire from a central position, where you can marshal those flows to foster personal growth, loving relationships, and a meaningful, whole life. From that place of wholeness, you'll be able to meet your emotions and learn their language.

Remember to revisit the practices on pages 58–60, and know that the five empathic skills you'll learn will help you as well. But the most valuable balancing tools you have (as you learned in the three empathic exercises on pages 33–36) are your emotions themselves, and we'll dive into their flowing and brilliant realm in Part II.

FIGHTING THE FLOW
(WARNING: FLOW *ALWAYS* WINS)

When we don't have a conscious and deliberate relationship with our free-flowing emotions, we won't understand the necessity of flow. We fight the idea of flow; we relegate certain elements and intelligences to the deep shadow, squelch the flows we can control, and attempt to live in a benumbed version of peace and quiet as tension piles up inside us. We get knocked over by physical pains and symptoms, when simply listening to our bodies could help us calm them. We are tormented by obsessive and compulsive thoughts, when simply inviting our minds into a dialogue with their brother-and-sister elements could ease them. We become powerless marionettes in response to our raging and distrusted emotions, when simply listening to their messages could help us heal. Or we lose our way in response to uncontrollable visions and ideas, when simply honoring them could bring us back to center. When we fight the flow, the flow usually surges up and knocks us down, which, tragically, makes most of us renew the battle. It's a terrible thing to watch (and a terrible thing to experience), this futile war people wage with flow, but it's all around us. When we don't understand that flow is the natural movement in all elements and all life, we can't create alliances between our elements and our intelligences, and we can't achieve equilibrium; instead, we fight what can only be a losing battle.

Our modern world is a battleground littered with bodies and souls in unrelieved discomfort. The flows never stop, no matter what we do. We fall in battle, heal a little bit, raise our heads weakly, and boom! Another wave pounds us into the ground. We learn to hate flow in all its incarnations, rather than learning to move and dance with the flows that will never and can never cease.

When we're in the midst of this losing battle, we tend to grab at strange things to alleviate our discomfort. Beyond just repressing and squelching the flows in our elements, many of us try to approximate equilibrium with distractions (for instance, by using balancing practices *instead* of inviting an element fully into our lives) or addictions (including sugar, nicotine, and caffeine). We often try to use addictions or distractions to help us access or deny a problem element (or a problem emotion), and this can help us navigate the flow for a little while. Of course, addictions and distractions don't bring balance, wholeness, or true flow, but in a culture that separates every element and intelligence, categorizes every emotion, and seriously distrusts flow, addictions and distractions *can* sometimes provide a little peace.

Look at it this way: When we assume that flow and emotions are a problem, we'll start problem-solving, and we'll end up with a solution based on our assumption that flow and emotions equal trouble and disease. If we believe that emotions are the cause of all our troubles (because we've been taught to distrust flow and therefore cannot attain equilibrium no matter what we do), addictions and distractions may seem to be our only answer. If we can instead welcome our flowing emotions as necessary and irreplaceable—as the water elements in our fully functional psyches—we won't need to go into a problem-solving mode. We won't need to banish our emotions or strap them into chairs and force them to confess their sins. We'll just want to understand them, flow with them, and work as their partners if we can. That's the process we're in the middle of. But what if you're using addictions or distractions right now to manage your emotional life? What can you do?

That's completely up to you, but before you make any decisions, you can take an empathic look at the specific relief addictions and distractions provide to offset the stagnation and disruption in the psyche. Bringing awareness to distracting habits, practices, and behaviors can break the hold distractions have on you, just as understanding what addictions provide will help you understand what kind of relief you're seeking. We don't use drugs or distractions by accident, by mistake, or without reason. There is a very important place for addictions and distractions in an unbalanced psyche. Living without the resourced village inside us is jarring and perilous, which is why so many of us turn to addictions and distractions just to get through the day. When we have no useful center, we're agitated by the very forces that keep us alive—by flow, by movement, and by change. We know this instinctively, but when we don't live at the center of ourselves, we don't know what to do about it. No one is home to tell us what to do, the flows batter and torment us, and we have no peace or calm in which to make worthwhile decisions. We turn to addictions and distractions not because we're broken or stupid, but because we're desperately trying to restore our lost energies and bring balance to our aching psyches.

There is a perfectly logical reason for us to turn to addictions and distractions—so let's drop down under the surface and take an empathic look at the relief addictions, distractions, and painkilling practices bring to us. Then let's soar above the situation, and envision an entirely new kind of life where addictions and distractions are no longer such a necessity.

6

Avoidance, Addiction, and Awakening

Understanding the Need for Distractions

IF WE POSSESS A fully resourced psyche, we can moderate and regulate our many flows, listen to and observe any inner turmoil, and compassionately restore balance to our psyches. However, if we don't have that central ground from which to work, our quaternity of elements and our multiple intelligences won't be properly moderated. We'll be buffeted and battered by ungovernable flows of thought, emotion, sensation, and visions, rather than moving gracefully upon each of their currents and eddies. When we don't stand at the center of ourselves, nearly every part of us falls into trouble of some kind.

Many of us learn to press on in the face of such trouble. We find a way to cope—not flourish, not soar, not enjoy and embrace, just flat-out cope. Most of us turn to some form of dissociative practice, whether it's avoidance of the trouble, distraction from the trouble, or addiction to a substance that separates us from the trouble. Most of us, instead of learning to navigate our flows, find a way to live beside our dreams, beyond our emotions, in spite of our thoughts, away from our vision, and out of our bodies. I often say that our entire culture is having an out-of-body experience, but it's more correct to say that there's no one at the center of our selves to guide or comfort us; therefore, we cling to any form of relief we can find. Avoidance, distraction, and addiction are absolutely commonplace in our culture because imbalance is absolutely commonplace in our psyches.

Moving toward balance means moving away from distractions, addictions, and avoidance behaviors. However, that movement is unusual, because distractions are absolutely everywhere. We all distract ourselves on a daily (and even hourly) basis. We're all living in a kind of holding pattern; we fly over or under our issues as a matter of course. Note how many people use coffee, not as a drink, but as a substitute for sleep and normal focus. Watch people drive—they're talking on phones, eating, or reading, but they're not focused on the road. Notice that television has become a staple in nearly every household and in nearly every child's daily life. Look at the massive amount of time we spend surfing the Net and filling our minds with trivia. We're all wired and distracted for most of our waking hours. We use distractions to manage our work lives, our relationships, our families, our health care, our thought processes, and especially our emotions. We distract ourselves from our goals and dreams, from our loves and hopes, from our troubles and traumas, and from our deepest wishes and our truest selves. We distract ourselves from moving into wholeness, most likely because we haven't been taught that wholeness is real and attainable.

Moving away from distractions, addictions, and avoidance behaviors means moving away from our utterly distracted society and into our own keeping. This movement can be quite difficult, which is why going cold turkey on any distracting practice or substance is not recommended. Moving away from distractions and addictions requires a great deal of support, but it also requires a deep understanding of why we all distract ourselves so much of the time. It's helpful to move backward in time and ask ourselves, "What happens right before we grind the coffee or plunk down in front of the tube or reach for the chocolate, the cigarettes, or the alcohol? What occurs in the moments before we start exercising, shopping, chanting, or painting obsessively? What triggers our movement toward distractions and avoidance behaviors?"

Here's a hint: it's watery, it's powerful, it always tells the absolute unblinking truth, and it lives in the shadow of each of our psyches. In every case, right before we distract ourselves, there's always an emotion trying to come into consciousness—not a thought, not a vision, not a physical sensation, but an emotion. Even when we distract ourselves from physical pain, such as a headache or a sore muscle, it is not so much the pain, but our feelings *about* the pain that hurl us into distractions. Even when we distract ourselves from disturbing visions or cycling thoughts, it is the emotions we have *about* those visions and thoughts that send us into avoidance behaviors. If we could move consciously into those emotions rather than into distractions, we would learn brilliant things about ourselves and our situations.

The key to bringing ourselves out of our avoidance-distraction trance is to know what emotions are, what the water element does, and which emotions we're avoiding and why. When we can bring some measure of consciousness to our avoidance behaviors, we can learn to flow with situations (as emotions do), rather than running from them. When we can learn to decipher our emotional messages, as we'll do in Part II, we'll be able to meet our emotions with intelligence and grace. When our fully resourced selves can live freely, our need for distractions will lessen naturally. We may still require help to break our old habits or to mend the damage caused by addictive substances, but if we can simply feel our emotions, we won't require full-time distractions just to make it from one moment to the next.

When our psyches are not resourced, the conflicting currents in each of our dishonored elements and ignored intelligences create a raucous and destabilizing cacophony. Therefore, dissociation and distraction function as survival skills that offer a sense of distance when we're overwhelmed by stimuli. We'll dissociate in whatever way we can: we'll drop into distracting practices like surfing the Internet or gaming, reading obsessively, or watching excessive TV and movies, or we'll enter into addictions and compulsions. Addictions, distractions, bad habits, repetitive behaviors, compulsions, and dissociative practices all help us function in spite of chaos. Each brings a specific kind of relief to us, and each can relieve our distressing symptoms for a while.

BRINGING EMPATHY TO OUR
ADDICTIONS AND DISTRACTIONS

We reach out for addictions and distractions not because we're weak or unprincipled, but because something is seriously amiss inside us. When we can observe avoidance, distraction, and addiction from an empathic perspective, we can bring clarity to the experience of addiction and distraction. If we can understand what sorts of relief distracting substances or practices give us, we can understand why we gravitate toward each one.

THE LANGUAGE OF EMOTIONS

As we focus on what we might be seeking in our distraction of choice, we're not looking for pathology—we're trying to understand what we achieve with addictive substances and dissociative practices. These are powerful activities, and each brings a jolt of energy or a moment of blessed calm to our overwrought psyches. We have very good reasons for turning to distractions and addictions; the key to transforming these distracting habits into awareness is in understanding why (and when) we need them. The idea that we can "just say no" is absurd: there's no way any of us can say no to distractions and addictions until we fully understand why we say yes.

Inside each addictive substance and distracting practice, there is a specific quality that can help us alleviate our specific turmoil. For instance, consider the quality inside alcohol. Alcohol irrigates the system; it brings a moment of flow to people who cannot balance water in their psyches, and it can help release or anesthetize repressed emotions. Unfortunately, attempting to irrigate the system with the false fluidity of alcohol—instead of learning to honor the water element itself—does not balance or heal anything.

Another group of substances and behaviors can give us a sense of flying free and unencumbered as the air and fire elements do. The speedy, flighty distractions of caffeine, stimulants, methamphetamine, cocaine and crack, inhalants, excessive Internet surfing, sugar, sex addictions, gambling, overspending, and shoplifting can help people lift out of their emotions and their bodies. These substances and practices can bring an airy swiftness and a fiery sense of power to people who cannot yet feel comfortable when their feet are on the ground. Stimulants offer the specter of vigor, brilliance, quickness, and instant fun, but soon enough more and more of them are needed, not to fly, but just to get up in the morning. The stimulants, because they don't balance the quaternity, end up slowing us down to a crawl.

An interesting new attempt to increase brain power with stimulants—called brain doping—is taking hold on college campuses and in high-intensity workplaces. Many neurologically normal people are now taking drugs meant for attention deficit disorder, such as Adderall and Ritalin, or a drug meant for narcoleptics, Provigil. There is quite a black market for these drugs, which reduce the need for sleep and help people

focus intently on tasks that are otherwise too boring to keep their attention (or that they put off until the last possible second). Though these
drugs are useful in cases of ADHD or narcolepsy, if we look at brain
doping through a quaternal lens, we can see that they rope the intellect into doing the person's bidding with a kind of inhuman focus; they
also quiet the emotions and the visionary aspects of the psyche, and
they disrupt the body's normal sleep cycles. What is fascinating about
brain doping is that a 2009 neurological study showed that daydreaming,[3] which was once thought to be irrelevant to intellectual tasks, is
actually a process wherein large parts of our brains are keenly activated
and engaged in high-level problem-solving. So the brain dopers, by forcing their minds to maintain constant focus, are probably reducing their
intellectual capacities and making themselves less intelligent and less
resourceful, not more. Constant, unwavering focus does not honor or
support the intellect.

A subset of the speedy substances—the fiery hallucinogens such as LSD,
peyote/mescaline, psilocybin mushrooms, *ayahuasca*, Ecstasy, out-of-body
spiritual practices, trance dancing, and many tribal substances—create a
sense that the spirit is lifting away from the body, the mind, and the emotions. However, the hallucinogens can cause dissociation and make it
difficult to get reintegrated again. This is a problem, because we don't need
further dissociation; we need practices that can help us come back to earth.
We need to allow our bodies, our multiple intelligences, our emotions, and
our visionary spirits to have equal say (and equal freedom) in our fully functioning psyches. When that is done, when we have balanced our quaternities,
we won't need or want to dissociate or send our awareness away.

There is another category of substances and practices that I call the
anesthetics. The anesthetic drugs and practices—painkillers, cigarettes,
heroin, marijuana, excessive reading or TV and movie viewing, and overeating—help numb the body, the emotions, and the thoughts so that part
of us can live in peace and quiet. Each of the anesthetics, in its own way,
creates a barrier against pain, emotions, thoughts, or other people. These
drugs and practices attempt to deal with flow by ignoring or suppressing
it. Each anesthetic can certainly provide a moment of stillness, but artificial stillness usually creates excessive flow in response, which is why the

anesthetics can be so powerfully addictive. By artificially squelching flow, the anesthetics actually encourage the psyche to increase its flow.

Remember that flow is natural and that it always increases when repression occurs. If we use an anesthetic to repress our emotions, our emotional intensity will usually increase when the anesthetic wears off. If we suppress our uncomfortable thoughts through some sort of anesthetic practice, our thoughts will probably intensify when the suppression is lifted. If we use anesthetics to create barriers against the world outside us, we'll inadvertently create a rush of flow toward ourselves; we'll almost provoke the world to batter at our false barriers. I see this most pointedly in the smoking habit. Smoking creates a smoke screen around the user—a seeming barrier against the world—but the false boundaries (and the physical deterioration that smoking causes) eventually break down smokers' ability to set real boundaries. Smokers then become less able to deal with the world. Soon they must smoke on a schedule in order to anesthetize their jangled and unprotected psyches. But the pain isn't truly addressed, the emotions don't actually go away, the thoughts don't subside permanently, and the world doesn't stop turning.

All addictions and distractions can help us move away from problems. They can provide entry into certain elements, and they can certainly provide relief. However, dissociative substances and practices should be treated as momentary crutches, because they all have unwelcome side-effects in the short run, and damaging effects in the long run. There are times when dissociative substances and practices can stabilize us, but it's always in our best interest to learn to channel our flows, address our emotions, and moderate our internal village of skills and abilities without addictive or dissociative stabilizers.

When we can nurture the village of elements and intelligences inside us, we can respond to the inner and outer world with agility and grace. We can use our eagle natures to help us do a flyover of troubling situations, and we can listen respectfully to the voice of fire instead of forcing it into the forefront with dissociative practices or substances. We can manage our workloads properly and trust our minds to work in their own way instead of doping our brains and forcing our minds to work like little machines. We can create a dialogue between our minds and our emotions—feeling, naming, feeling, naming—always coming closer to the issue at hand, rather than flooding, speeding up, or anesthetizing ourselves. We can honor our bodies with rest, good food, and a healthy environment, rather than running from our emotional reactions to pain or illness and stuffing them with stopgap anesthetics or stimulants. In short, we can heal our lives from the inside, rather than grasping at external sources of energy, suppression, or dissociation.

As we continue onward, we'll gather the tools and supports we need to keep ourselves whole and stable without the constant need for distractions, addictions, or avoidance behaviors. We'll learn to center and ground ourselves, and work with the flows in each of our elements. We'll learn to let our emotions (not distractions or addictions) provide the energy we need to deal with the many flows of life, and those natural flows will teach us how to ground ourselves in the present moment—where all our true power exists.

WHEN SUFFERING CEASES TO BE SUFFERING

Remember that we're learning to move in the way properly honored emotions do, which is from imbalance to understanding to resolution. Staying with imbalance until we understand it (without distracting ourselves) is a vital part of moving to resolution. The philosopher Baruch Spinoza wrote, "Suffering ceases to be suffering as soon as we form a clear and precise picture of it."[4] If that's true—if clear understanding of our suffering leads to resolution—then using addictions and distractions to relieve our emotional suffering will actually *cement* it. If addictions and distractions artificially erase our difficulties and separate us from consciousness, that means they actually stop us from moving consciously through our suffering. If we're strung out or distracted and avoiding the issue, we won't be able to gather clear information about that issue. We won't feel the pain or discomfort because we'll be numb; therefore, we won't be able to understand why we're suffering. Without this understanding, we won't be able to form a clear and precise picture of the issues that led us into the suffering. We'll just artificially remove our awareness from the situation; therefore, our suffering will continue unabated.

If we drink to deal with our emotions, we might feel better in the short run, but we won't address the very real trouble in our relationship with our water element. If we refuse to feel our way through our issues, we won't understand why our emotions are so unbalanced in our psyches; therefore, we won't be able to grow or evolve. If we have to artificially speed ourselves up to deal with life, we'll look functional and quick-witted (for a while), but we'll fly right past the emotional issues we most need to address. This flyby will eventually make us amazingly ignorant. If we use hallucinogens to access our fiery vision (while knocking out our bodies, our emotions, and our minds), we'll create frazzled psyches that can't possibly put our visions to any kind of use. Similarly, if we endlessly anesthetize ourselves against emotional pain, we won't have a conscious connection to the part of us that is most distressed.

Distraction and dissociation can give us a blessed vacation from suffering, but if they become habits, they will make us incapable of dealing masterfully with that suffering. If we don't understand Spinoza's premise that suffering *will* cease when understanding has been reached, we'll see suffering as an immovable, intractable thing, and we'll require dissociative substances and practices just to stay alive. However, when we can stand upright at the very center of the village inside us, we will no longer be endangered by the very things that give us life—by movement, by change, by confusion and pain, by emotions, and by flow. When we're home at the center of our souls, we'll be able to form clear and precise pictures of the situations that trouble us. We'll be able to observe and benefit from the flows of our thoughts, feel and use the flows of our emotions, marvel at and rely upon the flights of our visionary spirits, and listen closely to the sensations in our bodies. Pain and suffering will no longer send us running to the nearest bar (alcohol or chocolate); rather, our suffering will lead us into a deeper understanding of ourselves. If we can learn to navigate the flows within us, we'll be able to transform our suffering into clarity.

If you use any addictive, distracting, or dissociative practices, you don't need to feel ashamed of yourself or quit cold turkey, but you should know what you're doing with your distraction of choice and why you're doing it. Bless yourself for keeping your life going in any way you could, and turn your awareness toward your addictions and distractions; they can pinpoint the areas where you're most in need of support. If you gravitate toward alcohol, you can study how your water element fits into your psyche and your life. If you find yourself pulled to the speedy drugs or practices, you can look at how your mind and spirit interact with your body and your emotions. If you're reliant on the fiery drugs or practices, you can learn to bring your vision into your body and live your vision in your everyday life. If you're smoking to create boundaries and a sense of comfort in social situations, you can study your relationship with your sense of self and your boundary-defining anger. Each of the distracting substances and practices can help you become aware of how you've learned to operate in the world, and where you're most in need of healing and balance.

Check in with anything you use to get into or out of certain states, whether it's an obvious addictive substance or not. Check in with your exercise, your artistic expression, your intellectual hobbies, and your meditative or religious practices, as well as any alleviating food you might use. Just take a moment to discover if you're using any of these things as a crutch to get through life. Anything that stands in for proper emoting, sensing, thinking, or intuiting can disable you in the long run just as much as the more obvious addictions can.

THE BUDDHA AND THE BUNNY

There's an insightful Buddhist saying: "Suffering is discomfort multiplied by resistance." I repeat this saying to myself when I move toward distractions. If I can just sit with an uncomfortable emotion, I can understand myself more deeply. But if I resist the emotion and turn toward avoidance and distraction, I actually begin to suffer—maybe not in the moment, when I'm watching too many videos, playing too many online games, or eating too much chocolate, but when I put my distractions aside, where am I? It's a few hours and a few hundred calories later, and I still haven't dealt with the original emotion. Will it return with more insistence next time, or will it burrow itself down further into my psyche? Whichever thing happens, the original emotion is in a less healthy position, my awareness has been pulled away from it, and I've set myself up for an emotional imbalance I may not be able to address the next time it appears. If the emotion rockets back out with more intensity, I suffer. If it represses itself so I can't find it, I suffer. If I resist the original discomfort, that discomfort increases in intensity until I'm in full-blown suffering. My distractions don't make me more capable or more aware; they just take me out of commission for a while. Though I may experience a sad sense of fun in my distraction of choice, the discomfort remains, my resistance increases, my emotional agility decreases, and my suffering is certain. It is as if I am placating an upset baby with toys, rather than helping it learn and grow.

Let's look at a real-life experience with a baby who won't stop crying, no matter what we do. It's hard to be there with all the noise and unhappiness. We make soothing sounds and try to alleviate the distress. We check for binding clothes, wet diapers, hunger or thirst, but the crying increases with the baby's frustration. We shush the baby, we rock her, but she keeps crying, so we try to make her laugh. We find a toy. We get Mr. Bunny and make him do a dance. "Look at Mr. Bunny! Mr. Bunny hops on his head! Mr. Bunny's funny! Let's laugh with Mr. Bunny!" When the baby finally begins to laugh, we feel much better. Whatever was bothering the baby, well, that's forgotten now, thank goodness. We have peace, and that's what matters, right? However, what if we could say to the baby, "You feel really sad. Things are hard right now." Usually, the baby will stop crying much faster if we just let her feel, if we just support her in the way she feels at that moment. I've found that even very young babies, if you support their feelings, will be able to calm themselves or make some movement toward the source of their problem. Crying can move discomfort into conscious awareness, even in young babies, and from that place of awareness, even young babies can communicate their true needs.

If we get in the way with jostling and distractions, the crying will probably stop, but the baby will have missed an important growth experience. She won't have been able to let her feelings tell her what's wrong, and she won't have been able to make a conscious connection between her discomfort and an important issue inside her. What's worse, we won't have helped her strengthen her connection to her own water element, which means we'll move further from our own water element as well. When we wave Mr. Bunny around, we stifle awareness in others, but we also dim our own awareness and become less able to deal with life as it is.

Unfortunately, that's how we've set up our lives and our culture. If there's trouble or pain somewhere, we rarely sit with it and honor its truth. We rarely support the emotions or follow them from imbalance to understanding to resolution. Instead, we bring out some form of Mr. Bunny and terminate our discomfort. But in so doing, we multiply it into suffering that hurls us right out of our psyches. We don't honor the discomfort or the trouble; we just distract the baby inside. We learn in this culture, from our earliest moments, that discomfort must not be allowed to run its course or inform us in any way—that anything is better than discomfort. Young or old, rich or poor, we all rely on distraction and avoidance as a matter of course; it's the defining movement in our training and in our culture.

MAD DOGS AND MR. BUNNY

I see the tracks of our culturewide lust for distraction most vividly on the walls and store windows of the ghetto, barrio, or tenderloin areas in our cities. I'm not talking about the graffiti; I'm talking about the startling number of products and ad campaigns geared directly to the poorest and most devalued members of our society. Have you seen these ads, screaming out with bright colors on walls that haven't been painted in twenty years—ads for malt liquors and cheap fortified wines with names like Night Train and Mad Dog; ads for expensive, logo-laden clothing; ads for CDs and videos with the newest Latino or African-American stars; and ads for the newest lottery games, rich with the promise of a better life? As a culture, we spend obscene amounts of money targeting the people in these neighborhoods, rather than listening to them or alleviating their situations. We can't help but hear the discomfort and distress of these people, but our culture doesn't dare address the insidious, built-in factors that create such a crushing underclass in America. Instead, we spend billions of dollars to distract our poorest citizens with kicky street-lingo ads for shoes, jeans, gambling games, and bizarre liquors you'll never, ever find in middle-class grocery stores. See Mr. Bunny dance?

Could you get into the center of your psyche and imagine the society we could create if we were to sit with people in pain and honor them as they spoke from within it? Because the most broken people in a society tell us where our society is most broken. When we're distracted, we can't remember that. We can't see the part we all play in the creation and nurturance of poverty, because we're distracting ourselves by chasing after money as if it will heal us. Our culture doesn't stop to feel its own discomfort about inequality, racism, substandard education and housing, lack of affordable child care and mental health access, and unfair employment practices. No, it resists the discomfort honest exploration would bring, and in so doing it creates intractable suffering. That suffering certainly plays itself out in our ghettos, but it also plays itself out at all levels of our culture. The suffering that is endemic to the ruling upper classes makes many of its members blame the poor for the desperation in our inner cities, which does precisely nothing to address the situation. I don't mean to place blame on any group of people, because wherever we are in the financial or social strata, each of us has learned to distract ourselves and make excuses for our troubles; therefore, very few of us can address those troubles emotively or coherently. In response, the troubles get bigger, and the suffering becomes more powerful—and Mr. Bunny (not the Buddha) becomes the central figure in our culture.

Distractions, addictions, and avoidance behaviors have become the norm at every possible level of our culture. We've been trained since birth to avoid trouble and glorify distractions; therefore, moving away from distractions and into functionality can be very difficult. What I've noticed is that the difficulty isn't in breaking the specific habit or detoxifying from certain chemicals; it is in making a movement that is so very atypical. Just as we're doing with the emotions, we need to remove the taint of pathology from our movement toward addictions and distractions. We need to understand that our culturewide refusal to deal with discomfort has dropped all of us into suffering. Therefore, our movement toward distractions has in many cases been the only thing that has kept us upright in the midst of suffering. There is a certain blessing that needs to be given to the substances and behaviors that have helped us survive our suffering. Distractions are a part of our cultural legacy and a part of our Judeo-Christian split between body and spirit. They are, in most psyches, the only relief available. There is no shame in this—it's just how we've been socialized. We *can* resocialize ourselves, though. We can create an interior culture of equilibrium and enlightenment.

Before we go forward, though, before we learn to create equilibrium inside ourselves, we've got to address a huge underlying motivation for distractions and addictions. Our honest need for addictions and distractions cannot be brought into the light until we drop fully into the shadowy realms from which they spring. Our culturewide suffering, our genuine need for addictions and distractions, and our dishonoring of emotions doesn't spring from our individual souls. Our lust for distraction does not spring from the fountains of human knowledge; it comes directly from the heart of unhealed trauma.

We can't go further into the world of emotions until we look at trauma seriously, because it severely impacts our lives, our families, our culture, and our species. There is unparalleled information in the heart of trauma, not just for those of us who survived assault or abuse, but for our culture as a whole. Even though more than half of us survived trauma in childhood—sexual, physical, or emotional—there is no real understanding of the effect unhealed trauma has on society as a whole. There are certainly people in psychology and other healing arts working on the issues that affect trauma survivors, but there hasn't been serious sociological or anthropological study of the effects traumatized people have on their culture.

If more than half of us were deaf, we would expect to find a vastly different society than one where deafness was not so prevalent. If more than half of us could only speak Spanish, we would expect to see a culture quite different from one where German or English predominates. These are simple analogies, yet they mask complex questions: How did a people as bright and verbal as ourselves miss the fact that unrelieved trauma (especially in childhood) impacts our society at every level? How can we know that the vast majority of prostitutes, convicts, mental patients, addicts, and alcoholics survived childhood trauma without understanding that this mass of tortured humanity is trying to show us that trauma has an enormous influence on individuals, and through them, on our entire culture? Each one of us is intimately connected to trauma, either in our own lives or through the people closest to us. And how people deal with their trauma has a direct impact on their distractibility, their addictive tendencies, and their emotional skills; therefore, the behavior of the traumatized half of our population has a direct impact on how our society functions at every possible level.

7

Unintentional Shamans

The Role of Trauma in Soul-Making
and Culture-Building

No DISCUSSION OF TROUBLE in the emotional realm should ever occur
without a concurrent discussion of the impact of unhealed trauma,
because unhealed trauma takes a massive toll on our culture. If you are
not a trauma survivor, then one of your parents, siblings, mates, children, teachers, friends, or peers is. You probably learned from them, as
we all do, to distract yourself, deny your feelings, and avoid your pain;
therefore, we must address trauma before we can successfully enter the
emotional realm. Understanding trauma is especially important if you
want to understand rapids-level emotions such as panic, rage, despair,
and the suicidal urge. These intense emotions tend to arise after dissociative trauma, and if you don't understand their purpose in the healing of
trauma, they might destabilize you unnecessarily.

The definition of trauma is individual; you know it when you see
it or when you've experienced it. Trauma can occur when you've been
assaulted or attacked, but it can also occur during surgery or dental procedures, in response to the death of a loved one, or even from witnessing
someone else's trauma (especially if you have very active mirror neurons).
You can also be traumatized emotionally when important people yell at
or insult you, or when you're embarrassed in front of others. However,
not everyone responds to trauma in the same way you and I might, and
some traumas heal on their own. The way to tell if you've got unhealed
trauma is to check in and see if you can deal with and approach all of your

emotions without dissociating, distracting yourself, or avoiding them. For most unhealed trauma survivors, emotions are very difficult things indeed.

FOLLOWING THE TRACKS OF TRAUMA

When I began my healing work in childhood, I saw that physical trauma caused dissociation in the animals who were brought to me. When I worked with humans in my teens, I observed that sexual trauma (especially in childhood) dissociated people in essentially the same way. In many cases of trauma, a person's sense of psychological boundaries is weakened, and his or her ability to connect to the world and other people is often disrupted. Traditional therapy is often useful in addressing the mental and emotional components of trauma, but it can be less successful in addressing the boundary damage and the tendency toward dissociation.

Throughout my life, I have met survivors of physical assault or emotional abuse (and surgeries and ill health) whose sense of boundaries is in very much the same shape as that of the sexual assault survivors I worked with. I learned through them that the damage that results from any kind of trauma—molestation, beatings, emotional cruelty, painful surgeries or hospitalizations, or even frightening dental work—is remarkably similar and remarkably common. I was surprised to learn that the skills I taught to trauma survivors—grounding, focusing, welcoming their multiple intelligences, healing their boundaries, and channeling their emotions—were applicable to almost everyone. Many of us, it seemed, were dealing with some form of dissociative trauma, boundary loss, lack of grounding and focus, or disconnection from our lives. Many of us, even those who couldn't be placed in any accepted trauma category, were having unhappy out-of-body experiences and great difficulty with emotions. I had to expand my understanding of trauma to include the vast population of dissociated, emotionally disconnected, and mentally overwrought people I began to see.

My definition of dissociative trauma grew to include any sort of stimulus that could send a person's attention hurtling away from his or her situation. I began to see dissociation as a widespread survival skill, not just for the situations we all agree upon as traumatic, but for a vast number of agitating or overwhelming everyday situations. I also saw that trauma survivors tended to affect the people around them; they tended to create an atmosphere that provoked dissociation and avoidance behaviors in their circle of friends and family. Some trauma survivors did this by unconsciously visiting traumas (emotional or physical) on the people around them, but some did it merely by being emotionally unavailable in their relationships (which sent the people around them into discomfort and avoidance behaviors). I saw that dissociated and distracted people tended not to support integration and awareness in the people around them; they often created a ripple effect of distraction and unconsciousness in their environments.

An example of this ripple effect can be seen in early scholastic environments, where children who are learning to shut down their empathy (which requires powerful avoidance behaviors) are driven to create an emotionally dangerous environment of ridicule and threats. In this environment, it is nearly impossible to remain whole; the healthier children usually lose their emotional footing and their ability to stay integrated, while the offending children become emotionally deadened. The entire environment can become toxic—dangerous to the emotions and the psyche as a whole. In response, many children disconnect from their emotions in order to survive.

Empathically speaking, traumatic and dissociative behaviors are almost always contagious. Our disavowed (though never absent) empathic skills always alert us to traumatic behaviors and dissociation in other people. Dissociated people often have poor boundaries, and they tend not to be aware of boundaries in others, which makes them somewhat hazardous, emotionally and socially. Traumatized and dissociated people almost shake up the air around them; we really can't help but notice them. But since our empathic skills are hidden from us (for the most part), we cannot make heads or tails of what we perceive. Often, we simply dissociate in response to the jangling and undecipherable disruptions we sense. I observed this situation regularly when I did talks or workshops for my books, where one or two dissociated people would start a chain reaction of dissociation in the room. Of course, my audiences usually consisted of trauma survivors who already knew how to dissociate, which is why I always started my talks by running them through a quick empathic practice that reset their boundaries and helped them get grounded (we'll learn that practice in the skills chapter). But in nearly every talk, there would be a dissociated latecomer who missed the practice. Invariably, no matter where this person sat or how silent their entrance was, waves of dissociation would fan out in response to his or her presence in the room (people would lose their concentration or focus, begin dozing or fidgeting, become emotionally wrought, or their attention would wander). Not everyone would dissociate (some people were so relieved to be integrated inside a strong boundary that they refused to budge), but often, more than half the audience would lose their grounding, their boundaries, and their focus. Emotional and psychological states can be very contagious!

Notice in your own life the people with whom you're most comfortable and relaxed—often, those people are grounded and stable. They have what I call "good psychological hygiene." Now think of the people who disturb and jangle you—those people are often filled with unrelieved traumas, chaotic emotions, and scattered focus. These people have poor psychological hygiene: they don't have or respect boundaries, they don't deal responsibly with their emotions or yours, and they avoid conflict (or create too much of it) so that their relationships suffer. Each of us usually prefers to be around calm and stable people with good psychological hygiene—who seem to be few and far between in this age of distraction. The movement of culture has been to separate spirit from body, and mind from emotion. As a result, many of us have poorly moderated quaternities or dissociated personalities; we cannot focus ourselves properly, and our hygiene is bad.

Our society (in truth, *most* societies, if we look at the worldwide prevalence of racism, war, genocide, and civil strife) is teeming with unhealed trauma and unrelieved dissociation. As a species, we have been socialized to dissociate and distract ourselves from life as a matter of course, and as a result, most of us aren't fully aware of how or why we dissociate. In most of our psyches, there's nothing awake that could call our attention back into our bodies when we realize we're dissociated, nothing aware that could listen to and honor our emotions, and nothing whole that could harness and direct the movements of our minds. The conflicting flows in our often warring quadrants knock us around, and even if we weren't traumatized in any of the classic ways, most of us are drawn like magnets toward the distracted and dissociated behaviors that infect our culture. Distraction, avoidance, and addiction form the major impetus in most psyches and most societies; nearly every one of us is dissociated in some way. Either our spiritual lives are separate from our everyday lives, or our emotions and our intellects operate from within opposing and bitterly warring camps. As a result, most of us exhibit the disruptions I see in trauma survivors: we have poor boundaries around our psyches and poor focus—but we don't have to stay that way.

THREE RESPONSES TO TRAUMA

I've observed two basic ways that people respond to their dissociating traumas: either they learn to traumatize themselves, or they learn to traumatize others. When survivors respond to unrelieved trauma by traumatizing themselves, they usually repress it and re-create its atmosphere in their inner lives. The trauma and its aftereffects settle into their inner landscapes and create feelings of powerlessness, dread, and hopelessness. Physical and psychological symptoms such as behavioral or sleep disorders, hyper- or hypoactivity, depressions, learning disabilities, dissociative episodes, and chronic pain often follow unhealed traumatic incidents. In people who choose to keep their unhealed traumas clamped down inside themselves, these symptoms often lead to addictions or compulsions, codependencies, neuroses, or abusive relationships. Many trauma survivors tend to live in an endless, slow-motion replay of their original wounding (I certainly did). They live lives of desperation, lives that won't work properly no matter what they do.

The second response is to turn around and become a traumatizer of others—to express traumatizing behaviors upon others as a way to relieve the disturbing effects of the trauma. Survivors who traumatize others experience feelings of powerlessness, dread, and hopelessness— just as the self-traumatizers do—but these survivors don't clamp down on their pain or contain it; rather, they visit it upon others in an attempt to understand, deaden, or master it. Their response is to become abusers themselves, to don the cloak of the traumatizer in a desperate and horrifying bid to regain the power they lost in their original wounding.

My molester was certainly in this second category, as all molesters are. Cruelty is a learned behavior that springs directly from unhealed trauma. When I was a child, and I would lash out at my friends and family with my hair-trigger temper, I was expressing my abusive trauma onto them and making their lives miserable. Expressing my trauma didn't fix anything—it just created more trauma.

Notice, though, that these two responses—repression and expression—are the same ones most of us choose in regard to our emotions. There is a repressive response where the trauma is compressed into the inner self and an expressive response where the trauma is inflicted upon others. And just as it is with the emotions, neither response resolves the trauma or heals us. Repressing the trauma shoves memories, feelings, insights, and terrors into the unconscious, and without full consciousness, that material can only fester. Expressing the trauma, on the other hand, shoves the disturbing material onto the souls of others. Expression does not heal or address the pain in any way. It only ensures a brutal world and a destroyed ego structure for the traumatizer. Additionally, these repressive and expressive behaviors translate themselves directly into the emotional skills of trauma survivors.

If people choose to repress their traumatic material, they tend to repress their emotions as well. Repressers create an abusive internal environment by forcing memories, realizations, and emotions into their unconscious and subconscious realms. A represser's trauma stays alive and fully activated because it is never addressed with consciousness or clarity; therefore, the traumatic suffering continues unabated. Remember that "suffering ceases to be suffering as soon as we've formed a clear and precise picture of it." When we refuse to look at our suffering, it cannot cease, because no clear picture of it can be formed. A represser's central self is inhabited not by an awakened village of resources, but by dishonored emotions, unheard thoughts, ignored pains and sensations, and unrelieved torment. In such a psyche, dissociation, distractions, addictions, and avoidance behaviors are necessary.

When people choose to express their traumatic material and visit it upon others, they tend to be emotional exploders. Expressers create an abusive external environment by hurling their emotions, memories, and behaviors onto the people in their lives; they hurt everyone around them and consequently destroy their own ego structure. Again, no useful consciousness or integration is possible because their internal world is filled with trauma and ego devastation, while their external world is filled with violence and turmoil. Expressers gain no power, no peace, and no consciousness; rather, they keep their trauma alive in devastating ways so that suffering is ensured for all. In such a psyche, dissociation, distraction, addictions, and avoidance behaviors are also necessary.

Though society's criminal is certainly the expresser of trauma, repressers also tend to drag turmoil in their wake. Repressers don't do quite as much visible damage to the people around them as expressers do, but because their inner lives are so tumultuous, they don't relate coherently with others. Repressers are so busy keeping their trauma contained that they aren't full partners in any relationship. Because repressers avoid, distract, and dissociate as a matter of course, they destabilize their own lives and the lives of the people around them. Repressers don't support consciousness inside themselves; consequently, their lives and relationships tend not to support full consciousness either.

Whichever choice we make, whether we repress our traumas or express them onto others, we'll be almost completely tied up in the task. As a result, we'll have very little focus available for the task of living whole and conscious lives. Both choices—expression and repression—create very poor boundaries and very poor psychological hygiene.

The devastation of trauma is all around us, and we don't know how to help people who are essentially not among the living. In response, we don't think clearly about trauma. We offer hundreds of therapies, systems, medications, and distractions to erase the traumas—just as we do with the emotions—but we never stop to consider another choice. We don't ask the voice of fire to tell us why trauma is so prevalent or how we can bring ourselves back into our bodies after traumas occur. We don't listen to the call of water when it asks us to dive under the surface and feel the powerful emotions trauma brings forward. We run from the sensations in our bodies that ask us to viscerally feel the trauma again because we don't understand that certain aspects of traumatic flashbacks can heal us (but *only* if we approach them in the correct way). Then we hide in our logical intellects and create more systems and therapies to stop trauma, to erase trauma, and to end trauma, as if trauma were unnatural (it's not).

We don't even consider that there might be a third response, just as there is with the emotions. This third response to trauma is to channel it from within an awakened psyche, to enter it consciously, to dive into the emotions, the thoughts, the visions, and the sensations—and to turn the trauma on its ear. This response is the one I've been striving toward and working with for the last forty years. It's much better than responses one and two, I can tell you.

THE SOCIOLOGICAL ASPECTS OF TRAUMA

When I realized that traumatic and dissociative behaviors were nearly universal (and that expression and repression were at the center of the trouble), I brought more vision and emotion into my thought process. I moved away from the accepted definition of trauma as a singular event and into an overview of trauma as it moves through cultures and throughout time. I had already seen firsthand that the lingering symptoms of trauma could indeed be healed when dissociation was understood as a rupture between body and spirit. If trauma survivors can meet their traumatic memories and incidents from within the center of the village inside them (and agree to neither express *nor* repress their traumas), they can bring all parts of themselves to bear on the issues that led to their dissociation; they can channel the flows of information in all parts of themselves and come back to center. However, if trauma healing is attempted without that full-bodied understanding of which parts dissociate and where they go, healing is unlikely at best.

As my studies deepened, I was astonished to learn that dissociation itself was not the real problem at all; it's simply an innate survival skill we all use as a matter of course. We all distract ourselves, avoid issues, and dissociate every day—it's absolutely normal. The real problem arises when we can't reassociate or regain our equilibrium after a shocking or agitating incident occurs. Strangely, I also discovered that trauma is not the real problem either, because trauma is a fact of life. Trees fall, dentistry happens, stressors occur, cars veer, people yell and hit, and molesters prowl; danger is everywhere. The issue is neither in the danger *nor* in the dissociation, but in the fact that we don't have the resilience to bring ourselves back to center once the danger has passed. That resilience springs naturally from a fully resourced psyche, but without that stable and agile foundation, resilience is unlikely. When we don't have access to our whole selves, we can't tolerate flow, which means we can't channel our thoughts, emotions, sensations, visions, *or* traumatic memories. If we can't move our traumas along naturally, we'll have to keep them alive in endangering ways that force us to distract and dissociate. The trauma then expands as our dissociative and avoidance behaviors begin to travel and infect the people around us and eventually our culture as a whole.

There is a chicken-and-egg situation here: Did we become unable to resolve trauma because we don't have a fully resourced village inside us? Or did we lose access to the village inside us because we don't understand how to reintegrate ourselves after trauma? In either case, our centuries-long inability to resolve trauma in ourselves, our families, our communities, and our societies has increased the population of unhealed trauma survivors in each generation. In response to this nearly universal trouble in the psyche, humans have for many centuries nurtured religious doctrines, spiritual teachings, scholastic systems, medical and psychological modalities, and socialization structures that, in essence, *support and encourage* dissociation, distraction, imbalance, and emotional illiteracy. The separation between body and spirit, the overemphasis on small parts of the intellect and the dishonoring of the emotions, these behaviors and mindsets aren't restricted to one culture or one set of doctrines. Severe intrapersonal resourcelessness and the inability to restore focus and health after traumatic incidents exist throughout most world cultures. I wanted to know why.

I wanted to know how individual pain and trauma grew into a worldwide inability to deal with emotions or think coherently. I wanted to know what evolutionary purpose was being served: Why would the majority of a population choose to hold on to trauma or visit it upon others (in word or deed) when it was so clearly devastating? Why did dissociative behaviors run through audiences and crowds like wildfire? And why were both Eastern and Western spirituality so intricately tied to transcendence and dissociation from the body, the intellect, and the emotions? This last question led me to study spiritual traditions that were *not* transcendental; it led me more firmly into Taoism and indigenous belief systems that honored the grounded earth and water elements.

I studied tribal wisdom, mythology, Jungian interpretations of myths and dreams, shadow work, trauma-healing practices, and anything else I could find. These all led me back to the assertion made by mythologist Michael Meade about childhood sexual trauma: that it is an initiation done at the wrong time, by the wrong person, in the wrong way, with the wrong intent, *on* the wrong person—but it is an initiation nevertheless. Just like a tribal initiation, childhood sexual trauma creates a separation from the regular world and a wounding that changes the initiate forever. As I found so poignantly during my book tours, however, *all* forms of trauma create essentially the same troubles in the psyche that molest survivors endure; therefore, all trauma can be seen as initiatory. My goal then was to understand not trauma, but initiation.

THE JOURNEY INTO THE UNDERWORLD— AND THE JOURNEY BACK OUT

Mythologist Michael Meade has explained the three stages of tribal initiation:

1. Being isolated or separated from the known world
2. Having an ordeal or brush with death
3. Being recognized and welcomed back as an initiated person

Tribal initiations are performed as a way to guide tribe members through life's transitions. Rituals and ceremonies guide tribe members from conception through birth, from birth into childhood, from adolescence into adulthood, from marriage and mating into elderhood, and from elderhood into death and ancestral status. Many tribal societies create a container and a foundation from which all growth and transition can be understood and overseen. Stories and legends, dance and music, art and culture, and deep connectedness create tribal identity, while initiation marks important passages in individual and tribal life. Tellingly, most quaternal or five-element cosmologies spring from indigenous cultures.

In nonindigenous cultures, that wholeness is not in evidence. Much has been said about the freedom and individuality nontribal societies enjoy, but just as much has been said about the price paid for that freedom. Our individualistic Western culture has grown in ways tradition-bound tribal societies cannot, but we've also decayed in ways tribal societies have not. Our disconnection from Mother Earth and the quaternity is an unhappy result of splitting away from tribalism, yet our growing ability to tolerate diverse cultures and create complex communication systems that connect all people is a happy result. Neither way of life is ideal; both have their healing and destructive aspects. The healthiest society is probably somewhere between the two opposites in that sacred middle realm, but we're not yet in that sacred place. The opposing social structures have made contact, but it is not yet fully conscious contact. Much of the movement toward spirituality in nonindigenous cultures is a movement toward ancestral wisdom—toward ritual, ceremony, initiation, and connection to the deeper currents of life. Conversely, many tribespeople feel stifled and trapped in the amber of their ancient tribal customs.

We nonindigenous peoples live in a quandary: we value our freedom from tradition and tribalism, while at the same time we're drawn inexorably toward them. This should not be surprising since we all come from tribal societies in the first place. Each one of us can hearken back to African or Middle Eastern tribes, to Celtic or Viking tribes, to Asian or East Indian tribes, to Native American tribes, or to the island tribes of the South Pacific. Our tribal selves still live inside us, and our ancestral DNA has hundreds of thousands of years of indigenous memory that competes with a mere handful of hundreds of years of modern life. Our ancestors still speak to us from within the voice of fire. Our bodies still resonate to season, place, and rhythm. Our multiple intelligences still know how to translate symbols and impulses from deep within the subconscious. Our emotions still remember their sacred function as carriers of deep wisdom, just as our psyches still require ceremony, ritual, and initiation in order to live and grow properly. We moderns have moved out of our tribes for the most part, but tribal wisdom has not moved out of our psyches.

Traumatic injury in childhood has been equated with a kind of unconscious initiation ceremony—not because it is a spiritual or ceremonial experience, but because the movements within it mimic the movements of the first two stages of real initiation. Understanding the stages of initiation (and the ways in which traumatic incidents mimic initiation) will give us a greater understanding of what trauma does to the psyche, to our culture, and sociologically speaking, to us as a species.

Stage One: Separation from the Known World

In tribal initiation, stage one is an organized, expected removal from the parents and the everyday patterns of the tribe. Tribal children are brought up to expect initiation; they and their families prepare for it and are fully aware of its presence in their lives. In trauma, however, there is no preparation. Traumatic stage one is a disorganized removal from the known world—a sudden, shocking, and wholly unexpected end to normalcy. The stranger approaches, the loved one betrays you, the doctor comes near, or the play becomes ugly—and it begins.

Stage Two: A Brush with Death

Tribal stage two is an organized ordeal, such as a walkabout, a ritual scarring,[5] or a solitary journey. Though there is pain and fear involved, there is also a container created by the tribe and the overseeing adults. The walkabouts and journeys occur on tribal lands where trackers abound; the scarring and ornamentations are usually performed by adults who have a certain expertise at what they do; and the ordeal has a definite end-point, which the initiates are aware of on some level. In trauma, there is no organization to the ordeal and no promise of an end. Traumatic stage two is the out-of-control moment of the assault—the beating, the yelling, the unwelcome touch that separates spirit from body, or the beginning of the operation. The traumatic brush with death has no container, no safety hatch, no ancestral guidance, and no clear end-point. In regard to surgeries performed on children, some would say that surgical procedures are performed by expert adults, and that they have a clear end-point; however, since they often involve restraints, anesthetics, and the specter of death or disability that cannot be discussed openly—especially by children—they often create lasting traumas.

Stage Three: Being Welcomed as an Initiated Person

Tribal stage three is the celebration, during which the entire tribe recognizes the new person and welcomes him or her as an initiated and valued member of the tribe. The initiate does not return home as the same person; expectations change, responsibilities shift, and a new life begins. Sadly, in trauma there is no stage three; there is no welcoming back for trauma survivors. Traumatic initiations are usually performed in secret or are an established part of the shadow life of the family or the neighborhood. There is no one to tell the trauma victim that he or she has survived a deathlike ordeal and has come out the other side as a new being. There is no conscious acknowledgment of the sudden end of childhood or normalcy, and there is certainly no celebration.

In traumatic initiations, stages one and two occur without sense or reason. The regular world stops, the horror begins, and there is no protective ceremony, no overseer of the process, and certainly no welcoming back. Therefore, there is no way for trauma survivors to take their place as conscious and initiated members of society. When stage three does not occur, initiates (tribal or traumatic) are left in limbo. This is why the third stage of any initiatory process is crucial. Without it, the initiation and the initiate are unfinished, and the tribe is incomplete.

When Stage Three Does Not Occur

Tribal knowledge says that if stage three is not completed (for whatever reason), the initiate must cycle through the first two stages of initiation once again. Initiation is a three-stage process that does not conclude until all three stages have been completed. I have found that the psyche concurs with tribal wisdom on this point. The rule in the human psyche seems to be that stages one and two of trauma will be repeated until stage three occurs. Suffering ceases to be suffering only *after* we have formed a clear and precise picture of it, and that clarity only occurs in stage three. We cannot form a clear picture of traumatic suffering from the sudden separation of stage one or from the unfinished ordeal of stage two. There must be an end to trauma and an understanding of trauma before we can truly exit our traumatic initiations.

In initiatory tribal cultures, an unfinished initiate will be cycled through the initiation ritual once again, and he or she will be welcomed properly at the successful conclusion of the completed ritual. In noninitiatory cultures where unfinished trauma reigns, the psyche will revisit stages one and two in whatever way it can—by repressing the trauma and re-creating it in the inner world, or by expressing the trauma and re-creating it for others. The trauma will be kept alive because the initiation ritual will still be in progress. When there is no welcoming and no validation of the life-altering ordeal that has been survived, there will be no possibility of exiting the traumatic initiation. The psyche will intentionally cycle through stages one and two until resolution is achieved. In nonindigenous cultures such as ours, we call this cycling post-traumatic stress disorder when it is repressive, and abusiveness or criminality when it is expressive.

When we can understand the essence of initiation, however, we can see that both responses to traumatic initiations—both the repressive self-abuse and the expressive abuse of others—are unconscious repetitions of stages one and two. When we cycle unrelieved trauma through our inner or outer world, we're still very much in the process of initiation. We continue to separate ourselves (or others) from the known world, and we continue to enter or create ordeals in the desperate hope that stage three—the welcoming back—will occur. We may drop into unmanageable depressions, addictions, or neuroses. We may ingeniously seek out jobs and relationships that remind us of the atmosphere of our original traumas, or we may traumatize others. For many of us, these behaviors will lead to therapy or recovery, which can provide a kind of stage three.

In therapy or recovery groups, we can be welcomed into a world where our suffering is understood. We can help ourselves and other survivors make sense of turmoil, and we can speak freely and openly about our traumas, thereby ending the cycling. Though healing often occurs in these situations, many people remain attached to their therapists or their recovery or healing groups for years or even decades, simply because it's the only place they're seen in any stage-three sort of way. To stand up and say, "Hi, I'm Bob, and I'm an alcoholic," and to have the whole room be proud of your honesty, to have the whole room respond with, "Hi, Bob," is a stage-three experience. We may laugh at twelve-step groups and self-healing junkies, but these therapies provide many of us with our only experience of being welcomed by a tribe that sees our initiation for what it was.

For others who are not as lucky, stage three occurs in prison, where they're welcomed by a tragic group of fellow initiates. Prison life can be incredibly tribal (and incredibly unconscious), and initiations occur there as a matter of course. Tribes are based on skin color, gang affiliations, and criminal background, and in these tribes people experience a kind of brutal welcome. The trauma does not usually end; rather, tribe members are often organized and taught to be more skilled at traumatizing themselves and others. The true essence of stage three—the welcome into a new life after stages one and two have been concluded—doesn't often happen in prison tribes. The rough prison welcome doesn't put an end to trauma, but *any* welcome is better than no welcome at all. This is why it's so amazingly difficult to break away from criminality and prison tribal life; something in the psyche is fed when initiations and welcomings (however crude) occur. The tribal parts of our brains respond to tribal rituals, even if we have no conscious understanding that the rituals are occurring. Prison tribes (and the tribal street gangs that so often lead to prison) provide a powerful and seductive facsimile of welcome for the most damaged and resourceless members of our society. As a result, the criminal underclass becomes a powerful tribe of its own, one that supports and exploits trauma survivors at the very same time.

In both instances, in therapy groups and in prisons, trauma survivors are moved to a kind of stage three. However, neither welcoming process seems to allow trauma survivors to take their place as respected elders in our larger culture. In prison tribes, the trauma stays alive and spreads like wildfire through the prison and eventually back into the culture. No true healing occurs because the trauma is still being repressed and internalized, or expressed and lived out. Prison tribe members often become stronger and more skilled, but unless something unusual (like the William James Association Prison Arts Project) intervenes, convicts don't generally take their place as functional elders in prison or in society as a whole; they usually only function within a very small area of influence. In therapeutic tribes, on the other hand, a certain level of healing occurs (in that traumas are no longer being avoided or expressed chaotically), but in many cases, these tribe members do not enter fully into awakened elderhood either.

When the welcoming tribe is composed of similarly traumatized people, initiates often get the wrong message about belonging and identity, and many healing and recovery tribes don't foster a deep connection to our larger society or culture as a whole. Instead, the identification tends to limit itself to the trauma at hand. One becomes a survivor of a specific set of circumstances instead of becoming a fully initiated adult. One becomes a member of the alcohol tribe, the sexual assault tribe, the abused child tribe, or the prison tribe—but rarely a fully welcomed and valued citizen of the world. A form of stage-three welcoming does occur in these therapeutic tribes, but it is not true stage three, because it does not reliably provide our larger culture with true adults, sacred elders, or soul warriors. This kind of welcoming, then, is still attached to and embroiled in the first two stages of traumatic initiation. Much acknowledgment and healing does occur in these therapeutic tribes, but the deep and transformative movement into the completeness of stage three often does not.

In my empathic healing practice, I saw people who had been through many kinds of therapies, including these unintentionally tribal modalities. In most cases, I saw people after they had moved into "survivor" status—they were no longer victims, they had fully identified their wounds, they understood them intellectually, and they could monitor themselves for signs of traumatic reenactments or post-traumatic behaviors. Yet still they felt unfinished, as if something had been forgotten. They were right—many things *had* been forgotten, such as their visionary fire elements, which could tell them where trauma came from (and where it's going), or their earthy bodies, which in many cases still held on to traumatic events, no matter how much intellectual understanding had been achieved. There was also their oceanic emotions, which constantly attempted to lead them (or force them) into a deeper understanding of their trauma. These survivors were often quite confused; their therapeutic tribes had pronounced them cured, yet their physical symptoms, their emotional upheavals, and their spiritual or visionary emptiness continued unabated. Clearly, something was unfinished.

Moving into survivor status is important, but it does not fully satisfy the psyche's definition of stage three. Something deeper must occur, and that requires our entire village of elements and intelligences working together so that we can restore ourselves to resilience and equilibrium.

THE VILLAGE THAT WELCOMES YOU HOME

When your fully resourced psyche can be brought to bear on your trauma (however and whenever it occurred), the sacred wound at the center of your trauma can be revealed. The first task in restoring your wholeness is to reintegrate yourself (we'll learn how throughout the rest of this book). This reintegration is a form of self-welcoming that paves the way for the blessed movement into stage three. When the village inside you is reestablished, your traumatic memories can be addressed in deep and ceremonial ways, because your far-ranging eagle nature will be able to provide an overview of the situation. When your full awareness is embodied once again, true healing can occur because your suffering *will* cease when your consciousness is brought to bear upon it. When your vision and your multiple intelligences can track the trauma's origins, you can take your honorable place in the currents of time and culture—not just in the culture of your specific trauma, but in the whole of human history. When your psyche is reintegrated and all of your resources return to your psyche, trauma ceases to be trauma; instead, it becomes a portal through which you pass on your way to wholeness.

When we left our indigenous tribes, we gained much in the way of individual freedom, but we lost much of our understanding of the necessity of ceremony and initiation, and we forgot that our souls still require initiations, rituals, and ceremonial woundings so that we might grow into whole and conscious individuals. We've forgotten the deep rules of the psyche. We've forgotten our fiery myths and stories; therefore, our knowledge of sacred wounding has moved into the background and into the shadow. As a result, our movements toward initiation and ritual have moved into the shadow as well. The remembrance of the sacred aspects of the first two stages of initiation has left our conscious minds, but our profound need for the first two stages has never faded.

Initiation occurs whether we want it to or not, because it is a necessary passage in our lives. When we don't understand this, we create unrelieved suffering around our traumas. We run from our memories, our traumas, our sensations, our bodies, our emotions, and our lives. We try to hide in intellect-only or spirituality-only systems in the desperate hope that our traumatic memories and behaviors will just *go away*—but they never do. They can't. Stages one and two *must* repeat until stage three occurs. If we remain in a dissociated state, we'll be unable to move to stage three; but when we can consciously bring our full selves back together, we can become adequate to the soul-making task of moving to stage three.

This movement toward integration is empowering because it addresses the central issue of trauma, which is surprisingly not the pain or the horror of the incident, but the lingering sense of powerlessness and disconnection that results from not being able to move to stage three. I have observed that when trauma is treated as an individual tragedy (rather than a multicultural phenomenon), and post-traumatic behavior is treated as a pathological (rather than a natural) response, it cannot be dealt with in a way acceptable to the psyche. Trauma survivors can do much to become less disturbed and more functional, but true healing requires a fully resourced psyche in which the body and spirit communicate freely, and the multiple intelligences and all of the emotions are welcomed and honored. When this internal balance is restored, the movement to stage three is assured.

When the psyche has been reintegrated, there is no longer a knee-jerk rush toward distraction, avoidance, addiction, or dissociation; therefore, the inner world becomes a stable place in which clear thinking can occur and the emotions can be honored and channeled. When the emotions are allowed to contribute their brilliant and unceasing energies to the psyche, they provide a flowing conveyance into and through the underworld of trauma—they provide the energy and information needed in each part of the journey. When the psyche is integrated, the body can awaken and contribute its memories, abilities, and knowledge to the process, while the emotions can help relieve and ameliorate the pains, symptoms, and behaviors the body brings to consciousness. In this healthy, fluid environment, the logical intelligences can contribute their airy brilliance to the healing process. They can study healing and psychology; they can bring meaning to spiritual visions, emotional impulses, and physical sensations; and they can put the trauma into historical and cultural perspective. Through it all, the visionary spirit can provide an overview, not just of the trauma, but of the emotions, the thoughts, and the physical sensations that contribute to the healing of trauma. From the center of these well-moderated elements and intelligences, the psyche can regain its balance and resilience.

When we can heal trauma from a fully resourced perspective, we become deeply connected to the very center of our selves, but more than that, we become reconnected to the center of our troubled society. When we're whole, we can see that traumatic avoidance, distraction, and dissociation form the basis for most people's lives. When we can acknowledge the trauma at the center of the human heart (rather than repress or express it), we can consciously channel our trauma and understand the dissociative foundation upon which most lives and societies are based. From that understanding, we can make conscious decisions about our position in relation to dissociation, distraction, and avoidance. We can decide what role we want to take in our tribe of dissociated and quaternally unbalanced people. We can decide to take our honored place as elders, rather than remaining unconscious automatons.

By diving into the trouble and moving to stage three, we can finally make sense of our suffering, and in so doing, we can end it—for ourselves and for others. I call the conscious movement into trauma a soul-making journey because when we can dive into our wounds with our full complement of intelligences and abilities, we're no longer mere survivors of specific incidents; we become fully resourced soul warriors. From the sacred ground of stage three, we can keep our understanding of trauma alive, not by cycling through it with repression or expression, or by identifying ourselves as its powerless victims, but by remaining conscious of it and its aftereffects as we strive for social and political justice.

When we move consciously to stage three, we learn that we're not broken apart by our wounds; rather, we're broken open by them. Therefore, more energy, more information, more love, more art, and more soulfulness can flow through us. We become not half-alive survivors of trauma, but beautifully scarred elders, visionaries, and healers of our tribes. We become living shrines who carry sacred knowledge for our entire culture. We become able to take a meaningful position in the world, not in spite of our wounds, but because of them.

It has been my greatest honor to be involved in these profound journeys from mere psychological survival into the sacred territory of stage three. Many survivors never make the journey—that's true. Our prisons and streets are filled with survivors who become twisted and brutal and desperate in their endless cycling between stages one and two. Our everyday lives are filled with survivors who live in a waking nightmare of distraction, avoidance, and misery as they pretend not to be trapped in the same two stages. But my unusual healing practice brought me into contact with those brave survivors who continue to hope, love, strive, and believe in stage three, even though their lives have given them no reason whatsoever to do so. They stand before me with their thousand-year-old eyes that have seen the horror of human cruelty, and they share their desire to be well so they can be of real use to the world. They want to dive in and enter stage three so their individual traumas can end and they can take their sacred place in the trauma-centered tribe all around us. Though it may seem backward, I have found my greatest belief in humans and my clearest vision of joy through the work I have been honored to share with survivors of dissociative trauma.

THE END *WILL* BE BEAUTIFUL

The French author and trauma survivor Jean Genet spoke to the heart of this three-stage healing process in his harrowing written account of his own post-traumatic journey, *The Thief's Journal*: "Acts must be carried through to their completion. Whatever their point of departure, the end will be beautiful. *It is because an action has not been completed that it is vile* [italics mine]." When we cycle unconsciously through the dismal first and second stages of unrelieved trauma, our actions are vile—not because we're vile or life is vile, but simply because we don't move to completion. When we don't know of the third stage, all we can see is the vileness of trauma. We cannot grasp the beauty and power that live on the other side of the wound, and we cannot see an end worth working toward. In response, we repress our true emotions, memories, and traumas, and tumble into desperate and unconscious post-traumatic replays. We attempt to distract or dissociate ourselves from our wounds, but our denial only intensifies our cycling through the first two stages of unconscious initiation. We may seek practices, substances, or therapies that provide some relief from our painful symptoms, but we don't stop feeling vile somehow.

UNINTENTIONAL SHAMANS

We also don't understand that the vileness is a function of *not* moving to completion and *not* moving to stage three; instead, we internalize the vileness and lose our way.

I see in many trauma-healing modalities, though they are well-meant, a terrible short-circuiting of the true healing process, of that beautiful movement to completion. Many trauma-relieving practitioners use techniques that attempt to erase the trauma from memory. There are techniques that involve breathing, bodywork, eye movements, hypnosis, and even tapping on certain areas of the skin. There are also numbing techniques that run survivors through traumatic memories exhaustively until there's no emotional content left at all. I call all of these processes *erasure* techniques. They attempt to heal trauma by deleting it and its aftereffects from the psyche—which might be a good idea, except for the fact that traumatic initiations have a sacred function in the soul and in the culture. Many healers in the trauma field, because they don't understand the soul's three-stage process, try to erase the trauma from the psyche. They want to remove the trauma; they want the baby to stop crying and start laughing at Mr. Bunny. Unfortunately, that's not the genius path, that's not the soul-making path, that's not the path that will heal the culture, and that's not the path to stage three. My experience is that taking the opposite path—of diving directly into the trauma from within a fully resourced psyche—helps people not only to heal, but to enter fully into the most profound currents of life.

The erasure techniques have some value in extreme post-traumatic responses (long-standing insomnia, self-mutilation, amnesia, psychosomatic illness or paralysis, and so on), but most of us don't fall into that category. Most of us have been taught to function fairly well around our traumas through ingenious avoidance or addictive behaviors. Most of us deal fairly well with our dissociation and repressive or expressive behaviors. We're not whole or well-moderated, but we do all right. Most of us don't need the drastic erasure techniques, but we gravitate toward them because they have a sirenlike quality. Though I was as interested as anyone in these erasure techniques, I have found that I cannot recommend them in any but the most catastrophic cases. (However, a truly grounded and soul-honoring trauma-healing modality does exist: please see Dr. Peter Levine's works in Further Resources on page 399.) Many of the erasure techniques

III

do indeed work; they erase the memory of trauma from the conscious mind, but while the memory of the trauma may fade, the psyche remains unstable. The erasure techniques are symptomatic fixes that don't lead to stage three. Rather, they may remove the memory of stages one and two so that stage three cannot occur. The erasure techniques are the ultimate in avoidance behaviors; in their attempt to avoid pain, what they actually avoid is true wellness and soul-making.

If we understand trauma not as a mistake or a tragedy, but as our initiation into the deeper currents of life, we won't want to erase our memories. Even if our initiations were performed in the most appalling and unconscious fashion, they were still initiations. If we understand the sacredness in even the most profane traumatic initiations, we won't want anyone fooling around in our emotional landscapes and erasing our pathways to the center of our own souls. When we can complete the act begun in trauma—however vile it may have been—the end *will* be beautiful. If we can honor the trauma and let our emotions transport information consciously and honorably within our whole selves, we'll move consciously and powerfully into that third stage, and we'll be new beings.

Reintegrating the village inside ourselves is the important first step in the healing of dissociative trauma, but it is the emotions that actually help us move into and out of the memories and sensations that are associated with the original wound. Our emotions transport us to stage three. With their help, we can make the profound journey into a visceral understanding of the troubles—and the beauties—of our human culture.

8

The Role of Emotions
in the Resolution of Trauma

Water Will Carry You Home

EMOTIONS ALERT US TO specific trouble, and they do so without any subterfuge. If we're aware enough to listen to them—if our attention is focused and our minds are centered—our emotions will be able to contribute exactly what we need to move into and then out of any trouble imaginable. When we become able to hear and respond to our emotions effectively, we become able to understand the deepest language of our souls. With the support of our fully awakened emotions, those unceasing and abundant energies, we'll be adequate to any situation, any issue, or any trauma.

There is a wonderful Taoist proverb that tells us: "The glory is not in never falling, but in rising every time you fall." If we see life as glorious only when everything is perfect and untroubling, then we'll be totally inadequate to the process of living in the real world; we'll actually be traumatized by the turbulence of life itself. If we want to be able to meet life on its own terms, we've got to have whole and adequate psyches from which to work. We've also got to have access to all of our emotions—not just the peaceful ones.

When we view trauma from a fully resourced perspective, we can understand balance and equilibrium as flowing and malleable things that respond to their environment. Instead of pathologizing each of the uncomfortable or miserable symptoms of unhealed trauma (the rages and panics, the flashbacks, the self- or other-abuse, the nightmares, the depressions,

113

the eating disorders, and so on), we can listen closely to each one. We can understand that healing cannot occur until the original wound has been addressed to the satisfaction of the soul. From this knowledge, we'll understand that a dissociated person's panicky sense of danger all around is *factual* rather than pathological, because a person without a good connection to his or her body is endangered in every waking moment. We can then view the behaviors that spring from that dissociation in an entirely new light. We can see the constant eruptions and disruptions in the psyche not as signs of illness, but as the psyche's valiant attempt to bring severe imbalance into conscious awareness. With a full-bodied understanding of the situation, we won't attempt to erase those disruptive responses; instead, we'll follow their tracks to the heart of the trouble. When we can do that, the symptoms will decrease naturally, because they will have been heard and attended to in a fully resourced way. We'll be able to break the trancelike cycling between stages one and two and move decidedly and triumphantly to stage three. No matter how the trauma began, the end will be beautiful.

This beautiful movement is not any kind of avoidance technique. It is also not an antiseptic or dainty process; it's an oceanic, fiery, muddy, windblown process that creates not mere survivors, but fully initiated soul warriors. This is why it is so unusual in our culture; it doesn't look or sound like what we call healing. It isn't peaceful, anesthetized, or predictable. This movement to stage three is a vibrant and utterly singular process, which is why our access to the full village inside us is so vital to the outcome. When the psyche is moving out of the first two stages of dissociation and trauma, it shakes and jerks and kicks—just as animals do when they come back from dissociative trauma. The body shakes off its memories, the mind shakes off its trauma-centered beliefs, the spirit unshackles itself from horror and dissociative practices, and the emotions flow and surge in response to the healing movements throughout the psyche. Everything begins to move again, not in the distracted way our culture moves, but into a deepening process that brings all previously lost parts of the psyche together into an integrated whole. In an integrated psyche, the body does not imprison, the intellect does not chatter, the spirit does not pontificate or hallucinate, and the emotions do not torment; instead, each element and intelligence offers its specific information and abilities so that true healing can occur. When there is an awakened self at the center of all this flow, it can welcome, work with, and channel all of it—without self-criticism or avoidance behaviors.

CREATING THE CEREMONIAL SPACE: ANGER AND FEAR RETURN

The first emotions that usually arise when people begin healing from distractions, avoidance behaviors, addictions, or traumatic dissociations are the various mood states of anger and fear. Both emotions have been utterly pathologized, which is a tragedy, because they are intrinsic to the process of coming back to wholeness. Anger restores the boundaries we lose during trauma (and after we distract and dissociate), and fear restores the focus and intuition we lose when our instincts are overwhelmed. Together, anger and fear set the container or sacred space from which we can retrieve our honorable, intuitive, resilient core selves. When anger arises, whether it takes the form of rage, fury, hatred, envy, jealousy, apathy, or shame, it signals that real healing is underway. The channeling task for any of these angers is to use their intensity to restore the boundary around the psyche and create a sacred ritual space in which true healing can occur.

We know from the empathic exercises we did on pages 32–36 that free-flowing fear is our focused intuition and our instincts. When fear arises in any of its mood states—as fear, worry, anxiety, confusion, panic, or terror—it signals that new instincts are flowing into the psyche. The channeling task for the fears is to make conscious movements that restore a sense of focus, resiliency, resourcefulness, and intuition. Even panic— that despised emotion—has a vital role in the resolution of trauma. Panic arises in order to return the psyche to the shock phase of stage one. If it is welcomed and channeled properly, panic will utilize its massive store of energy to end the desperate cycling between stages one and two. When anger and fear, in whatever forms they choose, are openly welcomed and channeled in the whole self, the movement to stage-three healing can truly begin. When boundaries have been restored and instincts are once again available, a surprisingly powerful (and humorous!) level of resource-fulness I call "Jackie Chan" energy awakens and begins to perform a kind of martial arts cleanup of the trouble in the soul. When this emotional revitalization occurs, the rest of the emotions can then perform their own sacred healing tasks.

Sadness in any of its mood states—whether despair, dejection, or despondence—can then come forward to help release unworkable attachments and rejuvenate the psyche. Depression can come forward and report on aspects of the self that have been lost, squandered, or shoved away. Grief can come forward when profound loss has occurred; it can revive the entire self by moving it into and through the deepest waters of the soul. Shame and guilt can pinpoint boundary violations created from the inside (either from the behavior of a poorly managed personality, or from engagement in destructive relationships), and help break those agreements once and for all. The suicidal urge—when it is brought forward in a reintegrated psyche that is properly restored and resourced with anger and fear—can release the soul from torment by illuminating and exterminating the soul-killing stances being nurtured in the psyche. If the suicidal urge can be honored in a grounded ceremonial manner, it will contribute its brilliant, death-defying certainty to the absolute restoration of the soul.

Each emotion, when it is welcomed in the full village of a resourced psyche, can signal the presence of imbalance. Then, each properly channeled emotion will contribute the specific information and intensity needed to alleviate that imbalance and heal the psyche. Once the healing has been achieved, the emotion will move on, as all emotions should. When the emotions are welcomed and their messages can be translated in honorable ways, they are no longer dangerously primal; instead, they become brilliant and unceasing energies with which true healing and enlightenment can be achieved. When anger and fear are allowed to come forward and create the psyche's container, all emotional work (and indeed all healing) can proceed.

The problem is this: anger and fear are probably the most reviled emotions we have. There is certainly good reason for this revulsion in a world where emotions are only repressed or expressed; both emotions are so powerful and disruptive that we all have horror stories about them, and we've had no option but to force them into the shadow. However, when another option exists—when the fully awakened village inside us knows how to properly channel these two emotions—their power becomes a healing force. As we move into Part II, we'll speak to and honor these two noble emotions that make true healing possible. But while we're in the territory of trauma, it's important to stop for a moment and focus ourselves empathically on anger.

There's a belief that all anger is bad, which does a terrible disservice to people trying to heal from dissociative traumas or avoidance behaviors. The healing tasks of anger have been all but forgotten, and this ignorance endangers every one of us. In its free-flowing state, anger helps us create, maintain, and restore our boundaries and the boundaries of others. And what is missing most seriously in dissociated and distracted people is a clear, powerful, anger-supported boundary wherein the work of true healing can occur. When we tell angry people to drop their real emotions and behave in more manageable ways, we in essence ask them *not* to restore their boundaries. In so doing, we make the work of legitimately angry people nearly impossible.

THE COMPLEX RELATIONSHIP BETWEEN ANGER AND FORGIVENESS

Our troubles with anger have prompted us to shove anger into the shadow while we glorify its supposed opposite: forgiveness. Though forgiveness may seem to be much better than anger (and it can be, if anger is merely being repressed or expressed), forgiveness can actually trap people in the first two stages of trauma. When anger is not brought forward honorably, the movement to stage three cannot occur, because there will be no container or boundary wherein that sacred movement can occur. Forgiveness is a beautiful and necessary movement, but it has to be arrived at honestly, and it has to come about emotively. We can't throw anger out the window and don forgiveness as if were a costume.

The simplified relationship between anger and forgiveness goes like this: anger is bad and forgiveness is good. That's the simpleminded essence of it. If you forgive your traumatizer, you're good. If you're angry at your traumatizer, you're bad. Forgive and forget, and you'll be healed. Stay angry, and you'll be sick. So forgiveness and anger are set up as opposing forces—good and bad, right and wrong. However, if we look at the relationship between anger and forgiveness in a fully resourced way, we find something infinitely more complex. In practice, anger and forgiveness actually work together (and often at the same time) in any real healing process. Though anger and forgiveness may seem to be opposing forces, they are in truth completely equal partners in the journey to stage three. Each has its place, and each can only proceed with the support of the other.

When you're integrated and fully resourced, your anger will alert you to boundary violations. If you can channel anger properly, you can restore your boundaries and your sense of self—without hurting anyone. When your psyche is properly protected again, you can then forgive the person or situation that damaged you, because you'll have moved to stage three. You'll have identified the wounding, dealt with your emotional responses, and restored your psyche to wholeness. The other person might not have changed, and the original situation might not have either, but *you* will have changed. Your anger will have completed the cycle and moved you into a new position of strength from which you truly can forgive. However, if you try to move to forgiveness *before* your boundaries are restored, your forgiveness will be incomplete. You'll still be walking around with holes in your psyche; therefore, you'll still be in stages one and two. And the rule in the psyche is firm and clear: stages one and two must repeat themselves until stage three occurs. Forgiving from stages one and two—before your boundaries have been restored—will backfire, because it has to.

Forgiveness is not an emotion, and it can't take the place of one. It is a decision made by your whole self after your true emotional work has been done. You can't move to forgiveness until your emotions move you consciously through stages one and two, because your emotions are the only things in your psyche that can move energies, memories, and imbalances into your awareness. Your body can hold your pain, and your mind and spirit can remember your pain, but until you know how you *feel* about your pain, you won't be able to unearth it. If your pain is tucked very deeply into your unconscious (as traumas usually are), only strong and urgent emotions will be able to dislodge it. Therefore, the movement to the true forgiveness available in stage three often requires not just anger, but rage and fury; not just fear, but terror and panic; not just sadness, but despair and suicidal urges. Real forgiveness is not a dainty or delicate process—it's a visceral and deeply emotive awakening from a trancelike state. It is, in essence, a return from the dead. Real, foundational forgiveness is a messy, loud, thrashing process of coming back from death into life. It looks on an empathic level like those animals I helped heal as a child. There's shaking, kicking, grunting, trembling, and spitting—and then it's done.

Real forgiveness isn't a polite and teary gesture, made with a bowed head and demurely folded hands. Real forgiveness would never, ever say, "I see that you were doing the best you knew how, and I forgive you." No! Real forgiveness has an entirely different take on the subject. Real forgiveness does not make excuses for other people's improper behavior. Real forgiveness does not tell itself that everyone always does the best they know how, because that's preposterous. Do you always do your best? Do I? Of course not! We all make mistakes, and we all do things we're not proud of. Real forgiveness knows this; it doesn't set itself up as an advocate for the tormentors in your life. It doesn't make excuses for the disruptive behavior of others—because that sort of nonsense only increases your cycling between stages one and two.

Real forgiveness says, "I see that you were doing what *worked* for you at the time, but it never, ever worked for me!" Real forgiveness knows that real wounding took place; therefore, real fingers have to be pointed so that real movement through the underworld of suffering can occur. When that real movement has been made, real forgiveness raises you up off the ground, wipes off the spit, pulls the twigs out of your hair, and testifies, "You can't hurt me anymore! It's over and I'm free! You have no power in my life!" Real forgiveness is a process that creates true separations from torment and tormentors, and true separations require the proper application of boundary-restoring anger, or they won't mean a thing. When your anger-supported boundaries are restored again, forgiveness will be as easy as falling off a log. Forgiveness naturally follows the honorable restoration of your sense of self. Anger and forgiveness are *not* opposing forces; they are completely equal partners in the true healing of your soul.

When people hear that forgiveness is good and anger is bad, they generally do that first kind of demure, head-bowing forgiveness. It looks very evolved and saintly on the outside, but it has very bad effects in the inner world. Forgiveness performed from the unconscious position of stages one and two does two things: it excuses the behavior of others, and it reduces our ability to be conscious and present with the pain we truly feel. When we rush to forgiveness, we lose our connection to our original wounds. Forgiving before we've fully engaged with our wounding only short-circuits the healing process. We tell ourselves we're done because we've forgiven, but the wound and all of its attendant emotions only moves into the shadow. The pain goes underground—and then it goes haywire.

I've seen, for example, people forgive their fathers from stages one and two and then distrust all authority figures, or create insanely close relationships with people who behave just as their fathers did. The anger moves off the father and then oozes unchecked through their psyche and the world. I've seen people forgive their grandmothers before they've moved to stage three and then hate all women or all signs of the mature feminine, or enter into relationships and jobs that mimic exactly the emotional atmosphere of their early lives. Again, the grandmother is protected to a certain extent, but the individual and the world he or she inhabits becomes utterly toxic. When we forgive before we're done feeling the effects of our initiatory experiences, we artificially remove our gaze from the actual wounding event or person. We lose our connection to our emotional realities and to the wounds we carry, and then those wounds careen and lurch unchecked throughout our lives and our culture. Forgiving from stages one and two creates nothing but more wounding.

In true forgiveness, we return to the original stage-one initiatory moment (to that sense or feeling) with the help of our boundary-defining anger and our intuition-restoring fear. Both emotions move us through imbalance and into understanding, and then they contribute the energy we need to move to blessed resolution. Working with our strong emotions (by learning their language and channeling them, rather than expressing or repressing them) restores our focus and our equilibrium. With the help of our emotions, our wounds become not never-ending tragedies, but specific portals through which we can discover our true resilience. Channeling our emotions properly allows us to arrive whole at the very center of our psyches—and from that place of restored equilibrium, forgiveness is a natural and simple thing.

Jesus said we should forgive seventy times seven times, and I don't think he meant that we should find 490 people to transgress against us. I think Jesus was trying to tell us that deep wounds require more than just one pass through forgiveness before they are truly healed. Forgiveness, then, becomes a practice in itself. First, we might forgive after a bout of properly channeled fury, and we'll get our boundaries back—our authentic and honored anger will help us rediscover our strength and separateness. Next, we might forgive after a bout of consciously welcomed terror, and we'll retrieve our instincts—our honest and welcomed fear will help us become safer and saner in each day. Then, we might forgive after a bout of deep despair, and in awakening our crushed and broken hearts, we'll become able to love again—even through pain and betrayal.

I've seen this process unfold many times in survivors of childhood trauma, whose wounds seem to wrap themselves throughout their psyches. I always suggest that these people go to the library and find books about the developmental processes that were occurring at the time of their traumas (such as the *Your Two-Year-Old* or *Your Five-Year-Old* books).[6] It's fascinating reading, because early trauma insinuates itself into the learning and socialization processes of survivors. Depending on their age at the time of the trauma, people might have trauma responses swirled into their language skills (as I did), their hand-eye coordination, their eating behaviors, or their ability to attach and belong. Trauma at an early age can also predispose the brain toward learning and behavioral disabilities, and even ongoing depressive or anxiety disorders. For childhood trauma survivors, the process of forgiveness is quite lengthy (just as Jesus said it would be), because the trauma grows up with them. There's not one decisive forgiveness episode; instead, forgiveness is a gradual process of strengthening and unwinding, strengthening and unwinding further, and so on. This gradual process helps trauma survivors separate their innate selves from their traumatic behaviors. Their authentic emotions lead them into their real troubles, and then help them restore themselves to wholeness. Their bodies can safely recall the trauma, while their minds translate freely, their emotions flow unencumbered, and their visions are welcomed. Sometimes this healing process requires the help of therapeutic tribes, while at other times it is a solitary movement, but the process is always totally original, deeply emotive, and stunningly beautiful.

Real forgiveness is an intense healing journey with no shortcuts, no magical techniques, and no road map—it is a soul-making and culture-healing process that requires the fullness of a village inside you. Real forgiveness frees people and shoots them forward in consciousness, and that sort of movement only occurs in a resourced psyche where the body, the multiple intelligences, the visionary spirit, and all of the emotions are allowed to move freely. Real forgiveness can't exist without true anger, true despair, true fear, and true emotional integrity. Anger and forgiveness are not bitterly warring enemies; they are essential and irreplaceable aspects of the process of fully healing and restoring the entire self, and this process can only be undertaken in a soulful, and therefore emotive, way.

9

The Steadfast Promise

Why Love Is Not an Emotion

As we prepare to learn the five empathic skills in the next chapter, I thought you might like to get an empathic sense for emotions by looking at something that *isn't* an emotion: love.

When an emotion is healthy, it arises only when it's needed, it shifts and changes in response to its environment, and it recedes willingly once it has addressed an issue. When love is healthy, it does none of these things. If emotions repeat themselves endlessly, or appear with the same exact intensity over and over again, then something's wrong. Yet real love is a steadfast promise that repeats itself endlessly through life and beyond death. Love does not increase or decrease in response to its environment, and it does not change with the changing winds. Love is not an emotion; it doesn't behave the way emotions do. Real love is in a category of its own.

Those things we've learned to equate with love—the longing, the physical attraction, the shared hobbies, the desire, the yearning, the lust, the projections, the addictive cycles, the passions—those things move and change and fluctuate in the way emotions do, but they're not love. Love is utterly stable and utterly unaffected by any emotion. When we love truly, we can experience all our free-flowing, mood state, and raging rapids emotions (including fear, rage, hatred, grief, or shame), while continuing to love and honor our loved ones. Love isn't the opposite of fear or anger or any other emotion. Love is much, much deeper than that.

For some people, love is merely adoration, which is a form of good-shadow projection (see pages 220–21). These people find the person who best typifies their unlived shadow material—good and bad—and live in a sort of trance with them. Though I wouldn't call that sad game "love," it's what passes for love in many relationships: you find someone who can act out your unlived material, attach yourself to them, and enter into a haunted carnival ride of moods and desires. When the projections fall and you see your adoration target for who he or she truly is, you become disillusioned and try to reattach your projections, or even seek another person to project onto. But that's not love, because real love doesn't play games with other people's souls, and it doesn't depend upon what you can project onto your partner or what you can get out of the relationship. Real love is a prayer and a deathless promise: an unwavering dedication to the soul of your loved one and to the soul of the world. Emotions and desires can come and go as they please, and circumstances can change in startling ways, but real love never wavers. Real love endures all emotions, and it survives trauma, betrayal, divorce, and even death.

The truth about love is this: love is constant; only the names change. Love doesn't just restrict itself to romantic relationships. Love is everywhere—in the hug of a child, in the concern of a friend, in the center of your family, and in the hearts of your pets. When you're lost and you can't seem to find love anywhere, you're listening to love in human language instead of listening to the language of love. Love is constant; it's not an emotion.

If you want to explore love as an emotion, you'll have to read a book by someone who wasn't raised by animals and isn't an empath, because I sense a visceral difference between love and emotion. I can be furious with people I love, frightened of them, and utterly disappointed in them, but the love never wavers. If my loved ones are too damaged or dissimilar for our relationship to work, I don't stay with them (and I don't let them keep my credit cards!), but I don't stop loving them. Love lives in a realm far deeper than the emotions, and in that deep and rich place, words don't carry a lot of meaning. So I'll let words about love fall into the meaningful silence all around us, and we'll move on.

10

Building Your Raft

The Five Empathic Skills

THE FIVE EMPATHIC SKILLS in this chapter will help you create a raft to navigate competently through your emotions, your thoughts, your sensations, and your visions. When you can focus yourself and work skillfully with the village of elements and intelligences inside you, your emotions will become your allies and your guides. The raft you'll create is a grounded and body-based process that you'll perform with your eyes open, your mind engaged, your emotions and visions welcome, and your body comfortable. When I taught these skills in classes, we would all talk, laugh, drink water, and move around the room, and I've modified them over the years so that most of these skills can be used anywhere: at work, in the car, and even during conflicts or disagreements. As an empath, I've got to be able to move emotions through me whenever I get overloaded, wherever I may be. These simple skills help me do that.

We'll certainly bring our bodily-kinesthetic intelligence, our intellectual and verbal skills, and our visionary abilities into this empathic work, but these skills are primarily imaginal, which means that they rely on the power of imagery. Our watery intelligences comprehend imagery, movement, intention, and nuance; therefore, the skills you'll learn here actually rely upon and recruit the logic and language of the emotions. Through these skills, you'll immediately become more able to access your emotional realm, because you'll be working in a way that activates your innate emotional aptitude.

Before we learn these skills, however, let me remind you that if any of your emotions are making you miserable, it's important to get yourself checked out by a doctor or therapist. Remember, you can wear tracks in your brain by the way you learn to express your emotions; you can actually teach your brain to fall into depressions or rages or anxieties if you're not careful. Additionally, chemical imbalances can trigger repetitive emotional states, and early childhood trauma can lead to lifelong anxieties and depressions as well. Therapy, antidepressants, and antianxiety medications can be tremendously helpful; there is help available to all of us now. And there will still be work for you to do with all of your emotions whether you're on medications or not. Please make sure you're safe, comfortable, and well-cared-for before you begin.

ENTERING EMPATHIC PRACTICE

When your emotions are in their free-flowing states, it's a simple thing to work with them; however, when they move to mood states or to raging rapids, you can become overwhelmed. These empathic skills will help you maintain your equilibrium. The first skill (Getting Grounded) uses the healthy, flowing forms of sadness and fear to help you focus and ground yourself and connect your body to the earth. When you're focused and grounded, you'll be able to access the village inside you, and you'll be able to move emotions through you, rather than blocking them, repressing them, or expressing them ineptly. The second skill (Defining Your Boundary) uses the healthy, flowing forms of anger and shame to create a firm boundary around your psyche, so you'll have the privacy you need to work with your thoughts, sensations, ideas, visions, and emotions. The third skill (Burning Contracts) teaches you to channel your emotions in responsible and honorable ways. The fourth skill (Conscious Complaining) is yet another emotion-channeling technique that sounds silly but is surprisingly healing. The fifth skill (Rejuvenating Yourself) gives you a simple, empathic way to rejuvenate yourself whenever you need to and wherever you are. With the help of these five skills, you'll be able to integrate and balance your quaternity, access your multiple intelligences, work consciously with each of your emotions, and laugh while you're doing it.

Each of these skills may take a little getting used to. In my own case, I could work with my boundary almost immediately, but I couldn't ground myself at all, because as a skilled dissociator, I didn't want to be near my body or in this world. I couldn't drop into my body or into the deepening and grounding of sadness because I was afraid. I finally learned to ground myself over a period of months, but that ungrounded time was a blessing because I experienced all the objections a person might have to being grounded—and it made me a better teacher. For other people, grounding is easy, but creating a boundary is a jarring experience—something they've never done or even considered doing. Therefore, their work would focus on creating privacy for themselves and others. Each person's response to these skills is unique and revealing as to the condition of his or her psyche.

But don't worry in any case, because each of these skills supports the others; if you can perform any one of them, you'll tend to become more balanced. At first, each skill may feel strange, but soon it will feel strange to be without them! I knew I'd reached a turning point in my grounding abilities when I started to stub my toes when I was *ungrounded*. My body grew so accustomed to being grounded that I lost my coordination when I wasn't consciously connected to my flowing sadness, to my body, and to the earth. Or when people first learn to work with their boundaries, they feel as if they're working on something imaginary, but soon they feel shivers or their ears will pop when their boundaries need their help. These are empathic and body-based skills, which means that your emotions will translate them for your body and make them visceral and tangible almost immediately. We don't merely imagine our grounding and boundaries; we actually become able to feel them, talk with them, argue with them, and work with them effortlessly.

GETTING GROUNDED

The call to *be here now*, or to be in the present moment, comes from many enlightenment traditions, though there are many definitions of what that call means. For me, being here now means that I am fully aware and focused in the present moment, neither dissociated nor distracted. When I am fully aware, I don't require avoidance behaviors, addictions, excessive practices of any kind, or perfection; rather, I become able to deal with life as it is because I am connected to myself and my surroundings.

When I examine the idea of being here now through a quaternal lens, I see that each of us already owns something that can only be here now: our bodies. Our minds and spirits can be just about anywhere, while our emotions are often ignored or trapped in the amber of unexamined issues, but our bodies can *only* be here now. Our bodies cannot move backward into the past, and they cannot run into the future; our bodies can only live in the present moment. Therefore, if we can center our attention in our bodies, we'll be here now. It's as simple as that.

Centering our attention in our bodies in the present moment is uncommon in our culture because so many modern people make distinct separations between the physical (or profane) world and the spiritual (or divine) realm (or the seeming perfection of the intellectual realm, if their split is between body and mind). The body isn't usually seen as something to celebrate; it is often treated as something to master, escape, tolerate, or subdue. This is a shame, because bringing your focus into your body is an excellent centering tool, and it's also a way to reintegrate yourself if you're dissociated, distracted, or barreling toward avoidance behaviors or addictions. When you have proper grounded focus, you can direct the flows in each of your elements, and you can learn to navigate those flows rather than being pushed around. When you can navigate, you won't need to distract yourself or avoid your emotions, because you'll be able to focus your attention properly.

When an electrical circuit is grounded, it is more reliable because it can off-load excess current into the ground (instead of into an appliance, a fixture, or you!). Learning to ground yourself works in much the same way electrical grounding does—it allows you to release excess energy into the earth when you need to. There is also a relationship between energetic grounding and the idea of being grounded and competent in the world. When a person is said to be grounded, they are considered capable, knowledgeable, and solid in their abilities. Our empathic form of grounding brings these same qualities to you, and your level of groundedness relates directly to your competence in the inner and outer world. When you're ungrounded, you can easily be knocked around by competing flows or spikes in your psyche, but when you can get focused in your body and ground yourself, you can direct and moderate those flows, ground out any spikiness, and stabilize yourself.

If you've ever studied martial arts, you'll recognize grounding as a form of running your *qi* (life energy) downward. In most serious martial arts, students aren't allowed to jump and kick until they have good balance and are connected to their center of power and strength. Connecting to your qi source (which is located in your lower belly beneath your navel or in your solar plexus, depending on the tradition you follow) and connecting yourself to the earth creates focus and balance. From that balanced place, your movement into deepening practice and strength flows naturally; you become more agile, more focused, and more able to respond masterfully to internal and external stimuli.

If you are dealing with unrelieved trauma, dissociation, or addiction, grounding is a very useful tool. Grounding releases traumatic material from within your body, which calms most dissociative urges. When you're grounded, your need for alleviating substances and practices will most likely diminish. Grounding calms and regulates the flows within your psyche so that you can moderate and direct your thoughts, your bodily sensations, your visionary awareness, and of course, your emotions.

Exercise: Grounding Yourself
In the exercises on pages 32–36, you experienced the two free-flowing emotions that help you ground and focus yourself. Free-flowing sadness helps you connect with your body as you release tension, and free-flowing fear brings you calm, alert focus. Now let's bring them together.

To ground yourself, sit or stand comfortably, and breathe into your belly. Imagine that you're gathering warmth and light in your belly, and as you breathe out, imagine that your breath and light or warmth are moving down through your body and into your chair (if you're seated). Breathe in again, and imagine that light as a cord that's moving down into the floor beneath you, into the foundation of the building you're in, and down through the layers of soil and rock beneath your building. Breathe in again, and continue letting this light and warmth make its way downward. Just ground the circuit and thank your sadness.

Now, breathe normally, and let's make sure that you're not releasing everything. If you feel tired or heavy, you may just be tired, because many of us don't get enough sleep, but you want to be focused and present so that grounding doesn't make you so relaxed that you just want to take a nap. Understand that you're not *draining* your energy; you're just redirecting some of its flow downward. You're grounding the circuit. The heaviness will relieve itself as your body gets used to being connected to its home planet again.

As you feel this downward movement, stand or sit up straight and lean forward a bit—as you did when you were listening for that quiet sound. Get a sense of what it feels like to be grounded. Use your flowing fear to focus yourself and sense what's happening in your body. Keep breathing normally. Imagine filling your head and neck with your breath, and breathe down and into the earth again. Stay focused, and if it feels right, make loose spiraling movements with your arms or your body as you connect to the ground.

Imagine your breath and that light moving down and away from you, as if you're reaching down under the ground with a very long pole. Feel your grounding cord moving ever downward until it reaches the center of the earth, however that looks to you. Anchor your cord in some way; you can imagine your cord connected to the center of the earth on a lighted chain with an anchor, you can see it as the roots of a tree that wrap themselves around the center of the planet, or you can imagine a bright waterfall that creates a pool at the center of the earth. Any image that works for you is the correct image. Keep breathing normally.

If you're seated, get up and walk around. Did your grounding cord remain attached to the earth, or did you lose it? If it walks with you, great, because you need it to go where you go. If it disappeared, please breathe in, imagine gathering light and warmth in your belly, and breathe down to the center of the earth again. But this time, imagine wheels or use some other imagery or felt sense that will allow your sense of grounding to move with you. Remember that this skill is made of imagery and intention, which means that it doesn't need to behave like a physical object. It can go where it likes, move through any substance, and stay with you no matter how quickly you move—you can even ground yourself from an airplane at altitude.

Grounding has real benefits, but it's an imaginal process, which means it works in the imaginal realms the psyche loves best. This work is empathic; it's created out of intention and gossamer, so it doesn't have to be arduous, perfect, or particularly logical. We need our logical intelligence to help us make sense of things, but when we're accessing our emotions, we also need to rely on imagery, our intrapersonal intelligence, and our empathic abilities.

Empathically, being here now, being calm, focused, relaxed, and present, means welcoming our fear and our sadness. Perhaps now we can understand a little bit about why being here now is so hard for people that they have to turn it into a mysterious meditative process. These two emotions—fear and sadness—aren't things that people usually feel welcoming about. But we've experienced it ourselves: free-flowing sadness can help us relax and release things we don't need. It's a gorgeous emotion, and we don't need to be in a sad mood to access it. It's the same with free-flowing fear, which gives us this alert, quiet, gentle ability to be completely awake and focused in the present moment. Thank you, fear and sadness!

Here's an exercise that utilizes your free-flowing fear and sadness: Focus yourself and breathe normally. Feel the connection between your body and the center of the earth and bring your calm focus to bear on your interior state right now. If you've got any tension, confusion, or emotional upset inside you, breathe into that area and envelop it with your breath. Gather the tension, breathe it downward, and let it slide down into the ground. Try that again. Breathe into your area of tension (wherever it is), gather that tension, and exhale it down and into the ground. Let the tension ground away from you, and sense the relief your body feels when you let things go. If you need help, move your hands down your body and your legs, and describe grounding to your body in a literal way. Maintain your calm focus, and let your body tell you when it feels done. When you use your sadness and fear together, you won't release too much or exhaust yourself; your fear will help you remain focused and alert. Use this technique as often as you like; grounding helps you release tension consciously.[7]

It's a good idea to ground yourself each morning and stay grounded at all times if you can (if you can't just yet, don't worry—you'll get the hang of it), just as you'd ground an electrical appliance whether you were using it or not. Grounding supports and encourages flow throughout your body, which in turn helps your emotions awaken and come into the present moment, which in turn helps your intellect calm itself, which in turn helps your visionary spirit become more accessible. Grounding is the master skill in this process because it helps you focus yourself inside your body while you connect yourself to the earth. Grounding also gives you a way to cleanse your emotional realm. If you can breathe in, gather your confusion or tension, and then send it down into the earth, you can refocus yourself. Grounding helps you remain centered in the outer world by giving you a way to cleanse and stabilize yourself in the inner world.

Grounding is the opposite of dissociation; when I was a dissociator and I felt discomfort in my body, I'd lift away and leave my body behind. I did nothing whatsoever with the discomfort—I just flew away. With grounding, I listen to my body, I help it deal with discomfort or upsetting things, and I take charge of the situation. I don't just run away and leave my body to deal with discomfort all by itself. When I ground myself, I integrate the village inside me. Grounding is also an excellent way to connect yourself to the world around you. Grounding certainly heals you, but it can also heal your relationships, your family, and your community by making you more conscious of yourself, your thoughts, your feelings, your behavior, and your environment. When you can ground your tension and any intense emotions, you won't need to blast other people or repress everything and become flattened.

Some pointers: Grounding restores healthy flow to your body, and healthy bodies need to move. You can support grounding by moving your body regularly. You don't need to do formal exercise; you can just shimmy, shake, dance, or move parts of your body in spiral patterns. Anything that breaks up stagnation will increase your ability to ground yourself. Another way to support your grounding is to eat enough fresh, whole food, and get adequate protein and adequate rest (hungry, tired bodies can't ground easily). Watch your intake of stimulants, including coffee, tea, chocolate, and sugar, because they tend to mask fatigue that should be dealt with through sleep and rest. If you're not rested, it's hard to be focused, and if you're not focused, it's hard to remain grounded. However, if you can accept your ungrounded state and engage your imaginal capacities, you can figure out why you're ungrounded—or where you've lost your footing in the world. Then you can do something about it. Sometimes you'll feel grounded and focused, and your connection to the earth beneath you will feel palpable. At other times, you'll feel ungrounded and disoriented, and you won't be able to locate your grounding cord. Remember: this process is not about perfection; it's about wholeness, which means it encompasses peace and turmoil, grace and clumsiness, competence and incompetence, and the whole range of life experiences.

If you need some visceral support, you can ground yourself in the shower by imagining yourself grounding as the water flows down your body, onto the shower floor, and into the drain. Additionally, any time spent by a body of moving water (or with calm animals) is naturally grounding. Finally, any art form (dancing, singing, painting, ceramics, playing music, and so on) that helps you express yourself and focus your attention on creation will help with both centering and grounding. Art heals!

A note about focus: Honor the flowing nature of healthy focus. If you can allow yourself to distract, avoid, and dissociate when you choose to, you'll bring dissociation and distraction into your conscious awareness. The key to consciousness is to remain conscious, even when you need a break from consciousness itself. When you're daydreaming, drinking wine, eating chocolate, chanting, creating art, exercising, or using media because you want to, then none of these substances or practices needs to destabilize you. If you accept distractions and avoidance behaviors as normal and necessary, you'll behave normally around them. You'll know that something in your psyche—some part of you—is not able to engage with a feeling or a situation just yet. So you'll give yourself a break, always knowing that you can come back to center whenever you like. This awakened movement between clear focus and diffused consciousness gives you equal access to the center of your defined and grounded awareness and to the dreamy and ephemeral parts of your psyche. When you can move gracefully between focus and diffusion, you'll restore your resilience and flow.

In terms of the grounding part of this practice, it's important to stay grounded as much as you can, because grounding allows your body to off-load tension and charge, just as the grounding in an electrical circuit does. In some instances, I check my grounding several times throughout the day.

DEFINING YOUR BOUNDARIES

When you're focused and grounded, you'll be able to center yourself and restore flow to your psyche. As you become more skilled at staying present, you'll begin to notice how many people are uncentered, ungrounded, and unaware—and how hard it is to maintain your focus amid all the commotion. Our culture supports distraction and dissociation at every possible turn; therefore, remaining centered and integrated can be rather difficult. In order to stay focused and grounded, you'll need protection and definition; you'll need a sacred space where you can work without interference, and you'll need a strong and flexible boundary around yourself. Luckily, this boundary already exists. In the metaphysical community, it's called the *aura,* and while it has had a lot of wacky metaphysical connotations attached to it, your aura is simply your personal space. In the neurological community, this personal space is now understood to be your *proprioceptive* territory, and it is created by specific neural and muscular networks throughout your brain and your body. Your proprioceptive system maps your body and your position in relation to everything around you; it helps you stand, balance, move, and understand your body's relationship with its environment.

Your proprioceptors map your body and your environment so that you can interact competently in the physical world. Your proprioceptors map your home, your car, your tools, your workplace, and all aspects of your physical habitat. In most of us, the proprioceptive sense of personal space extends out to the reach of our arms and legs, and this is the exact dimension that most aura readers consider to be the size of a healthy aura. In the rest of this book, I will focus on the proprioceptive construct of your personal boundary; however, if you prefer to think of this area as an aura, go ahead and substitute the word "aura" for "boundary." At this point in my studies, I see them as one and the same thing.

If you can't yet wrap your mind around the idea of personal space, no problem. Your proprioceptors are brilliant at mapping territory, including imaginal territory such as your avatar in a video game or the imaginary box you create when you're pretending to be a mime. Your proprioceptors are ready and able to help you create an imaginal boundary that will actually become real to you in time. (For more information on the proprioceptive system, see the excellent book *The Body Has a Mind of Its Own* by science writers Sandra and Matthew Blakeslee.)

In truth, your boundary is already a real thing; you can sense it when people stare at you, and you can feel its exact dimensions when you're in a crowded elevator. Your personal boundary is the neural and visceral manifestation of your personal space. However, in our distracted and dissociated culture, most of us don't see ourselves as distinct individuals with clear boundaries. Most of us aren't focused enough to protect or define ourselves, and we tend to respond to our tattered boundaries by dissociating, distracting, and avoiding our inner lives because we're so scattered and unprotected. However, when we can ground ourselves and focus our attention in our bodies, we'll begin to create definition in our psyches. This definition will then allow us to firmly delineate our personal boundaries with the help of our innate proprioceptive and imaginal skills.

When you can restore your flow with grounding, you can focus yourself calmly and release trapped and confusing thoughts, emotions, or sensations and restore your sense of self—this also delineates your boundary. When you're focused and grounded, all you really need to do is become aware of your personal boundary once again. However, if you can't yet focus or ground yourself, this simple boundary-defining process may alleviate your difficulties by creating a sense of privacy and delineation for you.

Exercise: Defining Your Boundaries

Please seat yourself comfortably and ground and focus yourself, if you can (if not, it's okay). Now stand up, and reach your arms straight out to either side of you (if you cannot use your arms in this way, please use your imagination). Imagine that your fingertips are touching the edges of a lighted bubble that encompasses your private, personal space. Reach your arms out in front of you, and then raise them above your head. Feel how far your personal boundary is from your body. It should be an arm's length away from you at all points—in front of you, behind you, on either side of you, above you, and even underneath you. When you can imagine this area all the way around you, drop your arms and let them relax.

Close your eyes if you need to and imagine that this oval bubble, which is around and above you and even underneath the floor, is now lit up in a bright neon color. Choose a very bright and lively color (if you can't visualize, imagine a clear sound or a distinct movement at this distance from your body). Make your boundary quite obvious in whatever way you can. This is all you need to do to define your personal boundary—it's a very simple exercise. Feel yourself standing inside this oval bubble, as if you're a yolk standing firmly inside the protective eggshell of your own boundary.

As you sense your boundary around yourself, get back into your calm focus if you can, and ask yourself: "Do I claim this much room in the world?" As you connect with your brightly lit boundary, ask yourself if it's normal to feel completely in control of this area around your body. For most of us, the answer is absolutely not! For most of us, our personal boundary is our skin itself; we don't live as distinct people who have enough room to live and breathe fully.

Remember this as you work with your boundary. You may feel frustrated at first because you may not know, psychologically speaking, how to maintain a proper boundary or take your own place in the world. Don't feel alone in this, because it's a situation we all face. Nevertheless, you *have* your personal space, and you have a right to it. In fact, it's the area your brain identifies as yours, even if you didn't know it existed before today. Now that you *do* know, get acquainted with your personal boundary. Get a feeling of having some space in the world, of knowing where you begin and end, and of having some privacy.

Now thank the emotions that helped you create your personal boundary. Thank your free-flowing anger and your shame. Anger helps you observe and respond to boundary violations coming from the exterior world, and shame helps you observe and avoid boundary violations that may come from your interior world. Shame helps you protect your boundary and the boundaries of other people.

Isn't it funny that flowing fear makes us focused and intuitive, while sadness grounds us, and anger and shame set our boundaries? People generally avoid these emotions, yet look at what that means: if we kick fear out the window, we lose our focus and our intuition; if we avoid sadness, we won't be able to let go or get grounded; and if we throw anger and shame onto the trash heap, we lose our definition and our honor!

As we can all see, trouble with boundaries, intuition, grounding, and relaxation—and endless trouble with the emotions— are normal everyday problems for people. But we know that our emotions are the secret to grounding, focused intuition, and healthy boundaries. So take a moment to sense your calm listening state, and thank your fear. Feel your grounding, and thank your sadness. Connect with the feeling of being safe and protected inside your own personal space—you can light up the edges of your boundary again—and thank your anger and your shame.

Defining your boundary helps you avoid enmeshing with people and breaking *their* boundaries. Also, when you're properly defined, it becomes easier to be empathic in a nonempathic world, because you begin to know when you're sensing another person's emotion or situation and when you're not. What I notice when I have a good boundary is that I can experience other people as themselves instead of needing to control or change them. I can't do it all the time—who can? However, when I'm grounded, focused, and well-defined, my interpersonal intelligence gets a lot smarter.

It's perfectly all right if your connection to your boundary is uncertain at this time. This skill—creating a strong boundary around yourself and becoming aware of your personal proprioceptive territory—can be difficult because the condition of our personal boundary is intimately connected to many of the supposedly troublesome emotions. As a direct result, most of us don't have a good connection to the boundary-restoring anger and shame that could help us revitalize our personal space, or to the intuitive and instinct-restoring fears that could make us fully aware of our surroundings. Trouble with boundaries is everywhere, but it's nothing to be too concerned about. In fact, this trouble can be instructive when you know how to interpret it.

For instance, if your personal boundary is hazy and indistinct no matter what you do, you'll know that boundary-restoring anger isn't yet flowing properly in your psyche (you may be inhibiting it with repression or wasting it with dishonorable expression). That's an easy situation to address when you have emotional channeling skills and an understanding of anger's rightful place in your emotional landscape. Or if, instead of being faint and tiny, your boundary puffs itself out further than arm's length and engulfs everything and everyone around you, you'll know that boundary-honoring shame (anger toward yourself) isn't yet balanced inside you (repressing shame deadens your sense of honor, while flinging shame at others inflates your territory in disrespectful ways). That's also an easy situation to address when you have emotional skills. Or if your personal boundary squeezes itself close to you no matter what is happening around you, you'll know that the brilliant instincts of fear aren't being allowed to take their honored place inside you (repression and confused expression both misuse the intuitive and protective information fear brings forward). Each of these boundary troubles responds beautifully to grounding, focusing, and emotional channeling—all of which we'll be doing throughout the rest of this book.

Be aware, though, of how you create definitions and boundaries now. When you're feeling tired and vulnerable, do the mood states of anger or peevishness come forward? That's one way to create an emergency boundary. Anger sets a boundary and lets people know not to mess with you (but attacking people with your anger often breaks your boundary even further, which activates more anger, and often rage, and then you're in trouble). Or do you feel anxious, worried, and fearful when you're tired and vulnerable? Fear brings forward a great deal of intuitive "on guard" focus to keep you safe in the absence of a true personal boundary; however, the overuse of fear in its mood state can destabilize your body and your boundary, which can bring on full-fledged anxiety attacks! Or do the mood states of sadness or depression come forward when you're fatigued and vulnerable? Both emotions can create emergency boundaries by taking you out of commission so you can't engage with the world around you (however, being disengaged for too long can turn your sadness into unmoving despair, or trap your depression in an unending cycle).

Perhaps you move toward addictions or distractions when your personal boundary isn't functional—you might reach for the anesthesia of overeating or the fiery intensity of caffeine, or you might create a false boundary around yourself with a cloud of cigarette smoke. In each case (whether you misuse emotions, distractions, or substances), you sense a problem with your boundary and respond to it—unconsciously, perhaps, but you certainly *do* respond. Even if you can't feel, visualize, or imagine your personal boundary as the lighted oval I've described, you're already working with it, as you have been since the day you were born. Now that you can center and ground yourself, you can work with your boundary more intentionally. You can let your moods tell you about the condition of your personal boundary—and by delving into each of your emotions (as we'll do in Part II), you'll be able to understand and heal your boundary. Soon you'll be able to maintain your personal boundary in skilled and focused ways, rather than creating emergency boundaries with moods or distractions.

Exercise: Breathing with Your Boundaries

Here's a simple exercise to help you become more aware of your personal boundary right now: Ground and focus yourself if you can. Sit comfortably and imagine your arm's-length personal boundary as brightly lit or very distinctive. Choose a very intense color for your boundary, such as lime green or electric magenta; your boundary should be exceedingly noticeable to you (if you can't visualize, try to create a noticeable sensation or movement at the edges of your boundary). Take a deep breath and imagine your boundary expanding a few inches in all directions (just as your torso does when you inhale). As you exhale, imagine your personal boundary resuming its healthy arm's-length distance from your body at all points. Notice that your brightly lit personal boundary reaches under the floor. Breathe in again, and make sure that the edges of your boundary expand slightly in all directions—even underneath you. Breathe out, and allow your boundary to resume its correct distance from your body. You're done! You can breathe with your boundary as often as you like. It's a simple and healing way to help your proprioceptive network connect viscerally with your new sense of a personal boundary.

Some quick pointers: You can use your imagination as a placeholder for your personal boundary if you can't envision or feel it just yet. For instance, you can fill your entire personal space with your favorite natural environment: You can imagine yourself surrounded at arm's length by a shoreline, mountain, or desert scene (again, you don't have to *see* this scene—you can hear it, feel it, or even smell it if you can't visualize). You can use your nature scene to calm the area around your body, which will help you inhabit your personal space psychologically. If you can imagine yourself enveloped in your favorite mountain or oceanside scene, you can surround yourself with an incredibly healing sense of peacefulness. If you like, you can also invite totem animals to help you set your boundaries; you can imagine birds of prey or hunting animals guarding your territory, and in time you'll be able to guard it yourself. Any symbolism that works for you should be called upon. This is your personal, sacred territory, and you have every right to fill your personal space with images that make you feel whole. Also, imagine lighting up your boundary and breathing with it every day. Soon, it will be able to protect and define you in health-building ways.

Your personal space should be a sanctuary of solitude that no other people can enter—though you can populate it with totem animals, angels, or ancestors if they make you feel more secure. However, no living people and no expectations from the outside world are allowed in this sacred place. This is your inner village, and you're the chief here.

As you become more acquainted with focusing your awareness and protecting your personal territory, you may notice certain situations or relationships that tend to knock you out of your center. Pay attention. Don't berate yourself or feel as if you're losing your skills. In most cases, you're simply responding to dissociation or distraction in the people around you. It's natural (because we're social primates) to unconsciously mimic the behavior of others. Beyond that, though, dissociation is understood at some deep level in the psyche to be a sacred movement into initiation.

I've noticed that we drop our boundaries and dissociate not just to conform, but also to create a kind of ceremonial boundary around the dissociated people in our lives. It's as if we unconsciously move to the dissociated position of stages one and two to comfort or aid the dissociated people around us. We lose our grounding and our boundaries and dissociate in order to create a kind of sacred space—though we don't realize it. This "contact" dissociation doesn't help at all, but it is a very common response. As you become more skilled at grounding and defining yourself, see if you can stay centered inside your own body and behind your strong boundary when dissociated people or dissociating situations present themselves. If you can stay focused and defined, you'll create sacred space in a new way, by providing dissociated people with a model of integration. It's very hard to do at first, but soon you'll be able to remain integrated in the midst of chaos and distractions. When you can separate yourself from the dissociated and distracted behaviors that infect our culture, you'll be a walking example of calm, focused sacred space.

Your brightly defined boundary should be in place at all times, wherever you go, because it can be likened to the skin of your proprioceptive body. You wouldn't allow the skin on your physical body to wither or degrade; you need it to protect your organs, glands, bones, and muscles. The same is true for your boundary: you should keep it healthy because it protects and envelops your personal territory and the village inside you. Your boundary can be defined and renewed on a daily basis (or more often, if you're a very sensitive person).

BURNING CONTRACTS

The third skill in this process supports the definition of your personal boundary by helping you release trapped emotions and behaviors. The skill of burning contracts brings together each of the skills you've learned so far and invites all of your elements into an active and focused healing that frees your soul from bondage.

When you can focus, ground yourself, and set your boundary consciously, you become able to navigate the flows of life. You become able to remain centered during difficult times (rather than dissociating); you become able to ground emotions, attitudes, and sensations out of your body (rather than reacting to them involuntarily); and your healthy boundary enables you to see yourself as distinct from the world around you. From your position of clarity and strength, you can create a sacred space in which your elements and intelligences can interact intentionally with one another. When you can access all parts of yourself mindfully, you will attain equilibrium.

The empathic practice of burning contracts supports your equilibrium by allowing you to separate yourself from behaviors and attitudes that destabilize you. This practice helps you envision your behaviors and attitudes as *tendencies*, rather than concrete certainties. When you're grounded, focused, and well-defined, you can view your behaviors not as life sentences, but as inclinations you can choose to support or release, depending on your intentions. If you've got trouble with certain emotions, you can burn your behavioral contracts with those emotions and restore your emotional flow. If you're unhappy with a distracted or addicted behavior, you can burn your contracts with it and free yourself from its clutches. If you're unable to function in relationships, you can burn your contracts with those relationships—not to end them, but to reorganize the behaviors that control your interactions with others. This empathic process of burning contracts helps you meet each of your behaviors, attitudes, and stances from a grounded position. It also leads you into emotional channeling. Emotions move energy and information, and the practice of burning contracts relies on the movement, energy, and healing intention inside each of your emotions.

Exercise: Burning Contracts

To burn a contract with an idea, behavior, stance, or relationship, begin by focusing and grounding yourself. Illuminate your boundary with a very bright color (if you can), and breathe normally. Imagine unrolling a large piece of blank parchment paper right in front of you (if you can't visualize, use your hands to unroll this imaginary parchment). This parchment should have a calming feeling to it; it shouldn't be bright or jazzy. It should be a gentle color that can absorb whatever you place onto it. Keep this roll of parchment *inside* your personal boundary for now (placing this scroll or parchment inside your boundary helps you create sacred space for this process).

With your parchment in front of you, you can project, envision, write, speak, or just think your distress onto it. You can project your emotional expectations—how you're supposed to feel and express yourself—onto the parchment. You can project your intellectual stances—how you're supposed to think, what you're supposed to think, how you're supposed to be intelligent. You can project physical rules—how your body is supposed to look and perform for others. You can project spiritual expectations—how you're supposed to meditate, pray, or behave in relation to spirituality or religion. Or you can project entire relationships (images of yourself, your partner, and the ways you relate to one another) right onto the parchment. When you can get these behaviors, relationships, and ideas out in front of you, you can begin to individuate from them. In this sacred space, you can see yourself not as a victim, but as an upright individual who *decides* to act, relate, or behave in certain ways—and who can decide to act and behave differently.

As these behaviors, beliefs, and postures move out in front of you, you may feel emotions rising up inside you. This is absolutely fantastic. It means your psyche is awakened to the process and is bringing emotions forward to help you separate from these entrapping ideas and behaviors. Remain focused, intensify your grounding if you need to, and brighten your boundary so you'll have a greater sense of definition around yourself. Welcome your emotions—whatever they are—and use them to move these ideas and behaviors out of the shadows of habit and into your conscious control. If you feel angry, throw these ideas onto your parchment or imagine a color, movement, sound, or quality you associate with anger, and place it alongside your images. If you feel fearful, speed up your movements and fling these ideas out of you. If you feel sad, lay these ideas on your parchment slowly and mournfully. If you feel depressed, darken the images or your parchment (or slow your movements to a crawl) and welcome your depression to this process. Don't fight your emotions or pretend you're feeling something else. Don't surround yourself with Mr. Bunnies if you're enraged.

Remember that you're focused, grounded, and safely protected inside the sacred space of your personal boundary, and you don't have to repress, distract, avoid, or dissociate here. This is what channeling your emotions feels like. You can use whatever emotion comes forward to dislodge unworkable ideas or behaviors, and in so doing, you'll restore your flow. That's what emotions do: they move energy and information from one place to the next and restore your flow. Rely on them, and you'll achieve real separation from old attitudes and behaviors, and real understanding of your authentic self. If you're not sure how to work with certain emotions, please skip forward to the chapters on each emotion in Part II (but return to this process as soon as you can).

If your first parchment becomes full, move it aside and create a fresh one. Keep working through the situation until you feel some sense of completion. When you feel done for now, and your parchment (or parchments) is full of words, images, feelings, or sounds, please roll it up. This parchment embodies the contract you've forged with this behavior, belief, attitude, or relationship. Roll this contract tightly, so the material inside can't be seen or heard any longer; in this way, it becomes less powerful immediately. Tie your contract with a cord, if that feels right. Grasp your rolled-up contract, and imagine tossing it outside your boundary and away from you. When it lands, imagine burning it up with whatever emotional energy feels right. You can blast it with anger, strike it with fear, engulf it with sadness, or use your depressive energy to create a funeral pyre. Your emotions will provide the exact intensity you need to destroy the contract and set yourself free.

When the contract is burned to a crisp, refocus yourself, check your grounding, and brighten your personal boundary once again. You'll probably notice changes in your skills—you may feel a difference in your grounding, the nature scene around you (if you created one) may have changed, or you may notice changes in the condition of your boundary. If so, congratulate yourself—your imaginal and proprioceptive systems are communicating with you empathically! Note each of the changes, and gently bring yourself back to center; you should feel grounded and your vibrant boundary should be a healthy arm's length away from you at all points. That's it!

Burning contracts is the central skill of the emotional channeling process. It allows you to move energy and information from one place to another while you bring your behaviors, attitudes, and stances into your conscious awareness. It also helps you raft through the eddies and rapids of your emotions. Instead of haphazardly expressing your emotions at the outer world (or haphazardly repressing them back into your inner world), this process helps you work with each of your emotional reactions. Your grounding skills allow you to stay focused and integrated, even when strong emotions flow through you; your defined personal boundary creates a sacred space in which you can do your empathic work in safety and privacy; and your ability to imagine your behaviors and stances as contracts (rather than unchangeable destinies written in stone) allows you to amend and destroy them at will.

When you can free yourself from old behaviors, stagnant attitudes, or unworkable relationships, you will no longer require constant distractions, addictions, or avoidance behaviors, nor will you need to dissociate in response to your backlog of unlived and dishonored emotions. When you can bring your entire village to bear on your issues, you'll regain your resilience and your equilibrium.

If you can remain upright and conscious during periods of emotional upwelling, your emotions will help you end your suffering by allowing you to form a clear and precise picture of your suffering. If you don't honor your emotions—if you hurl them outward or shove them inward— you'll never understand what's going on in your life. However, if you can channel your emotions in an awakened way, you'll become whole. In essence, strong emotions call your soul to ritual.

You can burn contracts at any time, and in any place. No one needs to know you're doing it. Once you're focused and grounded, you can imagine your personal boundary as a brightly colored ceremonial bubble around your psyche. Within that sacred space, you can do whatever work you need to—in complete privacy. You can pull out a parchment at work, while you're driving, or even when you're in the middle of an argument (though it's very hard to remember your skills when you're fighting!). This process is fully portable. It's a fully embodied, emotionally welcoming, empathic process that was created for people with busy lives; it can be used whenever and wherever you like.

Your contract burning can be done as often or as infrequently as you like. Some people burn contracts every morning or every few hours, while others perform a big housecleaning once a week (or once a month). Your frequency will depend on how much of your life is tied up in contractual or reactive behaviors. If you're able to meet each new situation with new focus, you probably won't need to burn contracts very often. But if your life doesn't flow smoothly (or you constantly trip over old behaviors, distractions, and attitudes), you may benefit from regular contract-burning sessions. Burning contracts restores your flow and kick-starts your life again, but it has protective aspects as well. If you can burn your contracts with old stances and mindsets, you won't be trapped in reactive behaviors. Burning your contracts, because it utilizes the imaginal and emotive language the psyche likes best, will move you to a new place in consciousness, where you'll no longer need to waste your time on unfulfilling behaviors or objectionable attitudes. Burning your contracts can set you free.

CONSCIOUS COMPLAINING

Focus, grounding, and definition are states to aspire to, but no one can maintain them at all times. The brain doesn't appreciate constant focus, and life is a drag if all you do is work. Resting, daydreaming, fooling around, laughing, napping, and playing are extremely important in a whole and happy life. Learning to flow means learning to relax; it's important to keep things light. However, if you can't ground, focus, or define yourself when you *want* to, that's a horse of a different color.

It is easy to get into troubling moods or stagnant places and forget all your skills and all your emotional wisdom; it's easy to fall into emotional repression and incompetent expression. When this happens (and it will), your ignored and mismanaged emotions will intensify and repeat themselves—because neither repression nor improper expression can ever address the issues your emotions are trying to bring forward. If you continue to ignore your emotions (and you will), they'll become louder and more aggressive. Soon, they'll arise in response to totally unrelated situations. Cycling depressions and rages, anxiety attacks, and obsessive worry are all examples of emotions that have become trapped in a bothersome feedback loop. What started out as mobile emotions become monotonous, tormenting, and chronic responses to the world.

When your emotions are welcomed and honored, they move easily and quickly—they arise in response to real situations, they contribute precisely what you need, and then they retreat cheerfully. In contrast, a disruption in the healthy flow of your emotions creates a dam that destabilizes your entire psyche. Certainly, your emotions will get trapped behind that dam, but if the clog persists, the rest of your elements will be disrupted as well. If your emotions are allowed to fester and stagnate, your mind will soon become disturbed by all the trouble. This disturbance often ignites repetitive thoughts that (like your trapped emotions) never go anywhere. Your body will also begin to react to your lack of flow with fatigue and distress, and you'll often dissociate or run toward your addictions just to take a vacation from it all.

If this is your current situation, worry not! You can use each of your new skills to address this. For instance, you can ground and reintegrate yourself through relaxation and deep breathing or by simply taking a walk in nature or taking a hot bath. Then you can define your boundaries to create sacred space and burn your contracts with your cycling thoughts and emotions. However, there is a much easier way to restore flow to a clogged-up psyche: I call it *conscious complaining*.

I first learned of the importance of complaining in Barbara Sher's wonderful book *Wishcraft*, which puts forth the idea that wishes and dreams are not silly diversions, but actually crystal-clear pointers for your most important work. Sher writes that if you dream constantly of writing, training horses, traveling, going back to school, or becoming a clown, that dream is actually a specific treasure map that will lead you to the central vocation of your life. This is not an ordinary self-help book. Sher has truly lived the material inside it and knows that moving toward dreams is often the most terrifying, ridiculous, infuriating, and impossible task imaginable—which is why so few people attempt it and why so many attempts fail. Sher's assertion is that if you don't look at the problems, the terrors, and the impossibilities in a conscious way, you simply won't survive the often harrowing process of bringing your fiery dream into this world. She suggests taking regular time out to complain, both to "de-steam" and to get a clearer understanding of whatever it is that's holding you back.

Though Sher suggests finding a complaining partner, I've modified the practice, because there are very few people in this world who can deal with the amount of complaining I can produce. Most people are so uncomfortable in their own skin that they can't let me be uncomfortable in mine; they want to stop me, fix me, or help me see the world in a pep-pier light (which is just another form of repression if I'm in a foul mood). I've gone a different way and turned my complaining practice into a soli-tary one, which has been a real lifesaver. Now every time I lose all faith or come up against impossible obstacles, I can whine, moan, kvetch, and reinvigorate myself with the grim truth of what I'm experiencing. When I'm done, I'm not depressed; instead, I'm often able to get right back to work because I know exactly what the problems are and just how hard life can be. This practice doesn't bring me down; it lifts me up because it clears all the complaints out of my system and restores my flow.

Exercise: Conscious Complaining

Here's how to complain consciously. You can be grounded or not, inside your strong boundary or not—it doesn't matter. All that matters is that you're in a foul mood and you have some privacy. You start your com-plaining with some sort of phrase, like "I'm complaining now!" If you're inside, you can complain to the walls or furniture, to a mirror, or to what-ever strikes your fancy. If you're outside, you can complain to plants and trees, animals, nature, the sky, the ground, or your god. If you're a strong complainer like I am, you might want to create a complaining shrine for yourself, with supportive pictures of grumpy cats, bratty kids, barking dogs, political cartoons, and whatever else calls to your complaining nature.

When you've found your perfect complaining site, let yourself go, and give a voice to your dejected, hopeless, sarcastic, nasty, bratty self. Bring dark humor out of the shadows and really whine and swear about the frustrations, stupidities, impossibilities, and absurdities of your situation. Complain for as long as you like (you'll be surprised at how quickly this works), and when you run out of things to say, thank whatever you've been whining or yelling at. Thank the furniture, the walls, the ground, the trees, your complaining shrine, or your god for listening, and end your conscious complaining session by bowing, shaking off, and then doing something really fun. That's it!

People who try this practice are astonished to find that complain-ing doesn't pull them further down into the doldrums. Actually, it has precisely the opposite effect because it breaks through stagnation and repression and lets you tell it like it is—without repercussions. You restore your flow again, the truth is told again, the decks are cleared, and you get an important time-out. And because this is a solitary practice, there is no danger of losing face or hurting someone else's feelings; instead, it's like a quick lube for your soul. Afterward, you'll find that you can revisit your struggles with renewed vigor and vision.

Conscious complaining is especially helpful in a life of striving, good works, and personal growth, where complaining is often considered less than saintly (this is a shame, because all by itself, a lack of permission to complain can cause unresolving, repetitive mood states like worry, depression, and apathy). When you don't pay attention to the difficulties of trying to live a conscious life in a sea of distractions, the conscious life becomes less and less appealing, and the distractions start calling to you and shimmering seductively. If you only make time for work, and you never make time for play and rest, or for kvetching, moaning, whining, and complaining, your psyche will become flat and barren. Your flow will evaporate, you'll deteriorate into perfectionism, and you'll have no fun at all. Many parts of you will demand a vacation from all your striving and perfection, and that's when distractions will start to loom. Conscious complaining gives a voice to your struggles, and in so doing, it restores your flow, your energy, your sense of humor, and your hope. It sounds contradictory, but you just can't be happy unless you complain.

Complaining versus Positive Affirmations

Positive thinking and affirmations are the opposite of conscious complaining. The idea behind positive thinking is that each of us holds on to thoughts that get in the way of our health and well-being. Thoughts like "I'm unlovable" or "No one can be truly successful" or "Life is too hard" can really slow down our forward progress. Positive thinking techniques teach us to unearth and then replace those thoughts with more helpful affirmations, such as "I have love around me all the time" or "Success belongs to me" or "Life is absolutely wonderful." It seems like a good idea, right?

Though it can be quite healing to ferret out interior statements that crush your well-being, positive thinking tends to be too much of a quick fix (and it tends to be emotionally repressive as well). If you look at the practice from a fully resourced perspective, you'll understand the problem. Positive affirmations look at issues (like a lack of love or happiness, or an eating disorder) and apply a kind of reverse psychology upon the psyche. Instead of sitting with the issues and honoring the feelings involved, positive affirmations tend to override the situation with enforced statements that negate the true-but-discomfiting messages in the psyche. Affirmations such as "Food is healing and slenderizing for me" or "I am surrounded by kind and loving people" *do* provide a more pleasant inner dialogue, but they don't tell the truth or honor the truth that is trying to come forward. These affirmations don't speak to the myriad issues behind the eating problem, and they don't heal or address the broken and weary heart—and the psyche knows it. Most positive affirmations elevate verbal-intellectual statements above emotional truths and bodily realities. In essence you're *telling* yourself how to feel instead of *feeling* the way you feel.

Empathically speaking, I haven't seen or experienced deep or lasting change with positive affirmations. I've seen people deal with the surface of their issues, and I've seen them get some of the things they affirm, but I haven't seen them deepen or mature into wholeness. Look at it this way: If you place a conflicting or overriding verbal statement into the midst of strong emotions or sensations, you'll set up warring factions within your psyche. Each of your affirmations will deny or repress the truth of the situation, which means that your psyche will have to increase the intensity of the original emotion or sensation in order to get you to listen up, take effective action, and restore your balance. Positive affirmations attempt to deal with issues in an incomplete and distracting way.[8]

Conscious complaining is healing because it speaks to your real issues from within your actual sense of things: it addresses your actual concerns, it wrestles with them until flow is restored, and then it's over. Conscious complaining doesn't sugarcoat or attempt to transform anything. Instead, complaining tells it like it is, and your psyche likes that a lot. You allow yourself to be yourself, you allow your emotions to tell it like it is, and no one gets hurt. When you can stand up and complain in a conscious way (rather than just whining without any purpose), your vision and your focus return, your emotions flow, your body releases its stored-up tensions, and your linguistic intelligence has the fun of translating everything you feel into choice words and phrases.

Positive thinking is helpful when it's true, just as "negative" thinking is helpful when it's true. If the phrase "I'm wonderful and marvelous!" comes barreling out of your psyche, it's a sign of happiness moving through you in its own way and its own time. Embrace it! It's true! You *are* wonderful and marvelous! Similarly, if the phrase "I can't go on this way!" comes out of your psyche, it's a sign of sadness, fatigue, depression, or grief moving through you in its own way and its own time. Embrace it! It's true! You *can't* go on this way—so don't try! Use your skills, bring your emotions forward, and deal with the truth of what your psyche presents to you—whatever that truth may be. Dance with your marvelousness in its time—and complain, cry, whine, and burn contracts with your despair in *its* time. Then move on to your next emotion, your next idea, your next vision, or your next task. True emotional health isn't an unmoving and unchangeable sense of slap-happiness—it is your ability to flow and respond uniquely to each of your emotions (and each of your elements) in turn.

Support your real self, your emotional truth, your intellectual agility, and the factual conditions of your whole life by setting aside regular conscious-complaining time. You can even make it into a kind of meditative practice. Conscious complaining will restore your flow, refocus your attention, revitalize your psyche, and release your happiness, laughter, and joy in natural and healing ways. Flow is the key!

REJUVENATING YOURSELF

Our fifth and final empathic skill, which is rejuvenation, helps you refresh yourself so you can meet each new experience with focus and intention. This empathic rejuvenation exercise is very simple, and it takes almost no time at all. However, you can turn it into a long and luxurious practice if you like.

Exercise: Rejuvenating Yourself
If you're ready, please sit down, breathe in, and ground yourself as you exhale. Just let it go. Now lean forward with good posture, focus yourself,

THE LANGUAGE OF EMOTIONS

and imagine that your personal boundary is very bright and distinct at the correct arm's length distance from your body—in front of you, behind you, on either side of you, above you, and below the floor. Imagine your boundary as whole, distinctive, and vibrant.

Now in your personal space between your body and the edge of your boundary, I'd like you to imagine your favorite place in the world at your favorite time of day. For instance, feel yourself surrounded by a mountainside on a late spring evening, or beside a creek in a redwood grove at dawn, or in a cave on a tropical island where you can see and hear the ocean. Choose your favorite place, and imagine it surrounding you. Remember that you can feel or smell or sense this scene if visualizing isn't your skill. Just surround yourself with that feeling of beauty and relaxation and delicious, sensual pleasure.

You may feel your focus soften here, and that's perfectly fine. This is an interior exercise, and you don't need to be completely aware of the outside world. Let your focus drift naturally.

As you sense your gorgeous nature scene around you, breathe some of it into your body. Take a deep breath, and imagine breathing this peaceful, beautiful place into your body. Imagine embodying the way you feel when you're in your favorite place. Breathe this feeling into your chest and your arms and your hands, and breathe it down into your belly. Breathe it into your lower belly and breathe it down into your legs and feet. Breathe it into your chest and up into your neck, your face, and your head. Fill yourself with this feeling of peace and beauty.

When you feel full, let your body, your emotions, and your focus soften and relax. You can stay here for as long as you like, but for now, let's finish up so that we can move onward. To complete this rejuvenation practice, bend over and touch the floor with both of your hands, and let your head hang down. Just relax. You're done.

You can keep this nature scene around you at all times, or you can bring it forward only when you want to rejuvenate yourself. For me, it's fun to be where I am—in a traffic jam or on a plane or in a meeting—and also be swimming in the warm water at Ke 'e Beach on Kauai or listening to a stream in a redwood grove. Empathic skills are excellent!

After any contract-burning session, it's important to rejuvenate yourself so that old behaviors won't be able to reanimate themselves. When you clear a space in your psyche with contract burning, it's important to refill yourself consciously. If you don't consciously refill that empty space, it will be filled unconsciously, and you don't want that! If you don't have time to rest and rejuvenate yourself after you burn contracts, just take a moment to fill your boundary area with a luscious bright light. This takes less than five seconds, and it will hold you over until you can take good care of yourself. You can perform this rejuvenation practice every morning or evening, once each week, or whenever you like. Sometimes you may feel like rejuvenating yourself hourly—go ahead; these are *your* tools now; you can use them however you like.

I notice that rejuvenating and self-soothing abilities aren't prevalent in our society. Most of us know how to tune out and distract ourselves, and most of us know how to jack ourselves up with stimulants, but we seem to have less knowledge about how to soothe and replenish ourselves. For instance, napping has been shown to provide almost miraculous health and memory benefits, but how many of us make time for napping or resting of any kind? Physical touch has also been shown to be a necessary aspect of physical and psychological health, but most of us cordon off physical touch so that we only receive it during short hugs, sexual contact, or massages that we pay for.

Singing, dancing, doing art, playing, fooling around, laughing, and day-dreaming are also soothing and healing, but most of us seem to make little time for these activities. Instead we work and exercise intently, eat quickly, sleep restlessly, and don't have the time or energy for the simple, lovely pleasures of life.

If you've found a way to carve out rejuvenation time in your life—time where you're able to read, dance, sing, play a game, daydream, hang out with friends, watch the sunset, or laugh and play—congratulations! This is a wonderful way to call your attention and vitality back from all the places it rushes to, so that you'll be more resourced, more agile, and more available to live your life in a grounded and focused way. It's important to maintain a balance between the work you do when you ground and define yourself and channel your emotions, and the work you do when you just let go and enjoy yourself. Both are important in your whole life.

Something to be aware of: one rest and relaxation option many of us gravitate toward is home entertainment, either filmed, televised, or online. This is natural and normal because humans are storytelling primates for whom stories and dramas are a bit like brain food. However, we've all experienced the seductive, addictive pull of movies and TV or the way hours can disappear when we're surfing the web, IM'ing, or texting. As you bring more awareness to all parts of your life, take a clear but gentle look at the time you spend on entertainment or the Internet. These can be fun diversions, but they can also turn into serious distractions if you become entangled in them. If a great deal of your free time is spent in front of the TV or the computer, ask yourself what you're receiving in return for all your time, if anything. Are the stories on TV calming your emotions? Does lazing around in front of the tube give your body a chance to rest while the shows keep your mind focused outside of yourself? Does web surfing or messaging give your intellect lots of fun things to think about and research? Or have you simply fallen into an addictive cycle? Just ask. The answers will be different for each of us.

Also ask yourself what your priorities are in your real life—the life you live when you're away from the TV, the computer, and your messaging. Is your house clean? Are the bills paid? Do you spend enough time with your family? Or are you so tired that all you can manage when you get home is to crawl inside the tube or the Internet and get away from your life? When you bring your awareness to these activities, you can decide how you want them to fit into your whole life. If they seem to loom over you, or if your life is imbalanced by them, skip back to the chapter on addictions and see what you might be seeking in these entertainments. Or burn your contracts with these activities and see what messages your emotions have about them. You have skills now; you can bring awareness to anything you do, and make changes if you want to.

CHANGE AND STASIS—UNDERSTANDING THEIR DANCE

Change is a skill in and of itself. These empathic skills will awaken many sleeping parts of you and allow your emotions to come forward—and this will constitute a large change in your inner landscape. You may feel unusual and discomfited at first, which is normal. Any change in your psyche alerts the opposing force of stasis, which is the part of you that values tradition, normalcy, and the status quo. Neither change nor stasis is unnatural; both are absolutely necessary in living organisms. Depending on your viewpoint, though, each one can appear to be healing or destructive. If a change benefits you, you probably like change, but if it doesn't, you may see change as troublesome. If you're happy with the way things are, you probably love stasis, but if you're desperate for change, you might see stasis as a tormentor. Regardless of your momentary preferences, however, both change and stasis are equal participants in any real movement. Change tells you that new situations or influences are acting upon your system, and stasis allows you to maintain the situations and influences already in place. The way to ensure effective change is not to erase stasis (as if it were vile) but to understand that change and stasis are equal partners in your psyche.

As you learn these new skills, pay close attention to your reactions. If certain skills feel utterly strange or even impossible, pay attention and support those reactions. Make no mistake, these skills are unusual. We're so group-centered that we know what to say, what to wear, what to own, and how to act—but we don't know how we feel or what our inner voices are saying. These skills reawaken the part of us that feels, sees, hears, and senses our inner voices, which can be a startling thing. If these processes feel unusual, that's fine; they should! Unusual and unaccustomed feelings are signs that your internal sense of stasis is reacting to the changes you're making. If you can breathe with your struggles (rather than fight them) and welcome their presence, you'll be able to glide through any discomfort. Soon these skills will feel natural to you; they'll become a part of your new stasis, and your psyche will become agitated when you're *not* using them. Welcoming change and stasis makes any movement proceed more gracefully.

If these skills bring forward very unsettled feelings, however—if you feel fearful, enraged, or very displaced—take a break, especially if you've got trauma in your past or you're healing from addiction or dissociation. These skills (because they bring all parts of you back home again) signal to your psyche that a certain level of safety has been attained. In some cases, that signal will prompt your psyche to begin pouring forth memories, feelings, flashbacks, and issues because it wants you to figure them out as quickly as possible. This is an excellent movement, but it can be startling if you don't expect it (and if you don't have all your skills in place). If any skill truly unsettles you, stop and move back to your stasis position. Go to the chapter (in Part II) on the emotion that best describes your reaction to this process. When you understand the healing task for that emotion, you can come back here and make another attempt at these skills.

Know that you're completely in charge of this process. You can pick and choose among these skills, create your own versions of them, or ignore them if they feel unnecessary. Listen to yourself, make room for the voice of your stasis, and make your changes at your own pace. You're in charge.

INCORPORATING THESE SKILLS INTO YOUR LIFE
When you have access to one or more of these skills, you can use them in whatever way you see fit, and you can mix them up to match the condition of your soul. I don't attach time guidelines to these skills, because I can run through all of them in less than two minutes, or I can move slowly and prayerfully and take an hour or more. It totally depends on my needs and my time constraints. I'll offer a few general guidelines here, but trust and honor your own information. You are the expert in your own life.

Grounding and boundary definition are good everyday skills, but your focus can and should be able to wander (just make sure you can focus yourself when you need to be fully aware). You can burn your contracts as often or as infrequently as you see fit, and you can use your complaining shrine regularly or just keep it for ceremonially cranky occasions. Your rejuvenation practice should be used regularly because we tend to be so forgetful about taking care of ourselves. I set a schedule for it so I don't forget.

Notice if any of your skills change without your conscious permission. This is always a signal from your inner self about the current condition of your soul. If you created an oceanfront sanctuary inside your boundary, but it suddenly changes into a crystal cave or a rustic cabin (or disappears altogether), pay attention; your psyche speaks clearly through such images. In fact, pay attention to changes in any of your skills; your psyche will use them to communicate empathically about your deepest issues. Don't fight the changes. Instead, use all of your faculties to decipher the images your psyche transmits. If you can't make heads or tails of the situation intellectually, bring forth your emotional skills, your physical ability to grapple with issues, or your fiery vision in order to gain perspective.

Remember to move your body regularly as a part of your meditative practice. Exercise, change positions, shake and shimmy, yawn, and vocalize as much as you can. You might want to do these things in private because they can look quite silly, but movement is essential in all parts of your psyche. Your body should move freely, your mind should think and plan without restraints, your visionary spirit should dream and meander to its heart's desire, and your emotions should react and respond authentically. When you can nurture this sort of freedom in your psyche, you won't require repression, unskilled expression, distraction, avoidance, or dissociation because you'll be able to flow with and moderate your elements properly.

As you reintegrate the village inside you, ask your mind to support your emotions with its excellent ability to name and translate things. Ask your body to keep you in touch with your emotions as they move through you (or get stuck). Ask your visionary spirit to keep you connected to the larger issues your emotions are trying to address. And remember that your goal is wholeness—not perfection, but wholeness. This means you'll be brilliant and stupid, solemn and ridiculous, brave and cowardly, beautiful and ugly, hardworking and lazy, and so on into infinity. This practice welcomes all of your elements and intelligences, and gives you a solid foundation from which to function in the world as it actually is. You'll become not a flattened, dissociated, and emotionless person who seeks impossible perfection; instead, you'll become what you truly are: a vibrant and flowing soul capable of meeting any situation with focus and agility. You won't be knocked over by your strong emotional flows or have to watch in agony as your air, fire, or earth elements stomp on your water element, because your ability to ground, define, cleanse, and rejuvenate yourself will give you the full-bodied resilience you need to rise every time you fall.

When you have empathic skills, your emotions will become your allies instead of the big bullies they can be in a badly moderated system. Soon your emotions will begin to move, flow, and resolve themselves naturally— if you let them, they'll come in, attend to the issue at hand, resolve it, and then go on their merry way. As we move into each of the emotions ahead, please remember the mantra for any emotional state—including the joys—which is, "This too shall pass." All emotions will pass through you naturally if you just let them flow.

These skills form the raft you need to navigate the watery realm of your emotions. If you feel unsure of any of them, you may want to work with this chapter for a while. However, if you're ready to move forward, please wade with me into the exquisitely soulful ocean of your emotions.

PART II

Embracing Your Emotions

THE GUEST HOUSE
This being human is a guest house.
Every morning a new arrival.
A joy, a depression, a meanness,
some momentary awareness comes
as an unexpected visitor.
Welcome and entertain them all!
Even if they're a crowd of sorrows
who violently sweep your house empty of its furniture,
still, treat each guest honorably.
He may be clearing you out for some new delight.
The dark thoughts, the shame, the malice,
meet them at the door laughing,
and invite them in.
Be grateful for whoever comes,
because each has been sent
as a guide from beyond.
—Rumi

11

Wading into the Water

Awakening All of Your Emotions

WELCOME TO THE REALM of water—to emotions, flow, depth, reconciliation, and the language that teaches you not just what things are called, but what they *feel* like, what they are. From this point forward, you'll engage with your empathic intelligences, which are fluid, deepening awarenesses that lead you consistently from imbalance to understanding to resolution. The empathic skills you just learned will make it possible for you to remain standing when water is awake in your psyche and everything around you is in flux. From the center of the grounded and resourced village inside you, you'll be able to navigate and mediate the many flows in your psyche.

In this second half of the book, I've separated the emotions into categories in order to simplify your movement into the water, but as your awareness deepens, you'll find that—just as it was with your elements and intelligences—you can't truly separate your emotions from one another. Emotions don't fit into tidy compartments; there's a tremendous amount of interplay between most emotional states. Emotions move under, over, and through each other in a healthy psyche, and they hide behind or crush each other in an unhealthy one. Therefore, this practice requires emotional agility—not because the emotions are inherently dangerous or hard to understand, but because emotions flow and change constantly while they relate to you and to one another in unique and event-specific ways.

Emotional agility does not come from cataloging and manipulating your emotions, but from attuning yourself to their continuous flow and realizing that all emotions are present in your every waking and sleeping moment. Your angers always attempt to set boundaries for you, your fears always try to lend their intuition to you, your sadness always tries to help you let go and move forward, your shame always keeps an eye on your behavior, and so forth. All of your emotions are in constant flow. Your job is not to organize them into neat little compartments, but to welcome their lively energies into your life.

WELCOMING EMOTIONAL FLOW

The primary rule of emotional flow is this: all emotions are true. All emotions tell the absolute truth, either about the specific situation that brought the emotion into play, or about some area of the psyche. Even irrational, trapped, or repetitive emotions tell the truth about *something*— whether it's about a past trauma, a lost memory, a physical imbalance, or a severe reaction to certain stimuli. *All emotions are true.* This doesn't mean that all emotions are *right* or that you should take their word for everything! Some emotions can make you want to beat the living day-lights out of people, while others can drag you into hell or make you feel intense hatred for yourself. Some of your emotional reactions can display prejudices you didn't know you had, while others can make you lust after things that would damage you; therefore, you don't just follow your emotions like a brainless fool. However, you must understand that your emotions are true. Your task is to welcome that truth and support your emotional flow by bringing a full village of perspectives to each of your emotions.

These perspectives require a different vocabulary than most of us are accustomed to. Empathic people don't say, "You shouldn't feel that way," or "You're too sensitive," or "There's no need to get emotional!" No, empaths separate themselves from the emotionally deadening attitudes and behaviors that infect our culture; they create sacred space in which the truth of the emotions can come forward and be acknowledged. This is why your skills are so important. They help you call your soul to ritual and create sacred space for emotions in yourself and other people. But of course, if the people around you are experiencing severe depression or cycling anxieties or rages, you'll help them find support (major depressions, anxiety disorders, and rage disorders can damage the brain and the endocrine system, so they're nothing to fool around with).

When you understand emotions empathically, your emotions (and the emotions of others) won't threaten or destabilize you. If you meet with fear in yourself or others, you'll know great instincts live just beneath it. If you come up against anger, shame, or jealousy, you'll know the honorable restoration of boundaries is close at hand. If you find depression, you'll look for the ingenious stagnation at its very center, and if you meet the suicidal urge, you'll know that a rare and exquisite rebirth will soon occur. You'll be able to welcome even the most unsettling emotions and channel their necessary messages in useful ways.

Common knowledge says that wading into your emotions is inadvisable because you might not get back out. For instance, if you start crying, you'll never stop, or if you let yourself get angry, you'll take everyone out in a blaze of gunfire, or if you really feel your depression, you'll kill yourself. However, when you wade consciously and purposefully into your emotions, the exact opposite is true. If you give yourself over to crying, your sadness will move through you and cleanse your soul; then the crying will stop on its own, and you'll be rejuvenated. If you channel your honest anger appropriately, it won't hurt anyone. In fact, the strongly honorable qualities inside anger will restore your boundaries and protect you and everyone around you. Similarly, if you truly welcome your depression, it will show you amazing, life-changing things about why your energy has gone away.

Emotions don't cause trouble by themselves; they simply bring energy and information forward. If you don't honor them—if you don't wade in—you'll not only stop your growth and evolution, you'll also cause your emotions to fester and stagnate. *Not* wading in is what causes emotional torment! Never-ending depressions, cycling rages, unresolved anxiety attacks—these are clear signs of emotions that aren't being attended to in appropriate ways.

Be aware, though, as you step into the river of emotions, that your emotions may feel troubling to you. In some emotional states, you may feel as if you're getting in way over your head. If so, remember the scuba divers who orient themselves by following their air bubbles to the surface.

Let your thoughts bring you up and out of the currents of emotion if you get overwhelmed—but know that your intellect can't address your emotions all by itself. Your emotions will continue to move in their own ways, no matter how many facts and thoughts you stack on top of them. Moving into your airy logical intelligences during an emotional channeling session should be considered a short vacation, during which you come up for air, shake yourself off, and then return to the emotion when you're refreshed. The same holds true for your earth and fire elements; feel free to move away from troubling emotions by eating, dancing, resting, exercising, meditating, praying, or daydreaming (or whatever earth or fire practice you choose), but get back to your emotions when you're settled. When you can stand upright in the center of the village inside you, you won't need to hide in one element or run from another.

Remember that the mantra for any emotion is, "This too shall pass." Healthy emotions flow.

BRINGING EVERYTHING TOGETHER

Maintaining flow in each of your elements doesn't have to be an arduous or time-consuming process. You can maintain your bodily flow throughout your day by simply making circular movements with your wrists or ankles when you're at your desk, or by yawning, stretching, vocalizing quietly, or shaking off when you have the privacy to do so. You can easily support your intellectual flow by allowing your mind to plan, organize, and scheme freely, or by bringing mental tasks like puzzle-solving, math games, or wordplay into your life. You can maintain your emotional flow by welcoming moods and emotions into your day, surrounding yourself with art and music (even if that means just doodling or humming to yourself), and expressing yourself in wordless ways. You can also support your fiery spirit in simple ways, by welcoming your dreams, daydreams, and visions, and by allowing the spirit of things to speak to you. When your fire element is activated, you'll find meaning everywhere—on the bumper sticker of the car ahead of you, in phrases that pop out of songs or magazines, in sightings of wildlife, or in snippets of overheard conversations. As you honor each of your elements in your everyday life, the village inside you will become fully adequate to the task of living a whole and conscious life.

When it's time to channel your emotions, invite each of your elements into the process: Allow your emotion to come forward, without repressing it or expressing it all over the place. If it's very intense, or trapped in an unresolving feedback loop, engage your intellect and ask the correct questions for that emotion. Or bring your body into play and physically describe the shape of the emotion, its color (if it has one), its temperature, and its movement pattern. In so doing, you'll be able to treat your emotion as a message and a sensation, instead of a curse. You can also bring your fiery vision into play and allow your eagle nature to track your emotion through your body, your life, your family, or your culture. Then you can use your healing skills to focus and ground yourself, intensify your boundary definition, burn your contracts if your emotion is trapped in a feedback loop, or rejuvenate yourself if your struggles with your emotion have destabilized or exhausted you.

These practices can be used at any time (and in any place), because they allow you to take your sacred space with you wherever you go. You can ground yourself, set your boundaries, and burn your contracts anywhere—at work, in the car, in the ticket line at the airport, or wherever you find yourself. Your rejuvenation practice can even be modified for use in public places (you can simply brighten your boundary for a quick revitalization and perform your full-body rejuvenation at a later time). If you can't always make time for your complete meditative practice, bodily movement can break up stagnation in your body, and it can also relieve stagnation in your other elements as well. If you can create symbolic movements to unblock repetitive thoughts, trapped emotions, or spiritual malaise, you can restore your fluidity and awareness. You can also use your hands when you ground yourself, light up your boundary, burn contracts, or perform your rejuvenation practices; you can use your hands to describe the processes you're imagining.

It's also fun to combine conscious complaining and empathic skills, which really helps clear out the congested ideas and attitudes that trap you in old ways of emoting, thinking, or relating. I like to complain, move around, and destroy entrapping contracts at the same time: "Here's the way I think I have to act—BAM! And here's the horse it rode in on—KAPOW! Things are hard, and I'm tired of striving! Life really stinks right now! BOOM!" I have fun with the process and laugh a lot. Then I can get back to work, take a nap, or go out and play with a new attitude and fresh vitality. Conscious complaining is marvelous.

As we go into deeper territory with the emotions, I don't want you to take my word for anything or shut down any part of yourself as you read. What I'd like is for you to stay focused within your unrepeatable whole self, where you can make your own decisions about each of the emotions you encounter. If an emotion just won't move or respond to you, or if certain emotional states are repetitive and troubling, reach out for help. Also, there will be times when you see something in an emotion I haven't seen. Excellent! Call your multiple intelligences into play, bring your emotions to the forefront, and let your village of resources decipher the situation. Use your own best judgment, reach out for support when you need it, and keep yourself upright. We're both empaths; my information doesn't outrank yours!

12

Anger

Protection and Restoration

Includes Rage, Fury, and the Healing of Trauma

GIFTS
Honor ~ Conviction ~ Proper boundaries
~ Protection of yourself and others ~ Healthy detachment

THE INTERNAL QUESTIONS
What must be protected? What must be restored?

SIGNS OF OBSTRUCTION
Repressive: Enmeshment, self-abandonment,
apathy, depression, boundary loss
Expressive: Cycling rages that create harsh boundaries;
hatred and prejudice; isolation

PRACTICE
Channel the fiery intensity of anger into your boundary instead
of repressing it or exploding with it—*then* speak your truth or
make your correcting actions. This will reset your boundaries in
healthy ways, which will protect you and your relationships.

IF I WERE TO personify anger, I would describe it as a mix between a
stalwart castle sentry and an ancient sage. Anger sets your boundaries
by walking the perimeter of your soul and keeping an eye on you, the

people around you, and your environment. If your boundaries are broken (through the insensitivity of others or in any other way), anger comes forward to restore your sense of strength and separateness. The questions for anger are: "What must be protected?" and "What must be restored?" Both protection and restoration can occur quickly when you move anger's heated intensity into your imaginal boundary. This gives you something immediate and honorable to do with your anger. With the intensity of anger, you can reset your boundary and restore your sense of self. All by itself, this simple movement will address your anger and circumvent any need for internal or external violence, because your boundary will be properly restored. When you're fortified in this way, your ferocity will recede naturally, which will allow you to speak and act from a position of strength, rather than from brutality or passivity.

If you instead repress your anger, you'll be unable to restore your boundary because you won't have the energy you need to protect yourself; therefore, further damage will inevitably follow the initial affront. If you choose to dishonorably express your anger at the person who offended against you, your boundary will be dangerously unguarded, just as it would be if your castle sentry left his post and went out on a rampage. When your anger is used as a weapon and your territory is left without a sentry, your psyche will have to pour more anger into the situation. If you habitually express your anger, you'll end up expressing this new infusion of anger as well, and you'll break your boundary (and the boundaries of others) even further. This is how escalating rages and furies get started— the problem doesn't come from the essential energy of anger, but from the unskilled and dishonorable use of anger when it arises.

When your anger flows freely, you won't even know it's there; it will simply help you maintain your boundaries, your inner convictions, and your healthy detachment. Free-flowing anger will allow you to laugh compassionately at yourself and set your boundary mercifully because both actions arise from the inner strength and honorable self-definition anger imparts. When your anger is not allowed its natural flow, you'll have trouble setting and maintaining your boundary, you'll tend to dishonor or enmesh with others, and your self-image will be imperiled by your reliance on the capricious opinions of the outside world.

Anger also comes forward when you witness others being made vulnerable through injustice or cruelty. Anger is a social emotion in that way; it doesn't want to see anyone get hurt unnecessarily. When any of us chooses to unmask or to be vulnerable, the resulting openness is healing. However, that same level of openness and vulnerability, if it comes about without our permission, is nearly always threatening and invasive. And whether you're being hurt or I am, my anger will be alerted. This invasion may also bring up fear, sadness, depression, or shame, but it is anger that both signals the injury and creates new boundaries after any invasive incidents. Because there is usually a layer of emotion right under anger, anger is often misrepresented as a secondhand emotion, which leads people to view it as unimportant or counterfeit. This is a dangerous mistake.

All emotions travel in groups and pairs, and all emotions are intimately connected to one another. You don't call sadness counterfeit, even though it often arises alongside fear and shame, and usually leads to joy when you've truly let go. You don't call fear counterfeit, even though it usually travels with anger, and often leads to contentment when you've skillfully addressed your fears. Similarly, you shouldn't call anger counterfeit, no matter which emotions travel with it or which forms of happiness arise after you skillfully restore personal boundaries. Anger's basic message is one of protection, for yourself certainly, but also for others. Anger will even protect your other emotions by running out in front of them in times of danger. If you've ever been paralyzed by terror and had your anger rescue you and shout down whatever was petrifying you, you already know how helpful anger can be. Anger is just as irreplaceable as sadness, fear, joy, or any other emotional state. There is a special alliance between anger and sadness (see pages 296–301) that contributes incredible strength and elasticity to your psyche, and another alliance between anger and fear (see pages 238–240) that promotes brilliant, instinctive focus. But these alliances only flourish when each of the emotions can behave in its own specific way.

Healthy anger sets your boundary and helps you engage more effectively because it allows you to relate authentically and respectfully. When you have an awakened connection to your anger and a clear sense of your own boundary, you'll be able to honor boundaries and individuality in others; therefore, your relationships won't be based on power struggles, projections, or enmeshment. However, if you don't have access to your vital, bound-ary-defining anger, you'll be undifferentiated, certainly, but you'll also be dangerous to the people around you. If you repress your anger, you'll endan-ger others by creating a passive and poorly defined boundary that will lead you to enmesh yourself in their lives. And if you dishonorably express your anger, you'll create an imposing, fear-inducing boundary that will degrade the stability of everyone around you. When you can instead channel this noble emotion properly, you'll be able to maintain your boundary—and pro-tect the boundaries of others—with honor.

WHY WE'RE NOT ALL ONE

Many people think that if we could just shed our sense of entitlement or separateness and accept that we're all one, then peace would surely result, and anger would vanish. This idea seems logical at first, but if you sit with it awhile, you'll see that it doesn't come from empathic intelligence. It depicts boundaries and self-preservation as impediments to peace and relatedness—when both are actually *prerequisites* for peace and relatedness. You cannot relate coherently to another person if you don't know who you are (or where you begin and end), just as you cannot nurture peace or honor the needs of others until you understand and meet your own needs. The idea that we're all one, though it seems fine at first glance, proves to be deeply flawed when you look at it with all of your intelligences.

When we drop our vital, anger-supported boundaries and ignore our individual needs and wishes, we become spectacularly unprotected (we lose the "skin" of our psyches). This then sets off a chain reaction of emotional disturbance and psychological instability. I've noticed that when people try to maintain such a self-abandoning position, they often fall into cycles of depression (which often arise when you lose your connection to your healthy anger and your individuality) or anxiety (which arises when you lose your instincts). When anger is driven into the shadow by the "all one" mindset, turmoil results. It has to, because when the psyche is unprotected, anger becomes incredibly necessary, and if anger is continually forced into the shadows, it can only erupt in shadowy ways.

Let me say, though, that the "all one" mindset is not completely untrue from a five-element perspective. In fact, in our fiery, visionary spirits (which, if neuroanatomist Jill Bolte Taylor is correct, may actually reside in the right hemispheres of our brains)[9] we *are* all one. If we can intimately connect with our spirited vision through focusing and grounding, we'll always have access to a deep and abiding sense of oneness with all life. Oneness in spirit is healthy and natural, and it doesn't require the destruction of boundaries, the denial of anger, the separation of elements, or the abandonment of self.

Intellectually, we can work to become one with others. We can work toward agreement and learn to think alike, but oneness in the intellect often requires the restriction of the gusting and flowing movements the air element likes best. Oneness in the air element usually requires the squelching of individual thought processes and the denial of individual emotional reactions (which, sadly, forces the entire water element into the shadow). Though we can all easily agree intellectually about the basics—such as love, health, safety for children, and security—ideological disagreements about how to create or sustain those basics have kept our war industries thriving since the beginning of human history. Oneness in the air element cannot be supported in the real world, because it is a form of intellectual imprisonment. We cannot all think alike, nor should we try to. Intellectual freedom is an absolute necessity.

In the watery emotional realm, it's pretty easy to become one with others. It's called empathy when it's skillfully done and enmeshment when it's not. However, it's not healthy to be utterly empathic with everyone you meet (trust me!). Your emotions need to flow in your own life, not in your friend's, or your spouse's, or your family's. If you maintain a constant, unwavering level of empathic receptivity without any balancing or cleansing practices, your life will become completely disordered, which will throw your angers into high gear as they try to restore your fragmented boundary. You'll move from anger to rage in a split second, you'll suffer through cycling guilts and depressions, and you may even drop into suicidal urges or the "soft suicide" of addictions.

The honorable sentry of anger begs you not to attempt emotional oneness with others unless you have highly developed skills and know exactly what you're doing. Even then, I can report from many decades of empathic experience that it is far better to teach others to make empathic contact with themselves than it is to translate their emotions for them (which can lead to unhealthy dependencies). It is far better to respect the sanctity and native intelligence of others and use your empathic skills inside your own psyche. Besides, it is actually easy to create sacred emotional space for the people in your life in a nonenmeshing way—by simply welcoming all emotions as true and necessary. This level of empathy won't hurt anyone because it doesn't require you to erase your boundaries, throw away your anger, or move all your furniture into other people's emotional lives.

In your earthy body, oneness is impossible. There is no way to become physically one with another person. We can't climb into other people's bodies; we can't even trade blood or body parts unless the procedures are done very carefully. There is no way on earth to achieve bodily oneness with anyone else—it's a ridiculous notion.

Similarly, in the center of the village inside you—in your personality—you cannot attain oneness with any other personality. You are a unique and irreplaceable creature; your central nature has never existed before, and it will never exist again. Your personality can't ever be one with any other personality, because you are a complete original. Please remember this as you work with your boundary-defining anger; it will help you understand and support your need for bodily sanctity, intellectual freedom, emotional distinctiveness, and personal autonomy.

Spiritual oneness does not require any effort; you simply welcome your fiery vision by focusing and grounding yourself inside your vibrant, anger-supported boundary. Then you'll have free access to fiery oneness through your visions, dreams, and daydreams. True and healthy oneness is a very simple thing to achieve; all you have to do is become one with your own visionary fire element, which means learning to integrate yourself with the help of the defining capacities your healthy anger contributes to you.

THE MESSAGE IN ANGER

When you channel your anger properly, it will restore your boundary and your sense of honor. When you go on a rampage, you dishonor every soul you encounter (including your own). Similarly, when you weaken your boundary with repression, you become enmeshed with others and lose your sense of distinction and clarity, which paves the way for all sorts of crimes against honesty and humanity. If you can instead channel your anger into your boundary and light it afire, you will create a radiant sacred space around your soul that will enable you to focus yourself, ground yourself, and work with the many flows in your psyche. When you're centered and grounded inside your strong, anger-supported boundary, you'll be able to speak, act, protect, and restore honorably—you won't need to retreat into a repressive deflation or explode into an expressive rampage.

Let's look at a specific example: Imagine that someone offends you by calling you an idiot. This will usually bring anger forward, and anger exists to help you maintain your sense of self while protecting you and the people around you. If you choose to express your anger, you'll most likely respond in an equally offensive manner. Though this counterattack may help you restore your sense of self in that instant, it will nearly always ignite increased anger in the offending person (who, you must realize, is already boundary-impaired, as is evidenced by the initial attack on you). In most cases, your counterattack will only increase the conflict, which will further endanger you and your attacker as your interaction deteriorates into mutual belligerence and hostility. When anger is expressed in knee-jerk and dishonorable ways, it cannot protect or restore anyone; instead, both parties will walk (or limp) away stripped of dignity, compassion, and honor. In this graceless exchange, the protective, restorative, and honorable intensities inside anger are utterly squandered.

Now consider going in the opposite direction: Imagine stifling and repressing the anger that comes forward when you're called an idiot. You'll most likely ignore the offense or make excuses for the offensive person— neither of which will restore your boundary or protect the boundary of your offender (if repression is your habitual response to offenses against you, please see the section on the relationship between anger and sadness on pages 296–301). Anger comes forward not simply to protect you, but also to give you the strength you need to meet your opponent honorably during conflict.

This is a crucial point—when people are allowed to offend against you without consequence (though this may seem to be a compassionate way to deal with improper behavior), they will be just as damaged by the exchange as you are. Certainly, your own boundary and dignity will be injured in the attack, but if you do nothing—if you say nothing—you'll also ensure your attacker's descent into abusiveness and isolation *by refusing to honor the conflict that has presented itself for healing.* If you refuse to engage with people when they behave improperly, you dishonor them and the relationship. When you repress your anger, you degrade your own sense of boundaries and honor, certainly, but you also disrespect your opponent and ignore the uncomfortable truth of the situation. This has a devastating effect, because when you refuse to address your genuine emotions, you invite discord and deception into each of your relationships and every area of your life.

Now let's look at a third response: Taking honorable hold of your anger and channeling it properly means allowing your anger to arise when you're attacked. It means welcoming the potent surge of indignation and honoring the fact of the attack, instead of brushing it away with pseudospiritual gentility (or launching your anger on a search-and-destroy mission). The channeling of anger is probably the easiest task in the emotional realm, because anger sets boundaries, so all you have to do is imagine adding the intensity of anger to your boundary. You just choose a color, heat, sound, or sensation to represent your anger and pour it into your boundary. You can even set your boundary on fire if you're really steamed (I call this the "flame on!" boundary). This quick movement honors your anger and increases your focus so you can halt the attack in its tracks, focus yourself, and ground yourself strongly, all of which will help you see clearly. When your own boundary is restored, you'll understand that your opponent feels endangered or diminished and is trying to create an emergency boundary in unskilled ways: by smashing yours and weakening you.

Instead of counterthrusting and increasing your opponent's sense of danger (or ignoring the conflict and increasing his or her abusive tendencies), you can protect yourself skillfully while modeling proper anger behavior. And remember, because we're all empaths, your opponent will certainly sense that something new is going on, and he or she may learn through your example. When you're centered and grounded, you won't have to lash out or fold into yourself, because from within your restored personal boundary, you'll be able to protect yourself and your opponent while continuing to maintain your boundary throughout the exchange. You can also set a verbal boundary by questioning your opponent's behavior ("I'm sorry, but why are you picking a fight?") or by bringing some self-effacing humor forward to defuse the situation ("I know I can be a goofball, but 'idiot' seems awfully harsh, don't you think?"). When your anger is honored and welcomed into anger-inducing situations, it will no longer be a mindless hooligan or an unsuitably softened weakling; instead, it will take its rightful place as the honorable sentry of your soul and the soul of anyone fortunate enough to cross your path.

The Taoist saying "The glory is not in never falling, but in rising every time you fall" is especially valuable in gaining an understanding of the honorable use of anger. Let's face it: your boundaries will be threatened regularly, your self-esteem will be destabilized, your most cherished beliefs will be attacked, and your sense of right and wrong will often be violently disrupted. The task of a whole person is not to hide from these necessary diminishments, but to fall and rise again with honor, compassion, and integrity. Healthy anger does not (and should not) stop you from falling; instead, it gives you the strength to rise every time you fall. When you repress your anger, it is as if you're trying not to meet the challenges of life, as if not noticing your injuries will somehow keep you from falling (if this is your modus operandi, please reread the section on anger and forgiveness on pages 117–22). When you express your anger dishonorably, it is as if you're trying to control life, as if your ferocity will make falling unnecessary. Sadly, neither position will bring you valid or practical strength. Repressers fall very far (often plummeting into depressions and cycling anxieties) because they separate themselves from the strength their healthy angers bring, which makes them incapable of rising again. On the other hand, dishonorable expressers also fall in tragic ways—into violence, abusiveness, extreme isolation, and self-immolating behaviors—because they hurl their angers in every direction, which leaves them boundary-impaired and unable to rise again.

When you can channel your angers, you won't be invincible. Actually, you'll continue to fall all the time, but you'll also rise just as surely because you'll be able to restore your focus and your boundaries at the drop of a hat (or the rise of a hackle, in truth). When you're attacked or affronted and your anger surges forward, you'll be able to channel its intensity into your boundary and rise up from the floor. When you channel your anger in this way, its intensity won't be a liability. In fact, its intensity will correlate directly to your ability to define, focus, and ground yourself. Your anger will enable you to define yourself succinctly and draw a line in the sand, as it were. No one will be able to feel your anger when you channel it in this way, because you won't express it or focus it on anyone—you won't make angry faces or say angry things; you'll just make your boundary stronger and more vibrant.

In an honorable engagement, your anger will give you the strength to recognize your wounds and your fall, which is something expressers and repressers cannot do. They waste their energy and endanger themselves by pretending the fall hasn't happened. If you can channel your anger properly, you'll see your fall clearly, not from a stance of victimhood, but with an awareness of the skill of your opponent and the extent to which you were open to attack.

Anger only arises in response to real threats. If I were to yell at you, "You are a Lithuanian sheepherder!" you would probably just laugh. My attack would gain no hold on you; therefore, your anger would not rise. However, if I were to whisper, "You're not very good to your mother, are you?" your anger would probably flare up in a split second, because I would have hit a very sore spot. If you repress your anger in the pretense that I didn't wound you, this spot will remain unhealed and unaddressed (and I'll be able to bring it up whenever I want to best you). However, if you express your anger all over me in the pretense that you're too fierce to be wounded, you might feel better in that moment, but you'll have done nothing to clean up your relationship with your mother—and you'll now have unfinished business with *me*. However, if you can honor the wound I've caused, immediately channel your anger and reset your boundary, you'll be able to respond honorably to the accuracy of my attack—because, let's face it, I nailed you.

First, you can tell me that I've hurt you and ask me to explain myself; clearly, I have some vital information for you (or you wouldn't be so steamed up). If I'm able to speak coherently about what I see, we'll be able to uncover important information about your real or imagined treatment of your mother. If the situation between us remains heated, you can continue to pour your anger into your boundary (and continue to rise every time you fall). This continuous boundary-setting won't necessarily reduce the pain of your relationship with your mother (or silence me), but it will bring much-needed focus to your psyche. With that focus, you can set a boundary between yourself and my projections, ground any areas of discomfort in your body, burn contracts with me, your mother, and your attitude toward her—or any of a thousand other things. In this honorable exchange, you will surely fall, but you will just as surely rise. You'll clarify your relationship with me, gain a new understanding of your connection and contracts with your mother, and honor your true emotional responses (whatever they may be) from within the sacred space created by your anger. When you honor your anger and recognize your wounds, you'll gain more than just strength. You'll gain clarity, wisdom, the capacity for mercy, and the ability to rise from any fall.

When you learn to channel your anger, you'll discover that all angers arise in response to people or events that are important to you. In order for a boundary violation to occur, you must first give a person or situation significance in your life. Anger, in its strange way, is an honoring of the person or situation before you, because things and people that are unimportant cannot anger you! This is the most difficult thing to face when you're angry. It's easier to snap, "I don't care about that idiot (or that stupid thing)!" If, instead, you can use your powerful anger to reset your boundary and burn your contracts with whatever has angered you, you'll honor the fact that you're a sensitive person who has come upon a deeply important issue. You'll learn vital truths about the issues you need to face and the relationships you need to mend or honor.

Healthy anger is one of the most decisive and self-defining emotions you have. It exists to protect you, your moral structure, and the people around you. Remember that your anger and your personal boundary are intimately connected. If you have trouble with boundaries, you've got trouble with anger, and vice versa. Support your healthy anger by studying the boundary skills on pages 135–37, and support your boundary by working honorably with your anger!

The Practice for Anger

Anger of any kind always goes into your boundary, either as a heat, a color, a sound, a sensation, or a movement. If it helps, you can imagine yourself as the sun and feel your anger shining or emanating out of your body and into your boundary. This practice welcomes and channels your anger quickly and succinctly while it resets your boundary, protects your body from overwhelm, and invigorates your psyche. With this burst of energy and protection, you can deal honorably with the angering situation, rather than hurting yourself or others through repression or dishonorable expression.

When your boundary is reinvigorated, you'll be able to focus your attention and ground yourself strongly; both actions will help you remain upright and functional in the conflict. If your opponent is projecting an incredible amount of intensity at you, your angers will most likely intensify in response. Continue to pour these new angers into your boundary (if you keep them bottled inside your body, you'll most likely erupt). This is the central skill in the anger practice—to continue pouring your anger into your boundary as you speak or argue, rather than retreating into the old habits of squelching your anger or hurling it at others. If you get really hot, imagine the heat grounding you strongly, and feel free to warn your opponent or take a break from the conflict for a moment. When I do this, I stomp away to complain privately (albeit loudly) or burn my contracts with my opponent with flamethrowers and bombs. In essence, I honor the intensity of my anger without destroying my opponent's soul. When I return (usually in less than two minutes— empathic work is incredibly swift), my opponent and I can reenter the fray, which never contains the same intensity as when I left. Usually, other emotions arise from within the honored anger, and these help us move the conflict in new directions.

Remember the anger questions: "What must be protected?" and "What must be restored?" These questions will help you maintain the conflict honorably as you continue to protect and restore your boundary and the dignity of your opponent. Know that your task isn't to win or lose, but to gain an understanding of your wounds and your vulnerability so that you can strengthen yourself in meaningful ways. You cannot strengthen yourself by repressing your anger or by going on a rampage with it; you can only gain useful strength through conscientious engagement in the anger-inducing conflicts that present themselves for healing. Remember this: conflicts will occur, you'll be affronted and wounded, and you will fall—because every setback is necessary for your growth and evolution. Your healthy anger doesn't make you invincible; it gives you the strength to rise every time you fall, with dignity, compassion, and humor.

When you've resolved your conflict, take a few private moments to reground and refocus yourself, burn a few contracts, move your body, and rejuvenate yourself. Anger releases incredible amounts of energy into your system, so it's a good idea to refresh yourself and bring every part of you into the present moment, where you're a much different person than you were when the conflict began. When you're done, thank your anger and let it know it's totally welcome in your soul as a sentry, a boundary setter, a conflict mediator, and an honorable protector.

HONORING ANGER IN OTHERS

Many people mistakenly respond to anger in others by affecting a falsified calm, as if there's no reason to be angry. Though this may seem helpful, it's actually a form of repression that severely isolates the angry person. If you can instead set your boundary and match the quality of the anger that has presented itself for healing, you'll create sacred space. The angry person will no longer be isolated or ashamed because he or she will have an ally in you. Through this alliance, you can support others in restoring their boundaries—by letting them complain and de-steam, by commiserating with them, and by maintaining your own boundary throughout the engagement. This simple honoring won't require a great deal of your time or energy. You won't need to counsel, create solutions, or become a sage, because when people can get in touch with the reasons for their anger, they can usually find their own solutions within a few moments. Conversely, if people are cajoled, studiously ignored, or shamed out of their angers, they won't understand why they got angry in the first place, and they'll be unlikely to learn or grow.

Anger arises when protection is required; therefore, you should take heed and protect yourself before you engage. The analogy about the use of airplane oxygen masks is helpful here: in an air emergency, you should put on your own mask before helping others with theirs. In an anger emergency, you should set your own boundary strongly before attempting to intervene. You don't need to feel angry; you can just brighten your boundary with the color or quality of felt sense you use when you're angry. If the person you're trying to support is raging, you can set your boundary on fire. In essence, you can protect yourself while you match the intensity of the situation, so you can understand how the person is feeling and become an ally in his or her struggle.

It's very helpful, when dealing with angry people, to repeat to yourself silently, "What needs to be protected and what needs to be restored?" This will help you stay on task and allow the angry person to work honorably through his or her anger. Don't try to create boundaries for angry people or "teach" them in any way; interference will actually degrade their boundaries further (which may bring their anger down on you). Just keep setting your own boundary—this practice alone will maintain sacred space and an emotionally welcoming atmosphere, which is the most healing and empowering thing you can do for yourself or anyone else.

Though it may seem contradictory, habitually angry people are actually deeply caring people, because anger always runs in direct proportion to concern (people can't get angry about things that have no significance to them). When people in your life are habitually angry, bless them—they're feeling too much of the world for their comfort, and their boundaries are in tatters. Their hearts are usually in pain, not because of their anger, but because they don't know how to address their profound concerns in healthier ways. Habitually angry people see the injustice and boundary violations all around them, and they feel those violations right inside their bodies, so they lash out with anger in the desperate hope that they can control the world and stop the pain. They can also be extremely depressed underneath all their raging. Their explosive behavior doesn't work at all, and habitually angry people are hard to be around, but in their essence, they are our deepest humanitarians and our greatest strivers for peace. That may seem counterintuitive, but it's the absolute truth, as you'll soon learn when you honor the anger in other people instead of shaming it, ignoring it, or counterattacking. Bless the angry people in your life; they are dealing with foundational issues of honor, certainty, protection, restoration, and boundary setting.

WHAT TO DO IF YOUR ANGER GETS STUCK

If anger causes any unpleasant aftereffects, just sit with them empathically. Anger should create changes in your body, because it contains intense heat and activation. You should feel energized, empowered, and even a little antsy; however, if you feel uncomfortably jangled and fired up, headachy, or nervous in the pit of your stomach, you may have forged a contract that helps you feel terrible when anger arises. Most of us carry some form of this contract because we've been shamed out of our anger since day one. We've also done some terrible things with our anger, so these contracts were probably quite protective and valid when we had no skills. Now, however, we have skills, so we can look at these contracts with new eyes.

Healthy anger, like any other emotion, comes up, addresses an issue, and then moves on. If anger lingers, disturbs you, or creates tension headaches or stomach upsets, its flow is being impeded in some way. If you feel unwelcome or uncomfortable sensations attached to your anger, know that you may have some sort of punishing connection with anger (this can come from just about anyone or anywhere). If you can imagine this connection as a contract (or contracts—there can be many) and burn them, your anger will be able to flow properly and become the healing force it was meant to be.

Here's how to do it: Focus and ground yourself and brighten your boundaries with a fiery light or felt sense. Now, imagine a contract materializing right in front of your troubled areas (or in front of your entire body if you're really fired up). Take a deep breath into the area of your discomfort, gather it, and imagine breathing this discomfort out onto your contract as you exhale. Repeat this process—take another deep breath into the area of your discomfort, gather the discomfort once again, and imagine breathing it out onto your contract. Stay focused behind your boundary and observe this punishing contract from behind your eyes; in this way, you can gain some perspective on it. Know that this contract is separate from your free-flowing anger—and from you as a person.

Keep breathing into whatever sensations, thoughts, feelings, or images you sense, gather them, and breathe them onto your contract. If your first contract becomes loaded with material, move it aside, create a fresh contract, and continue working. When you feel done for now (punishing contracts often require many contract-burning sessions), roll up your contract (or contracts), throw it out of your personal space, and burn it with whatever emotional intensity you feel. Let it go. You're done! Follow this session with your favorite rejuvenation practice, then go out and play!

Be aware: Repetitive angers, especially in men, can be signs of an underlying depressive condition. If you're regularly angry, incensed, riled up about injustice, or peeved, please check in with your doctor or therapist. Anger is an intense emotion; if you express it constantly, you can easily send your brain chemistry and your endocrine system into a tailspin. Also, if your brain chemistry or your hormones are unbalanced, you may express your anger continually, even when another emotion might be more appropriate. In either case, please seek help and support.

There's a wonderful saying for situations of emotional disturbance: "You can't step into the same stream twice." If your emotions are allowed to flow, they'll respond differently each time they arise; however, if they're dammed up (through repression, unskilled expression, shaming messages you've absorbed from others, or chemical and endocrine imbalances), they'll repeat themselves monotonously. Watch for this in your emotional life. No emotion should become so ingrained and stagnant in your psyche that it appears with the same intensity every time it arises, becomes your emotion of choice, or creates lingering physical symptoms. Watch for emotions that have no differentiation or that cause lasting repercussions in your body or your behaviors—and know that it's not the emotions that are causing the trouble. Something unhealthy is going on. If you've got unhealthy beliefs about your emotions, you know what to do: burn your contracts and move on! However, if burning your contracts doesn't work, then please seek help.

ENTERING THE RAPIDS: RAGE AND FURY

Rage and fury are states that arise in times of extreme distress, either when anger has not been heeded, or when tremendous boundary violations have occurred (or vital personal sensitivities have been ignored). As such, the physical and emotional environments of enraged and furious people must be examined carefully. Their angers may have been building for years, and their jobs or home lives may be unbearable. Uncontrollable bouts of rage and fury can also cause (or stem from) organic imbalances. If your rages and furies persist unchanged after you've channeled them a few times, a visit to your doctor is necessary.

Rage and fury are rapids-level emotions that carry tremendous power. Expressed rages and furies nearly always endanger you and others, while repressed rages and furies wreak terrible damage throughout your psyche. However, when the powerful intensities of your rage and fury can be channeled into fierce boundary definition and the focused annihilation of overwhelming and destructive contracts, they will heal and strengthen you in amazing ways. The intensities inside rage and fury will restore your boundary in an instant, separate you from abusive and endangering behaviors, and move you bodily out of any victimlike behavior. Channeling these powerful emotions helps you think on your feet and act in the present moment—where nobody gets hurt.

Furies and rages arise when the intensity in anger isn't quite enough to deal with the situation—when the boundary violations are severe and even life-threatening. In relationships, they appear after repeated attacks on your sense of self. Fury and rage step forward to tell you that people can only abuse you twice if you (1) don't communicate your discomfort, or (2) don't leave when your communication is ignored. Both emotions exist to give you the strength to incinerate your contracts and end your relationships with the infuriating people or situations in your life. You may not need to sever all contact with your abusers (that's not what burning contracts is about), but you do need to allow fury and rage to step forward and help you end the abuse. Rage and fury aren't going to let anyone tell them what to do, where to go, how to feel, or how to live—and this is precisely the attitude you need to destroy abusive contracts. Rage and fury say that enough is more than enough, and that all the abuse or boundary violations that went on before end *now*, in this instant, no questions asked, no excuses accepted. The ferocity inside rage and fury can give you pinpoint accuracy and the certainty you need to make swift and decisive moves away from entrapment and diminishment and into a fully resourced stance.

The Practice for Rage and Fury: The Only Way Out Is Through
The key to channeling rage and fury is to welcome it, without hurling it onto others or slapping it down and affecting a mask of falsified virtuousness. Rage and fury only arise when you're in true danger. They signal serious,

ongoing threats to your moral base, your sense of self, your health, and even your life or the lives of others. Rage and fury aren't responding to everyday concerns with everyday anger—they're the next step up. Expressing them throws their messages and their potency right out of your life, while repressing them is almost like sitting on a pile of dynamite. Channeling them is the only real choice, which is why the mantra for any of the rapids-level emotions is: "The only way out is through."

It is extremely important to pour your rage and fury into your boundary the second you feel them. Their intensity can disrupt your body if you try to repress them (or if you bring them to a boil in preparation for an attack on others). Rage and fury both call for the incendiary "flame-on!" boundary, which honors their intensities immediately while setting your boundary forcefully. When you're inside such a fierce boundary, you'll feel all the strength and intensity of your rage and fury without needing to take yourself or others out of commission. Again, no one will be endangered when you channel your emotions in this way because you're not focusing your rage or fury in word or deed—you're marshaling your own energies in your own private territory. You're increasing your focus and your ability to ground and stabilize yourself. You're protecting your body from damage, and you're protecting other people from harm. You're doing the right thing.

Once your boundary is intensely delineated with the ferociousness of rage and fury, you should burn contracts right away—with flamethrowers. If you're in a conflict, it's good to excuse yourself in such a way that your opponent knows you're not leaving the conflict permanently, but that you're protecting him or her while your rage and fury are present. Get away if you can, and burn your contracts like crazy (or complain like there's no tomorrow). Don't try to sit still or hamper your movements; these emotions bring a great deal of heat and ferocity with them, so feel free to let loose with stomping, howling, and shaking. Fierce movement honors your rage and fury without hurting anyone, and it clears out your body at the same time. You can even kickbox inside your boundary and use your hands and feet to smack contracts (or complaints) away from you before you burn them. You'll be surprised at how quickly your rage and fury will move on when you welcome them in this way (because this too shall pass). They'll give you specific information about the damage you've endured, they'll give you the energy you need to restore your boundaries, they'll help you move your body in empowering ways, and they'll help you incinerate your contracts with the behaviors and relationships that brought them forward in the first place.

When you've channeled your rage and fury, you can return to the original conflict because your boundary and self-awareness will be restored, your body and psyche will be cleared out, and you'll be revitalized; therefore, the previously enraging situation won't influence you in the old ways. If you were once a represser, you will no longer be the boundary-impaired and self-abandoning person who agreed to the original contracts or situations. If you were once an expresser, you'll no longer be the explosive and unstable person who caused chaos and discord everywhere you went. Your properly channeled rage and fury will allow you to act powerfully and succinctly—without hurting yourself or anyone else.

Bless your rage and fury, and know this: they only appear when you're in grave danger. Rage and fury rise up, sword in hand, to save your life. Welcome them, and they'll protect your unrepeatable soul. Channel them properly, and that sword will be transformed into a ceremonial dagger with which you can cut away the behaviors and beliefs that entrapped you in dangerous relationships and situations.

Please contact a doctor or therapist if your rage and fury persist unchanged after you've channeled them a few times. Repetitive cycles of rage and fury can exhaust every part of you—so take good care of yourself and reach out for help if you're having trouble. You may need to fortify your body and your brain chemistry before you can work with your intense angers in this way. If you're a trauma survivor, please read on, but also, please reach out for proper medical and psychological support.

RAGE, FURY, AND THE HEALING OF TRAUMA
Rage and fury have important functions in the psyches of unhealed trauma survivors (who are often dissociated and nearly always boundary-impaired). Many trauma survivors dissociate or distract themselves to escape their traumatic memories and flashbacks, which unfortunately ensures their

further suffering. Suffering can only cease when full awareness is brought to it, and when people dissociate, they remove their awareness from their bodies and their everyday lives. This makes grounding and focusing impossible, which then degrades their boundaries and their sense of personal space; therefore, dissociated and distracted people almost never have functional boundaries—not empathically and not psychologically. Most dissociated people exhibit interior instability due to their lack of focus and definition, but most also exhibit classic interpersonal instability (they tend to choose unworkable jobs or relationships that further their suffering) because they aren't able to make conscious choices in their lives. Most unhealed trauma survivors and dissociated people also have a tendency to erupt in rages and furies, which makes perfect sense when you understand the constant assaults they endure due to their lack of boundaries. All emotions come forward with the exact amount of energy needed to address the situation—no more, and no less. If people's wounds are deep and ongoing, then their emotions have to be deep and primal in response (put another way, if the emotions are intense, then so are the wounds, and vice versa).

The full healing of trauma is a process of coming back from near-death into life again. This process is not neat and orderly, and it is never emotionless. It follows the deep logic of the soul, where the remembrance of the original wound and the knowledge of the three stages of initiation reside. When we connect with this deep logic, we can understand the function of rage and fury in the lives of unhealed trauma survivors; we can see their fierce boundary energies surging forward to replace that which was lost in the trauma. We can also see that everyday levels of anger aren't called for, because traumatized boundaries have not simply been affronted or impaired. Boundaries broken in trauma (especially in childhood) are often completely destroyed. They often need to be rebuilt from scratch, and only rage and fury carry enough energy for that task. Rage and fury, then, aren't always signs of dysfunction or instability; rather, they are specific healing responses to the instabilities created by trauma.

Rage and fury are fiercely protective emotions that only arise in times of extreme need; they're absolutely necessary for rebuilding devastated boundaries and for establishing sacred space for the journey through the three-stage healing process. When a boundary is created with the intensity of rage and fury, the psyche will have the strength it needs to pass through the first two stages of the traumatic initiation on its way to the blessed liberation of stage three.

CREATING SACRED SPACE FOR THE
JOURNEY TO STAGE THREE

The empathic process of trauma healing does not come with maps or guidebooks. It is an intense and unique journey undertaken in the soul's own time and in the soul's own way. Though it is most usual for rages and furies to come forward first, this does not always occur. For some people, the first emotions that come forward are the fears, terrors, and panics that often travel alongside traumatic flashbacks. We will certainly study fear and panic in the chapters to come, but it is important to create strong anger- and rage-supported boundaries first. If you don't have a good boundary, you won't be able to ground or focus yourself. And if you try to go through the flashback process in a disheveled and unprotected state, you'll probably throw yourself into a crisis. Don't. You have time to get your feet under you, and you have time to prepare yourself for the journey.

The flashback process is incredibly important because it returns you to the atmosphere of your original wounding (stages one and two). When you're in a fully resourced position, you'll know that you've already survived the trauma, which means you're already a full-fledged survival expert. Moving through your flashbacks from this stance is essentially a process of housecleaning—you release any trapped stances or emotions through grounding and contract burning while you ask your proper empathic questions, move your body, and even kickbox your way through the situation (this full process is detailed in the chapters on fear and panic). However, if you're not properly grounded, focused, and defined, you'll have no ground to stand on and no skills at your disposal, so the traumatic replay will almost certainly knock you flat, just as it did the first time. You'll most likely dissociate, repress, or explode with whatever emotions you feel, or run for the nearest drug or distraction just to survive the pain.

Our empathic healing process helps you stop running, because it gives you the tools and information you need to face your traumatic memories head-on. When you can channel your rage and fury into your boundary, you can immediately create sacred space in which to do your deepest work. When you can ground yourself, you can stabilize your body no matter what sensations bubble up. When you can focus yourself inside your boundary, you can bring yourself back to center no matter what thoughts or visions come forward. When you can burn contracts, you can move anything out of you—behaviors, memories, flashbacks, pains, or even entire relationships. When you can channel your emotions, you can use them to help you burn old contracts and complete your traumatic reenactments in victorious ways. Then, when you're done, you can rejuvenate yourself and restore flow to every part of your soul.

When you're ready, you'll be able to perform this full-bodied movement to the third stage of initiation. For now, though, your first task is to create the sacred space in which that work can occur—to channel your angers, rages, and furies into your boundary and into intensified grounding. These preliminary steps will stabilize your boundary system and increase your ability to maintain your focus. Using your anger and rage to increase your grounding will also help your body release traumatic sense-memories, perhaps of the car hitting you, the flame burning you, or the hand touching you. Your grounding will also help you dislodge the emotional debris you picked up during the trauma, and it will help your logical and linguistic intelligences (which store all the thoughts, plans, schemes, and decisions you made during and after your trauma) begin to relax their hypervigilance so that you can think clearly again.

Setting your boundary with rage and fury gives your fiery spirit a fully defined space in which to settle and interact; grounding your body helps you release trapped sensations and discomfort as you restore flow to your emotional realm and help your mind think clearly once again. This in turn supports your central nature by giving you full access to each part of the village inside you, which means you'll no longer have to wage futile battles with your emotions, your thoughts, your sensations, your fiery visions, your memories, or your flashbacks. When you can channel your rage and fury properly, you'll be able to rebuild your boundary, increase your focus, and heal your soul. Rage and fury are your guardians and your sentries. Learn to attend to them in honorable ways, and they'll protect you, heal your traumas, and save your life.

Remember to welcome your anger in all its forms: as your free-flowing ability to set and maintain your boundary, as your mood-state ability to understand when injustice is occurring, and as the raging rapids that surge forward when injustices have gotten completely out of hand. Welcome and thank your anger.

13

Apathy and Boredom

The Mask for Anger

GIFTS
Detachment ~ Boundary-setting ~ Separation ~ Taking a time-out

THE INTERNAL QUESTIONS
What is being avoided? What must be made conscious?

SIGNS OF OBSTRUCTION
Monotonous indifference, impassivity,
or distractibility that halts creative action

PRACTICE
Honor your need to be separate and detached
without taking yourself out of commission.
Use the anger beneath apathy to reset your boundaries
in healthy ways.

REPRESSION IN ANY EMOTION causes trouble throughout your psyche, but anger is so vital to your health that repressing it actually brings up a specific state in response. This "masking" state of apathy (or boredom) arises when you're unable or unwilling to deal with your true anger. Apathy is not an emotion, but it does protect you. However, since it stems from repression, it can lead to trouble if you're not aware of it. It's fine to feel apathetic, but it's important to know what's happening in your emotional realm when apathy appears. In unmasking apathy, you'll learn about the anger trapped within it (and how that entrapment is sometimes a helpful thing), and how to support yourself in addressing the true angers beneath your mask.

When you don't have the time, energy, or ability to work with your anger properly—when you don't protect your boundary or the boundaries of others, when you feel unable to speak out against the injustices you see, and when you feel incapable of affecting your surroundings, you'll often fall into the masking state of apathy (also known as boredom). In a masking state, you cover up your inner truths with a protective attitude that can distance you from uncomfortable situations. Apathy squelches emotions by affecting an "I don't care; I can't be bothered; whatever" attitude. Apathy seeks distractions such as TV, fun food (as opposed to nourishment), new loves, travel, money, shopping, instant fame, instant meaning, and a quick and easy way out. Apathy is a dissociated state, usually related to being stuck in the wrong environment for your needs. Because it masks emotion, though, apathy is powerless; it longs for change, but it doesn't have the emotional agility to make conscious change happen.

If your apathy is allowed to flow freely in your psyche, you'll let yourself take small vacations from focus and industriousness—you'll be able to daydream, detach yourself with diversions or comfort foods every now and then, or plop yourself in front of the tube or a mindless book when you need a break. You won't fight your movement into distractions by throwing yourself into overwork or hypervigilance. If you welcome your apathy, it will move on quickly, but if you inhibit it (or wallow in it), you'll plummet into imbalance. Here's how to maintain your equilibrium around your need to detach yourself and take a time out.

THE MESSAGE IN APATHY

Apathy often masks anger and depression (see page 327), both of which arise in response to inappropriate environments and degraded boundaries. You can see apathy trying to slap a boundary together—trying to define itself with material possessions, addictions and distractions, sarcasm, or perfect-world scenarios. Apathy points to a loss of boundaries, and to a distinct and urgent need for change, but it does so in an ineffectual and distractible way. Apathy chatters and gripes all day, but it doesn't ever accomplish anything. Conscious complaining (see pages 146–49), then, is an excellent antidote for apathy because it takes powerless griping and turns it into an intentional and defined practice.

Apathy and boredom can serve important functions in many situations where effective action cannot be undertaken. Adolescents, for instance, whose lives are controlled by schools and parents just as if they were still toddlers, are often plagued by apathy. Since we no longer have rituals for the complex transitions of adolescence, we don't notice or honor the ascent into adulthood, nor do we honor the individual who's trying to emerge. The human trapped in adolescence is ripe for ongoing bouts of boredom and apathy; she's in an environment too small for her soul, and she can do nothing but wait until trudging, stubborn, endless time sets her free. Apathy helps to mask and staunch the incredible angers within her—angers that might incinerate the only home she has. Therefore, in our incredibly unaware culture, boredom in teenagers can be seen as a *good* thing.

Apathy and boredom in adults is another story altogether. Boredom is a sign of becoming a product or a victim of your environment, instead of an active and aware participant. Boredom in adults (who have choices and options teenagers can't even imagine) is often a sign of emotional repression, avoidance, and dissociation. However, this is no reason to consider apathy and boredom as entirely odious things. We *need* the masking state of apathy if we're unbalanced or dissociated and can't use our emotions properly, and many of us use apathy to provide the flow that should come from our emotions. For some of us, apathy and the distractions it requires are the only things that can get us from one place to the next. We get bored with one job and take another; we tire of one relationship and grab on to someone else; we trudge away at work to get enough money to buy this perfect car or take that perfect vacation; we survive. We don't understand ourselves, and we don't live full lives, but our apathy keeps us going and provides a certain shielding from our deep issues (and the deep issues in our culture). The mindless activities apathy and boredom require can even protect us from falling into the true depressions and anxieties that underlie many distracted and dissociated behaviors.

We struggle against our natural depressions and anxieties with incredible amounts of boredom-relieving stimuli—most of us have instant, in-home access to TVs, phones, music, and computers. We can be tuned-in to noise, other people, or trivial information twenty-four hours a day. There's no longer any socially approved time for rest, quiet, contemplation, or privacy because we've created a world that doesn't have room for that. We scrabble around for money, housing, and relationships; we obsess about our health, our appearance, and our families; we attempt to heal ourselves or others in what often seems a futile race against the ravages of time; and we have very little peace. People as preoccupied and stimulated as we are certainly aren't going to drop into a meditative or contemplative mood when we slow down; we'll either collapse into fitful sleep or fall into deep depression and anxiety about all that we haven't got, don't know, or didn't do. So instead of slowing down, we surf the Net, turn on the TV, or use our favorite addiction or distraction to ignore our need for rest (or our squashed emotions and dreams) in order to keep all of our balls in the air.

Apathy masks our true selves and gets us through the inanities of modern life. It helps us believe that another car, the right lover, a different job, or the perfect slice of pie will cure us. Apathy lets us be shallow, and sometimes that's all we can manage. Sometimes, all we can do is mask our true feelings and stay on the surface with our meaningless activities. Our emotionally deadening culture makes us believe that deep empathic living is impossible, as if true feelings or brilliant visions would slow us down unnecessarily or prevent us from meeting the rent, raising the kids, or turning the thankless crank. That's not true, of course, but the overriding message in our culture tells us that we can't stop to feel or dream because we have to keep moving. In response, we become highly distractible automatons. This next practice can help us become living, breathing human beings again.

The Practice for Apathy

It's important to make distinctions between apathy that arises from your unwillingness to rest and apathy that arises from your inability to set boundaries and channel your anger appropriately. Here's how to tell the difference: If you're filled with apathy right now, honor it, but feed it with a deeper version of what it wants. Take the reins and become its master, instead of letting it pull you around by the nose. For instance, if your apathy wants a perfect lover, work on making yourself a valuable love partner instead of passively waiting for some super person to appear. If your apathy wants a better house, a better car, a better body, or a better wardrobe, put your best critical energy into your current house, car, body, or wardrobe, and make those things better right now. If you begin to act consciously and deepen the demands of your apathy, you'll be able to unearth your true issues. If your apathy is a response to your refusal to rest, this practice will uncover your fatigue and probably some sadness (see page 295) or depression (see page 327). Please set your boundary strongly, ground yourself, and replenish yourself by performing your rejuvenation practice as often as you can for a few days (and, of course, rest!). Also, have yourself checked for a sleep disorder; they are amazingly prevalent and astonishingly underdiagnosed. If these suggestions don't relieve your fatigue, or if you drop into depression, please skip forward to the practice for depression on pages 334–37.

If your apathy is a mask for anger, this practice will bring your anger forward. You might feel indignant, perturbed, open to attack, or trapped in your current surroundings. Please skip back to the anger chapter, set your boundary strongly, burn your contracts ferociously, and protect yourself with the information and intensity your anger brings forward. If apathy and boredom are habits for you, you may need to perform this practice a few times before you break the cycle—but the cycle will end when you bring your full awareness to it.

It is important to listen to your apathy but not to follow its demands mindlessly, because mindless action only invites more mindless action. Break the cycle mindfully by answering your apathy and boredom in conscious and honorable ways, but remember that both apathy and boredom act as tourniquets or shut-off valves for your anger and your energy when you're not in a position to effect change. If you're truly unable to affect your surroundings, let your apathy be, and simply deepen your responses to its demands.

We've all been in scholastic or work situations where we really can't do much besides go through the motions, and in these situations, apathy and distractions can be a godsend. When I look back at the binders I've kept for college classes, I can tell how tedious they were by the amount of doodling I have in my class notes. In some classes, I had the time to draw an entire town, mock up a website, and recall all the steps of the quadratic equation. My apathy protected me and my classmates, because otherwise I would have been interrupting the class to alleviate my boredom or show up the professor. Apathy rocks!

However, if you *can* effect change, but you've been hiding from your responsibilities and diminishing your boundary in the masked state of apathy, please focus and ground yourself. Ask the questions for apathy: "What is being avoided?" and "What must be made conscious?" Listen to your answers, peer out from under the mask of apathy, and find out what you're really feeling.

HONORING APATHY IN OTHERS

Honoring apathy in others is a difficult task because apathetic people seek separation in unhealthy ways—they isolate themselves or throw their energy away rather than setting their boundaries properly. This often weakens them to the extent that they cannot engage in relationships without losing their way. There's a terrible feedback loop in apathy, where isolation or frantic activation lead to the need for more isolation or more *stuff*. You cannot break that feedback loop for anyone else—it's an inside job. However, you can model honorable engagement. You can set your boundary strongly when you're in contact with apathetic people—not just to protect yourself, but to protect them from you as well. Think of apathetic people as being without skin, and be aware that any unfocused or ungrounded contact from you may weaken them and subsequently intensify their apathetic cycle.

If you can allow apathetic people to complain, and lend an ear to their pain, you may help them uncover the anger, fatigue, or depression beneath their apathetic masks. Continue to set your boundary throughout the engagement and welcome the true emotions when they arise—they're the only things that will break the cycle of apathy. When you can create a sacred space for emotions in other people (even when they refuse to do so for themselves), you may be able to help them awaken and restore their focus and balance once again.

14

Guilt and Shame

Restoring Integrity

GIFTS
Atonement ~ Integrity ~ Self-respect ~ Behavioral change

THE INTERNAL QUESTIONS
Who has been hurt? What must be made right?

SIGNS OF OBSTRUCTION
Crippling, repetitive guilty feelings that do not instruct
you or heal your relationships; or shamelessness where
you are endangered by your own behavior

PRACTICE
Channel this intense emotion to set a strong boundary
and create a sacred space in which you can atone for your
transgressions, amend your behaviors, throw off manufactured
shame, and heal your heart and your relationships.

GUILT AND SHAME ARE forms of anger that arise when your boundary has been broken from the inside—by something you've done wrong or have been convinced is wrong. While anger is the honorable sentry that faces outward and protects your boundary from external damage, guilt and shame are the sentries that face inward and protect your internal boundary (and the boundaries of others) from your own incorrect or ill-conceived behaviors. Guilt and shame are vital and irreplaceable emotions that help you mature into a conscious and well-regulated person. With their assistance, you'll be able to honorably monitor your behavior, your emotions, your thoughts, your physical desires, your spiritual longings, and your ego structure. If you don't have conscious access to your free-flowing guilt and shame, you won't understand yourself, you'll be haunted by improper behaviors, addictions, and compulsions, and you'll be unable to stand upright at the center of your psyche.

When the healing influences of free-flowing guilt and shame flow gracefully through your psyche, you won't be painfully shame-filled or guilt-ridden; instead, you'll have a compassionate sense of ethics, the courage to judge and supervise your own conduct, and the strength to amend your behaviors without inflating or deflating your ego unnecessarily. When you successfully navigate through your honest guilt and shame, you'll feel proud of yourself, and you'll move naturally into happiness and contentment. Unfortunately, since all forms of anger are tragically misunderstood and reviled, guilt and shame have been suppressed mightily (and expressed brutally and insidiously), to the extent that most of us cannot connect shame to happiness in any way whatsoever. Guilt and shame have been labeled useless, false, toxic, addictive, and unnatural, and both have been thrown onto the trash heap. This is a reasonable response, because we've all seen and experienced the damage wreaked by raging guilt and shame. Unfortunately, we've lost our conscious connection to the healing forms of these vital and restorative emotions. We've rejected guilt and shame so completely that we don't know which is which anymore, why they exist in the first place, or that guilt isn't even an emotion at all.

THE DIFFERENCE BETWEEN GUILT AND SHAME

In my early teens, I read a popular self-help book that branded guilt and shame as "useless" emotions. The book presented the idea that we're all perfect and, therefore, shouldn't ever be guilt-ridden or ashamed of anything we do. That idea seemed very strange to me, so I went to the dictionary and looked up "guiltless" and "shameless" and found that neither state was anything to celebrate. To be guiltless means to be free of mark or experience, as if you're a blank slate. It's not a sign of intelligence or growth, because guiltlessness exists only in people who have not yet lived. To be shameless means to be senseless, uncouth, and impudent. It's a very marked state of being out of control, out of touch, and exceedingly self-absorbed; therefore, shamelessness lives only in people who don't have any relational skills. Both states—guiltlessness and shamelessness—helped me understand the intrinsic value of guilt and shame.

Fascinatingly, in a dictionary definition, guilt isn't even an emotional state at all; it's simply the knowledge and acknowledgment of wrongdoing. Guilt is a state of circumstance: you're either guilty or not guilty in relation to the legal or moral code you value. You cannot *feel* guilty, because guilt is a concrete state, not an emotional one! Your feelings are almost irrelevant; if you did something wrong, you're guilty, and it doesn't matter if you're happy, angry, fearful, or depressed about it. When you don't do something wrong, you're not guilty. Feelings don't enter into the equation at all. The only way you could possibly ever *feel* guilty is if you don't quite remember committing an offense ("I feel like I might be guilty, but I'm not sure"). No, what you feel is *shame*. Guilt is a factual state, while shame is an emotion.

Shame is the natural emotional consequence of guilt and wrongdoing. When your healthy shame is welcomed into your psyche, its powerful heat and intensity will restore your boundary when you've broken it yourself. However, most of us don't welcome shame into our lives; we obscure it by saying "I feel guilty" instead of "I feel ashamed," which speaks volumes about our current inability to identify and acknowledge our guilt, channel our appropriate shame, and make amends. This is unfortunate because when we don't welcome and honor our free-flowing and appropriate shame, we cannot moderate our own behavior. We'll continually do things we know are wrong, and we won't have the strength to stop ourselves. In our never-ending shamelessness, we'll offend and offend and offend without pause—we'll *always* be guilty—because nothing will wake us to our effect on the world.

If we continue to use the incorrect statement, "I feel guilty," we'll be unable to right our wrongs, amend our behaviors, or discover where our shame originated—which means we'll be unable to experience true happiness or contentment (both of which arise when we skillfully navigate through any difficult emotion). If we don't come out and correctly state, "I'm ashamed of myself," we'll never improve. I'll say it again before we go deeper: guilt is a factual state, not an emotional one. You're either guilty or not guilty. If you're not guilty, there's nothing to be ashamed of. However, if you *are* guilty, and you want to know what to do about the fact of your guilt, then you've got to embrace the information shame brings to you.

THE MESSAGE IN SHAME

Shame is one of the master teachers of emotional channeling. You don't have to lift a finger or study anything to learn to channel shame through your body and your boundary; shame will pour forth in a tidal wave without your help or permission. It will stop you in your tracks, turn you bright red, and leave you speechless and dumbfounded. Though shame actually strengthens you in the long run, it breaks you down in the immediate moment. If you've got no internal skills, you won't be able to tolerate this necessary fall from grace (or discover why your shame arose in the first place). Shame takes you out of commission in a split second; if you're dealing with your own shame in a skillful way, this downtime can be a blessing. However, if you're responding to manufactured or applied shame, this downtime may unnecessarily cripple you.

When shame arises in response to your own authentic and addressable flaws or missteps, it flows appropriately (and often a step or two in front of your behavior). If you welcome your appropriate shame, you'll stop yourself before you do something crazy, before you say the wrong thing, or before you enter into unhealthy behaviors or relationships. Appropriate shame will help you turn away from your own maliciousness, charlatanism, and thievery—even when no one's looking. It will keep you punctual, polite, and upstanding, and it will lead you gently but firmly away from the path of temptation. Free-flowing and authentic shame will watch over you and ensure that your behavior is honorable and correct. Shame will also keep your other emotions gently in check by giving you the inner fortitude to navigate through them (instead of squashing them like bugs or hurling them at others). Authentic shame will stand at your inner boundary and monitor everything going out of your soul and everything occurring within it. With its honorable assistance, you'll become a conscientious and well-moderated asset to yourself and our world. As a result, you'll experience authentic self-respect, which will lead you time and time again to true contentment and happiness. Interestingly, your appropriate shame will also inoculate you against being victimized by charlatans and schemers, because your willingness to shine a light upon your own shadowy behaviors will make you aware of those behaviors in others instead of trapping you in an enmeshed nightmare with them (in the wise words of W. C. Fields, "You can't cheat an honest man").

IDENTIFYING AUTHENTIC SHAME

Most of us were not taught to welcome or work with our authentic shame and remorse (which all of us feel naturally, especially when we've hurt someone); instead, most of us were taught about shame by being shamed. Authority figures such as parents, teachers, peers, and the media often attempt to teach and control us by applying shame from the outside, instead of trusting our natural ability to moderate our own behaviors. As a result, most of us repress any natural shame we might feel (which makes us unable to effectively monitor our behavior) or express our shame all over others in unfortunate attempts to disgrace and control them. This sad behavior has disconnected most of us from the strengthening influence of authentic shame, and filled us with staggering amounts of manufactured and applied shame.

When we don't have a healthy connection to our own shame, we're often coerced into embodying other people's ideas of right and wrong ("Good girls don't act that way; big boys don't cry; we don't get angry in this family; no one likes a smarty-pants; no one will love you until . . . "). In this onslaught, we become overwhelmed by untruths, foreign messages, damaging contracts, and inauthentic shame. In response, our authentic shame often surges forward to fight off the foreign shame. If we could grab on to this natural shame, we could use its intense heat to set our boundaries fiercely, and incinerate the foreign messages and manufactured shame careening through us. Unfortunately, since most of us have no skills and no practice for shame, we tend to crumble in front of all shame, whether it belongs to us or not. Usually when our authentic shame moves forward, we become overwhelmed and essentially dissociate from our emotional selves. We fall into an incoherent shame spiral (where we're simultaneously drawn toward and repelled by shameful and forbidden behaviors) and wrestle in futility with seemingly senseless amounts of foreign *and* authentic shame.

This spiral is unnecessary, and you can halt it by learning to identify your authentic, free-flowing shame, which is actually sensible, momentary, and empowering: your hand goes out for a cookie, you realize you don't need it, and you walk away. That's authentic, free-flowing shame working properly. Afterward, you feel strong and aware. In authentic shame, there's no spiral because you simply live by a moral code. You floss because you like clean teeth, you avoid drugs and crime because they're uninteresting, and you treat people respectfully because it feels right. Authentic shame places gentle and authentic brakes on your impulses, so much so that you won't really feel them. Improper behaviors won't loom over your psyche or call to you with seductive intensities, because your authentic shame will help you stay awake and functional. That's what your free-flowing shame feels like. Manufactured or applied shame, on the other hand, makes you nearly comatose. You'll eat *all* the cookies, even if you're not hungry. You'll treat yourself and others shamefully, and you won't be able to control yourself, because you won't have access to the brilliant and integrity-restoring messages of your own authentic shame.

When you can identify your authentic shame, you'll be able to brighten and define your boundary, ground yourself firmly, call your intellect into the situation, and examine (and destroy) the contracts that are attached to any excessive or inauthentic shame you might carry. However, if you have no skills, the intensity of shame may incapacitate you, so much so that you'll actually stop moving forward or challenging yourself in order to avoid making any new mistakes (which could intensify your shame in even more paralyzing ways). Or you might become shameless in response to the shame roaring inside you. You'll act like a cranky two-year-old or like an adolescent in full-scale rebellion; you'll break rules you agree with, just to prove you're independent; you'll blurt things out and turn bright red only *after* the damage has been done;

you'll eat and buy and do the wrong things; you'll fall for scam after scam; and you'll have no authentic direction.

If you're entangled in a losing battle like this, you'll come back to the same destructive behaviors over and over again, almost as if you're drugged. There will be nothing awake at the center of your psyche; the village will be deserted; your intellect, your visionary spirit, and your body will be devastated by your shame spiral; and your emotions will rage uncontrolled. You'll pray for willpower, God's help, and anything else you can think of, but if you can't welcome the strengthening influence of your own authentic shame, you won't have the resolve you need to effect conscious change or restore yourself to wholeness.

We all use shame to raise children, to train each other, and to get our way—it's how we do things in our boundary-impaired culture. That's not going to change any time soon. Your task is not to change the culture from the outside in, but to change yourself from the inside out—to strengthen yourself so that you can individuate and create your own true boundary once again. It's extremely important to oppose and renounce foreign and applied shame and to restore your authentic morality and integrity, but you can do this only by welcoming your authentic shame inside your own soul. When you can take hold of your own shame and consciously halt your spiral, you'll be able to stand upright and look around you with new eyes. You'll be able to identify and release the foreign and applied shame inside you, and you'll be able to identify and avoid any new shaming messages coming from any outside source (you do this by strengthening yourself when your boundary weakens in response to another person's opinions or criticisms). Most important, you'll be able to refrain from expressing your shame onto others, which will change the culture around you in profound ways—from the inside out.

Your authentic shame surges forward when something is seriously amiss, either in your behavior or as a result of having had behavioral control forced upon you. If you can honor and welcome your shame, it will give you the strength you need, both to amend your own ill-considered behaviors and to throw off the foreign tyrannies that disrupt your authenticity. If you can use your skills to separate yourself from the shame-inducing messages of others, you'll free up incredible energy, and with it, you'll be able to hear your own code of ethics. You'll also be able to respect and honor the boundaries of others, no matter how much shame you may be dealing with at any given time. With the help of your free-flowing shame, you'll always have an internal sentry that returns you again and again to the honor code of your individual morality.

The Practice for Shame

The practice for shame involves many skills, but the first task in working with shame is to welcome it with open arms. When your shame arises in the presence of others (it usually appears first as an internal pull in the gut, a flush of heat, a momentary speechlessness, or a sense of internal caution), it's important to stop, quickly ground yourself, intensify your boundary, and focus on your shame. If your shame stops you before you say or do something shameful, you can thank it and make your necessary preemptive corrections. If you don't know why your shame has come forward, you can ask yourself or the people around you if you've done something incorrect ("Who, or what, has been hurt?"), and apologize or make amends if necessary.

This is a big first step in learning to work with shame—to deal with it immediately and openly the moment it appears. Most of us skate right over the top of our momentary shame and continue on with the very act that brought our shame forward in the first place (which ensures our fall into repetitive or rapids-level shame). The way to halt a shame spiral and interrupt its feedback loop is to meet your shame immediately (and use it immediately) to set your boundary, restore your integrity, and make amends ("What must be made right?"). If you can openly welcome your shame, it will recede naturally (and swiftly) once it has helped you make your correcting actions. Then your contentment and happiness will arise naturally, and you'll move forward as a smarter, stronger, and more honorable person.

If you're unable to channel your shame in this simple way, and you feel it intensifying, you may need to excuse yourself and find a quiet place where you can channel your shame in private. When you can get away, you should pour your shame into your boundary, because if you allow this confusing shame to stay inside your body, its intensity may throw you off-kilter. Shaming messages may bubble up from every corner, memories or sensations from long-repressed shameful incidents may resurface, and you'll almost certainly be overwhelmed and incapacitated. Channeling your shame into your boundary will revitalize your sense of self and set sacred space for your shame, but it will also calm your body and give your mind the peace it needs to differentiate between you and your emotions (this differentiation is an absolute necessity when you're dealing with emotions that have been dishonored and denatured). Functional judgment is a lifesaver when shame arises, so bless your intellect and welcome it into this process. Don't let your logic shout down or disable your shame; instead, let it take its honorable position as the translator of the vital information your shame is trying to bring forward.

After you move your shame into your boundary and calm your body, please ground yourself strongly. Grounding will help you release any trapped bodily shame you might carry (such as body-image distortions, eating disorders, sexual shame, compulsions, or addictions). As you ground yourself, you may feel uncomfortable sensations arising in your body. This is a wonderful sign; it means that your body has become a conscious and equal partner in your emotion-channeling process. In many cases, the parts of your body that have been shamed will actually carry physical as well as emotional pain. Maintain your focus, and use your skills to ground any areas of discomfort. If your discomfort persists or intensifies, place a contract in front of the troubled area and project the discomfort onto the contract, so you can understand what your body is trying to make conscious (this may take a few channeling sessions).

When you're grounded and centered within your vibrant, shame-supported boundary, the heat and intensity shame carries will give you the energy you need to shine a spotlight on your own behavior and examine your contracts with whatever has brought your shame forward. In this sacred space, it will be easy to differentiate between authentic shame that belongs to you and manufactured shame that was forced upon you. The difference will become clear almost as soon as you visualize your contract. When your shame is authentic and personal, you'll only sense your own behaviors flowing onto your contract. You'll see or feel yourself doing or saying something you know is wrong, and you'll feel appropriate chagrin coupled with an impetus to correct your behavior and make amends with anyone you've hurt (including yourself). When you destroy authentic shame contracts, you'll feel intensity toward them but not a great deal of violence.

However, when you bring forward a contract filled with applied or enforced shame, you'll sense a cacophony of images, noise, and static barreling out of you. You'll hear the voices of shaming authority figures, you'll sense images of disciplinarians, and you'll most likely lose your focus, and time-travel back to the moment you picked up the shameful message in the first place. This contract will probably become full very quickly (if so, move it aside and create a new one), and when you burn it, your shame may intensify into an inferno. This intensity is a wonderful asset when you have skills, but it can knock you out if you don't (which is why most people refuse to deal with their shame). A great deal of intensity gets trapped inside you when shame is applied from the outside. When you can ground yourself strongly, focus yourself, and burn your contracts, this intensity will free you. Roll up these contracts, wherever they came from, fling them out of your personal space, and destroy them with the fierce intensity of your shame.

When you're channeling rapids-level manufactured or trapped shame, each of your skills will help you remain stable. Your grounding will help you release any shame trapped in your body or your psyche; your inner focus will give you a private place from which to operate when your whole being is aflame; your ability to burn contracts will help you identify and release any and all trapped shame messages (no matter where they originated); and your ability to rejuvenate yourself will revitalize you. Please be sure to take regular rejuvenation breaks (see pages 151–52) when you're working with shame. Massive healing changes will occur when you burn contracts with applied shame, which means your stasis tendencies will be on full alert. When you consciously replenish yourself, your ability to support stasis will be as conscious as your ability to create change.

Shame is a major stumbling block in every psyche, and as a result shame-channeling sessions can be quite lengthy. Don't let this process take too long, though. Listen to your body, your mind, your spirit, and your other emotions; if any part of you gets tired or antsy, pay attention. Roll up your contracts, burn them fiercely, and go directly to rejuvenation or some form of play. Don't allow your channeling practice to become grim and perfectionist (especially when you're working with shame). Let your emotions know you're always available for shame-channeling sessions in the future, and take care of yourself in the present. Take your place at the center of your village and remember that you have emotions, but you aren't made of them. Give yourself the freedom to be lazy, to be resistant, and to be unwilling to drop into the deep waters at a moment's notice. Don't let your emotions take over; instead, keep thinking, keep sensing, keep dreaming, and keep moving with fluidity and laughter, because shame has most likely been applied to you since the moment you took your first breath. You don't need to clear all of it out by this afternoon! You have all the time you need, and if you make this clear to your shame, it will calm down and allow you to move at a relaxed and therapeutic pace.

And remember this about shame: when you can successfully channel your authentic shame, you'll feel proud of yourself (deservedly so), which will bring your authentic contentment and joy forward. You won't read that in most pop-psychology books, where shame is usually trashed and demonized, but it's true! Authentic shame is essential to your health and your relationships—and you won't feel happy without it. Shame says this: "We're here to help one another, to transform ourselves, and to make amends. This doesn't mean life should be a chore. This planet is not so much a place of punishment as a place of grace, or the opportunity for grace. In each day, each of us has the chance to do it right and make it right, with the brilliant assistance of our appropriate shame."

WHAT TO DO IF YOUR SHAME GETS STUCK

Coming back to consciousness after a long bout with repetitive shame can be rather involved, because shaming messages and labels can form a tremendous amount of your identity. You may have become accustomed to branding yourself with shame-based titles ("I'm a loser, an alcoholic, rage-aholic, post-traumatic compulsive gambler, and I bite my nails!") that pigeonhole you and intensify your shame. It's vital to examine your self-talk as you're coming out of a shame spiral, because those old titles and labels can throw you back into the old identifications. As you're healing, it's helpful to substitute empowering phrases in order to break this cycle (not "positive" affirmations, but empowering, choice-based phrases). For instance, if your smoking bothers you, and your habitual phrase is "I can't stop smoking! I've tried a hundred times. I'm just an addict!" you can change your feeble words into forceful words and assert, "I won't stop smoking! I refuse to. I love smoking!" You can even go on a pro-smoking rant and enumerate all the ways smoking has added to your life. You can celebrate your smoking as a conscious choice.

When you can move your smoking out of the reach of your futile shame spiral, you'll be able to look at your decision to smoke with new eyes. When smoking is a choice (and a darned *good* one, yeah!), you can take a look at it from a more empowered place. You can make decisions about your smoking from within your natural moral code, instead of from a shameful feedback loop. You can bring your physical reactions about smoking to bear, you can use your intellect to examine and research smoking, you can explore your emotional attachments to cigarettes and nicotine, and you can ask your visionary spirit to help you understand why you might need a smoke screen around you at all times. Your natural shame can then bring forward its authentic reservations about your smok-ing, which you'll now be able to hear as an intelligent, upright person who has thousands of options, instead of as a cowering addict whose entire soul has been overwhelmed and imprisoned by nicotine. Wherever you go from that place, you'll remain standing. You'll be able to focus yourself and incinerate any number of contracts with your unwanted behaviors—or with any belittling messages or labels that careen around in your psyche—and you'll be able to move forward as a whole person, instead of a powerless victim of your environment, your upbringing, or your chemistry.

BOUNDARY TROUBLE:
WHEN SHAME GETS *REALLY* STUCK

If you don't find a great number of shaming titles in your psyche, yet you still struggle mightily with repetitive shame, you may have boundary trouble. When your boundary is weakened or unsuitably inflated, you may tend to enmesh with others simply because your personal boundary isn't sufficiently defined. If your shame is constant and unrelenting, or if you find yourself inexplicably unable to speak up or take appropriate action, your shame may be in a feedback loop of another kind.

When your personal boundary isn't well-defined, your anger may move to its mood state to help you protect and restore yourself. If you constantly repress or explode with this anger (as rage, fury, hatred, or apathy), your boundary trouble will intensify. Then your shame will come forward, too, because now you're not only dealing with affronts from the exterior world, but you're actually hurting yourself and others by mismanaging your anger. In this situation, your shame will try to silence and inhibit you simply because your boundary is too weak to protect you (which means you really shouldn't be out in public), or so large that it inadvertently interferes with the boundaries of everyone around you (which means you'll be offending against others as a matter of course—even though you don't mean to).

If your shame is your constant and unwelcome companion, please skip back to the boundary-definition exercises on pages 135–37, and pay close attention to maintaining an arm's-length boundary (no more, and no less) around you at all points. Then pour your shame into your boundary, and let it revitalize your personal space. If you let shame and anger take their rightful places as your sentries and behavioral mentors (instead of your tormentors), you'll be able to live, act, and react consciously, instead of exploding or deflating simply because your boundary is impaired.

As you learn to define and care for your personal boundary, make sure that you conscientiously channel each of your anger energies (rage, fury, hatred, apathy, and shame), instead of repressing them back into your inner world or expressing them haphazardly at the outer world. When your boundary is refortified, you'll protect yourself and everyone around you from enmeshment, boundary damage, and repetitive shame spirals.

HONORING SHAME IN OTHERS

There is an emotion I watch for in situations where people have done something that is truly wrong: appropriate shame. If a friend offends against me, and I call him or her on it, I wait to see if appropriate shame and remorse come forward. If they do, I know that the offense is over and that I don't have to harp on it anymore. On the other hand, if a friend offends against me and then refuses to own up to it or apologize, I know that he or she has a problem with shame. If so, I keep a close eye on this person. I usually let friends screw up three times, but if they continue to behave shamelessly, I walk away. Setting a boundary isn't just an imaginal skill; it's important to surround yourself with honorable people, and separate yourself from people who can't manage their behavior ethically.

Appropriate shame is something we should all support in ourselves and others. If we discipline a child, and it's clear that he or she is truly sorry, the discipline needs to end immediately. What you want to see is appropriate shame arising in response to the original affront—not to your strict discipline. Continuing onward with the shaming after a child has shown remorse is abusive, and it often leads to a hardening in the child's soul. That hardening, as we've all experienced, can lead to shameless behaviors that can make people untrustworthy. When someone behaves shamelessly, they're trapped in a reaction to bad parenting or bad teaching, which is why I give everyone three chances. We can all learn and grow beyond our childhood wounding, but sometimes people just don't want to. Bless their hearts is what I say as I walk away.

If you are parenting or working with children, it's important to help them connect to their authentic shame in healthy ways. A great way to do this is to let them be involved in setting punishments, if any, for their misdeeds. When I suggest this, many parents scoff and imagine that children will choose extra ice cream as a punishment; they won't take it seriously because they're all little outlaws. But what I found in parenting, teaching, and coaching is that children are very solemn about their acts of contrition. Most children feel remorse deeply, and the punishments they create for themselves are often comically medieval. As the parent or authority figure, you can easily lighten their suggested punishments and help children find a way to make amends without (as has been suggested by various little ones I know): never eating again; paying $2,000 to the police; or giving all of their toys to homeless kids. When children can be involved in deciding upon their acts of contrition, they can connect to their shame in healthy ways (as long as you stop them from inflicting retributive self-flagellation upon their own souls).

Of course, none of us grew up this way; therefore, we and most of the people we know struggle mightily with shame. It's not a topic anyone really wants to bring up, so it can be difficult to create sacred space for shame in people who have no skills. Our scandalous abuse of shame has endangered us all; therefore, when shame arises, most people just dissociate and lose their way. Even verbal expression, which is usually a good idea with other emotions, may throw people directly into a shame spiral, because if the shame is foreign in origin (or dishonored by repression or incompetent expression), it will increase in intensity as soon as it is brought into the open. Shame is so vital to the sanctity of the soul that when it is released, it will work unceasingly to expose inferiorities and restore integrity. If people have skills, they can grab on to their shame and raft through the rapids to safety; however, if they don't have skills, they'll just go under.

My appropriate shame tells me that working with shame-filled people is either a job for trained therapists who can provide a skill set and support for people going through the rapids, or that it's an inside job for people who have accumulated the skills on their own (through this book or in any other way). I would caution you strongly against attempting to deal with a shame cycle in a person who has no support structure. I applaud you for wanting to create sacred space for shame in others, but sometimes the most sacred act is to let people know that they are in the rapids and that there's no shame in reaching out for more help than a friend can provide.

TRAUMA SURVIVORS AND "TOXIC" SHAME

Trauma survivors are often overwhelmed by shame, sometimes because they blame themselves (they often feel "guilty" for having caused their traumas somehow), but usually because they were actively shamed during or after their traumas. Some abusers (or other emotionally incompetent people) blame survivors for being in the wrong place at the wrong time. Many trauma survivors are incapacitated by repetitive and unresolving shame, or are undermined by their own futile and rebellious attempts to defy the powerful shame they feel. This disruptive post-traumatic shame spiral has been labeled "toxic" by many mental health providers. While this intense and repetitive shame certainly has toxic effects when it is expressed or repressed, it is not toxic at all when it can be channeled.

In fact, this rapids-level shame can lead trauma survivors directly to the blessed third stage of healing.

Channeling shame of this magnitude can only be done in a sacred context, so if you're not quite up on your skills yet, you should reach out for support. Many therapists can create sacred space in their consulting rooms, and many trauma support groups can be healing, as well, because when you can see your supposedly shameful behaviors reflected identically in the souls of your fellow survivors (or explained by a therapist), you'll be able to remove the stigma of pathology from your soul. You'll see that post-traumatic shame spirals are common and not specific to you, and you'll understand that powerful shame exists not to break you down and incapacitate you, but to halt your forward movement as a precaution when your movements are certain to be incorrect or shameful.

If you're dealing with unhealed and unresolved trauma (where you're distracted, boundary-impaired, and dissociated), you'll be cycling through stages one and two, and you'll most likely seek traumatizing situations or relationships in order to intensify your cycling in the desperate, unconscious hope that you'll finally shoot forward to stage three. In this dire situation, your psyche won't want you to move at all, and it will stop you in any way it can while it tries to rebuild your ravaged boundary and put out the fires that keep erupting in your soul.

It is very easy to crumble in the face of this sort of turmoil, which is why skills, support, and sacred space are absolutely necessary. Whether you choose to take this journey on your own or with the help of a therapist, your ability to ground and focus yourself will enable you to halt any distraction or dissociation you might experience, just as defining your personal space will begin to relieve your boundary impairment. When you're grounded and reintegrated inside your sacred space, you can channel (or be helped to channel) any emotion that comes forward while you incinerate your contracts with any shameful memories, labels, or foreign messages that disable you. Empathic skills help you consciously enter the territory of the first two stages of your initiation with resources, focus, and the knowledge that this too shall pass. Your shame can then help you stand upright and face any memories or behaviors that have tripped you up or shamed you; it can provide the heat and focus you need to forgive yourself and make amends to people you may have hurt unintentionally—and it can restore your dignity and honor.

When intense shame appears, it contributes the focus and impetus you need to perform serious soul-work. If you don't have the skills you need just yet, please seek out competent therapeutic help, but remember to bless your shame and welcome it into your healing process. Authentic shame is not here to punish you; it's here to strengthen your inner boundary and your determination so that you can halt your shame spiral, rid yourself of applied and manufactured shame, restore your integrity, and heal your soul.

If you can welcome your shame, you can begin to identify the different forms shame takes, rather than just falling into shame spirals. Welcome your free-flowing ability to effortlessly support ethical behaviors in yourself and others; welcome your mood state when you've done something wrong; and welcome the raging rapids that surge forward when something shameful has not been addressed consciously or honorably. Welcome and thank your shame.

15

Hatred

The Profound Mirror

Includes Resentment, Contempt,
Disgust, and Shadow Work

GIFTS
Intense awareness ~ Piercing vision ~ Sudden evolution
~ Shadow work

THE INTERNAL QUESTIONS
What has fallen into my shadow? What must be reintegrated?

SIGNS OF OBSTRUCTION
Fierce, laser-focused attacks on the souls of others
without concurrent self-awareness

PRACTICE
Retrieve your shadow material from your hate partner by describing
in detail the serious faults you perceive. Say hello to your lost self,
pour your hatred into your boundary, incinerate your contracts with
these despised behaviors, and restore your psyche to wholeness.

THOUGH HUMANKIND'S EXPRESSION OF hatred has created unrelieved suffering throughout history, hatred is actually a natural, healthy, and exceptional emotion. Hatred is a laser-focused form of rage and fury that arises when your boundary is devastated, not through an attack per se, but through a more intimate and interior hazard that you're not yet able to confront on your own. Hatred is not mere dislike, where something unpleasant leads you to separate yourself from another person. Hatred is also not fear, where you intuitively pick up on another person's improper or threatening intentions. No, hatred is an intense flare of rage and fury, which means you're dealing with boundary devastation and the near-complete loss of your equilibrium. If you can immediately grab on to your hatred and bring your full awareness to bear upon it, you can use its intensity to learn absolutely astounding things about yourself, your behavior, and the behavior of your hate target. In fact, many deep and buried issues cannot be fully revealed until the fierce energy of hatred arises, because without its powerful sentry capacities, its acute awareness and convictions, and its ability to instantaneously rebuild your boundary, you might not otherwise be able to make the profound leap from business-as-usual complacency into the sudden, piercing awareness hatred initiates.

Hatred signals boundary devastation, certainly, but its pinpoint focus also has a brilliant secondary function, which is to alert you to specific interior issues that hinder and endanger you. Again, hatred is not mere dislike, which goes away when you separate yourself from people who behave badly. No, hatred is a focused attack on another person (or group of people, if your hatred has erupted into racism, homophobia, xenophobia, or any other form of bigotry). Teaching someone to hate is a perfect example of terrible psychological hygiene. It's abusive to teach someone to share your hatred and, consequently, your devastated boundaries. Though it might seem fun to create a community of hate, everyone in it will be injured by tearing other people down in order to build themselves up. When hatred arises, you're responding to things you see in your hate target, but you're also shining a rage-powered spotlight on serious boundary issues buried in the shadows of your soul.

ATTACKS FROM WITHIN:
SHEDDING SOME LIGHT ON THE SHADOW

When repression is used within the psyche (or the society), the repressed material becomes trapped in the unconscious. This trapped and dishonored material does not disappear; instead, it gathers itself and forms what has been called the *shadow*. Many schools of psychotherapy (most notably the Jungian schools) focus their attention on the shadow because it contains some of the deepest information within the human psyche. Shadow work is a rich subject that deserves a lifetime of study (see Further Resources on page 399), but a quick overview of the shadow is important at this time.

In a nutshell, the shadow is the portion of the psyche we're not aware of, not because it's mysterious or hidden per se, but because we deny it. The shadow holds our squelched impulses, our unfelt emotions, our unacceptable behaviors, and our unlived dreams. Though many people see the shadow as containing only the "bad" parts of us, the shadow is not as simple as that. The shadow can also contain our artistic brilliance, our truest voice, our mathematical genius, our financial wizardry, and even our beauty, depending on which of our aspects we deny most ferociously. Each person's shadow is a completely different animal.

Robert Bly, in his exquisite work entitled *A Little Book on the Human Shadow*, put it this way: "The drama is this. We came as infants 'trailing clouds of glory,' arriving from the farthest reaches of the universe, bringing with us appetites well preserved from our mammal inheritance, spontaneities wonderfully preserved from our 150,000 years of tree life, angers well preserved from our 5,000 years of tribal life—in short, with our 360-degree radiance—and we offered this gift to our parents. They didn't want it. They wanted a nice girl or a nice boy."

This drama continues throughout our lives. First we turn down our radiance and our appetites out of love for our parents. Then we enter into peer relationships and scholastic situations that ask us to repress our emotions, our physical desires, some of our intelligences, and most of our visions. Eventually we end up as adults who are conscious of just a tiny slice of that original 360-degree radiance. The rest of our radiance lurks in the shadow world of repressed tendencies and abilities—and more often than not, that dishonored material leaks and strikes out when we're not looking. The shadow contains great power, not simply because so much of us is trapped within it, but because it takes tremendous effort to deny our wholeness. What we repress and ignore becomes dangerous, not because the material is dangerous in itself, but because we take such great pains to banish it from our consciousness.

So we all come into this world with a 360-degree soul, which is brave and cowardly, brilliant and stupid, gentle and murderous, caring and selfish, graceful and clumsy, and so on into infinity. As we grow, we're taught to suppress certain parts of ourselves (which is a normal part of our socialization) while we emphasize other parts. Each family, neighborhood, group, school, culture, and country forces a different set of unwanted talents and behaviors into the shadow while shining a welcoming light on the set of talents and behaviors that fit comfortably in that environment. So each of us has a shadow self, a constellation of abilities and behaviors we've been taught to suppress. However, when we see people who remind us of our shadow, we're often agitated in some way. Unfortunately, in our severely anger-impaired culture, that agitation is often expressed in crimes against decency and humanity—racism, sexism, homophobia, war, brutality, genocide, ethnic cleansing, and prejudice—or repressed into self-hatreds that rip us apart.

The expression and repression of hatred completely ruin the subject of hatred, and that's a terrible shame, because if you aren't aware of your hatreds, your name-calling, and your pettiness, you won't be able to discover the ways in which your psyche has been diminished. If you can't access your hatreds in a conscious way, you won't be aware enough to individuate; you won't be able to integrate the suppressed and lost parts of your whole, 360-degree self, and you'll completely miss the profound movements your psyche is trying to make.

If you express your hatred, you'll damage your hate target and launch yourself into a spiraling hate cycle that will totally disable you. But if you repress your hatred under a mask of pretense, you won't be conscious enough to uncover the issues that brought your hatred forward in the first place. Either way, you won't have the strength or agility you need to do your deepest work, and unfortunately you'll also intensify your hatred because your self-trashed boundary will now *require* the fiercely protective intensity hatred contains.

You have the right to feel hatred. In fact, there's no way to stop feeling it, unless you really want to hurt yourself with a steady diet of enforced repression. Hatred arises for a very important reason, and it should never be ignored. The only way out of hatred is to move through it, which means learning why hatred comes forward and how to honor its powerful, life-altering message. If you can take the reins and channel your hatred properly, you can fly through your most difficult issues and catapult yourself into new levels of awareness—without hurting yourself or anyone else. Hatred isn't the problem; not at all. In fact, the ferocity and power inside hatred can transform you, if you will just bring your empathic skills to bear upon it.

THE MESSAGE IN HATRED

I've always wondered, when we truly hate someone, why don't we just move on and live our own lives? Why do we stay so massively involved, with attacks and name-calling and endless complaints? Why can't we just let go? Why does hatred make us attach ourselves like parasites to the objects of our hatred? Therapist and author John Bradshaw answered these questions for me in a lecture with this saying: "Resentment is the strongest attachment." It's stronger than love and stronger than blood. (I am placing resentment and contempt into the hatred category because they carry very similar feeling— they're not identical to hatred, but they're close enough for our purposes.) I've seen and felt, when resentment, hatred, and contempt are present, a bizarre dance of glee and obsession. There's distinct relish in hatred and an utter craving for engagement and enmeshment that I couldn't grasp until I understood the fierce attachments beneath resentment and hatred.

When we express hatred, we fool ourselves into thinking that we're totally separate from our hate targets—that we're nothing like them, that we're stronger, truer, better, and more righteous. If this were the case, though, we'd have appropriate boundaries and the ability to treat people with respect. Resentment, hatred, and contempt don't arise when we feel strong and whole. No, they arise when our boundaries are ravaged by intense imbalances within us, and they bring with them the most concentrated anger possible. If we can channel hatred inside our own psyches, we can instantaneously reconstruct our boundaries, focus ourselves intently, and perform amazing feats of shadow-retrieval and evolution. When we express hatred (and let me remind you once again that hatred is not mere dislike) and focus all of our rage and disgust on the soul of another person, we're depending on them to live out parts of our own shadow.

This throwing of our unwanted material—this projectile vomiting of our own fierce imbalances onto the souls of others—can provide tremendous (though ultimately disastrous) relief.

Hatred arises when our suppressed material moves forward and destabilizes our sense of who we are. Hatred arises when our lost greeds, talents, longings, ferocities, and weaknesses bubble up from within our cauldron of suppression in order to be made whole. If we have internal skills and agility, we can raft through these powerfully disruptive moments and shoot forward in consciousness. We can grab on to our hatred and use its fierce intensity to set absolutely impenetrable boundaries, within which we can create white-hot crucibles for the contracts we've forged with suppression and internal tyranny. If we have no skills, though, we'll be unable to even tolerate these surging movements, and in most cases our lack of agility will send our shadowy aspects on a seek-and-destroy mission. Most often, we'll find people who typify our lost and stomped-on material (this is not a difficult task, since all humans carry all human traits), and we'll project our troubles outward through the expression of our hatred. In a very real sense, we'll use our hate targets as baggage carriers—these acts of projection can lighten our internal load for a while. The problem, of course, is that projection squanders our awareness, which means we won't be able to focus ourselves, restore our boundaries, protect ourselves, honor our true emotions, or respect others. When we project our material onto others, we lose our integrity, our honor, and our skills.

Let me take a giant step back and say that projecting material onto other people is a common practice—and it's not always horrific. Projection isn't a terrible thing; it's a human thing. We all project our shadow material, because we usually can't work with it in straightforward ways. (If we could, it wouldn't be called the shadow, would it?) In fact, most of us project our "good" shadow material onto others just as frequently as we project our "bad" material. For instance, when we admire a public figure, we often project our best selves onto them—we let them hold our talent, our courage, and our brilliance (these traits are suppressed into the shadow just as often as our uglier traits are). This is often a necessary passage, because most of us can't say, "My family raised me to be scientific, but I'll just ignore that and become a painter." No, we'll need to observe and idolize painters in order to bring our own art forward. We may even attach ourselves to certain painters (as if they personified painting) in a form of projection known as adoration. Carl Jung, who contributed massively to the understanding of the shadow, pointed out that projection is sometimes the only way we can become aware of our shadow material. He even went so far as to say that projection is the only thing that gets us out of our parents' houses. So adoring someone else's talent is a safe way to move toward our own.

However, you'll notice that strong adoration often moves to disappointment when our adored person acts like a regular person and not a divine being. This is the point when the projection slips, and we're supposed to let go and move into our own talent (and get back behind our own boundary). Unfortunately, most of us don't figure this out. We remain attached to our adored people and try to change them into our perfect vision once again, which launches us on a roller-coaster ride with them. When we find ways to reattach the projections, everything is peachy, but if they slip, we have to start all over again. It's an extremely unstable attachment that seesaws back and forth between infatuation and disillusionment. In many cases, this sort of adoration will even drop into hatred—into a fierce and shadowy attachment (think of stalkers and crazed fans, and you'll get the picture). This intense form of adoration, then, helps us understand what hatred is all about.

Hatred is a twisted form of adoration, and that's where that strange enmeshed glee comes in. Hatred is the underside of adoration, where the intensity, the shadow projection, and the enmeshment are identical in intensity, but different only in the material being projected. In the excellent shadow books of Robert Bly, Robert Johnson, and Connie Zweig (see page 402), each author points out that we can easily find our shadowy, unlived material by looking closely at the people we attach ourselves to through adoration *or* hatred. If people live out the beauty and talent we suppress, we usually attach to them through adoration, idolization, or infatuation. If they live out our ugliness, we usually attach to them through hatred, contempt, or resentment.

Most of us can understand the enmeshments we create with our idols and our adoration targets, but when we flat-out hate people, we're usually not aware of the strong and enmeshed attachments we create. Even hearing about it gives us the willies. Yet these are the facts: If we dislike someone, we can walk away; if we fear someone, we can run away; but when we hate someone, we do neither of these things. When we express our hatred, we attach ourselves to our hate targets with fierce glee.

When we find people who can really live out our unwanted material—our selfishness, our power, our arrogance, our brilliance, our ignorance, our sexual appetites, our stiffness, our mildness—there's almost a bacchanal in our souls. There's a kind of wild dancing and shouting inside us: "Look at those vile people! Look at them living all the things we can't!" We're mesmerized and fascinated, and we can't take our eyes off of them. We watch in sickened awe as they live out things we were forced to suppress—things so unwanted, so dangerous to our parents, teachers, or peers that they couldn't even be spoken aloud. We also watch in an angry disbelief because the ground doesn't open and swallow these bad people, God doesn't smite them dead, and night does not turn into day. In response, our own shadowy material begins to vibrate wildly, our suppression-formed self-image begins to crumble, and our angers and rages (not to mention our fears and terrors) pour forth in response to the incredible earthquakes erupting inside us.

When these earthquakes occur, most of us don't take this extraordinary opportunity to become aware of our own shadows and the enforced suppression we've suffered. No, most of us resist this deep movement, and instead vomit our hatred onto the people who live out our shadowy aspects—just as we vomit our enmeshed adoration over people who sing, act, or paint for a living. Whether we hate or adore people, we're igniting a twisted love affair in which our projection targets are forced to live out our shadows for us. When we enforce these shadowy contracts with others, our boundaries are stripped, our focus is thrown outside of ourselves, and our villages are in complete disarray. We also dishonor our targets—whether we hate them or adore them—because we force them to become something other than human.

If you can catch yourself at this point, you'll be able to perform the brilliant task of individuation, which begins the moment you realize that each of us carries all things human. Each of us carries greed and generosity, weakness and strength, bitterness and grace, tenderness and brutality, and on into infinity. You are all things, and the process of individuation is a process of remembering your whole self and making conscious peace with all of your elements, all of your tendencies, and all of your intelligences. When hatred arises, it's a signal from your soul: *Here are the things I can't live yet. Here is where I have lost my way.*

Your task when hatred arises is to channel your hatred honorably, because expressing your hatred and your shadow material will destroy your boundaries, while repressing your hatred and suppressing your shadow will drive you out of your mind and your body. The movement when hatred rushes forward is toward insight and integration of the suppressed materials that are struggling to make themselves visible. When you understand that honorable movement, you'll bless your hatred and your hate targets for showing you so clearly which parts of you are trapped in the shadow. Instead of remaining obsessed with your hate targets, you'll be able to disengage with honor and become upright and functional again. When you can channel your hatreds properly, you'll protect yourself and everyone around you from projection-based relationships of any kind.

The Practice for Hatred

Hatred says something true about your hate target, certainly, but it says far more about you. If you express your hatred, you may score some points at the expense of your hate target (and your humanity), but you won't learn a thing about the issues that brought your hatred barreling forward in the first place. Your job is not to point fingers, but to actually honor the brave soul who had the guts and the honesty to parade before you (even if he or she did it unconsciously) the lost and despised parts of your own psyche. Your job is to bless and protect your hate targets while you discover, digest, and integrate your own shadow material.

Therefore, hatred goes directly into your boundary immediately (if not sooner). This focused flare of rage and fury carries tremendous, life-altering energy with it, and this energy must not be squandered. It must also not be expressed onto other people, so this practice will have to be done in private or with the help of a companion (not your hate target!)

who has skills of his or her own. Hatred takes you into the raging rapids, where two specific mantras apply: "The only way out is through" and "This too shall pass."

Please set your boundary on fire and create a fiercely defined sacred space with the intensity of your hatred. Ground and focus yourself firmly, unroll a large parchment in front of you, and throw the image of your hate target onto it. Write, yell, project like mad, and get this image out in front of you. Complain out loud to this parchment if you need to. If it gets full, move it aside and create a new one. Keep projecting until you feel a shift inside you, then roll up your parchment(s) tightly so you can't read anything on it, fling it out of your personal space, and burn it with your hatred.

This first step protects your hate target from your rage. If you can create a flaming, powerful boundary around yourself, you can be brutally honest about your feelings inside your own sacred space while you protect your hate target from your wrath. Burning your contracts won't hurt other people, no matter how hot the fire gets, because you're not projecting anything at them, you're not talking to them, and you're not even looking at them—you're simply being honest about your real feelings in the absolute privacy of your own defined sacred space. In fact, the intensity of your flame will correspond directly to the level of separation you'll achieve. In this sacred ceremonial space, the intensity of your hatred will free you.

If you try to burn a hatred contract—a totally enmeshed, fiercely unconscious, and deeply twisted contract—with a little poof of peevishness, you won't move it at all! When you're in a hatred spiral with someone, you need a fierce and disruptive emotion to extricate yourself and rebuild your ravaged boundary from scratch. This is no time for gentility; you need the big guns. So go ahead and flame on—it will heal your boundary, your behavior, and your relationships. Your fierce emotions are only problematic when you fling them at others or stuff them into your shadow. When you can channel them properly, they will deliver the robustness you need to heal your serious imbalances. Bless your fierce emotions—they make deep soul-work possible.

When you've burned a few contracts with your hate target, you're ready to move on to the real work, which is to understand exactly what your hate target has been living out for you. You may want to get a pen and paper, because if you can write out (or just call out) the qualities that make your hate partner so odious, you'll be able to gain incredible clarity. It's important to avert your gaze from your hate target—to look down and to the side, to where shadow is—as you list the specific flaws your hate target carries ("What has fallen into the shadow?"). Get it all out of you; shine your spotlight on their selfishness and inconsistency, their brutality and ignorance, their lack of control, or their weakness. Then ask yourself if you have room for any of these inferiorities in your own life. If your answer is an explosive "Hell no!" then I'd say you've found your shadow.

When you know which parts of you have been trapped in the under-world, you can simply bring forward a contract for each lost aspect—for instance, for brutality, ignorance, or selfishness—and see what's in it. The powerful intelligence inside hatred will give you the intense focus you need to understand how these aspects dropped into your shadow and why you agreed to keep them there. Examining and then burning these shadow contracts will allow you to integrate your suppressed material ("What must be reintegrated?"). This won't turn you into a brutal, igno-rant, or selfish person; it will actually protect you because you'll no longer be tormented or seduced by brutality, ignorance, or selfishness in shadowy ways. When you reintegrate your shadow material, you won't suddenly enjoy brutality, ignorance, or selfishness, but you won't be endangered by them either. You'll be able to make healthy separations from people who live out those traits, instead of throwing yourself into twisted, hate-filled love affairs with them. When you can bring consciousness to previously unconscious aspects of yourself, you'll awaken your soul and restore flow to areas that were once suppressed and blocked. When you can bring your shadow material forward into the light of day, you'll immediately detoxify that material, and you'll reduce the amount of drag your shadow exerts on your soul.

When you can take your hatred in hand and channel it properly, you may even feel a certain gratitude and protectiveness toward your once-hated targets because you'll be able to see them as individuals, and not as the villains or heroes of your twisted fantasies. When you can see your once-hated targets as separate people with separate destinies from yours, you will have performed this healing in its entirety. Good work!

THE LANGUAGE OF EMOTIONS

When you've brought forward and burned a number of hatred con‐
tracts, you'll be in a very different place than you were in when you
entered this hate cycle. Please revitalize yourself by getting grounded,
resetting your boundaries, and rejuvenating yourself. Many people choose
to bring totem animals inside their sanctuaries after they've done shadow
work—as a way to maintain their newfound focus—perhaps falcons or
birds of prey, big cats, bears, crocodiles, or other predators. These are, of
course, imaginal representations of you, but it can be helpful to have these
watchful symbols keeping an eye on your boundary and your behavior.

When you're done for now, thank your hatred for holding up a mirror
to your soul, and let it know that it's welcome to return any time you lose
your way. Then go do something fun.

WAIT—DOES THIS MEAN I HAVE
TO ACCEPT *EVERYONE?*

After people perform this hatred exercise for the first time, they often
wonder if it's okay to dislike people for any reason, or if they should
just accept everyone, no matter what. Can you hear their anger trying
to create proper boundaries again? Can you see their judgment trying
to make good decisions? This is an excellent sign. This hatred exercise is
startling, and it often knocks people's feet out from under them because
they lose their sense of how to respond in the old ways. This sudden
change alerts their protective stasis tendencies, which seek new rules for
the new situation.

Here are the new rules: If you just don't like someone, that's fine. If
someone's behavior doesn't fit with your life, and you can walk away
from him or her without harm, do it! It's okay not to enjoy people and
not to be with them. It's okay to make adult judgments about whom
you will and won't spend time with. However, if you've got a lot of
furious intensity toward a person, and you can't detach until you change
or best him or her, that's not okay. That's enmeshment, that's projec‐
tion, and that's hatred. You have every right to feel your own hatred, but
no right to defile other people's souls with your unlived material. You
now have a practice for hatred that allows you to be honest about your

226

projections, your enmeshments, and your shadowy involvement in any hate-filled relationship.

I've noticed a fascinating tendency in people who try to transform their hatred into falsified love and acceptance (or enmeshed "healing" behaviors). I call this tendency the "cloak of the oppressor," which comes from one of my favorite sayings: "How often the liberator takes on the cloak of the oppressor." When we're not aware of our suppressed hatreds, they can easily hijack our attempts to accept or heal others. If we try to right wrongs, end injustice, and save the world before we've become integrated and upright, we tend to drag our unconscious shadow material right into the heart of our crusades.

For instance, I've seen countless unhealed trauma survivors in rescue-based relationships who end up retraumatizing the subjects of their efforts; women's groups that create social systems far worse than the allegedly villainous patriarchy could ever create on its own; environmentalist groups that pollute the public discourse so that no workable communication can take root; welfare programs so inhospitable and impoverishing that their subjects are actually better off on the streets; and victim's rights or therapy groups that unintentionally revictimize their members by trapping them in the first two stages of trauma. Our society is rife with unhealed shadow that makes many of our supposed liberators into our newest oppressors. Our misguided denial of hatred—our refusal to meet it head-on and channel it honorably—creates turmoil that is as unnecessary as it is unfortunate.

When you hate, your soul is ready to do some of the deepest work you'll ever experience. Do yourself and everyone around you a favor: get into a conscious relationship with your hatred and your projections. Don't repress your hatred, don't explode with it, and don't try to erase it by shellacking fraudulent acceptance on top of it, or you'll endanger yourself, your relationships, your "good" deeds, and your society. Channel your hatred properly, and you'll heal yourself and your world in awakened ways.

WHAT TO DO IF YOUR HATRED GETS STUCK

If, after you've performed your favorite rejuvenation practice, you're still fired up with hatred, please flip back to the practice for rage and fury on pages 183–85. These practices should help you dislodge any punishing contracts you have with your hatred and restore your flow once again. If these practices don't bring relief, remember that cycling angers or hatreds can cover up an underlying depressive condition, and depression is nothing to fool around with. Please take care of yourself and seek psychological or medical support if your hatreds are torturing you.

HONORING HATRED IN OTHERS

It is very difficult to create sacred space for hatred in other people if they have no skills and no awareness. Hatred is a rapids-level emotion that can cause real damage if it is handled dishonorably, and unfortunately, it is almost always handled dishonorably in our anger-impaired culture. Entering the sphere of a hate-filled person can be considered a five-alarm anger emergency, in which setting your own fierce boundaries is an absolute imperative. People who hate are not only dealing with severe boundary damage, but they're also being pushed and prodded by their own powerfully repressed shadow material. As you can imagine, anything you say or do could easily turn their hatred toward *you,* so you should approach very carefully.

I would go so far as to say that the true channeling of hatred is a solitary process (because it is so intensely personal); however, you can provide a steam-release valve for hate-filled people by simply allowing them to complain to you. This is a difficult task, and you'll have to keep grounding yourself and setting your boundary fiercely, but if you can let people talk themselves out, you'll provide them with the opportunity to bring all their material forward. This talking is a healing in and of itself, because people almost never get the opportunity to fully explore their hatred. Most of us stomp on hatred in others because it is so dangerous and frightening. We all know where hatred leads, and none of us wants to go there. Unfortunately, when we repress the hatred in others, we actually increase the pressure in their psyches, which increases the likelihood that their hatred will explode (or implode) in the near future. If you can meet these people where they are (instead of where you'd like them to be) and match their emotion by setting your own boundary on fire, you'll provide a healing alliance, so they won't be dangerously isolated in their hatred anymore. As it is with any emotion, it can be calming for a hate-filled person to feel that he or she has an ally. Emotional isolation is painful.

You won't have to become a counselor or a sage, because if you can simply welcome shadow-filled material into the light of day, it will immediately become less toxic. Their hatred will no longer be an unruly and menacing thing, because it will be out in the open, where it can be heard, addressed, and worked with honorably. Remember to silently repeat the hatred questions to yourself ("What has fallen into the shadow?" and "What must be reintegrated?"), and the twin mantras for intense emotions ("The only way out is through" and "This too shall pass") as you set and reset your boundary. Remind yourself that hatred contains powerful boundary-building and shadow-retrieving capacities, and bless the hate-filled people in your life. They're in the deep water, dealing with crucial, life-altering issues. If you can create sacred space for them, they may be able to catch their breath and bring their full awareness to the profound soul-work they need to do. If you cannot help, and the person cannot bring any awareness to his or her hatred, please take care of yourself and suggest (gently!) that the person seek support from a medical or psychological professional.

FUN WITH YOUR SHADOW

You can do some very useful shadow-retrieval work without needing to be overtaken by full-fledged hatred first. You can do this by writing down all of the qualities you see in someone you adore and in another person you gossip about now. Your gossip target will hold shadow for you (or you wouldn't spend time gossiping about him or her), just as your adoration target will—and both will bring startling insights to you.

If you can fully describe all of the qualities you see in your adoration target, you'll see a mirror image of your own soul's deepest wishes, dreams, and aspirations. You might not believe it at first, but it's true. If you can burn your contracts with your adoration target, and then imagine filling your personal space with these beloved qualities, you'll be able to begin integrating them into your life. Similarly, if you can describe or write out all the nasty qualities in a person you gossip about, you'll see a mirror image of the things you've been unable to express or live out. If you can burn your contracts with your gossip target, and then make room for these unwanted qualities in your personal space, you'll begin to integrate your lost aspects and heal your soul.

When you can perform these preemptive shadow-retrieval sessions, you'll most likely be struck by the dark comedy of your shadow and by the ways your hatred pushes you in the direction you actually need to go. I wrote the following poem about hatred in my late twenties. It's a true story, though the names have been changed to protect the ignorant.

ALL RIGHT!

As a child I despised orange,
hated its intensity, didn't want it near me—
hid in the soothing coolness of blue.
Got my colors done; no blue,
but orange, red-orange, orange-red, peach, melon, *apricot!*
After a while I swallowed my pride . . .
All right! I look good in orange!

As a teenager I despised scientists—scientists and college boys—
wrote anti-science fiction, huge immorality plays
about their cold, emotionless lives.
At 26, slammed into college
after finding out what life was like without it—
graduated valedictorian with a degree in . . .
All right! Science!

As an adult I despised poetry—poetry and advertising,
both equally excruciating, embarrassing ways
to promote a viewpoint.
Now, I've won an award for . . .
All right! Advertising!
And two for poetry.
Knowing all this, what do I now *dare* to despise?
Tall people!

You can create your own version of this creative process: When you feel hatred rising up in your soul, just ask yourself, "What is it in this dreadful person that I'm about to become? What essential part of me—what lost or suppressed aspect or talent—does this person represent?" Then set your own boundary very strongly, incinerate your contracts, avert your gaze from that poor soul to your own, and get to work—all right?

WHEN HATRED SEEMS JUSTIFIED: HATRED, FORGIVENESS, AND THE JOURNEY TO STAGE THREE

Many people who would never condone hatred in normal situations feel quite justified in hating people who choose to harm others. Many of us have a special hatred compartment reserved for criminals—especially murderers, rapists, abusers, and child molesters. These people don't live out unconscious parts of your shadow or mine; rather, they live out the shadow of our entire species. Those of us who survive contact with these people are often filled not just with anger, fear, and traumatic residues, but also with raging infernos and conflagrations of hatred. Though these hatreds are completely justified and understandable, their presence can make healing very difficult for two reasons. First, our culture has no hatred practice whatsoever, which means that these furious hatreds either get acted out in criminal behaviors or self-mutilations, or suppressed into devastating emotional disturbances, addictions, and manias, or unresolving cycles of depression, anxiety, and suicidal urges. When hatreds of this magnitude are ignored and dishonored, turmoil inevitably ensues.

The second serious impediment to healing from trauma is our culture's deluded perception of forgiveness. All survivors are cajoled, urged, and intimidated into premature (and frankly endangering) forgiveness by people who erroneously presume that hatred and forgiveness are in opposition to one another. In the section on anger and forgiveness (see pages 117–22), I spoke of the absolute connection between these two supposed opposites, but now that we've entered the rapids of hatred (which is the fiercest and most directed form of anger), we can speak more succinctly about the anger-supported process that leads inexorably to the third stage of initiation. In our empathic hatred practice, our honorable movement through the true emotive aftermath of trauma leads to deep forgiveness.

Once again I remind you that real forgiveness doesn't make excuses for other people's horrific behavior or set itself up as an advocate for your tormentors. Real forgiveness doesn't support the ludicrous fantasy that every-one always does his or her best (the healthier forgiveness phrase is "I see that you were doing what *worked* for you at the time, but it never worked for me!"). Real forgiveness knows that real damage has occurred, which is why anger, rage, fury, and hatred arise in front of it to help restore devastated boundaries. Real forgiveness creates a distinct separation from torment and tormentors, and this separation *requires* the boundary-restoring angers so that the passage through the underworld of suffering can occur. Anger (and rage and hatred) and forgiveness aren't opposing forces; they are completely equal partners in the passage to the blessed third stage of healing from trauma.

A personal example: In my late twenties, I was consumed with white-hot hatred, both for my primary molester (there were many after him) and for that bloodless concept of forgiveness people were forcing on me. My hatred isolated me severely, and its ferocity threw me back and forth—from furies and rages into appallingly grim suicidal depressions. I knew enough to channel the rages and depressions, but that loathsome forgiveness-is-saintly spiel kept spinning my head so that I couldn't see the hatred clearly enough to make heads or tails of it. I finally brought my linguistic and logical intelligences into the situation by searching through the dictionary, where I learned to my astonishment that forgiveness is the ability to show mercy. I had never heard that from any of the forgiveness pushers. No, they presented forgiveness as surrender, or as a renunciation of my need to acknowledge the damage I had endured. Fascinated, I looked up "mercy," which is the com-passionate treatment of the unfortunate, or a willingness to spare someone from harm. This was entirely unexpected—to learn that forgiveness could only come from strength, and the knowledge that you *could* hurt someone but consciously chose not to. I had never been able to take that position of power because I had never felt strong in relation to my molesters. I was too young, too small, and too outgunned in the original incidents, and that sense of impairment and inadequacy had grown up with me.

Traumas that occur in childhood can shape all further growth and development because traumatic postures tend to grow with the children—almost as if they are poured into the foundation of the house of their lives and hammered into the framing lumber along with the nails. However, there is deeper information underneath the trauma, and it surges forward with the intense emotions: the essence of a person can never be stolen, erased, desecrated, or destroyed. That essence seems to return on the wave of powerful, rapids-level emotions, as if the submerged, shadowy, but steadfast essence of the survivor is sending specific assistance into the very heart of the trouble.

If you know that anger resets boundaries and restores that which has been broken, you'll completely understand the need for rage, fury, and hatred in people whose boundaries have been brutalized. You'll see the deep logic of the presenting emotions and the intrinsic wholeness of the submerged person who is fighting to resurface with their powerful assistance. When you understand the healing and restorative powers of the emotions, you'll welcome them in whatever form they choose. You won't demonize this one, repress that one, or glorify this other one over here—and you won't allow forgiveness to loom above any of them. You'll understand that forgiveness is the end result of a deeply emotive process of coming back from the devastation of trauma and betrayal and into strength once again. You'll understand anger's profound connection to real forgiveness, and you'll understand the true definition of mercy: mercy can only arise from a position of strength that gives you the ability to harm, tempered by the ability to control your impulses and choose not to. That's the gift your properly channeled angers bestow upon you; they make you an honorable protector, not just of yourself, but of others. When you can channel your rages and hatreds into strong boundaries and use their intensities to absolutely obliterate your contracts with your traumatizer, you'll be able to achieve clear and authoritative separations. Your traumatizer will no longer haunt you because you'll have retrieved your strength and your instincts.

When I finally dove into this true forgiveness process, I was able to use my rage and hatred to destroy the nightmares and whisperings that taunted me, I was able to ground out the shadows of touch and revulsion from within my body, and I was finally able to clear the interference from my soul. This interference was easily identifiable because it always brought forth intense emotions. As I worked through my genuine emotional material, my molester stopped towering over me. I began to stand upright, and he became smaller and smaller, until I saw him not as a monster, but as a tragic and devastated figure and the object of my most profound pity. I

233

couldn't hurt him or wish him ill, because nothing I could do or dream of doing to him could approach the horror he created just by living in the way he did. Do you see? He has no power because no one is ever as powerless as when they hurt another—and he lives in a hell of his own creation. I have had to do a great deal of work to come back from the hell he created, but he destroyed his own soul by initiating a child into his diseased, traumatic nightmare. If I had stayed sick and virulently hateful in order to blame him—to prove that his crime was heinous—I wouldn't have changed anything for either of us. I would have only perpetuated a desperate and disempowering contract that ate away at both of us. But when I got well, I became free, and I became able to free others. Most important, I became able to be less murderous toward the people who had transgressed against me because I know now that the only person who gets hurt—truly, irreparably hurt—is the one who hurts others.

I sustained incredible damage to the foundation of my life's home, but my hatreds and furies came forward to prove that I still had unlimited strength at my disposal. With their fierce and unyielding assistance, I was able to wash away the filth and obscenity that clung to me—not through any bloodless, gutless erasure technique, nor through some half-baked fantasy of forgiveness. Instead, I dove into the awful truths of the first and second stages of my traumatic initiations armed with the powerful assistance of my own angers and hatreds (and with the certain knowledge that I had, in fact, already survived the assaults). With this support, I was able to ground myself firmly, incinerate hundreds of molest contracts, restore my boundary repeatedly, and finally stand upright as a fully resourced person. From that stance, forgiveness was a simple task because I had become clear enough and strong enough to extend true mercy. The trauma was over, and I had no need to stay enmeshed with my molester any longer. Hatred rebuilt my boundary, revitalized my psyche, separated me from horror, and restored my honor. The trauma was over.

If you can channel your own hatred and retrieve your shadow, you'll become your whole self again. You'll become a shadow-fortified (instead of shadow-persecuted) soul warrior who creates peace, true mercy, and honest forgiveness from authentic strength. Go you!

16

Fear

Intuition and Action

Includes Anxiety, Worry, and the Healing of Trauma

GIFTS
Intuition ~ Focus ~ Clarity ~ Attentiveness ~ Readiness ~ Vigor

THE INTERNAL QUESTION
What action should be taken?

SIGNS OF OBSTRUCTION
Constant worries or anxieties that decrease your focus and clarity

PRACTICE
Focus your attention on your fears. Prepare yourself,
act and move consciously, and revitalize your psyche with
the dynamic focus fear brings you.

As WE LEARNED IN our empathic practices, free-flowing fear brings you focus, instincts, and intuition. Fear hones your senses, alerts your innate survival skills, and increases your ability to respond effectively to novel or changing environments. When your fear flows freely, you'll feel focused, centered, capable, and agile. Sadly, our connection to free-flowing fear has been so disrupted that most of us have no understanding of fear whatsoever. Most of us think we know fear because we have experienced the mood states of worry, anxiety, trepidation, terror, or panic. However, none of these emotions is fear! Though we have all felt true fear (there is no way to survive without it), we have so completely confused it with anxieties and terrors that we have lost our ability to identify fear as the distinct and vital capacity it is.

Here are some examples: Have you ever avoided an automobile accident by instinctively maneuvering your car out of harm's way, or handled an emergency such as a house fire in a very calm and focused manner— only feeling anxious or jangled after the danger had passed? Each of us would most likely say that we felt no fear while the dangerous situation was occurring (and that the fear only arose afterward), but we would be absolutely wrong. Fear is the intelligence that takes over our bodies, our minds, and our emotions, and turns us into surprisingly masterful lifesavers. In fact, in those times when we're sure we feel no fear, when we're completely focused, brilliantly instinctive, and amazingly resourceful, those are actually the times when our fear is flowing freely.

Your task in the territory of fear is simple. All you need to do is learn to identify fear when it is flowing. For instance, when you're driving and checking both rearview mirrors, easing out of the way of slowed or speeding cars, signaling your intentions, and making eye contact with other drivers, your flowing fear is at work. Your instincts are fully engaged, you're constantly scanning your changing environment for novelties and dangers, and you're acting in a way that increases your likelihood of arriving at your destination in one piece. When fear flows through you, it makes you focused, lucid, and able to respond effectively to your environment. If you should come upon something startling or hazardous, your focus and readiness will allow you to act in ways that protect you and the people around you. Fear in its flowing state is your constant companion, not just in potentially endangering situations like driving, but in all situations.

When you're working at your office, answering phones, juggling schedules, carrying on two or three conversations at once, and tracking down supplies or contractors, your flowing fear (not your anxiety, your worry, or your panic) is on the job. Your entire being is engaged and focused; you're scanning through significant amounts of information, altering your behavior in response to changing demands, interacting with many people, machines, and businesses in unique ways, and ensuring that your business (and therefore your financial survival) will continue to thrive and respond healthfully to changing market conditions. When your fear flows freely, you become competent, capable, and intelligent in every area of your life. Most intuitive people aren't aware of this, but intuitive skills are intimately related to the instinctual energy of fear. Free-flowing fear gives each of us the capacity to identify, sort, translate, understand, and act upon the emotional and physical cues we pick up. There's no real magic to this (intuition is a function of lightning-quick neurological processes that aren't fully perceptible to our conscious awareness), but because our society has so completely vilified and rejected fear, intuition has been treated as a mysterious faculty instead of a normal, freely available, fear-supported skill.

Again, fear is not worry or anxiety, which jangle and nag at you when your instincts are in some way impaired (or when you're ignoring them for some reason), nor is fear terror and panic, which take over when your instincts have been utterly overwhelmed. Free-flowing fear will make you intuitive, agile, balanced, and safe—not because you meekly tiptoe through life to avoid all possible dangers, but because you can trust yourself, your instincts, and your resourcefulness in each moment. If you're generally capable, naturally intuitive, and focused, you're actually already connected to your flowing fear (even though you may not think of yourself as fearful). All you need to do now is to name your fear as itself, welcome it, and thank it for all its help. Fear is not your enemy. In fact, it may well be the best friend you have.

So what happened to fear, and why are most of us completely unaware of its true nature? I see three distinct problems that have led to this confusion. The first problem is that we don't name fear as itself—as our brilliant and innate capacity to act, move, react, and change our behavior based on the input we receive. We call fear our horse sense, our gut instincts, our little birdie, our survival skills, or even our guardian angel, but we don't call it *fear*, so we can't identify it properly. The second problem piggybacks on the first: because we can't identify fear when it's active, we often confuse the aftermath of fear (those jangled feelings we experience *after* we've escaped an accident or a hazard) with the fear itself. When our fear flows properly, it may take complete control of our bodies and minds, and steer us through hazards in utterly innovative ways. After the danger has passed and we've survived, our fear will retreat so that we can settle ourselves down. When our fear retreats, our bodies will need to discharge all their excess activation and adrenaline, our other emotions will need to scramble forward, and our minds will need to review and integrate our survival experience in any number of ways. Most of us, because we don't know fear, confuse this series of aftereffects with the fear itself. These jangled and fired-up responses are related to fear, and they need to be honored and attended to so that our fear can continue to flow properly, but they're not fear.

These first two problems can be dealt with rather easily, first by awakening to the true nature of fear, and then by understanding and working with the activation we experience in the aftermath of fear-inducing situations (we'll learn how in the practice on pages 244–45). However, there is a third area of confusion in our relationship with fear that comes not from fear itself, but from the relationship (or lack thereof) between our fear and our anger. This confused relationship, more than anything else, keeps us from identifying, honoring, or working with our exquisite and indispensable fear.

FEAR AND ITS RELATION TO ANGER

If you can imagine your healthy anger surrounding you—protecting you, defining you, and constantly monitoring your behavior—you can easily see that trouble with your anger will degrade your psychological boundaries, your relationships, your personal space, and your self-respect. If your anger is not channeled properly and honorably, you'll exhibit poor psychological hygiene. In this case, your fear will need to move forward in your psyche, not to increase your intuition and focus, nor to simply help you respond to change or novel stimuli, but just to help you make it from one moment to the next. I have been fascinated to note that our society's depression epidemic (depression is, among many other things, a sign of boundary impairment) has now mutated into an anxiety epidemic. Even at the societal level, trouble with anger leads to trouble with fear.

This following analogy may help illustrate my point: Imagine that you're driving on a rainy night in a car that represents your anger-supported boundary, while you (the driver) represent your fear. If your car is sound and free of leaks, if it has good tires and brakes, and if its windows are clear and the wipers work, your drive may be somewhat challenging, but not particularly daunting. When your car is in good shape, you can drive through most weather conditions without too much trouble, and if you should come upon a pothole, a darting animal, or a bad driver, the condition of your car will most likely help you deftly avoid those hazards. When your emotional realm is healthy, this is almost exactly the way your anger and fear work together; when your anger sets a good boundary and helps you define yourself in the world, your fear can pilot you through life without too much drama. However, if your car is a clunker with bad brakes, foggy windows, and old, streaky wipers, you'll have to be a hyper-vigilant driver just to make it through the storm. If you come upon any hazards, your car's condition will be a real liability, and you may not make it through the trip in one piece. When your emotional realm is unhealthy, this is almost exactly the way your anger and fear work together: when your boundary is decayed, ignored, and poorly maintained because you don't honor your anger, your fears will have to become hypervigilant and overly activated just to keep you upright.

Without your boundary, you'll be unable to monitor your behavior or identify proper behavior in others (which means your relationships will consistently unsettle you), you'll dishonor people or let them dishonor you for no good reason, and you'll be vulnerable most of the time. When you're in this sort of turmoil, your relationship with your fear will decay almost immediately. You'll have no privacy and no sacred space in which to regulate your emotions, and though your fear will move forward to protect you, its intensity may actually destabilize you when your boundary is weak. Fear asks you to focus yourself, but that's nearly impossible when you don't know where you begin or end; therefore, your increased focus will most likely turn into anxiety or paranoia. Fear also brings incredible amounts of energy and adrenaline forward to help you deal with threats, but if your boundary is weakened by your repression of anger, or overinflated by your explosive expression of anger, your increased energy will just leak or spike out of you. Everything that comes near you will be perceived as a threat (just as every new twist in the road is a possible death trap when your car is a lemon).

Remember that fear becomes activated when you encounter change. If you have no boundary, you'll be overtaken by jarring changes every time you walk through a room, step outside your house, encounter people or animals, answer the phone, or even open your mail. Without a strong boundary, you may experience amorphous anxieties, you may attack people verbally (or physically) or accuse them of plotting against you, you may stifle yourself and never speak up about your troubles, or you may drop into panic-attack cycles, simply because your fear has been forced to take an unnaturally forward position in your perilously unprotected psyche.

If your boundary is impaired, and you experience repetitive or unresolving worries, anxieties, terrors, or panic attacks, please take very good care of yourself because you're essentially dealing with an emergency. This emergency is not caused by your fear, but by the serious disturbances in your psyche that your fear is trying desperately to mend. Please visit your doctor or therapist as soon as you can, because anxieties and panic attacks take a huge toll on your body; they're not anything to fool around with. Until you can get there, though, try this and see if it helps: attend to this emergency by grounding yourself and imagining a contract in front of your body. As you ground yourself, allow any stuck or spiky anxieties and terrors to pour out of your body and onto the contract, and then destroy this contract with whatever level of intensity feels right. This empathic technique may help to calm your body so that you can focus yourself again. When you've destroyed a few of these contracts and are in a more relaxed state, please skip back to the boundary-definition section on pages 134–41, and make sure you fully understand what your boundary does. Then please reread the chapter on anger on pages 167–89 in order to restore the precise emotion you need to heal yourself (and give your fear a much-needed break!).

When your flowing fear is allowed to take its secure and proper position inside your well-defined boundaries, it will bring you an instinctive sense of readiness, focus, calm, and vigor. In fact, you won't seem "fearful" at all, just as you won't appear angry when you set your boundary properly. When your emotions are allowed to flow freely, they can heal, empower, and inform you in subtle ways so that you won't need to drop into obvious mood states. However, in order to create a space for this kind of healing flow, you must be enveloped in a protected and defined boundary wherein all your emotions can act and react harmoniously. This means that your emotional health is utterly reliant upon your ability to honor your anger, first and foremost. Remember the correct relationship between your anger and your fear: anger sets your boundary and protects your sense of self, while fear maintains your focus and readies you for any eventuality. They're a team.

THE MESSAGE IN FEAR

Free-flowing fear helps you focus yourself, identify where you are in relation to what you're sensing, and bring all your faculties into the present moment. Fear comes forward to give you the energy and focus you need to deal with change or novel situations. This often means that you have to stop what you're doing, or at least slow down. Unfortunately, most of us fight anything that tries to halt our forward movement, which means that most of us fight our fear. This is a serious mistake with serious consequences. Fear is not cowardice; it is the protective mechanism inside you that knows you're not adequately prepared for whatever is coming next. Fear stops you—not to immobilize you, but to give you the time you need to gather yourself and your resources. Flowing fear steps forward when you require extra skills—or time to take a breather—so that you can make it through the next moment. If you trust your fear and take time to focus yourself, it will give you those skills.

When you ask your fear the internal question, "What action should be taken?" your fear will tell you in no uncertain terms: "Stand still. Run! Speak out. Remain silent. Duck! Fade into the background. Walk forcefully. Move quickly to the left. Look stupid. Downshift and swerve. Yell! Roll into a ball and protect your head. Hide behind your book. Grab your children and get out of the house. Call 911. Listen carefully and slow your breathing. Don't worry—false alarm! Hit back! Don't hit back. Study and research before you commit. Take a deep breath and dive in. Go back home."

When your instincts are informed by your free-flowing fear, your actions will be unique to each situation you encounter. You'll have hundreds of options, and if you let it, your fear will help you choose the right one each time. Your fear is not cowardice; it is caution. It carries your survival instincts, which contain hundreds of thousands of years of resources and responses that helped your ancestors survive floods, fires, wars, stampedes, earthquakes, tornadoes, ambushes, famines, plagues, ocean voyages, riots, revolutions, inquisitions, and cross-continental treks. If you honor and listen to your fear, you'll have instant, in-body access to all of the information that helped your ancestors survive and reproduce, while millions of other people sickened or died in the very same circumstances. Think of it this way: the fact that you're alive proves that you and your ancestors are survival experts. If you listen to your fear, you'll have access to more expert information, instincts, and resources than you could ever possibly need.

However, if you fly over the top of your fear and charge ahead unheedingly—if you ignore, squash, or rationalize your fear away—you may make it through by the skin of your teeth, but you'll almost certainly initiate a feedback loop that will cause your fears to intensify or decay. Dishonoring fear (which most of us learn to do in early childhood) can lead to what is now called "anxiety disorder." This means that anxious and unhelpful levels of fear appear at odd times for no apparent reason, while focused and useful levels of fear aren't readily available when they're needed. This disorder does not originate in the fear or the anxiety; it often arises as a direct result of the way we've all learned to devalue, reject, and disable our fear (it can also arise as a result of chemical or endocrine imbalances, so please see your doctor or therapist if you're plagued by anxiety). Fear, like any other emotion, is supposed to arise when it's needed, deal with the issue, and then move on. If we don't welcome our fear because we're trying to be brave, fearless, polite, or whatever, we'll cripple our survival skills and throw ourselves into disarray.

Not listening to fear is almost a national pastime. Even when people learn something about the true nature of fear, they often continue to reject its primal wisdom. Many people have learned to thank their fears for warning them while they proceed with their fear-inducing event anyway. My observation is that this is a way to rationalize the fear away, as opposed to channeling it properly. While it's important not to let fear stop you completely (unless you're about to wander off a cliff!), it's even more important to find ways to work with, and not against, the instinctive brilliance your fear brings to you. When you can channel your fear properly, it will contribute a sense of self-preservation while it pushes you to study, prepare, and renew your understanding of courage as the capacity to live life on your own terms, rather than throw yourself headlong into fearless or daredevilish behaviors. While such behaviors (extreme sports, recreational drug use, and the like) often make juicy news segments, they can endanger your body and your life for no good reason. My observation of daredevilry is that it's a strange sort of emotional management technique that literally blows all the trapped and repressed fear out of the psyche in one big whoosh. Unfortunately, daredevils soon need bigger and more daring feats or an addictive repetition of thrill-seeking behaviors, because they tend to reject and walk over their everyday fears as a matter of course; they constantly repress their emotions and, as a result, begin to require fear blowouts just to keep themselves functional.

In truth, each of us (whether we're daredevils or not) has learned to impede, reject, and disable our fear in any number of ways. This is nothing to be ashamed of—it's how we were raised, trained, schooled, and controlled. It's also how we train and control ourselves, but it's not a life sentence. If you can connect consciously to your flowing fear (see the exercise on pages 35–36), its fine-tuned awareness will help you revive your instincts and your resources. Your fear will also reconnect you to your innate intuitive abilities. Your fear can give you free information and advice on any topic because it has its finger on the pulse of the true difficulties and obstacles you face. When you need answers about the future, your career, your relationships, or anything else, you should ask yourself what you fear. Fear, better than anything else, lets you know where you need to focus yourself in order to prepare for your next step.

Fear has another important function: it helps you know when you're encountering true change. When you're about to take on a new job, a new love affair, or any new direction in your life, your fear may move forward in its mood state. If you don't understand fear, you may stop yourself dead in your tracks or throw yourself fearlessly at the new thing; however, neither extreme reaction is helpful. If you can welcome your fear as a certifier of the newness you're facing, you can slow down, focus yourself, and rely on its instincts and intuitions to help you pilot your way safely and confidently into your new adventure.

The Practice for Fear

When you have free access to your fear, you'll tend to be calm and relaxed most of the time because your intuition will be fully activated, which means you'll be able to avoid unnecessary dangers without much effort. You'll tend to identify squirrelly drivers and maneuver around them long before they make offensive driving errors, and you'll tend to avoid unsafe people and areas, not because you feel actively anxious, but because something just seems to steer you in another direction. So your first task is to identify your fear and create a functional personal boundary in which your fear can work unhampered. You can do this by defining your boundary strongly, and grounding and focusing yourself inside your sacred space. When you have a strong boundary, the clear focus your flowing fear brings you, and the ability to ground out any wayward or distressing thoughts or sensations, you'll become intimately connected to your inborn instincts and intuition.

Your second task is to listen carefully when your fear asks you to slow down and prepare yourself for some sort of change. This request can come in the form of a queasy feeling in your stomach or in any other area of your body, in the sudden sense that you need to pop your ears or focus your eyes intently, in the sense that something feels "funny" or is nagging at you in some way, or in a sudden urge to make an unusual movement or change in your routine. As you reacquaint yourself with your flowing fear, it's helpful to create a phrase or bodily posture (such as saying, "Hold on; something's not right," or bringing your hands upward in a "wait" gesture) that will give you a few moments to check in with yourself and ask the fear question: "What action should be taken?" In most cases, your fear will alert you to some change in your environment. If so, simply note the change, make any necessary alterations to your posture, movement, or behavior, and thank your fear for alerting you. In other instances, your fear may arise when you're about to do something you know you shouldn't or when you're about to reanimate a behavior you've been struggling to change. Using your "wait" phrase or gesture will help you slow down enough to interrupt your old pattern and revive your healthier instincts.

If you can make room for your flowing fear in these simple ways, you'll make it easier for your fear to increase your intuition and instincts when you're in actual danger. If you know how to focus yourself and listen to your fear, you'll have full access to the resources you need to face and survive dangers unscathed (if it is at all possible to do so). Your fear, your intuition, and your instincts cannot make you invincible, but if you listen to them, they can provide you with the best survival information available to you.

LISTENING TO FEAR WHEN DANGER IS PRESENT

In instant-fear situations when you're in actual danger, you can also use your fear to strengthen your boundary; you can imagine the interior area of your personal space (inside your bright, anger-defined boundary) almost on fire with fear. This is an especially helpful technique if your emotions get stuck and your fear tends to agitate and immobilize (instead of prepare and instruct) you. If you can move your fear out of your body, you can use its intensity to strengthen your imaginal territory, calm your body, and restore your equilibrium—all of which will help you listen to your fear. With this simple empathic technique, you'll have access to all the benefits and resources of fear without being overwhelmed or incapacitated by them. Then, when you ask, "What action should be taken?" your fear will pilot you through the danger in any number of ways, depending on which responses will offer you the greatest chance of survival.

When you allow your fear to instruct your behavior, you may find yourself acting in absolutely unaccustomed ways: ducking when you're actually very strong, fighting back or dealing masterfully with the situation when you're actually very gentle, dropping all outward emotion when you're usually quite moody, or appearing emotionally agitated when you're usually quite calm. When your life is at stake, your fear will cause you to act in lifesaving ways that might never occur to you in any normal situation. However, you won't fight these instincts; you'll understand the genius of letting your fear and your hundreds of thousands of years of ancestral instincts take the helm. Your fear can think faster, move faster, and decide faster than you can, and if you let it, it will do whatever is necessary to keep you alive.

After the real danger has passed, and you're out of harm's way, your fear will recede somewhat so that you can calm yourself and review the situation. If you can take advantage of this cooldown period, your revved-up body will be able to shake off all its excess activation and adrenaline (actual physical shaking and shimmying are extremely beneficial), your emotions will be able to restore their normal flow, and your mind will be able to review the dangerous situation in many different ways. Unfortunately, most of us don't take advantage of this opportunity to cool down. We often clamp down our natural trembling, our emotional upwelling, and our mental excitation, and we pretend that nothing unusual has occurred. We tell people that we're okay, just fine, don't worry about it. This is extremely unwise, because this cooldown period allows us not only to shake off our excess activation (which is the only way we can return to normal functioning), but also to analyze our experience by running through it any number of times. This is probably the most healing aspect of fear: if it's honored and channeled properly, it gives us the immediate opportunity (while our memory is still fresh) to scrutinize and renegotiate our emergencies and traumas in many different ways.

These run-throughs, or flashbacks, can help you integrate those times when you were in danger. They are absolutely necessary for your future survival, because your survival skills don't just rely upon your ancestral instincts; they also rely upon your logical ability to examine and understand present-day situations where you're overwhelmed or endangered. When danger passes, your fear will recede just enough to help you cool down, but it will also keep you energized and on task so that you can mentally and emotionally replay the danger or trauma, and integrate your experience more fully. This replay process uses the material of the fearful or dangerous situation to help you delve into your strengths and weaknesses so that you can become more skilled and resourceful in the future. Sadly, instead of congratulating ourselves for surviving, thanking our fear for its excellent assistance, and bringing our entire village in to help integrate our experiences through review and scrutiny, most of us have learned to squelch this healing process. We interrogate this after-fear state

("I survived! Why am I scared *now?*"), ridicule it, or suppress it with avoidance behaviors, distractions, or addictions. This incompetent behavior then traps us in the hyperactivated after-fear state, which ensures our descent into unresolving wariness or anxiety.

If you can't or won't integrate your frightening experiences, you'll remain in a constant state of alarm and readiness: your adrenals will pump full-time, and you'll find yourself jumping, starting, and striking out at everything. Your body won't be able to relax, your sleep may become disturbed, and your eating habits may fall into disorder as well. You may also begin to cycle through memories of the frightening situation in a way that seems obsessive—you may experience persistent flashbacks, nightmares, phantom pains, disorientation, emotional volatility, and any number of behavioral disruptions. And here, in the territory of fear, is the entryway into the third stage of traumatic initiation—the welcoming back.

FEAR AND THE HEALING OF TRAUMA

If you can move consciously through the replays of a fearful situation, you can release your excess energy and adrenaline, cry, shout, shake all over, run around, recount your drama, or fall into an exhausted sleep—all of which will restore your flow and resilience. If you can consciously and intentionally work through your flashbacks with the assistance of your fear, you will return—in a safe and manageable way—to the isolation of stage one and the ordeal of stage two. From there, you can complete your initiation in triumph and welcome yourself to the blessed domain of stage three—where the end *will* be beautiful.

Going through a flashback looks like this: You focus and ground yourself inside your strong boundary and light your boundary on fire with anger (this creates a ceremonial container for this process). If your fear is extremely distressing, you should pour some of it out of your body and into your strongly defined personal space so that your body can relax a little. You can do this by imagining your fear as a light, a color, a sound, or a movement pattern, and seeing or feeling it flowing out into your personal space. You may even want to jump around and shimmy for a little while to release some of your activated fear. Then when you're centered, you can consciously replay the fearful situation from within your resourced sacred space.

The phrase "consciously replay" is crucial because it's important not to simply relive the incident (your fear already knows what happened; what it wants now is *new* information). As you move through the situation in your mind—and in this sacred space—you can work with it imaginatively; you can speed it up, slow it down, rewind it, manipulate it, and study it closely. You should also act out the trauma physically and role-play any number of alternate reactions. If you froze during the actual trauma, but you felt like running, you should imagine running, and perhaps run around the room. Then you can try freezing, yelling, swerving, punching, crying, or whatever occurs to you.

The key to resolving these flashbacks is to complete each movement that occurs to you, and to end your replay in a position of triumph (even if you didn't triumph in the actual incident). When you're in this sacred space, the facts of the situation almost don't matter; your task is to use your fear to learn, to try new things, to increase your options, and to add to your skill set. Remind yourself that you're already a survival expert (you survived, didn't you?). These flashbacks simply want to make you more expert, more skilled, and more resourced.

When you can see your flashbacks as brilliant survival tools, the replays can actually become fun and comical. You can move from a broken-down victim position into a powerful survivor stance. Your fear can contribute an agile, resourceful, and humorous "Jackie Chan" stance that will help you see yourself in an entirely new light. And if your flashbacks need to repeat themselves (because there might still be more survival information locked inside the situation), you won't see yourself as crazy or disordered; you'll be completely willing to enter each replay with focus and vigor. Then, when you've extracted all the information held in the incident, you can ground yourself, burn any contracts you need to, and rejuvenate yourself.

Even fears of the future (worries and anxieties about things that haven't happened yet) can be worked with in this way. If you can preplay fearful events in your mind, you can role-play any number of win-win scenarios before you get there and prepare yourself as best you can. Instead of squashing your worries with positive affirmations (which are complete lies if you're worried), you can access all of your elements and intelligences, work through worrying situations, and prepare any number of responses and plans to get you through. And if your fear increases as you imagine any worrisome event (which is a sign you should never ignore!), you might investigate the situation more closely, cancel the event, or change your involvement in a major way. If you listen to your fear, it will prepare and protect you brilliantly. Fear lets you know when something is amiss. Your task is to listen closely to your fear, help your body sense the direction of the fear, use your mind to respond to and prepare for the fear, and ask your vision to imagine a future where you survive victorious.

Actors say the only cure for stage fright—one of the most universal fears—is preparation, preparation, and more preparation. This is a good example of the wisdom of studying and listening to fear. Fear knows that this world is filled with dangers and novel situations, and in every way it tries to prepare you for them (if only you will let it). Fear stops you in your tracks when you're not prepared because it wants you to survive. Thank and love and honor your fear. It will awaken your intuition and your instincts, alert you to imminent changes, save you from making dangerous moves, protect you when danger is unavoidable, and help you rebuild yourself after danger has passed.

HONORING FEAR IN OTHERS

Honoring fear in others can be difficult, so prepare yourself for failure in this territory, because we've all been taught to slap down our own fears and the fears of everyone around us. Each of our psyches is crowded with knee-jerk statements that are antagonistic to fear ("There's nothing to be afraid of. Don't be such a scaredy-cat. No fear! I'm not afraid. There's no need to worry. Cowards die a thousand deaths," and so on), and these statements may burst out of you if you're not careful. The key to honoring fearful people is to treat them not as weaklings or overly reactive beings, but as intuitive people whose instincts have become activated. If you can shift your attitude, you can help fearful people connect to their intuitive abilities.

Fear works best when it is allowed to focus itself intently. A helpful opening question for fearful people is, "What are you sensing?" Let them know you take their intuitions seriously, and help them focus on whatever they're picking up. Ground yourself and set your boundary, because you may begin to sense the fear yourself when it is brought out into the open (this is why we so often suppress fear in others—we don't want to feel it ourselves!). When the fear is more focused, simply ask the question: "What action should be taken?" When fear is welcomed in this way, it will allow both of you to move out of harm's way with skill and agility.

If you have the opportunity to attend to people in an after-fear state, you can create sacred space simply by allowing them to feel their feelings. It's important to help them view their trembling, laughing, swearing, crying, or agitation as necessary parts of the intense experience they've just had—as an important cooldown period. This is a vulnerable time for people, so if you can protect them by placing your body between them and any onlookers while you verbally praise and support them (not in a condescending way, but perhaps just by stating the obvious: "Whoa! That was intense!"), you'll create a ritual container for them.

An important warning: Try not to hold on to people while they're in their cooldown period. Their bodies are processing massive amounts of adrenaline and energy, and if you grab on to them, you could interrupt their flow (almost as if you're a circuit breaker on their line). Gentle, minimal touch may be okay, but don't envelop them, or you could interfere with their process. If people reach out for you, certainly hold on to them, but wait until you're asked. Your proper position is to be an assistant; basically, you take your cues from them instead of taking the lead.

When they're ready, they'll want to verbally or mentally review the incident and examine it from a number of different vantage points. Here, too, let them take the lead. If you tell them what they "should" have done, they won't be able to find their own solutions (and anyway, you might be wrong). Follow their storytelling as a support person, and not as an authority. Fear itself is the true authority in the territory of survival, and if the person can connect with fear, he or she will become an authority as well.

When the trembling, laughing, crying, anger, and storytelling have moved through people, it's good to help them ground themselves with food, water, or hugs. However, it's important to wait until people have truly exited the cooldown period first, because eating, drinking, and touch help people focus themselves in the present moment and relax into grounding, while the cooldown period actually requires them to be focused on the past incident and somewhat hyperactivated. Don't rush this process. Wait until people have completed a number of retellings, until their emotions are settled, until any trembling and activated movement has ceased, until the color returns to their faces, and until they're able to breathe and speak normally. This cooldown period connects people to the healing heart of their own fear, it empowers and educates them, and it even protects them from decaying into post-traumatic disorders. Let this healing proceed at its own pace, wait until people are calm, and then offer the grounding of food, water, or touch (if it seems appropriate).

One technique that has been suggested recently is to engage the brain's cognitive processing centers soon after a fearful or traumatic experience has occurred. A 2009 Oxford University study had some subjects play the computerized block-stacking game Tetris after they had been shown unpleasant videos of injuries and accidents (the control subjects just sat alone after viewing the videos).[10] The subjects who played Tetris experienced far fewer incidents of post-traumatic flashbacks than subjects who were simply left alone. The hypothesis is that the brain is less likely to take the time to cement traumatic memories if its processing centers are engaged in other tasks. This seems to support the cognitive-behavioral approach, where anxiety-disordered people are taught to count backward from one hundred by threes when they begin to spin into an anxiety attack. In our elemental framework, we can see that letting the intellect work in its own way on a simple problem can help the emotional part of us settle down. Other suggestions for redirecting the brain include light-hearted movements such as dancing around the room or shaking off, or redirecting the senses with pleasant or delicious smells like vanilla, chocolate, cinnamon, or floral scents.

When fear is welcomed and respected, it alerts people to danger or novelty, prepares them to act decisively, contributes the energy they need to complete whichever action works best in each situation, integrates more survival data, and then retreats to its watchful (but not anxious or worried) free-flowing state—from which it continues to gather information, skills, resources, and knowledge. If you can remind yourself of this natural and empowering progression, you'll be able to create sacred space for fear—in others and in yourself.

WHEN FEAR GETS TRAPPED: WORRY AND ANXIETY

There are two distinct types of worry and anxiety. The first is a constant sense of dread, wariness, nervousness, and apprehension that arises when we're clogged with rejected and dishonored fears. There may be anxieties about going out of the house or making decisions, about natural disasters or attacks, about ill health, about the safety of our friends and family members, about money and finances, or about life in general. These amorphous anxieties don't increase our focus in useful ways; instead, they repeat endlessly, disturb our lives and our well-being, and don't resolve. This uncomfortable state is now called anxiety disorder, but the disorder does not come from anxiety; this hypervigilant behavior is actually a normal bodily reaction that occurs when we don't cool down or take full advantage of the healing information in our after-fear states (it can also be a symptom of chemical or hormonal imbalances, so please seek help if your anxiety torments you). Be aware, though, that therapeutic intervention can help with anxiety, but it can overemphasize specific worries while failing to address the situation that triggered the anxiety in the first place. We can deal with this or that worry, but if we continue to reject our fears, we'll continue to cycle into worry and anxiety. When this sort of feedback loop is activated, our healing task is not to shut down all fear, but to reconnect with flowing fear in conscious ways (see the fear practice on pages 244–45).

The second type of worry and anxiety is a response to fears of the unknown. With this form of anxiety, you'll feel a nagging sense of disturbance or distress, but you'll have no precise information to grab hold of. You may sense something amiss at a very subtle level—something about a person's voice, something about the way your car sounds, something about a smell or an image that seems out of place—but that's it. In situations like this, it's extremely important to focus yourself and take the time you need to sort out your perceptions, because your fear is giving you plenty of time to prepare yourself. This level of anxiety has a preparatory and predictive function: it alerts and readies you for something that isn't happening right now, but may happen in the future. I say "may happen," because this is the point at which you may be able to identify avoidable danger and get out of its way (or prevent it from happening in the first place).

Unfortunately, most of us fly right over the top of these subtle signals, sometimes because we don't trust our instincts, but often because we're in a rush or are trying to appear polite (or worse, fearless). Don't do this to yourself. Please reread the fear practice and acquaint yourself with this intuitive and instinctual emotion. It can literally save your life. In his book *The Gift of Fear*, security expert Gavin de Becker writes that almost every victim of violence he interviewed in his security practice was able to recall early and subtle cues and nagging feelings (which they nearly always ignored) that were trying to help them predict and avoid the violence that was just about to occur. Much of his practice is now dedicated to helping people listen to their protective and ingenious fears, regardless of whether those fears arise openly or in less obvious ways. Interestingly, Gavin de Becker is a survivor of childhood violence who dove into his wounds and returned with startling truths about fear that are lifesaving. He's a perfect example of someone who has completed the three-stage initiation process and is now a soul warrior and protector for us all.

Though worries and anxieties aren't always linked to physical danger, they always try to get your attention for crucial reasons. Pay attention and honor the signals your fear sends you. All emotions are true!

The Practice for Worry and Anxiety

If you're worried and anxious most of the time, pay close attention to your grounding. Connecting yourself to the earth and off-loading your tension is a wonderful way to calm and focus yourself so that you can feel safe. If you struggle a great deal with anxiety, you'll often experience serious chemical disturbances due to an increase in adrenaline, cortisol, and related hormones. Your body will need plenty of rest, contact with nature, restorative nutrition (adrenal and hormonal disturbances can trigger food allergies and eating disorders), and calming exercise like yoga, tai chi, walking in nature, or swimming—all of which can help you restore your balance. It's also important to reduce or eliminate stimulants (coffee, tea, sugar, chocolate, herbal energy-boosters, diet pills, excessive exercise, excessive sex, etc.) while you heal. When you're in an anxious feedback loop, your body can spiral into uncontrolled "fight or flight" behaviors—and stimulants will only add insult to injury.

When psychotherapists work with anxiety disorders, many adopt a desensitization and cognitive reframing technique that brings the intellect into the mix; this is a good approach. Let's say you're deathly afraid of spiders. In cognitive reframing and desensitization, your therapist would help you, in small steps, become able to tolerate spiders while you calm yourself with inner statements such as "The spider isn't after me—he's just walking on the wall." This process has been shown to greatly reduce fears, and for some people, it's enough. However, after running a heightened level of fear for extended periods, many people also need to address their hyper-activation with medications (such as beta-blockers or antianxiety drugs) that help to calm their exhausted bodies. Meditation can also be healing, but be cautious: certain forms of stillness and mindfulness meditation can increase anxiety in some individuals; if so, it's a good idea to switch to a moving meditation such as tai chi or qigong. Calming movement seems to be more healing than stillness for anxiety-prone people.

While strengthening your personal boundary is an important part of any fear work you do, it can be a difficult task when you're over-whelmed by anxiety. One way around that difficulty is to use conscious complaining (pages 146–49). Cycling anxieties trap you in a whirlpool of confusion and alarm; if you can swim the other way and bring your anger to your issues by complaining consciously, you can often break the cycle and restore your instincts and your sense of humor. If you can complain loudly and vociferously about something, you won't have to worry about it anymore because it will be out in the open where you can work with it in active ways. Conscious complaining helps you verbalize your amorphous anxieties, while it also restores your healthy anger and your focus. When your anger and focus have returned, you can calm and ground yourself, reconnect to your instincts and your intuition, and define your boundary once again.

Keep an eye on your boundary as you're coming out of an anxiety trance; when your fear is trapped in a feedback loop, your personal space can become small and puny in response to your lack of usable instincts. Pouring your anxiety into your personal space (once you have an anger-strengthened boundary again) will certainly help your body relax and heal itself, but it will also fill your personal space with enough energy to restore itself to its proper size. Your anxiety is only troublesome when it's trapped in your body; if you can channel it, it will restore your sacred personal space and give you access to unlimited intuition and information. Use it!

HONORING WORRY AND ANXIETY IN OTHERS

When people are stuck in the territory of worry and anxiety, they are near their fears but not yet able to work with them consciously. Anxiety and worry both point to real concerns, but they do so in a way that tends to confuse people. To create sacred space for anxious and worried people, you can support them in tracking their way back to their true and intuitive fears and their ability to act decisively. You can do this with a series of "What if..." scenarios that support and explore their anxieties (rather than suppressing or attempting to placate them). For instance, if a friend is overtaken with worry about an upcoming meeting, you can help him or her preplay a number of worrisome scenarios (dressing inappropriately, being late, babbling incoherently, etc.). In this host of worries, he or she will always find serious issues that really must be addressed before the meeting takes place.

We've all been taught to force our way through worries, but this is a real shame because they actually contain startling amounts of constructive (though not yet accessible) information. In this case, the underlying reality might be that the chosen clothes actually are wrong, that the chosen patter actually would sound like babbling, or that something in the work relationship doesn't feel right on some level. When free-flowing fear is uncovered, your friend will once again be able to connect to his or her own intuition and abilities. From that place, he or she can then make useful decisions and take corrective actions.

When you can help people create sacred space for the messages trapped inside their worries and anxieties, you'll make way for their flowing fear to focus and ground them so that they can hear their own true language once again.

Remember to welcome your fear in all its forms: as your free-flowing instincts, intuition, and capacity to focus yourself; as your mood-state ability to deal with danger skillfully and integrate it properly; and as the worries and anxieties that may be signaling an imminent hazard. Welcome and thank your fear.

17

Confusion

The Mask for Fear

GIFTS
Diffused awareness ~ Innocence ~ Malleability
~ Taking a time-out

THE INTERNAL QUESTIONS
What is my intention? What action should be taken?

SIGNS OF OBSTRUCTION
Being unable to decide, act, or believe in yourself
or your decisions

PRACTICE
Honor this time-out and stop looking outside yourself for
answers. Ask your internal questions; they'll restore your
instincts and your decisiveness. Intention ends all ambiguity.

THE MASKING STATE OF confusion arises when you can't or won't access your fears, and you've lost your instincts. Confusion actually tries to protect you by halting your actions, but it can easily spiral into a persistent and unresolving state. It's fine to be confused, but it's important to know why confusion appears. If you can unmask your confusion, you can revive your instincts and intuition, and discover why you're being prevented from taking decisive action.

When you're confused, you'll find yourself dithering, changing your mind constantly, and being nearly unable to focus or ground yourself. Confusion is essentially a form of dissociation that takes you out of commission when you've lost your way. It's a bit like apathy, which is also a masking state, but instead of being bored or lusting after shiny things, you can't decide *what* you want. In a confusion, you can't make decisions because they might not be the right decisions; you can't move ahead because you might move in the wrong way; you can't think clearly because you can't translate, store, or retrieve information properly; and you're often disconnected from the lessons of the past, so you tend to make the same mistakes over and over again. In confusion, your mind cannot focus itself, your emotions swirl around in unhelpful ways, your body loses touch with its instincts, and your attention flies off to a more peaceful perch somewhere above the commotion. If you fight your confusion and force yourself to make a decision, you'll almost certainly fall right back into the confusion again (or relentlessly second-guess yourself).

The practice for confusion is not to erase it or blast your way through it, but to take the time to discover why your psyche has become unhinged. Confusion stops you for a reason. My husband, Tino, who is a lucid dreamer, found the perfect cure for confusion in a dream in which he heard this saying: "Intention ends all ambiguity." Since then, if either of us drops into confusion about some decision, project, or relationship, we ask each other, "What's your intention?" This question immediately cuts through our fogginess and illuminates the struggles and difficulties we face. Our confusion lifts, our real feelings come forward, our focus and grounding come back, and we become able to think coherently and stand upright again. From this place, we can thank our confusion for stopping us, because we always find something seriously disordered in our instincts, our behavior, or our intentions. Knowing our intentions *does* end all of our ambiguity, and the saying is just as true if you say it backward: ambiguity ends all intention. Many thanks to Tino and the fiery dream realm; that vision is a definite keeper!

The Practice for Confusion

The practice for confusion is simple in theory, but sometimes difficult in reality. You simply ask yourself what your intention is—not which direction you should go, what choice you should make, or what thing you should do, but what your *intention* is. Confusion stops you when you're not following your instincts or your flowing fear (which is why you dissociate). Questioning your intentions will almost always help you pinpoint why your intuition and your focus have departed. In most cases, confusion arises to trip you up when your behavior or your motivations aren't compatible with your stated purpose in life. Pushing forward from a confused state will almost certainly take you far off your path; therefore, your confusion can be seen as an important emotional barricade. If you blindly push ahead, you'll almost certainly make a mistake, but if you can stop yourself and question your motivations and your intentions, you'll be able to reassess your position. When you can do this, you'll immediately realize (sometimes with a start, sometimes with a thud) why you've been unable to think or act. When you know your intentions, you'll know exactly why you've been so confused.

Here's an example of this practice: Let's say you're trying to decide between two jobs, but you absolutely can't. If you push forward and force yourself to decide, you'll probably become more and more conflicted until you drop into a serious confusion. Then you'll almost certainly make a decision you'll never feel comfortable about (but at least you decided—right?). However, if you can stop yourself and question your intentions, you'll most likely find that both jobs have serious and even insurmountable problems, and that the best decision would be to walk away from both of them. This can be a distressing discovery, especially if you've got to get a job right now because the rent is due. However, if you're dedicated to living a full and meaningful life, you'll much prefer scrambling for the rent this month and refocusing your job search over ignoring your intuition, selling your soul, and losing your vision. We all know people who took an ill-advised job just to pay the rent and are still working there—miserable and stuck—fourteen years later. Your confusion stops you for a reason!

Sometimes, however, questioning your intentions doesn't get you to the crux of the problem. In these cases, I've found that questioning each element one by one will illuminate the issue succinctly. I'll use a personal example: I was once offered a teaching gig on a cruise ship, which is not the way I want to work with people. However, I was absolutely doubled over with confusion about the job. I questioned my intentions and tried to get focused and connected to the village inside me, but the confusion raged on, and I didn't know what to do.

Finally, I woke up enough to organize my thoughts, and I asked each of my elements if they wanted to take the job. My fiery vision told me that this was not the image I held for my teaching career, so no, it didn't want the job. My airy intellect questioned the logic of doing something so clearly against my better judgment, so it didn't want the job either. My watery emotions were very clear—this job held no interest for them whatsoever. But my earthy body wanted to go on the cruise with a yearning that was flagrant! This was why I dropped into such confusion; I had a profound disagreement inside myself. My work then was to understand why my body lusted after the cruise (I desperately needed a vacation at the time), and to find better ways to meet its needs (I took some time off, took hot baths, went to the river, and scheduled some massages, which made my body very happy). Please note that I didn't punish or ignore my body—nor did I allow any of my other elements or intelligences to do so. My body's needs were absolutely valid, but there were much better ways to meet them than teaching on that cruise.

When you're confused, it's very important to understand that something aware inside you (sometimes very deep inside you) is actually working on your behalf. If you can stop yourself and reassess your position when your confusion arises, you'll be able to connect to that awareness and find your way back to the center of your meaningful, whole life. Confusion is not the problem—it's just a messenger. Stop yourself and listen closely to its message; it will help you find your focus, your insight, and your integrity once again.

HONORING CONFUSION IN OTHERS

Honoring confusion in others can be a bit tricky because you may be tempted to take an incorrect position as the knower of all things and the giver of all answers. Though your wisdom is important, it's far more important to support a confused person in restoring his or her own wisdom and instincts. If you become the answer expert, you'll only cement the confused person's helplessness and indecision. If you can remind yourself that others' confusion exists because they've lost their connection to their innate intuition and focus, you can gently steer them back to their own answers. You can do this by helping them work through their ambiguity. If they can state their intentions, their confusion and ambiguity will tend to lift immediately (if not, you can teach them to question each of their elements until they locate the roadblock in their psyche). Your task then, when people know what they want and need, is to continue to hold sacred space by supporting them in finding *their own* way back to center again. Confusion is not a sign of stupidity; it's a masking state and an ingenious roadblock. If you can help people honor their need for a time-out, you'll help them recover their instincts, their decisiveness, and their ingenuity.

18

Jealousy and Envy

Relational Radar

Includes Greed

GIFTS
Fairness ~ Commitment ~ Security ~ Connection ~ Loyalty

THE INTERNAL QUESTIONS
What has been betrayed? What must be healed and restored?

SIGNS OF OBSTRUCTION
Cycling suspicions that don't bring useful awareness to you or
stability to your relationships; or fevered avarice that places your
needs above all other things, including logic and honor

PRACTICE
Discern whether you're responding to disloyalty and unfairness
in others or to your own lack of self-regard and worthiness. In
either case, restore your boundaries *first;* then listen to your
intuition and honor the anger and fear inside jealousy and envy.

JEALOUSY AND ENVY ARE separate emotional states, yet they carry similar
messages: jealousy arises in response to unfaithfulness or deceit in an intimate relationship, while envy arises in response to the unfair distribution
of resources or recognition. Both contain a mixture of anger (including
hatred, so check your shadow!) and fear. Both attempt to set or restore

lost boundaries after they've intuitively assessed an authentic risk to your security or your position. If you can honor these two emotions, they'll contribute tremendous stability to your personality and your relationships. If your jealousy flows freely, you won't appear obsessively jealous or possessive; rather, your natural intuition and clear boundary will help you instinctively choose and retain trustworthy mates and friends. Similarly, if your envy flows freely, you won't appear openly envious or greedy; instead, your internal security will allow you to celebrate the gains and recognitions of others (even when they're undeserved) without ignoring your own need for gain and recognition. However, when you dishonor your jealousy and envy, you'll have trouble identifying or relating to reliable companions, and you (and everyone around you) will be disrupted by your disastrous attempts to bolster your self-respect and security by denouncing everyone else's, and grabbing everything you can get your hands on.

I call jealousy and envy the "sociological emotions" because they help us understand and brilliantly navigate our social world. Very few people share this view; our culture pathologizes most difficult emotions, but jealousy and envy seem to be targeted more universally than others. People who express these emotions are rarely honored; they are often called "insanely jealous" or "green-eyed monsters," which throws these emotions into the shadows. That's never a good idea, especially in regard to emotions that carry intuitive and protective information. Both jealousy and envy arise when you've detected a risk to your social and personal security. Shutting them down is like throwing a noisy smoke alarm out the window instead of finding out why it went off! When you stifle your jealousy and envy, you not only lose your awareness of the situations that brought them forward, but you lose your emotional agility, your instincts, and your ability to navigate through your social world and your relationships.

Many psychologists and laypeople have classified jealousy and envy as "primitive" emotions more suited to Neanderthals than to modern-day people. This is yet another example of misusing the intellect to pigeonhole and disrespect an emotional state. When the intellect is allowed to wage war on the emotions, the village inside us destabilizes, and functional intelligence decreases alarmingly. Classifying jealousy and envy as primitive and obsolete ignores the fact that the need for jealousy and envy hasn't declined in any population since the beginning of human history. If these emotions were truly obsolete, they would have disappeared by now. Since they haven't, our job as empaths is to find out why they're necessary. We'll start with jealousy.

THE MESSAGE IN JEALOUSY

Imagine yourself and your lover at a party. The two of you are entering into a committed relationship, you're appearing in public as a couple for the first time, and you're looking forward to the evening. As your lover moves off to get you a drink, he or she sees an ex-mate and smiles with such joy that you feel a sharp pain in your heart. You immediately push this pain away, and paste a smile back onto your ashen face in case some-one is watching you. Next thing you know, your lover and the ex are hugging and kissing each other in ways that make you wonder if it's truly over between them. When your lover disentangles and returns with your drink, what do you do? Do you repress your jealousy and present a happy face? If you do, your lover will probably appreciate it, but a little bit of your soul will collapse (and you'll probably fall into inadvertent sulking or brooding for the rest of the night). Or do you express your jealousy in its mood state and accuse your lover of betrayal? If you do, you'll gain the upper hand, but you'll damage your lover's self-image and reputation (there may have been no improper intentions). If these were your only choices—to hurt yourself or castigate your lover—jealousy would deserve its terrible reputation. Luckily, there is another option. If you can under-stand why jealousy arises (and what it brings to you), you'll be able to channel this powerful emotion honorably.

In the situation above, your free-flowing jealousy allowed you to read the situation accurately, because there is clearly a strong connection between your lover and the ex. Jealousy is a combination of intuition (fear) and self-protection (anger) that arises in its mood state when your most intimate and important relationships are threatened. Intimacy, and security in intimate relationships, is incredibly important to your health and well-being, so much so that you'll actually feel physically threatened when you sense betrayal from your mate. This sense of threat can cer-tainly be traced back through our lineage to more "primitive" times when mate selection and retention ensured physical survival in harsh climates. However, our intimate survival issues have not lessened in importance over the course of evolution, because each of us still faces present-day threats to our health, security, and well-being. Even when you're surrounded by creature comforts, you still require intimacy and security in your relationships because dependable mates still help to ensure your social and material status. Dependable mates still nurture and protect your children and your family, and they still provide intimacy, love, security, companionship, sexual communion, friendship, and protection. Healthy and committed relationships are vital to your social and emotional well-being, and in truth, to your very survival.

If your mate is unreliable, or your position as the primary focus of your mate is threatened (as it certainly was in the scenario above), your psyche will pour forth emotions and messages to help you face this very real threat to your security and well-being. There is no pathology in this—it's a natural and healthy response. However, if you don't listen to and honor your jealousy, it will tend to drag you into a feedback loop that can make your life very uncomfortable. If persistent jealousy is a major stumbling block for you, please look into David Buss's excellent book on the sociological and biological necessity of jealousy, *The Dangerous Passion: Why Jealousy Is as Necessary as Love and Sex*. It is an incredibly eye-opening book that defends jealousy as a natural and accurate emotion—even while it chronicles the horrific abuses caused by the repression and incompetent expression of jealousy. One fascinating finding Buss presents is that follow-up studies on couples who entered therapy to deal with one partner's "pathological" jealousy uncovered clear instances of hidden infidelity in an overwhelming percentage of the cases (and clear instances of crippling amounts of internal insecurity in the rest). In each case, the jealousy was pointing to a truly endangering situation of external or internal insecurity and acting exactly as it should have—to alert its owner to serious threats to intimacy, mate retention, and social well-being.

Remember that all emotions are true, even when they're unpleasant or filled with seemingly hazardous intensities. When jealousy comes forward, it does so for a valid reason. Your task is to acknowledge and welcome it rather than pretending you don't require security in your most important relationships. Jealousy is an important part of love and loving connections. In fact, true and abiding love, which opens your heart and soul in profound ways, will often call forth your jealousy. When you truly let another person into your heart, you essentially drop all of your boundaries—which means your psyche will need to protect this relationship that has now become a part of you. Jealousy plays an important role in this protective strategy.

The key to working with your jealousy is to identify when the sincere risks you perceive come from a betrayal by your mate, and when they come from your own sense of unworthiness or insecurity in the relationship. Just as it is with every other difficult emotion, there is no real alternative to channeling jealousy; the only way out is through.

The Practice for Jealousy

Jealousy contains anger, so you should send it into your boundary to help strengthen it after the shock-damage it has experienced. Jealousy usually feels rather fiery, either flaring and intense, or simmering and steamy; in either case, channeling it out of your body and into your boundary will reestablish your personal space and calm you so that you'll be able to get focused again. Setting your boundary with your jealousy will address your anger meaningfully, and from within your revitalized sacred space, you'll be able to address your shock and diminishment with renewed strength. Then you can access the fear-based instincts and intuition your jealousy brings to you.

If you attempt to take action (which is the correct response to the fear inside jealousy) *before* you restore your boundary with the anger, you'll most likely overcompensate and explode, or undercompensate and collapse. However, if your boundary is strengthened and stabilized first, your actions will arise from a position of grounded strength. When you create sacred space for yourself, you'll have full access to your intuition and your instincts, which means you'll have dozens of ways to respond (instead of the usual two: explode or collapse). You may decide to study the situation more carefully ("What has been betrayed?"), search your memory for any other incidents of betrayal (this is a brilliant use of the intuition inside jealousy), speak respectfully with your partner about your honest concerns, examine your own sense of worthiness and security ("What must be healed and restored?"), or perform a contract-burning session in order to become aware of the agreements you made as you entered into the relationship (faithfulness may not have been one of your original concerns, though it clearly is now!). Whichever action you take, you'll act as an upright and emotionally resourced person instead of a powerless victim. If you listen to your jealousy, it will increase your awareness and your ability to honor yourself and your mate.

If you throw your jealousy away by repressing it or exploding with it, your ability to identify and respond appropriately to faithlessness will deteriorate. Then the relationships you choose will most likely be so incompatible and destabilizing that you won't have the peace of mind you need to take care of yourself, balance your life, or examine your deepest issues. But if you can honor and listen to the brilliant information your jealousy brings you, you'll be fully able to withstand the often harrowing journey you must take to reach the core of any troubling relationship issue. At this core, you may discover not just information about your current mate, but foundational beliefs you hold about your self-worth and the worth of others, the familial programming you've ingested in regard to love and belonging, the contracts you still carry with your parents or care-givers (your first love relationships), or perhaps the ingenious tricks you've used to protect yourself against loss by unconsciously selecting incompatible people with whom you'll never truly be able to connect.

With the help of your honored jealousy, you may uncover intimacy contracts related to peer pressures, family rules and inconsistencies, media brainwashing, and just about anything else. If you can place those trapped and entrapping messages on nice big contracts and take a look at them, you'll begin to understand why relationships and jealousy have been stumbling blocks for you. Then you can use your jealousy to set yourself free. When you can roll your contracts up and wrap them tightly, you can encapsulate and enclose them as a way to separate yourself from their influence (now that you know what your contracts contain and why you agreed to them). Then when you can throw your contracts away from you and burn them with whatever intensity you feel (jealousy can make blazing bonfires out of those contracts!), you'll be able to take full advantage of the power of your emotions instead of being overwhelmed by them. Your psyche will be cleansed, your awareness will be expanded, and you'll retrieve your definition, your intuition, and your resources. Maybe the relationship that called forth your jealousy will continue, now that you're able to be a more conscious partner in it. Maybe it will fall away if your mate is untrue, or if you discover your own untruthful reasons for being in the relationship in the first place. Maybe you'll unearth serious feelings of inadequacy that require healing before you can truly commit yourself to any relationship. However your story unfolds, your honored jealousy will enable you to protect your heart and the heart of your mate. Don't treat jealousy as if it were an unwanted houseguest. Invite this guest in and embrace it fully; there's powerful healing knowledge inside jealousy.

If you've spent a lot of time in your life suppressing or exploding with your jealousy, you may find a world of emotions trapped behind it—especially angers and fears. You may find shame, hatred, rage, and anger bubbling up, or you may feel anxious, panicky, or confused. You may drop into apathy or depression, or you may move into sadness, despair, or grief. Don't pathologize these feelings! All emotions will move through you if you simply welcome them, channel them, and honor their brilliant information. If you need to, you can turn to the chapters that deal with whichever emotions come up for you, but know this first: increased movement and flow means you're doing everything right! Stand upright and congratulate yourself; your flow has returned! Use your multiple intelligences, feel your body, connect with your vision, and remember: you have emotions, but you aren't made of emotions alone. Emotions aren't your tormentors; they are your tools, your guides, your protectors, and your allies.

When you've moved through the contracts your jealousy can identify right now, please refocus yourself, refresh your grounding, brighten your boundary, and rejuvenate yourself as soon as possible. Jealousy helps you uncover and dislodge enormous amounts of information and old behaviors. This extreme change in your psyche will alert your stasis tendencies immediately—so you should rejuvenate every part of yourself right away. Refilling yourself intentionally makes your movements toward stasis as conscious and deliberate as your movements toward change. When you're done, thank your jealousy and let it know it's totally welcome in the future to help you choose, maintain, and watch over the most important relationships in your life.

WHAT TO DO IF YOUR JEALOUSY GETS STUCK

Persistent and unrelenting jealousy is rarely pathological. It's disruptive, uncomfortable, and often embarrassing (shame and jealousy often travel together, because both help you monitor your behavior and your relationships), but it rarely comes out of nowhere, for no reason at all. However, the raging-rapids form of jealousy is often so distressing (and hard to share with others due to jealousy's bad reputation) that it becomes easy to think of yourself as disordered. Though all of the skills in the jealousy practice above will help you move through any amount of trapped jealousy, this emotion is so powerful (and has been so powerfully dishonored) that approaching it may feel daunting and even impossible. If so, it's time to reach out for support. Traditional therapy can be very useful, as can cognitive-behavioral therapy. The most important thing to remember, though, is not to allow anyone to attempt to erase your jealousy in favor of some "nicer" emotion. Your sacred task in the territory of jealousy is to restore your boundaries, your intuition, and your ability to choose and maintain devoted relationships—not to forever rid yourself of the incredible healing force of jealousy.

HONORING JEALOUSY IN OTHERS

If you can simply help people honor and listen to their jealousy, you'll perform a great healing service. If you try to argue or shame people out of their jealousy, you'll disable their instincts and their boundaries. However, if you can welcome jealousy as valid and purposeful, you'll immediately calm and center the jealous person, which means that his or her boundaries and instincts will return. You won't need to be a sage or a counselor; jealousy comes complete with its own brilliant information and instincts, so all you really need to do is ask jealous people what they sense. This will help them honor the intuition inside their jealousy and validate the signals that have alerted them to trouble.

If people you know struggle with persistent cycles of jealousy, you can create sacred space by helping them see that their jealousy always arises in response to true threats to their well-being and intimate security. If they are entangled with a faithless mate, you can help them identify the situation by simply allowing them to speak. If the trouble is not in the mate, but in their own sense of insecurity (or their inappropriate choice of mates), you can also help them identify the situation by simply allowing them to speak. However, if their jealousy persists unchanged, you should help them find a good therapist who can assist them in uncovering the buried issues that disrupt their ability to experience healing intimacy. Jealousy is an intense emotion; if it is misused, it will spiral into a feedback loop and drop people into the rapids—which means they'll require more help than a friend can provide.

THE MESSAGE IN ENVY

Envy is similar to jealousy in that it contains a mixture of boundary-restoring anger and intuitive fear. The difference between the two emotions is that envy uses anger and fear to help you identify risks to your position and your security in your social group, rather than in your most intimate relationships. Envy alerts you to betrayals and affronts to your well-being, but it does so in connection to the fair and equitable distribution of resources and recognition, rather than to threats to your reproductive survival or your value as a mate. Envy is powerful because it responds to powerful threats to your social position and your connection to resources (money, food, privilege, protection, belonging, and status). Envy stands up for you in instances of unfairness or favoritism, or when resources have been (or seem to have been) pulled from you in deference to another.

Envy has been branded along with jealousy as a primitive and destructive emotion, but just as with jealousy, the need for envy also hasn't decreased in any population since the beginning of humankind. We are an inherently social species, which means that both jealousy and envy arise in order to monitor our social connections, social pressures, and social positioning. Both of these emotions help us function within our social structures. In more primitive situations, envy arose when an individual's position in his or her social group was seriously jeopardized by interlopers, shunning, or capricious authority figures ("What has been betrayed?"). In such cases, envy contributed the strength to reset boundaries and the intuition to understand which actions (among hundreds) should be taken to restore social position ("What must be healed and restored?"). If the individual's position had been destabilized, or worse, erased through banishment from the group, the strength and information inside envy would have given him or her the capacity and intuition needed to survive and perhaps seek a new group.

In the modern world, threats to our social position and our ability to gather resources haven't decreased in any way whatsoever. We now require more money, more resources, more things, and more infrastructures just to feed ourselves than our ancestors ever did. This means that the power and intuition in envy—which help us connect to and monitor our sources of material and communal security—are still incredibly necessary for our survival. Our key task is not to erase envy in favor of a more pleasant emotion, but to understand (and take full healing advantage of) its important intuitive and boundary-restoring capacities in our massively resource-dependent modern lives. Envy has a crucial protective function; it exists to keep us safely connected to the social structures and support we need to live and flourish.

Imagine this scenario: You've been at your job for six years, and you've worked your way up slowly. You now understand the structure, the hazards, the allies, the troublemakers, and the rumormongers. You know how to read your supervisor's moods, and you know when and how to suggest changes in ways most likely to be implemented. You enjoy your work and you've got a lot of vision, but you don't sense an opening for your vision to be fully supported. You think of leaving, but you couldn't match your salary or your accrued vacation at another entry-level position, and you've just reached the level of dental insurance where you can finally have your long-needed bridgework done at 30 percent of the cost. All in all, it's not a bad job.

Suddenly, a bright young man is hired on, and as you watch openmouthed and envious, he learns to deal with your supervisor and even the troublemakers in ways you've never imagined. If you don't know how to work with your envy, you'll probably make one of two ineffective choices. If you repress and stomp on your envy, you may look more professional, but since your envy has arisen in response to a very real threat, it will have to return (most likely in sneaky ways that will embarrass you). When your squelched envy sneaks back in, you may find yourself sniping at the newcomer (or your boss!) without meaning to, "forgetting" important work assignments, or making completely avoidable mistakes for no apparent reason. Repressing your envy will topple your boundary, decrease your intuition, and reduce your effectiveness to the point that you may actually endanger your position at work all by yourself. This new man may even be called in to help (or supervise) you! Repressing your envy takes you out of commission at a time when you need to be focused and completely able to think on your feet.

Your second ineffective choice is to express your mood-state envy in subterfuge or sabotage. You might engage in open sniping at the newcomer, secret alliance-making to maneuver around him, or subtle snubbing behaviors to force him out of the loop. Here's the problem: each of these warlike maneuvers will hurt and degrade you and the newcomer, disrupt your work environment, and perhaps disable the entire business—all of which will threaten your position in far more insidious ways than this newcomer ever could. If the newcomer is seen by higher-ups as your victim, you'll immediately lose face and become the grandiose and self-absorbed "bad sport." If the newcomer has better social skills than you do, he'll discover a way around you (which means he may have to destabilize your position at the company just to save himself). If your battles take up a great deal of your time and energy, your work performance will suffer. It's very easy to see why envy has such an awful reputation. Both the repression and warlike expression of this powerful emotion create nothing but harm to other people, your own position, and your ability to function wisely within your social structure.

Luckily for us, there is a healing third way to utilize the excellent anger and fear that live inside envy. When you honor and welcome your envy, you'll have the inner strength and intuition you need to reassess your position and the threat posed by this newcomer in valuable ways. Instead of crippling yourself with repression or attempting to cripple your new co-worker with sabotage, you can use the vitality in envy to strengthen and prepare yourself for the many changes this man will inevitably bring to your workplace. When you can restore your boundary and observe the situation from within your sacred space, you'll be able to withstand the shock of this man's sudden appearance in your established social group. You'll also regain the equanimity you need to scrutinize your own modus operandi with the help of the startling new information this man's arrival has brought to you. If you like him, you can welcome him to the job and learn about his valuable social skills firsthand, and perhaps add to your skill set by adopting (or at least evaluating) some of his techniques.

If you can't tolerate him, you can do some important shadow work (see the hatred chapter on pages 215–34), which will give you the strength you need to examine why your job strategies don't work very well, while his so clearly do. With this new information, you can reassess your job and your career path within the company, and perhaps see for the first time how deluded you've been about your ability to work within this corporate structure. This is not a fun experience, and sometimes it's disruptive, which is why envy comes forward. When your social position and your connection to the distribution of recognition and resources are threatened, as they clearly are in this example, you'll need an immediate infusion of boundary definition and intuition. You'll need to be able to think on your feet, act quickly, restore your sense of self, channel the appropriate shame you may feel if your behavior has been less than stellar, reset your boundary, and create and implement any number of win–win scenarios at a moment's notice. Envy gives you all of this, if you will only use it.

Envy contributes the precise skills and abilities you need to deal effectively with any threat or change to your social status or financial viability. Properly honored and channeled, envy doesn't make you war-like or submissive; it enables you to understand social structures, to work within those structures or leave them behind if you cannot work within them, to gather and nurture resources and recognition without devaluing others (devaluing others is an exceedingly poor social strategy), and to add to your social survival skills. When you dishonor your envy, you become destabilized, isolated, and endangered, but when you allow it to flow freely, it gives you the internal security and intuition you need to meet and respond to the many threats and sudden changes you'll experience in your struggle to gather resources and protect yourself honorably in our modern jungle.

The Practice for Envy

The anger inside envy is powerful, so it should go into your boundary as soon as you feel it. You can even imagine setting your boundary on fire in order to strengthen yourself (and to protect your envy target from harm). When you can honor the intense anger inside envy and move it out of your body, you'll be able to calm yourself enough to focus and access the intuition envy carries with it. Just as it is with jealousy, if you attempt to take action *before* you restore your boundary, you'll overcompensate and explode, or undercompensate and collapse. However, if your boundary is strengthened and stabilized first, you'll be able to ground and focus yourself inside your sacred space, where you'll have access to your multiple intelligences, your emotions, your bodily instincts, your vision, and your integrity.

It's important to be surrounded by your village of resources at times like these, because if you're not, you may hold on to your behaviors and attitudes as if they were precious heirlooms or vital organs, instead of decisions and strategies you adopted in the past for whatever good reason you had at the time. If you can treat your behaviors as strategies, you'll become able to explore and amend them (with contract burning) in favor of newer strategies that may fit into your present-day social situation in more advantageous ways. This is not to say that all envy-provoking situations require you to change your demeanor or your behavior. However, envy arises in response to real threats, either from an interloper, from an authority figure who may not have your best interests at heart, or from an internal sense of insecurity that lessens your capacity to fit effectively into your social milieu. The anger inside envy arises to give you strength, but the fear arises to give you the instincts and intuitions you need to make any number of corrective and healing actions. Envy contains both emotions because *both* emotions are necessary in the situation. This is not merely a time to act (especially not if your boundary is impaired!), nor is it merely a time to restore your boundary and your previous position (your previous position may be in jeopardy); change has occurred, and your envy arises to keep you protected, effective, and agile in the midst of that change.

If you can bring forward contracts with your envy target, with your superiors or the authority structures under which you labor, with your own position or title (in order to uncover the expectations you may have woven into this identification), or with anything else that arises naturally from within your envy, you'll be able to unearth many of your beliefs and stances. You may uncover core beliefs about your worth and value in social structures; childhood programming about your value to your parents and your family; sibling and peer issues that have been suppressed but are actually still directing your behavior today; and perhaps even the ways you try to assert your independence by refusing to fit comfortably into *any* social structure.

When your envy is welcomed and channeled honorably, it will help you uncover unhealed issues and traumas that continue to haunt your present-day behavior. When you've restored your boundaries, your intuition, and your social expertise, you won't have to collapse or explode with your envy because you'll be able to assess and face the threats that brought your envy forward in any number of different (and more valuable) ways.

Please be aware that mismanaging your envy can and does create trouble throughout your emotional realm—especially with your angers and fears. Don't be surprised if shames, angers, rages, hatreds, apathies, fears, anxieties, panicky feelings, and confusions come tumbling out of you while you're channeling envy. Any trapped emotion creates a dam in your emotional realm, and relieving it may cause your other emotions to surge forward for a while until your flow is restored. This is certainly an intense experience, but you've got the skills you need to raft through any surge of emotions. If you can notice and welcome these emotions (if you need to, skip to the chapters that deal with whatever emotions you're feeling), they'll contribute the information and focus you need to heal yourself, and then they'll move on as they should.

Please remember that your task is not to manage your emotions, but to become a fluid and agile conduit through which emotional energies can flow freely. It doesn't matter whether your emotions are pleasant, uncomfortable, mild, or intense—what matters is that you use your skills to welcome them, channel them, and honor their vital information. Remember the twin mantras for all intense emotions: "The only way out is through" and "This too shall pass."

When you've examined and destroyed the contracts your envy can identify right now, please refocus yourself, refresh your grounding, brighten your boundary, and rejuvenate yourself as soon as you can. The channeling of envy creates immense changes in your psyche; therefore, you should use your rejuvenation practice to refill every part of your personal territory so that your movements toward stasis will be as conscious and deliberate as your movements toward change. When you're done, bless your envy and give it an honored place in your emotional realm. It will give you the inner strength and awareness you need to observe and even celebrate the gains and recognitions of others while you nurture your own connections to resources, social support, and recognition.

WHAT TO DO IF YOUR ENVY GETS TRAPPED (OR DECAYS INTO GREED)

If envy is a huge stumbling block for you, and your envy doesn't move at all after you've tried to channel it a few times, you may need to call upon the support of a therapist. Trapped envy is powerful, and it can throw you into the rapids. I've noticed that serious and persistent envy often relates back to parental inconsistencies or sibling rivalries that were never dealt with properly. When a child experiences constant injustice and threats to his or her sense of entitlement as attention and resources are continually diverted to others, there can be serious boundary impairment. The opposite is also true, in that there can be serious boundary impairment in children who were raised with too much entitlement and, therefore, never developed a healthy sense of what constitutes *enough*. The unstable behavior that inevitably follows this boundary damage will then disrupt each of the child's other emotions and his or her social skills.

If the child grows to adulthood with no connection to healthy envy, he or she may become a distrustful, self-absorbed, and deeply greedy person who will do anything to best the other guy. The worldwide financial meltdown of 2008 is a perfect example of greed raging unchecked through financial institutions of every kind, eventually creating a vortex that sucked everything into itself, leaving many of us ruined simply because others—many of whom were already ludicrously wealthy—couldn't control their greed. When people and institutions don't understand the concept of enough, their envy mutates into rapacious greed and turns them into bottomless pits of unheeding, debased craving. The same is true for politicians and their governments: when politicians and leaders (who so often come from the overindulged upper classes) imbue their governments with their own sense of unearned entitlement, they tend to see every place on the earth as theirs to own or control. Our American government's warlike, jingoistic, xenophobic, and isolationist reaction to the attacks of September 11 is a perfect example of how unchecked greed for power only works for a little while—and then eventually pulls everything and everyone into hell with it.

Though the techniques in this book can help you heal from a childhood that twisted your envy into greed, you'll need a skilled therapist in your corner as you work through core issues of betrayal, emotional and financial abandonment or overindulgence, unheeding want, and confusion about what truly constitutes injustice. Reach out if you feel overwhelmed, and retrieve your instincts, your intuition, your boundary, your healthy shame, and your sense of honor.

HONORING ENVY IN OTHERS

Envy always arises in response to true threats to social standing and connection to resources and recognition, either in the outer world of social structures, or in the inner world of psychic structures. Unfortunately, when envy moves to its mood or rapids states, it can be hard to work with. Here's why: Envy tends to run alongside shame in most people because almost no one knows how to channel this tricky emotion. If people have chosen to repress envy throughout their lives, their shame will become uncomfortably activated due to their constant self-abandonment (crushing your envy will sometimes protect your envy target, but it always endangers you, and your shame won't like that one bit). On the other hand, if people have chosen to express their envy in warlike and self-absorbed ways, their shame will also be uncomfortably activated (your shame moves forward when you dishonor others, not just because you're behaving badly, but because dishonoring others is almost always a terrible social strategy). As a result, many people feel humiliated in the presence of their own envy.

Another impediment to working with envy is that it's got such an awful reputation—even worse than jealousy in most cases. We seem to have more permission to feel jealousy than we do to feel envy. If you can buck this trend and make room for envy in yourself and others, you can help to detoxify it and reduce its humiliating aspects, which means it will be less likely to cycle into greed. If you can create a sacred space and honor envious people by asking them what they sense, you'll help them connect to their own intuition and information again, which means they'll be able to identify the threats they face, explore their many possible responses, and revive their own instincts. You won't need to offer advice or be an all-knowing sage, because envy will bring its own powerful healing wisdom to the situation.

If you can support, listen to, and honor envious people by inviting them to speak and explore their perceptions, you'll help them discover where those threats originated and what to do about them. However, if a person's envy persists unchanged or cycles repetitively, you should help him or her seek a skilled therapist who can assist in unearthing the issues; when envy becomes trapped in a feedback loop, it can spiral people into intense suffering and/or ravenous greed, which means they'll require more help than a friend can provide.

Remember to welcome your jealousy and envy in all their forms: as your free-flowing sociological intelligence, as your mood-state ability to identify betrayal or unfairness and then restore and heal any violations, and as the rapids-level intensities that may signal serious threats to your social standing and security. Welcome and thank your jealousy and envy.

19

Panic and Terror

Frozen Fire

Includes Healing from Trauma

GIFTS
Sudden energy ~ Fixed attention ~ Absolute stillness
~ Healing from trauma

THE INTERNAL QUESTIONS
What has been frozen in time? What healing action must be taken?

SIGNS OF OBSTRUCTION
Cycling attacks of panic and terror that immobilize
and torment you

PRACTICE
Focus yourself on your internal questions. Remember: You've
already survived. Panic and terror exist to help you renegotiate
your trauma and move from survival into wholeness.

I'VE SEPARATED PANIC AND terror from the fear chapter because these emotions bring us survival skills that help us do three very specific things.[11] We're all aware of our "fight or flight" responses to danger; these two panic- and terror-based responses can protect us from harm, but there is another response that isn't as well known—it's called "freezing." In many dangerous or traumatizing situations, fighting and fleeing aren't our best survival options because we may not be strong enough or fast enough to avoid danger. If our healthy panic and terror can help us freeze and dissociate (or go into shock or numbness) in response to extreme danger, we can often survive the unsurvivable. Freezing is a brilliant option in many situations because it can dull our senses to excruciating pain, protect us from overwhelming stimuli, and present a corpselike demeanor to our attackers, who may become less interested in the attack when we exhibit no emotion and make no sound or movement (this is a possum's lifesaving strategy, and it works!). However, in the aftermath of panic and terror, there's so much activation that it's hard to revisit, renegotiate, and integrate the situation, as all fears ask us to do. It's especially difficult if your terror made you freeze, because people often equate freezing with cowardice.

If you've turned directly to this chapter and haven't read through the chapter on fear, you should go back and read it before you proceed. Our distorted relationship with fear makes our lives difficult indeed, but it makes the lives (and the healing) of panic sufferers almost impossible. If you don't understand fear, you won't have access to your instincts, focus, or intuition, which means you won't have the capacity to work constructively with the sudden actions panic and terror compel you to make. If you don't understand the purpose of fear, you may scorn your own and other people's freezing behaviors, which means you won't be able to view panic and terror with any useful insight. Understanding the message of fear (and its relation to anger) is imperative; please take time to understand fear.

When I observe panic and terror empathically, I sense incredible brilliance that connects us back through time and underneath our cultural conditioning to our most ingenious survival instincts. However, I also know that people who suffer from panic attacks are dealing with a paralyzing and debilitating condition, and that antianxiety medications and beta-blockers can truly help them. Unrelieved panic and terror can destabilize your endocrine system, your sleep cycles, your appetite, and your equilibrium. If you're a panic sufferer, certainly get thee to a doctor and calm your body and your mind. When you feel stable again, try the panic practice in this chapter and see if it helps you work with this rapids-level emotion.

Let me remind you again that panic-inducing traumas aren't restricted to serious assaults, combat injuries, or criminal acts. Traumas routinely arise from such mundane events as witnessing accidents or violence, from standard medical or dental procedures, or even from being emotionally assaulted by the everyday name-calling, prejudice, overstimulation, or isolation we all endure. If you experience panic attacks but you cannot track them back to anything you'd call a trauma, please look again. Our society trains us to dishonor, ignore, and dissociate from our thoughts, our emotions, our dreams, and even our physical sensations. If you're a sensitive soul and you've become dissociated in response to this unrelenting onslaught, your psyche will need to revisit each instance of dissociation in order to help you reintegrate yourself, add to your skill set, and come fully back to life. Don't make the mistake of relegating trauma or panic responses to the territory of violent crime or gory car crashes. You're a sensitive and unique organism, which means you'll respond to startling and overwhelming input in your own unique way.

If your panic has helped you to freeze or "zone out" so that you could survive a terrorizing or dissociating situation, your psyche will need to replay stages one and two of that trauma in order to scrutinize and integrate the experience. Unfortunately, if you don't understand panic and the brilliant survival skills of freezing and dissociation, you can easily plummet into an unhealthy relationship with freezing behaviors and experience panic attacks that can literally immobilize you. However, if you can understand that your sudden lack of movement and consciousness actually ensured your survival (you're alive, aren't you?), you can bring your full awareness to your panic cycles. If you can learn to see the act of freezing as the genius-level response it is, you can reenter that frozen state with vigor and courage, restore your flow, and move purposefully into the exquisite territory of the third and final stage of traumatic initiation.

If you need support in dealing with panic cycles that stem from trauma, please see Further Resources for the work of Peter Levine. He's a psychologist and medical biophysicist who has studied trauma and stress for over three decades. His books walk you step-by-step through trauma-relieving processes that are empowering, integrating, and fun.

THE MESSAGES IN PANIC AND TERROR

I'll rephrase something I wrote in the chapter on trauma: danger is a fact of life. Trees fall, dentistry happens, stressors occur, cars veer, people yell and hit, and molesters prowl; danger is everywhere. The issue is not in the danger or in the dissociation we experience in response to it, but in the fact that we don't have the resilience to reintegrate ourselves or regain our equilibrium once that danger has passed. Restoring our resilience is the key to reintegrating our psyches after traumatic incidents, but that task can seem daunting when rapids-level panic and terror are involved. Panic and terror can be debilitating, but they have something in common with every other emotion we have: they contain the precise amount of energy needed in the situation that called them forward—no more, and no less. Your emotions don't fill you with enormous amounts of energy for no reason!

When your terror and panic are activated in response to trauma, they move forward to increase your adrenaline in case you have the chance to fight or flee at any time during your ordeal; to help you freeze; to release heightened amounts of painkilling endorphins so you'll be more likely to survive any injury; and to help you dissociate if necessary. All this preparation takes a great deal of energy, which panic certainly contains. After the trauma has passed, your panic will retreat, but it won't disappear completely. Like fear, panic will stay activated in order to give you the energy you need to reintegrate yourself, shake and tremble all over, and replay your trauma in any number of ways. If you don't take advantage of this cooldown period, you'll remain in a hyperactivated state, and your panic will have to remain activated because the trauma won't truly be over. This hyperactivation often cycles you into panic attacks, which also contain a great deal of energy. This energy doesn't exist to torment you, but to help you navigate through your flashbacks and reintegrate yourself. Panic attacks don't occur without reason; they arise to help you confront your trauma ("What has been frozen in time?"), move through your replays any number of times, access new and different instincts and responses each time ("What healing action must be taken?"), and activate your body, your mind, your emotions, and your vision in service to your healing. It takes a great deal of energy to do this; panic and terror carry that much energy.

When panic attacks or flashbacks arise, your psyche is signaling very clearly that it's time to move to stage three, to replay the situation that sep-arated you from the everyday world, to explore the stimuli that brought your terror forward, and to move through your traumatic memories in instinctive and empowering ways. But it's hard to move at all—let alone move to stage three—when your terror and panic compel you to freeze and dissociate. It's like being on fire and being trapped in a block of ice at the very same time. This kind of panic fills you with heat and energy, yet it forces you into completely frozen immobility, which doesn't make any sense intellectually. However, when you can bring your fully resourced awareness to the situation, you can use your skills to honor both sides of panic. You can honor the enforced stillness by focusing yourself and sitting quietly, and you can honor the hyperactivated state by brightening your boundary intensely, grounding yourself strongly, and channeling the panic out of your body and into your vibrant and protected personal space.

Panic and terror bring forward enough energy to help you reinte-grate after trauma. If you can stay grounded and shoot the rapids with their assistance, panic and terror will help you renegotiate your trauma, restore your instincts, and come back to life. But make no mistake—it's an intense process. Panic can feel boiling hot and freezing cold, pains can come and go, screams can bubble up, and you may need to kick and yell or run around the room. When you come back from a deathlike experi-ence and reintegrate yourself, you'll need to tremble, shake, jerk, swear, kick, and fight—just like the animals in my childhood practice did when they returned to their bodies after being hit by cars or mauled by dogs. But then, when you're back in one piece, your panic and terror will sub-side naturally—as they're meant to—and you'll have your life back. When you're reintegrated, you'll once again be able to move, think, dream, sleep, feel, laugh, and love—not because you're perfect and unblemished, nor because you've erased all traces of trauma from your soul, but because you're fully resourced and whole again.

Here's an important point: This practice can help you reintegrate and channel your panic and terror properly, but it won't erase panic and terror from your soul. It can't! You need panic and terror; life is hazardous, and there will continue to be times when your panic will need to come forward to help you to fight, flee, freeze, dissociate, faint, or go numb. Panic isn't the problem. Problems only arise when this powerful emotion gets caught in a feedback loop, but those problems exist in all emotions— even joy! You're not supposed to erase your powerful and unpleasant emotions; you're supposed to become skilled at working with them. Your sacred tasks in the territory of panic and terror are to restore your flow so that panic can move through you when it needs to—during emergencies and traumas—and to restore your resilience after your panic has risen up to save your life. Panic is your ally.

If unresolving panic-attack cycles have been an issue in your life (and you're being treated effectively by your doctor), you should focus on your grounding skills so that you can release some of the activated energy that's trapped in your body. It's especially healing to increase your grounding from your solar plexus area, which is the home of your adrenal glands. It's the area that often takes the biggest hit during trauma, which means it often needs the greatest connection to the earth. In order to calm and heal your overworked adrenals, it's also important to limit or omit your use of stimulants—certainly the obvious ones: coffee, tea, soda, diet pills, herbal energy concoctions, cocaine, methamphetamines, and chocolate, but also the less obvious ones, such as sugar, gambling, overspending, and sex addictions. Stimulants, because they arouse your adrenals and separate your attention from your body, tend to drop you into cycles of unfocused worry and anxiety, and those are too close to panic and terror for your health and well-being. Chronic worries and anxieties are moderately disruptive to all of us, but they're seriously unsettling to anyone struggling with unresolving panic-attack cycles.

If you use stimulants to jack yourself up and out of your panic, you'll most likely need something to bring yourself down before bedtime. Please also look into your use of alcohol or the anesthetics (painkillers, cigarettes, heroin, antidepressants, marijuana, excessive reading or TV and movie viewing, and overeating), and reread the chapter on addictions (see pages 77–89) to get a clearer view of the assistance your psyche is seeking in your addictions and distractions. Please be gentle with yourself and know this: If your soul is injured and dissociated, you'll absolutely require distracting, alleviating, or energy-boosting substances and practices just to keep yourself going. There's no shame in your movement toward relief; there are just better ways to find it.

The Practice for Panic and Terror

If you're prone to panic attacks, please don't barrel into this practice unheedingly. You need help calming yourself and your body before you begin. You've also got to have all of your skills under you, and a strong sense for when you're dissociated and when you're not before you can work in this territory. You also have to be able to identify and channel all of your other emotions, because when panic gets trapped in a feedback loop, it creates a dam in your emotional realm—which means that any and all of your other emotions can get stuck behind it, so you'll need to be quite agile. Also, because unresolving panic attacks can disrupt your adrenal glands and your chemistry, you may need to strengthen your body in a number of ways before you attempt to channel panic and terror. I strongly recommend that you seek medical and psychological help; unresolving panic is debilitating!

The practice for panic and terror follows the basic steps you learned in the practice for fear (see pages 244–45). You focus yourself and set your boundary strongly. Then you ground any part of you that feels tight or uncomfortable. A body dealing with panic needs a lot of soothing, and grounding can provide a relaxing sense of relief. This increased grounding will help you unfreeze yourself, while each of your other skills will prepare you to revisit and renegotiate the original traumatic situation in order to create any number of new outcomes.

When you're in the territory of panic, you may find that you have enormous amounts of energy stored in your body. Good! Before you enter a flashback, it's helpful to pour this energy into your boundaries and your personal space. This technique helps you calm your body and revitalize your boundary, but it also helps you maintain your connection to the power and force of panic, which you can use during your replays to run like the wind, duck and feint, kick your way to freedom, scream bloody murder, or cry like there's no tomorrow. During your replays, you should treat your body as the survival expert it is and follow its wisdom. If you feel like curling into a ball, do it. If you feel like punching and kickboxing, do it. If you feel like trembling, howling, hiding in a closet, or shaking all over, do it. Every action you take will add to your survival skills and your resources.

However, there is a possible difficulty you may encounter: when you imaginatively revisit your original trauma, you may dissociate! Since panic can trigger dissociation (that's one of its vital functions), replaying the separation of stage one and the ordeal of stage two may cause you to experience dissociation and numbing again. This is certainly disruptive, but it is not actually an impediment to healing when you have skills. If you can't work through your replay in an integrated state—if you shoot out of your body like a grapefruit seed, or if you have no conscious memory of the incident—you can work with your traumatic material from an imaginative and dissociated position first.

Basically, you ground and focus yourself in the present moment—where you're safe—and imagine or envision a trauma similar to yours. Then you can imagine going in as a rescuer—of yourself! I had to use this technique to access my own sexual assault memories, because I was very young when the first attacks occurred, and the atmosphere and situations were so awful that I couldn't get near them in any useful way. Once I began to access and work with my traumatic experiences in this imaginal way, I was able to go in as my adult self and save my child self over and over again (there was a lot of yelling and shadowboxing going on in my house, I can tell you!). And it works just fine. Within a few days, my body began bringing forth its own stored pains (which I was able to work with and ground out), my mind became able to organize its fractured and disconnected memories (which allowed me to incinerate my contracts with the behaviors and beliefs I could now identify as trauma-based), and my emotions became more distinct and fluid (which gave me the information, courage, and resources I needed to go deeper into the replays).

After a few weeks of working from this dissociated position, I was able to get into my body, place myself in a few of the positions I remembered from childhood, and fight, scream, and kick my way out of the replays—always completing every flashback in a position of triumph. It was wonderful! My body reawakened, my mind became resourced, my emotions became my allies (instead of my tormentors), and my attention nestled itself firmly inside my body—because it didn't want to be anywhere else. Now I can stay in my body when traumatic memories come forward because I know I'm safe, agile, and resourceful enough to deal with them. For decades, I ran from those dreadful memories in order to be "happy." Who knew that jumping into them would bring forth strength, healing, laughter, and joy?

Each time you work through a panic cycle (whether you're dissociated or integrated), it's important to rejuvenate yourself (see pages 151–3). The channeling of panic and terror moves amazing amounts of energy through you and creates massive changes in every part of your psyche. These changes will alert your stasis tendencies, which will want to refill you in whatever way they can. It's vital to refill yourself consciously so that your movements into stasis are as conscious as your movements into change. It's also a very good idea to eat or drink something after you've channeled panic, because your body will need some soothing and grounding. If you can immerse yourself in water (in a pool, a lake, the ocean, a bath, or even a shower) you can help your body calm itself. Hugging and massage are also excellent grounding activities, but please wait a few hours or perhaps a day before you engage in sexual activities. Sex brings your partner right into your body, and your body will need some private time in order to reorganize itself. You don't need to swear off sex for an extended period, but you do need to respect your body's newness and sensitivity. You'll also need some time to heal from your adrenal fatigue, so it's important to give your body plenty of rest, relaxation, healing food, and time in nature (especially near bodies of water). It's also a good idea to see a therapist to get ideas about how to keep from falling backward into old panicky behaviors.

As you're working through your panic cycles, bodily movement will help you heal and reintegrate yourself. Yoga, qigong, and tai chi can help you restore your flexibility, while dancing, swimming, and sports can restore your flow, your strength, and your playfulness. Martial arts and self-defense classes are also wonderfully supportive because they teach you the honorable rules of engagement for physical conflicts. Model mugging workshops (where a heavily padded instructor teaches you to defend yourself as he or she attempts to mug you) are also an excellent idea, but be sure to tell the instructor you're working your way through panic and

THE LANGUAGE OF EMOTIONS

trauma. The model mugger needs to know that when you fight back, your panic may give you superhuman strength! Model muggers are heavily padded and expertly trained, but a word to the wise is never wasted.

Remember that this practice won't erase panic from your soul; it will simply restore your flow so that panic won't dam up your emotional realm. When your flow is restored, you'll be able to connect healthfully to all of your fears, and if necessary, to flee, fight, freeze, or dissociate in the future if that's your best survival option. Then when the trauma or emergency has passed, you'll be able to use the intensity in your panic to work through your replays with the support of the fully resourced village inside you.

WHAT TO DO IF YOUR PANIC GETS STUCK

If, after you've read through this chapter or tried to channel your panic, its cycling intensifies, it's time to seek professional help (which may involve medication) from a therapist or doctor. There is no shame in this at all. Panic-attack cycles can be extremely destabilizing, and you may require a great deal of support, therapy, healing, intervention, and time before you can restore your equilibrium. Reach out. Help is available.

HONORING PANIC AND TERROR IN OTHERS

This is not a job for friends and acquaintances! If someone you know is dealing with panic-attack cycles, please help that person find expert intervention and therapy. Also, let him or her know about Peter Levine's books (see Further Resources on page 399). Dr. Levine offers grounded and immediate healing techniques that remove the taint of pathology from the panic sufferer's ordeal.

A TALE OF TWO KITTIES (OR THE IMPORTANCE OF MOVEMENT IN THE RESOLUTION OF TRAUMA)

I learned a vital lesson about the healing aspects of physical movement from two of my beloved stray cats, Rufus and Jax. Both cats came to us through some sort of radar, because we didn't plan on having animals. Rufus was a muscular gray tabby who approached us by crouching in the manzanita grove beyond our driveway and crying pitifully whenever any of us appeared in the yard. My husband, Tino, began meowing back at Rufus, and over a period of weeks, got him to come near enough to eat regular meals. Rufus was absolutely traumatized and would run and jump at any noise or movement, but he always showed up for meals and meow sessions with Tino. Eventually, he allowed us both to touch him, and soon he demanded petting before every meal. He remained skittish, and he didn't like any stranger, but he became safe, well-fed, and willing to be loved.

Jax was a sleek black-haired adolescent whose mother (another stray) dropped him off at our house before she moved on. Though Jax had been raised as a stray, he had been protected by a very good mother and he was able to bond with us immediately. We were fascinated to observe the different ways Jax and Rufus responded to the world. Jax was always curious, while Rufus was always suspicious and often terrified. Jax enjoyed rough-housing and would often take a swipe at us in the middle of a play session (as if to teach us how to play fair), while Rufus needed to be touched in very specific ways or not at all. If we touched forbidden areas or moved in forbidden ways, Rufus would smack us very hard and end all contact by running away, often not reappearing for hours.

Jax and Rufus also responded to novel stimuli in nearly opposite ways. If Jax came upon a new smell, sight, or sensation, he'd react viscerally, pull back, shake off as if he had water on him, and then reengage with the novel thing until he understood it. Rufus, on the other hand, rarely allowed novel stimuli to come anywhere near him. If he was forced into contact with something new, he wouldn't shake off as Jax did; instead, he'd freeze and then run as if from a gunshot. The differences between them fascinated me, and they translated directly to human behaviors. Unhealed trauma survivors often hold their bodies rigidly and respond in very limited and stress-filled ways to their environments, while healthier people generally move more often, more easily, and in more and varied ways.

I experimented on my own traumatized body by changing my exercise from my usual regimented routines that only exacerbated my rigidity; I began dancing, stretching, and moving in unaccustomed and previously avoided ways. Many old memories moved into my consciousness, many buried pains came forward, and many unusual thoughts began to cycle. I used my empathic skills to support the unraveling of my traumatic postures, and soon, freer movement returned to my spine and my psyche, simply because I chose to move more like Jax than like Rufus. I saw that holding myself rigidly and protecting injured parts of my body were ways to hermetically seal my injuries and my traumatic memories. This was an excellent coping skill when I was little, but it created its own pain as I grew up. Restoring unstructured movement helped me release many physical remnants of my traumas, and it restored my flow.

We were able to apply a simplified form of this healing method to Rufus. Obviously, we couldn't teach him to dance or do tai chi, but we found ways to help him ease some of his body armoring by introducing different petting rhythms and by touching him in "forbidden" ways and then in "Rufus-approved" ways, over and over again while we soothed him. Sure enough, he became more fluid in his movements and more able to respond resourcefully to stimuli. He became much more able to deal with sudden noises, and he began to ask for petting whenever he saw us, instead of just at mealtimes. I don't know if Rufus will ever be the rollicking ball of fun Jax is, but he has made real progress.

If you've survived trauma, be aware of your own movement patterns and of frozen or numbed areas in your body. Do not pathologize them (freezing and numbing are excellent survival skills) or blame yourself for holding on to them. Sealing off painful or damaged areas is a very good coping mechanism, because until you have skills, the pains you carry can seem overwhelming. Restoring flow and movement to your traumatized body is an intense experience because memories begin to move, pains begin to appear, and thoughts and emotions begin to awaken. This is not an easy transition to make when you're undefined, ungrounded, and dissociated—and your psyche knows this, which is why the armoring remains in place. You need all your skills under you before you can restore authentic movement and allow your trauma to present itself for healing. When you have your skills, though, you can move through this healing process as a grounded and resourced survival expert.

Please remember that you may have armored yourself or dissociated in response to just about any painful occurrence, because you can almost never control when or how such painful events unfold. You were most likely not allowed to back away and shake yourself off when you were frightened (as Jax and all healthy animals do), nor were you likely allowed to gather your resources when overwhelming stimuli bore down upon you, just as you probably weren't allowed to tremble, cry, or cool down after the danger had passed. Most of us were told to hold still, stop crying, stop whining, stop backing away, stop fighting, and stop wriggling! Consequently, our natural instincts, responses, movements, and emotions were repressed and short-circuited. When you can reenter your traumas consciously and revive your instincts and your free movement again, you'll be able to shake off your traumatic residues and restore your Jax-like strength and agility. When you can restore flow to all parts of your psyche, everything inside you will become awakened, resourced, and able to respond to any hazard or opportunity you can imagine. Flow is the key.

Remember to welcome your panic and terror in all its forms: when it makes you flee, when it makes you fight, and when it makes you freeze. It knows what it's doing! Honor it for helping you survive, and use its intensity to revisit and renegotiate the dangers and traumas that brought it forward. Welcome and thank your panic.

20

Sadness

Release and Rejuvenation

Includes Despair and Despondency

GIFTS
Release ~ Fluidity ~ Grounding ~ Relaxation ~ Revitalization

THE INTERNAL QUESTIONS
What must be released? What must be rejuvenated?

SIGNS OF OBSTRUCTION
Unmoving despair that does not bring resolution or relaxation

PRACTICE
Release that which no longer serves you; this will restore flow,
tears, and healing water to your body and your soul. When you
can truly let go, rejuvenation and relaxation will surely follow.

WE'VE BEEN RELYING ON sadness in its free-flowing state to get into our
bodies, connect to the earth, and release things we don't need. Now we'll
visit sadness in its mood state.

Sadness is your psyche's water-bearer; it restores life-giving fluidity and
movement when you've become arid and inflexible. Sadness helps you
slow down, feel your losses, and release that which needs to be released—
to soften into the flow of life instead of holding yourself rigidly and
pushing ever onward. Sadness asks you to trust in the flow of time, in

the surprising flow of vision and inspiration, and in the ebb and flow of human relationships so that you may release yourself and others from contracts that aren't healing, and settle into the flow of deeper and more fulfilling relationships. Sadness also helps you release yourself from behaviors or ideas that take you away from your authentic self; if you can truly let go, the gentle nature of sadness will lead you to peace of mind that comes not from chaining yourself to a formal set of beliefs or ideologies, but from listening to your own innate wisdom.

Sadness also has an important biological healing component: tears cleanse your eyes and sinuses and release toxins (and excess tension) from your body. Crying is a potent detoxification process that helps you move fluidity through yourself in tangible ways. When you welcome your healing sadness and your tears and release that which must be released, you'll feel freer, lighter, and more focused in every part of yourself. This is probably the most important thing to understand about sadness: if you truly let go of your outdated attachments, you'll be rejuvenated and revitalized by its healing flow. If you refuse to let your sadness perform its healing tasks, you'll lose your sense of flow, your focus and agility will fade away, you'll experience excessive tension, and you'll have trouble finding or connecting to your deepest path and dearest loves. If you never let go, your heart's true knowledge will be obscured by your outworn attachments to unsuitable people and ideas. When you reject sadness, you cannot be rejuvenated; therefore, your vitality and your flow will be impeded by your unmet needs, your unsaid words, your unshed tears, and your grinding soul fatigue.

Welcoming your sadness is not just a process of allowing honest sorrow and tears back into your life; if it were that easy, we'd all have done it by now. No, we all have very good reasons for repressing and ignoring our natural sadness, and surprisingly these reasons don't have as much to do with sadness as they do with anger, or to be more precise, with how sadness and anger work together.

THE MESSAGE IN SADNESS
(AND ITS RELATIONSHIP WITH ANGER)

Many people think that anger and sadness are oppositional emotions, that the fierce strength in anger has nothing whatever to do with the sorrowful softening in sadness. In truth, anger and sadness are intimately connected in a wondrous and fluid dance; unfortunately, the steps to this dance seem to be hidden from us.

When you move into the softened releasing posture of sadness, you can uncouple yourself from the ideas, situations, or people you've outgrown or whom you attached to with improper intent (because you felt lonely, because you felt pity or responsibility, because you needed security or position, or because nothing better was available). Sadness moves forward to question your outdated or hollow attachments in a slow and persistent way, and it asks you to release them (and yourself) back into the flow of life. If you move through your sadness honestly, you'll encounter honest pain, honest sorrow, honest emptiness, and finally, an honest reconnection to and rejuvenation of your heartfelt self. Your honorable journey through sadness will rejuvenate your psyche, but stepping back into life without the camouflage of those outgrown attachments can feel very disorienting. Therefore, your anger will step forward to help you restore your boundary and protect your new position so that you can support and maintain your important changes (instead of falling backward into your old attachments as soon as you feel lonely or weakened again). Your healthy anger will strengthen your resolve, which means that you may appear somewhat unsympathetic to people who only knew you as a pushover. This transition is wonderful and necessary, but if you've been trained to see anger and sadness as oppositional emotions, this natural emotional progression may startle you.

Your healthy anger may also arise just in front of your sadness, in order to protect you while you perform your necessary release work. When you move consciously into your sadness—into a softened, deliberate, languid posture—your boundaries will most likely intensify in response, and your anger may wrap you in a protective cocoon. Have you ever moved into your sadness fully and felt an unusual heat emanating from your face or chest? Have you ever let yourself cry deeply and felt a sense of timelessness in those moments? That's your anger creating a protective boundary of privacy around the sadness in your psyche. Anger will often move forward during times of sadness to help you maintain a connection to your strength and security while tremendous change is occurring inside you. If you can welcome the heat and protection of your anger as the ally of your sadness, you can use your anger to surround yourself with a ring of fire so that you can move deeply inside yourself and make the serious changes sadness asks of you. When you're protected inside your vigilant, anger-defined boundary, you may be able to release a long-held idea or goal that no longer feeds you, because your anger will remind you that your strength doesn't rely on any exterior possession or accomplishment. And when the sentry of your anger calmly walks the perimeter of your psyche, you'll be able to alter or end a relationship that serves no one, because your healthy anger will help you make clean and respectful separations with honor and dignity.

When the noble sentry of your anger and the graceful water-bearer of your sadness work together, you'll be able to release outworn ideas or unworkable relationships while you restore your authentic purpose. When you release dead weight and restore yourself to a focused and upright position with the help of your anger and your sadness, you'll actually feel rejuvenated, wiser, and more aware (instead of empty or lost). You'll feel the pain of having been attached to people or ideas that could not meet your true needs, but you'll also feel deep relief at being once again on your own true path. Creating harmony between your anger and your sadness, then, is vital if you're going to work with either emotion effectively, because each contributes to and supports the other in a vibrant and purposeful way.

If anger and sadness aren't harmonized in your psyche, they can throw you into precarious behaviors. If you reject your sadness and use your anger all by itself, you'll just protect and restore, protect and restore, without asking if what you're protecting is worth keeping. If you can't access your sadness, you won't be able to identify or let go of things that no longer serve you, so you'll end up defending indefensible positions. You can feel this sort of imbalance when you're arguing strenuously with someone and suddenly lose your entire train of thought. The argument begins to seem absurd, and you become embarrassed about having started it at all. If you could disengage and apologize, your sadness would be able to come forward and help you release whatever essentially meaningless thing you were fighting about, but that doesn't happen very often.

Without a proper connection to your sadness, your anger will fight just to save face, even if there's no reason whatsoever to stay in the fight.

Similarly, if you use your sadness all by itself, without the protective assistance of your anger, you may release so much that you lose parts of yourself in the torrent. Without your anger's certainty and resolve, your sadness might release too many attachments. If you've ever felt that any movement toward sadness or weeping would be dangerous—that if you started crying, you'd never be able to stop—you were probably sensing a lack of healthy anger in your psyche. Without anger's presence, your sadness can add overwhelming amounts of water to your system, and you can be swept away. When your angers (and consequently your boundary) are impaired, you may express your deep sadness and find yourself not only ending relationships, but giving up your art, your dreams, and your self-respect in response to your sadness, which is a clear sign that your anger wasn't available to protect you while your sadness surged through you.

If your healthy anger has the freedom to do so, it will often protect you from dropping into your sadness when your surroundings aren't safe or emotionally supportive. Sadness asks you to drop all crutches and pretenses and get back to the center of your unrepeatable self—to feel things only you can feel. This is not a casual request; this is real soul-work. Your anger knows this, and it won't let you move into sadness until you're safe enough to do that work. You may experience this protective movement as an inability to cry unless you're completely alone, which is not a sign of emotional incompetence. There is real danger in crying or showing deep vulnerability in our society. Many people see crying and sorrow as unstable, weak, or even disturbed. Crying in public can threaten the image you craft for yourself, and it can make you lose face in the eyes of friends, family, and co-workers. Your anger understands this, and it tries to protect you and your position in the world. If you understand what your anger is trying to do, you'll be able to thank your anger and channel it into your boundary to strengthen your resolve. Then if it's at all possible, you can immediately find a private place in which to mourn and cry. If you don't understand why your anger is preventing you from moving into your sadness, you'll probably force your tears back into their ducts, repress your sadness, and go forward with grim resolve. Perhaps you'll cry later, during a phone company commercial, or perhaps you'll hurt yourself accidentally, so you'll have a justifiable reason to cry. The tears will come out eventually, but when you don't understand your anger or your sadness, you probably won't be able to feel (or even remember) your teary connection to the original saddening event.

In many cases, poorly moderated anger and sadness can get into a contentious relationship with one another. For instance, your movements into anger may amplify your sadness in unhelpful ways (you may cry or become despondent when you get angry, which won't help you restore your boundary at all!), while any movement toward sadness and release may bring your anger stomping onto the scene (you may find yourself lashing out with inexplicable fury when you're actually quite sad). As you can imagine, this sort of inner turmoil is terribly destabilizing. It's hard to maintain your balance while you're rocketing back and forth between boundary devastation, fury, fatigue, and despair. In no time at all, you'll lose your focus, your relationships will fall into disrepair, and you'll struggle with a great deal of shame—both for having hurt yourself and others with your poorly managed anger and sadness, and because it's embarrassing to be alternately rageful and then crushed by sorrow. When your anger and sadness are allowed to remain in conflict, you'll be neither protected nor softened; you'll just be battered by these seemingly adversarial emotions.

If you have skills, though, you won't have to put up with such chaos. When you can maintain your focus and your grounding, you can respond appropriately to both your sadness and your anger. That's where the dance comes in—where your sadness supports change and vulnerability, while your anger offers stability and protection. When your anger and sadness can work together, they can help you move with strength and grace toward their shared goals of clarity, release, rejuvenation, protection, and authentic wholeness. When you can dance with your anger and sadness, you won't second-guess or wrestle with any anger that arises in front of your sadness; instead, you'll realize that anger actually *should* move in front of your sadness because anger exists to strengthen you when your boundary and self-image are challenged (as they always are when sadness appears). You also won't second-guess your sadness or repress it simply because it isn't convenient. You'll be able to channel your anger into your boundary to create the time and space you need to address your sadness mindfully, and release your outworn attachments to the ideas, behaviors, attitudes, or relationships that brought your sadness forward in the first place.

LEADING WITH SADNESS (AND LOSING YOUR WAY)

In a well-moderated psyche, anger is the primary emotion—the boundary-setter and sentry of the soul—while sadness acts in a more interior way to restore flow, grounding, and integrity. In many people, however, this relationship is turned around in that sadness is their leading emotion, while anger limps behind, if it appears at all. This dynamic is present in what we would call soft or passive people, those who are very sensitive, malleable, and attentive to others, but not very well-protected or defined. Such soft people can't make good separations between themselves and the world around them, or work with their anger in conscious ways. In psychological terms, these people are often called passive-aggressives, but that sort of labeling crushes the spirit and converts a normal human behavior into a pathological condition. Leading with sadness is not a condition; it's a choice.

People who lead with sadness are often children of raging or addicted parents (or survivors of other ongoing violent childhood traumas). Having experienced firsthand the horrors committed in the name of anger, these children often shun anger completely in response to the carnage. This is not usually a move made in weakness; it's often an almost swashbuckling, death-defying decision. All children know that anger can protect them (that's obvious), but these children make a choice to live differently than their families or tormentors do—to feel differently and to behave differently. They make a choice to drop their anger completely, and this is a very brave, dangerous, and life-affirming choice. It's sad that the aftereffects of this choice are so tragic, because living in a rage-filled house (or through a brutalizing childhood) without a boundary is a very brave thing to do. Sometimes it's the only path to survival, because there's not enough room in most raging families or cruel authoritarian structures for more than one angry person. If you display your anger in these settings, you might be brutalized; it's better to drop your anger and survive.

Here's the problem: Brave survival skills (like raging, dissociating, freezing, fighting, fleeing, or dropping all anger) are fantastic and brilliant, but they're only supposed to be used in response to danger or trauma. Survival skills are perfect when you need them, but they're only meant for times of need. Survival skills contain tremendous power, but unfortunately, if you use them as a matter of course, you'll remain in an overly activated survival mode—constantly preparing for and anticipating danger, rather than coming fully back to normal life.

Survivors of repeated trauma learn to rely on their survival skills because there is so little chance for them to relax into their authentic personalities. As they grow, these survivors tend to present their survival skills *as* their personalities, which means they often gravitate toward situations or relationships where those skills will be called into play. For people whose survival choice was to lead with sadness rather than anger, those situations almost always involve mates, bosses, co-workers, or friends who have trouble with anger. As such, people who lead with sadness perform a fascinating function in our emotionally impaired society. Because they don't lead with anger and don't have strong boundaries, these softened people can often find startling truths in troubling events or deal in remarkable ways with enraged people. Softened people will attach themselves to furious people or enraging situations (or assaultive jobs), and instead of putting up defenses, they'll accept whatever is thrown at them. Often they'll process the assaultive turmoil in their own bodies in a kind of empathy, and gain a deep understanding of the inner torment of troubled people or situations. This can be a good skill if it's balanced with the protection and resolve of healthy anger, but in people who lead with sadness, this balance is rare.

People who lead with sadness often struggle with physical and emotional instability, cycling depressions and anxieties, unworkable relationships, and excruciating loneliness (even though they're usually surrounded by people). After a while, they realize they're trapped in a dreadful cycle of stabilizing unstable people and systems over and over again, in an exhausting repetition of the first two stages of their childhood traumas. Breaking this debilitating cycle and moving toward the liberation of stage three begins when they realize that leading with their survival skills (rather than their authentic emotions) ensures that they will remain in survival mode. The task of passive and overly softened people is to become reacquainted with the healing heart of anger, and to destroy their contracts with the depraved and dishonored anger they witnessed in their parents, authority figures, peers, or siblings.

Leading with sadness is a choice; therefore, it can be brought forward, looked at as a contractual decision, and dealt with in empathic ways. If you're an overly softened person, you can free yourself from the thankless task of incessantly healing angry people and abusive situations, and you can restore the honorable sentry of your anger to its rightful forward position in your psyche. When you can protect and restore yourself with your healthy anger, your already advanced ability to work with sadness will help you release your painful and devitalizing attachments to unworkable relationships, behaviors, memories, or ideas.

The Practice for Sadness

The practice for sadness is very simple: you just stop, drop into yourself (which grounds you almost automatically), and set your boundary strongly as you ask the internal questions, "What must be released?" and "What must be rejuvenated?" It's important to ask *both* questions because most of us link sadness only to loss, which is why our protective anger so often places itself in unfortunate opposition to our sadness. However, in true and honored sadness, there is certainly loss, but it's always followed by an amazing sense of quiet and utter relaxation. If you hinder your sadness by refusing to let go of your outworn or inappropriate attachments, or by allowing your anger to stomp on it, you won't experience the rejuvenating flow that always follows healthy sadness; therefore, you'll be unable to let go, your anger may intensify, and your flow will evaporate. In response, your sadness will have no choice but to decay into full-blown despair or depression, and you'll be in the rapids for no good reason.

The movement through true sadness is as simple as it is healing. All you need to do is to create sacred space for your sadness by setting a strong boundary (whether you feel angry or not). If you experience a great deal of anger when you're sad, you can channel your anger and illuminate your boundary very brightly. If you don't feel a lot of anger, you can just envision your boundary in a fiery color and proceed with that imaginal support. Usually all you have to do is get quiet, welcome the protective heat of anger, let your tears flow if they need to, release that which needs to be released, and relax into the flow of life again. Honestly—that's it! You may want to bring forward a few contracts, but sadness usually washes away old attachments or contractual entrapments all by itself—without the need for any special techniques.

If you drop into the trapped states of despair and despondency (see pages 306–10), you'll need to burn many contracts, but when you're in the territory of sadness, you'll have easy access to the flow you need to release yourself from inappropriate attachments. When you're done, you may not even need to rejuvenate yourself (unless you want to), because sadness brings incredible healing energies with it. Sadness arrives with its own tool kit to ground and comfort you, wash away old attachments and contracts, and heal your soul.

When you welcome your sadness and allow it to flow through you, you may become a little bit weepy at first, which can seem troubling if you don't understand the healing power of tears. Don't fight the flow, and don't underestimate the healing power of a good cry. Crying is an incredibly simple way to add the tempering influence of water back into your psyche. If you're tense and overstimulated, crying will help you cool off and soothe yourself. If you're rigid and unbending, crying will break down the boulders in your soul. If you're zooming around on too much intellectual stimulation, crying will restore healing humidity to your system. Crying helps you unwind and relax into yourself after hard work, loss, hectic situations, or self-sacrifice—so cry as often as you need to. It's the all-purpose healing balm of the soul.

As you move into a closer relationship with your healing sadness, be aware of your habitual responses to hectic situations. Notice how often you distract yourself when your tears and sadness attempt to come forward, and watch for any movement toward the siren song of "fun." When you're inflexible and desiccated and you need to bring flow and relaxation back to your life, notice how often you move as far as you can from your healing sadness. If you're like most people, you'll respond to tension and stagnation by trying to bring more joy to your life, which will never work because flow and relaxation live in the realm of sadness; they don't live in joy! Joy and its comrades (happiness and contentment) are lovely states, but they don't work in the way sadness does. Manufacturing joy, chasing happiness, and courting exhilaration—these are distractions and avoidance behaviors that cannot and will not heal you. When you require deep relaxation and deep release, you must move honorably and meaningfully into sadness. When you do, joy will naturally follow your sadness, and fun will naturally return to your life. This may seem counterintuitive, but it's the emotional truth.

HONORING SADNESS IN OTHERS

What do you do when the people around you are sad? The first thing most of us do when we're confronted with sadness is to smile and affect a cheery attitude. The more skilled among us might be able to listen supportively, but eventually we'll try to put a happy face on any sadness we encounter. Very few people are ever given the time or permission to feel truly sad for as long as they need to. We dry their tears, hug them, make jokes, and wave Mr. Bunny at them. Unfortunately, this lengthens their stay in the house of loss and stops them from receiving the rejuvenation sadness brings.

Because sadness is so misunderstood and dishonored, it tends to wander through our culture like an orphan, grasping on to anyone it can. If you don't know how to work with sadness, the sadness of others will probably travel into your tense and boundary-impaired psyche and incapacitate you in the way your own sadness does. For instance, if you've got a lot of unshed tears inside you, the sadness of others will make you cry. You won't have good psychological hygiene, and your boundary will probably drop just because you need to cry. However, if you can set your boundary and make room for softness and release inside your properly protected psyche, you can welcome sadness in others—without having to share it with them. Once you set your boundary and soften yourself a bit, you can easily make room for crying and sorrow in another person because you'll have the patience and the timelessness you need to simply sit and listen—without offering unsolicited advice or inappropriate cheerfulness. You won't have to become a sage or a counselor, because if you can just let the sad person speak in sacred space, their sadness will do all the work required. Trust this beautiful emotion—in yourself and others. It can and does restore the soul to wholeness.

WHEN SADNESS GETS STUCK: DESPAIR AND DESPONDENCY

Sadness arises in response to specific issues, it meets the situation and allows for conscious release, and it contributes rejuvenation, renewal, and relaxation before it moves on. When sadness is not allowed to run its natural course, it will decay into the troubled state of despair (also called despondency). Despair signals that the mood state of sadness has become imprisoned in a feedback loop where rejuvenation cannot occur.

Authentic sadness moves through your body in waves—sometimes gentle, sometimes powerful—and that fluid motion bathes and rejuvenates you. Despair, however, doesn't move at all; even if you cry your eyes out, it remains stagnant. Despair occurs when sadness is not experienced in its wholeness, when only the loss inherent in sadness is attended to, while its releasing and rejuvenating capacities are obscured. Despair is a sign of stagnation, and it can also be a survival tool for abuse victims who learned to respond with a despairing and brokenhearted posture (rather than with anger or vengeance) in order to elicit some leniency from their abusers. This sort of despair feels not like an emotional choice, but like a specific stance required for survival. However, despair is not a good long-range survival tool because it dams up the emotional realm and eventually destabilizes the psyche.

If you can ask your body to don the posture of despair, you'll immediately feel the difference between it and sadness. In despair, the natural softening and inward-turning posture of sadness becomes a nearly hangdog pose, and unfortunately, when you're trapped in despair, your anger will escalate into imbalance right alongside it. At first your anger might react in a useful way, perhaps creating heat or stillness so that you can experience your despair in private. However, because despair cycles endlessly with no resolution, your anger will begin to cycle along with it. You may begin to rely on rage or hatred to create emergency boundaries for yourself—either openly, or in passive and sneaky ways. Usually, despair will knock you into a tailspin that will cause you to unintentionally injure people as your dishonored anger careens unheedingly through your relationships. Your behavior will be so unpleasant that you may eventually find yourself alone and unwanted, which will reinforce your despair on a daily basis. When you make an unconscious decision to maintain despair and woundedness at any cost, it begins to cost more than anyone could ever imagine.

When your sadness is trapped, your mind and body will become clogged, and you'll probably dissociate to get away from the whole mess. Despair can imprison you, but if you can understand the purpose of despair, you can begin to free yourself from its grasp. It's vital to understand that staying in despair and refusing to release your sorrows puts you in a perverse position of power as the wronged or wounded one (my mother called it "the tyranny of the weak"). Being wronged, being wounded—these things do occur, and it's important to recognize and honor those times when you were hurt. However, your life must be measured not by what happens to you, but by how you deal with what happens to you. When you cement yourself into the territory of despair, you become a thing—a slate upon which the wrongs of the world are written, or a tally sheet of pain and trouble—instead of a fully human being. When you can break through despair and restore your flow, you can awaken and live again. You can move from the crumpled category of victimhood into the upright category of survival. Then, when you're able to ground yourself and burn your contracts with your woundedness and despair, you'll move from survival into grace.

The Practice for Despair

When you channel despair, you'll release a massive clog in your psyche. If you're not grounded and centered, you may be knocked down by the sudden restoration of your flow, so make sure that you ground and focus yourself before you begin. You may want to work in the presence of a therapist who can help keep you safe and focused. You'll also need to have many imaginal contracts at the ready, because much old and unhealed material will need to be felt, examined, and released. During the channeling of despair, it's important to prepare yourself to move through the emotions and attitudes that should have followed your original wounding.

Though your own mix will be unique, some form of fear, anger, depression, and grief should follow all seriously disruptive life events. When you become trapped in despair, though, these natural states can't flow properly. Therefore, when you channel your despair, you could find old angers that may have decayed into rages, old depressions that may have decayed into suicidal urges, or old fears that may have deteriorated into anxieties or severe confusions. Your emotions have little choice but to intensify themselves when there's a blockage. This is why a therapist may be necessary.

The proper channeling of despair will call all of your skills into play. Being focused and safe behind your bright, anger-supported boundary will reintegrate you and give you some much-needed separation from all the desperate torment despair creates. Grounding will help your body release the trapped sense memories of your wound or loss, all of the trapped emotions, and the self-talk that keeps you focused on how unfair and brutal life has been. Grounding will also connect you to healthy sadness in its free-flowing state, which will help you support the flow that's been missing. Your contract-burning skills will take a central role in helping you disentangle yourself from all the stances and behaviors you've adopted in response to your despair. You should also take full advantage of conscious complaining (see pages 146–48); it restores your feistiness and your zest. If you can complain loudly about a situation, it is very hard to remain in despair about it!

After channeling despair, you may feel a little worn-out. If so, congratulations! You've done some serious work, and you've freed up enormous amounts of trapped energy; therefore, you'll need to rejuvenate yourself. This finishing touch is important in cases of despair, because despair depletes your energy and your boundary. Rejuvenation will help you reestablish your sense of strength and balance. Also, as you're healing from your despair cycle, please make sure to welcome your anger and sadness in their free-flowing and mood states. It's important to honor and channel these protective and softening emotions; they'll restore your boundary and your flow, and protect you from dropping into despair again. Welcome them both.

If your despair does not move or shift after you've channeled it a few times, please seek more intensive help from your therapist or doctor.

Despair can cycle you into a serious depression, and for this you need to seek outside help.

HONORING DESPAIR IN OTHERS

Creating sacred space for despair in people who don't have skills is almost impossible. Because despair imprisons healthy sadness (the very emotion that restores flow to the psyche), it can erect a kind of life-sapping vortex around itself. You'll find yourself pulled into a despairing person's drama before you know it, but nothing you do will alleviate the anguish. You'll fix one problem or meet one need, and four more will pop up—because despairing people have no real investment in working through their troubles. They honestly can't invest themselves because they're not resourced and they're not living in the present.

Despairing people can also be somewhat dangerous in interpersonal relationships because they lead with their sadness (or this trapped form, anyway), which means their anger will leak out or surge forward in illogical and senseless ways. They'll tend to hurt you without meaning to or even being aware of having done so. If you try to help a chronically despairing person who has no skills (bless your excellent heart), you'll find yourself spiraling with him or her into a drama that has no end. Please know that in many cases, the most loving thing you can do is to let someone know when they're in the rapids and require more help than a friend can provide. Despair creates a difficult and entangling situation that is best left to trained therapists to unravel.

THE DIFFERENCE BETWEEN DESPAIR AND DEPRESSION

I make a distinction between despair and depression because I see them as very different states. Despair is almost a personality type. People seem to move their entire psyches into the house of despair; they filter everything they encounter through a despairing, crumpled, defeated posture. In depression, though, there's more of a cyclical relationship between many different moods. Depression includes despair, but it has more facets than mere despair, and in many cases it has an unusual connection to elation that despair doesn't have. I see depression as a constellation of many emotions and many factors, most notably a jarring estrangement among the elements and intelligences. The back-and-forth, seesaw nature of depression points to a deep and long-standing conflict in the psyche. When an emotional state repeats endlessly and doesn't ever resolve, there's always something underneath that can't be felt or expressed properly, but with depression there's much more going on than that. Depression is a cyclical movement through any number of repetitive states; it often incorporates despair, but it isn't made of despair alone. Depression is such a rich topic that it will be explored in its own chapter on pages 327–44.

Remember to welcome your sadness in all its forms: as your free-flowing ability to ground and relax into yourself as you let go, as your mood-state ability to access the fluidity of tears and rejuvenate yourself, and as the rapids-level depths of despair that can help you restore and rejuvenate your psyche after terrible loss. Welcome and thank your sadness.

21

Grief

The Deep River of the Soul

GIFTS
Complete immersion in the river of all souls

THE INTERNAL QUESTIONS
What must be mourned? What must be released completely?

SIGNS OF OBSTRUCTION
Unwillingness to accept or honor loss, death,
or profound transitions

PRACTICE
Stop, drop everything, and ask your internal questions.
When the river of the soul takes your weight unto itself,
you can release that which has died into the next world
so that you may live more fully in this one.

GRIEF IS A BEAUTIFUL, languid, and powerful emotion that arises when death occurs, be it actual death or the death of profound attachments, ideas, or relationships. Grief does not simply bring water to you as sadness does; grief drops you directly into the river of all souls. Grief transports you to the deepest places when you have no choice but to let go, when the loss of vital relationships or vital attachments feels like (or is) death itself. Grief will come forward in response to death, the end of a love relationship, the irretrievable loss of your health or well-being, the loss of a cherished goal or possession, or the stunning betrayal of your trust. Grief will also arise in response to never having had something we're all supposed to take for granted, such as health, strength, security, or a happy childhood. Grief enables you to survive losses by immersing you in the deep river that flows underneath all life. If you can't move into your grief, you'll only experience destabilization and dissociation in response to the shock of loss, injustice, inequity, and death, instead of being cleansed and renewed in the river of all souls.

THE MESSAGE IN GRIEF

When I call grief the deep river of the soul, I *mean* the soul; I mean the fully resourced village that incorporates and integrates our bodies, all of our emotions, all of our multiple intelligences, and all of our dreams and visions. Grief is so powerful, I think, because it has the job of defending our bodies and our emotions against the cultural training that makes our intellects and visionary spirits so domineering. Our visionary selves cannot connect fully to grief because they see no death and no loss. They soar into the future and above the world as it is; therefore, they don't really mourn or grieve death. If we overemphasize our fiery visionary aspects, we'll have a hard time connecting to grief, just as we will if we hide in our airy intellects. Our logical and linguistic intelligences usually try to circle around and dissipate grief; they like to talk about death and loss, find reasons for it, and make everything seem logical and tidy, which is the opposite movement to that which grief requires. Grief asks us to become quiet and stop all forward movement so that we may dive into the depths, but the intellect doesn't know how to go deep—not like the emotions can. The intellect usually tries to lift us out of the water and dry us off before we've really immersed ourselves in grief.

Our bodies and our emotions, on the other hand, have a visceral understanding of death and loss. They can no longer touch or see the dead, yet they can still feel the embrace of a lost lover or hear the laughter of a long-dead child. Our bodies miss lost limbs and remember pain. Our bodies and our emotions experience the reality of injury, loss, separation, injustice, and death every day. These two elements *know* grief, which means they can act as our guides and mentors. If we can stay grounded in our bodies and stop ourselves from flying off into purely spiritual or intellectual distractions in response to grief, we'll be able to receive the astounding healing grief offers. Though this sacred, downward grieving movement is vanishing from our society, it is an absolutely necessary movement—for our own souls, certainly, but also for the souls of our loved ones, our ancestors, and our world.

A few years ago, I saw a TV news report about a young child who had wandered into a neighbor's pool and drowned. The news crews got onto the scene quickly, and they caught the reactions of the large African-American family who had lost their little one. On the front lawn of the neighbor's house, the entire family (including teenaged boys) was wailing, weeping, hugging, and collapsing to the ground, calling out to Jesus. I was mesmerized by the grief, both because it was so visceral and because I had been socialized in white culture *never* to show true grief. In the funerals I had attended, everyone was hushed, dressed in their best and least comfortable clothes, looking uneasy, and offering bland platitudes. The mourners I knew sometimes cried, but they usually apologized for it. In my culture, there was no real grief, just polite sadness and uncomfortable silence. The grief of this family was real and honest, and I could clearly see the grief pulling them downward.

Like most people, I avoided the downward movement into grief for most of my life. As a child, I was fascinated by death and horror, and gravitated toward them as a moth to a flame. I, like many survivors, used painful events and scary movies to further hone my dissociative skills. Throughout my childhood, I'd enter into relationships with unstable people (or go to frightening movies) in an unconscious attempt to reenter the first two stages of my trauma. Because I didn't yet know about stage three, I cycled endlessly through a pathetic and endangering form of post-traumatic play. When trouble would inevitably detonate in the unstable people, or when terror would erupt in the scary movies, I'd simply dissociate and watch the ensuing carnage from afar. Engaging with traumatizing people and watching traumatizing entertainment allowed me to keep my dissociative skills—my only real defense—fully exercised and engaged. I prevented myself from dropping into the healing waters of grief by shooting out of my body when grievous situations occurred. I didn't stick around long enough to feel any proper emotions; therefore, I didn't learn to make the proper movements in response to pain, fear, sadness, or grief. All four of my grandparents died before I was eleven, but I didn't grieve or mourn for any one of them because I was unable to get near enough to my body to feel any loss. I never wailed. I never dropped to the ground. I didn't even cry.

As I entered into fire-only spiritual study in my teens, I became further separated from grief. I learned that there was no such thing as death and that life continues on in some form or another, no matter what. This very welcome belief system allowed me to imagine spirits moving in and out of life, but it didn't help me connect to my body or my emotions in any way; I was very ascendant in my outlook. The movement I made in my late teens toward an in-body experience of spirituality, helped me conceive of grief, but not actually feel it. I understood that grief was deeper than sadness, but I still had too much fiery metaphysical distance from life to be able to enter grief competently. Learning to grieve took me awhile. It took numerous African grief rituals (see the books by Malidoma Somé and Sobonfu Somé in Further Resources), and a lot of unwinding, but I learned to let my body and my emotions share their thousands of years of wisdom with me, and in my thirties I finally learned to stop, drop, and grieve.

As I wrote in the preface about the weekend my mother died, I didn't fight my grief at all. None of my thoughts, none of my visions of the future, none of it mattered because my *body* knew that she was gone. It didn't matter that my spirit could imagine her traveling to the other world because my *heart* couldn't feel her next to mine anymore. All the mental facts about her meds and possible reactions—they were all gibberish. A part of my body and a part of my heart were gone, and I needed to grieve Mom's death deeply, right there in front of her comatose body. So I did. Grief grabbed hold of me and plunged me into the river of the soul, into the river of all souls, where my position as a living person gave me a very important task. My job was to cry my living tears so that the river could be fed and renewed. Without those tears, the river was too shallow to carry Mom to the next world.

Now that I look back on my life, I see that my decades-long unwillingness to cry and grieve was my way to keep the dead alive. It was my way to stop death in its tracks. I thought this made me stronger, more spiritual, or more evolved than other people. It didn't. It just trapped me in an immature and unbalanced relationship with true loss and death. I was all intellect and vision—all air and fire. I could describe death, I could pontificate about death, and I could fly above death. But I couldn't feel death in my heart, and my bend in the river of all souls was devastated by drought. When I finally learned how to grieve in my thirties, the river began to flow again, and I felt my grandparents and all the ungrieved people and animals inside me breathe a communal sigh of relief as they finally resumed their journeys into the next world. My dearly departed couldn't take their rightful places on the other side of the river—as ancestors, as wisdom-holders, and as supports for me— because I had trapped them in a netherworld by refusing to get into my body and grieve.

If you're a primarily intellectual person, and this talk of spirits and the other world sounds like gibberish to you, think of it this way: if you don't grieve your losses, the people who have died either get erased from your consciousness (as if they were unimportant), or they hang around in your psyche (as if you're being haunted). Neither position is honorable or logical. It's important to honor your departed person's life and truly let them go so that you can live more fully, integrate your losses, and deepen as a person. This is also true for experiences or situations in which you lose something irretrievably. Thinking about it and intellectually releasing it is a good first step, but the real, fully human next step is to grieve properly. The logical intellect and the visionary spirit can't possibly dive down underneath life in the way that the body and the emotions can. They just can't, because it's not in their nature.

Both the intellect and the visionary spirit like to soar above and around life, and they don't understand the need to drop down *into* life. Grief, however, powerfully overrides the need to fly above or oversee or describe the process of death; grief asks us to wade right in and sink down under the water. If we don't sink into grief, we can't connect properly to death or take our places in its sacred and necessary rituals. In many indigenous traditions, it's known that serious public grieving helps the dead cross over into the next world; the sounds of wailing are said to alert the ancestors to the death and to create a pathway for the departed souls to follow if they get confused or lost. These stories tell us that if we living people don't cry and genuinely mourn our losses, the dead won't realize what happened, and the spirit world—the ancestors—won't be properly alerted. If we don't get into the river and mourn, there won't be enough water in the river, which means the dead won't be able to cross into the next world and become ancestors themselves. We the living help transport the dead to the next world through the quality of our grief and the quantity of our tears.

If grieving is necessary and sacred, then what a terrible legacy we create for ourselves and our dead in our grief-impaired culture, in which we move dead bodies into boxes and urns, and gather quietly in our somber outfits around tables full of food. We tell each other it was all for the best, or that little Bobby is in a better world now. Our minds devise perfect explanations, our spirits imagine the departed in heaven or nirvana, our feelings are anesthetized, our bodies are uninhabited, and we "hold up" very well (what an amazingly accurate description of grief impairment!). When we see someone actively dropping into grief and mourning, we often turn away. It's embarrassing; it's frightening; it's distasteful—it's just not done! We turn away from the grief around us because we don't want to feel anything that deeply. It's too threatening, so we straighten our clothing and turn away. And that's the real death—of compassion, of community, of feeling, and of understanding.

When we don't allow ourselves to grieve, we're repeatedly traumatized by death. When we refuse to feel the pain of loss, we refuse to honor our connections. We trick ourselves into thinking that we can guard ourselves against all pain if we just refuse to grieve (or think about or prepare for death). In that refusal, however, we make a deadly mistake: we move further and further away from ourselves, we fail to connect deeply to the people in our lives, we lose connection to the real flow of life, and we dry up inside—because there is no one in the river to honor our lost loved ones or our lost dreams. Each death and each loss, because we don't feel it properly, just stacks itself on top of the last death or loss—like papers on a disorganized desk—until we're filled with unfelt, unlived, unresolved deaths.

THE GRIEVOUS CONSEQUENCES OF NEVER GRIEVING

I watch people who respond to death by making death unreal and grief unnecessary, just as I once did. They rely heavily on their spiritual beliefs so that death doesn't touch them, or they hide in their intellects and create long, rambling stories about death and loss. After a while, they become numb and disconnected from the world. I see that numbing influence in fire-only metaphysical circles, where people eradicate their own empathy by explaining illness or poverty as the end results of improper thinking or incompetent prayer. This deadened mindset allows them to offer pontifications and admonishments, instead of loving support or compassion, to people in trouble. People with this coldhearted, benumbed spirituality can't see troubles for what they truly are; they don't realize that pain, illness, trauma, and grief are natural and deeply meaningful processes, without which no true spiritual or moral evolution could ever occur.

I see a similar numbness in air-only intellectual circles, especially in politics, where welfare moms and Mexican immigrants are blamed for their poverty; where sweatshops and *maquiladoras* are seen as unfortunate necessities in the competitive marketplace; where wars and torture are touted as necessary for the maintenance of democracy; where people of color are imprisoned and executed in inexcusably unequal numbers; where people use their brilliance to seduce the public into accepting the unacceptable in the name of progress; and where truly grievous actions occur, unheeded and unmourned, every hour of every day.

I also see that numbing clearly reflected in our violent culture and our ridiculously violent entertainment. People blather on about violent entertainment giving us a safe outlet for our own violent impulses, but that's so wrong! What a violent movie, book, or game does is inure us to violence. When we choose to watch bludgeonings, shootings, knifings, rapes, and molestations over and over again, what we're actually doing is anesthetizing ourselves. Our culturewide addiction to violent (and absurdly sexualized) entertainment hasn't given us any kind of outlet for our violent impulses; if it did, we'd have a less violent culture and less need for violent images. But we don't; the violence level in movies, books, popular music, and television keeps increasing as our ability to grieve keeps decreasing. You see, we're not flocking to violent entertainment in order to understand violence or our own impulses (true violence bears almost no resemblance to entertainment violence; trust me on this); what we're doing is asking the entertainment industry to traumatize and retraumatize us so that we can numb ourselves to pain, horror, and death. But it doesn't work because our grief still exists and still waits for us, no matter how much brutality or manipulative sexual behavior we gaze at.

If we can awaken from this anesthetized stupor, we can reintegrate our psyches and finally connect to our true grief. If we can shake off our fiery or airy delusions and take off our brittle armor and wade into the waters of grief, we can finally become truly alive. When we sink down into the waters of grief, we'll certainly feel the pain of loss, but we'll also discover our sacred position in the dance of all souls.

In indigenous wisdom traditions, it is known that if a culture doesn't properly grieve their loved ones into their death journeys, they cannot properly welcome their children into their life journeys. There is such poetic truth to that. When we can't grieve our deep losses and honor our dearly departed, we won't have ample room for our children, for the young souls in the world around us, or for the elders who are preparing for death. In America, this is certainly our current political and social situation; we don't feed or educate our youth competently (we don't welcome them properly), and we don't honor or protect our elders (we don't support them properly). If we could learn to fully grieve our losses and send our dearly departed to their proper places in the next world, we could learn to make room for new connections, new attachments, new loves, and new lives. We could make room for love and life in both worlds.

In Mexican culture, which honors its dead in an exquisite yearly festival called *Dia de los Muertos* (Day of the Dead), there is great wisdom about death. I found this saying on a Dia de los Muertos shrine bench at Chicago's O'Hare Airport: *La muerte nunca muere; la muerte es la ventana al otro mundo.* It means "Death is undying; death is a window to the other world."

GRIEVING AND THE IMPORTANCE OF RITUAL

We humans have a great deal of primal wisdom about grief because there's a greater preponderance of primal wisdom inside our brains than there is intellectual information. Much of that primal wisdom can be accessed through ritual.

All cultures have sacred grief, mourning, and funeral rituals, and while many portions of these ceremonies exist in our modern world, they are in most cases stripped of their emotive and sacred context. In just two or three generations, many of us have lost our vital connection to the spiritual and cultural traditions that help us create sacred space for the incredible shock of death and profound loss. We've moved our dead out of our parlors (parlors in traditional homes were actually built for wakes!) and into funeral homes, and we're slowly losing our connection to community-based grief rituals. However, we all see people creating roadside shrines at accident scenes, or impromptu candlelight vigils for sudden deaths in their communities, so we know we still have a tremendous underground capacity for grief rituals. Fortunately, ritual and sacred space respond to our individual intentions, which means we can create new and meaningful grief rituals for ourselves and our loved ones, even if we've lost connection to our heritage.

In most funereal traditions, certain elements appear with regularity. There is usually a "shrine of the dead," whether it's the actual coffin or body, a shrine or altar, a photo, an image, or a collection of items associated with the dead person. Mourners nearly always gather in groups separate from the shrine, and those closest to the dead are given a position of honor nearest to the shrine. Music is often used to delineate the space of mourning, and people often speak out to the mourners about the dead, usually by standing with their backs to the shrine (but not too close at this time) and facing the area of mourning. When the mourners are united in their collective remembrance of the dead—with their stories, their griefs, their songs, their laughter, their regrets, and their tears—they move forward individually and visit or commune with the dead by paying their respects directly to the shrine. When the mourners make their final good-byes, they either return to the area of mourning and close the ritual with song or sermon, or leave the space of direct mourning and gather to share food and companionship. Each aspect of this ritual helps delineate the dead from the living by creating a sacred space for the dead and a sacred community for the mourners to hold on to in this world. If these ritual components are overlooked, the delineation becomes blurred, and the mourners essentially cross over to a middle place where they don't truly release their dead or join fully into life again. They, and their dearly departed, become trapped in a netherworld.

Ritual exists to help us navigate and survive the necessary (and often wrenching) passages of our lives. Our unfortunate disconnection from meaningful ritual not only strips us of community and the sacred, but of our ability to live, love, feel, and grieve fully. Most of us have participated in funeral ceremonies (which are often excruciatingly stilted), but I think very few of us have truly experienced the full release of our dead into the next world, because we haven't been given the time or the space to make the profound movements grief requires of us. In our culture, funerals usually last a few hours, which simply does not allow enough time for mourners to create true communal space, let alone pay their full respects to the dead.

With my husband, Tino, I had the great good fortune to participate in a number of indigenous West African grief rituals with Sobonfu Somé, who is a ritual keeper from the ancient Dagara tribe (see Further Resources for books about the exquisite rituals of the Dagara people). This grief ritual lasted for two full days, but in Sobonfu's village, they last for three. I didn't think there was any way to maintain direct grief and mourning for an entire weekend, but now I don't see how anyone can truly grieve in less time than that. The practice for grief is steeped in ritual because grief is a lengthy and profound process; however, if you can simply focus your attention in your body, you can gracefully move into your own grief. Your body is a brilliant mourner, and if you trust it, it will convey you into the river of tears and bring you safely out again. Your body knows grief and will be able to carry you through the process if you put your trust in it.

The Practice for Grief
Your first task is to stay integrated by grounding and centering yourself instead of rushing off into distractions or dissociating completely (if you

leave your body behind, you'll lose your ability to grieve masterfully). Your second task is to create a shrine for the dead (or the loss) so that you can create a container for your mourning and some delineation between this world and the next. If your grief relates to physical death, your shrine can contain photos, personal items, or reminders of your dearly departed. If your grief relates to the death of a relationship, a goal, an idea, your health, your trust, or that which you never had, your shrine can contain any items that symbolize your loss. It's important to place something disposable in your grief shrine—something that can eventually be buried or burned in a funeral ceremony—so that you can ritualize the end of your mourning period as clearly as you ritualize its beginning and its unfolding.

Your grief process can be undertaken individually or in a community or family group. If you include others, let them place their own items in the grief shrine as well, and make sure their access to the shrine is not hindered. If you can place this grief shrine in an accessible, though private (as opposed to central) part of your home, you can delineate an area of direct mourning that you (and others) can enter and leave as you move through the layers of your grief. In this way, you can maintain your shrine for as long as you need to grieve. Two days, two weeks, two months—it doesn't matter how long the process takes (mourning periods differ from person to person and from culture to culture). What matters is that you have a secluded physical space where you can work through your grief in your own time, sanctify your loss in your own way, and release your dead into the next world through the quantity of your tears and the quality of your mourning.

When you move into your grief, you may feel a tremendous weight upon you. If you don't understand what's going on, you may feel crushed and suffocated by loss, and you may dissociate in response. If you can remember that the movement required in grief is downward, you'll understand the necessity of this heaviness, which anchors you and presses you into your body so that you can feel the weight—and the depth— of the situation. It's important to integrate yourself and take your place in the center of your full village so that you can keep a close watch on any mental explanations or spiritual sermons as you move into your grief, because grief requires that your body and your emotions work together without interference. You shouldn't repress your visionary spirit or your intellect; instead, you should balance and calm them while you do your grief work, and you can only do that from an integrated position. The proper questions to ask in grief are, "What must be mourned?" and "What must be released completely?" If your intellect is overly activated, it might chime in with "What needs to be explained and rationalized?" However, if you can calm your intellect and welcome it to your grief process, it will help you observe and translate the memories and thoughts associated with your loss. If your fire element is overly activated, it might add "What needs to be transcended?" If you can calm and balance your visionary spirit, it can contribute the eagle-eyed vision you need to be aware of the companionship and support that exists all around you during times of grief. Your moderating task is not to stifle your intellect or your spirit, but to help them take their proper supportive roles in the sacred rituals of grief.

When you move through grief with your skills intact, you'll feel pain, but it won't crush you. In true grief, your heart will break open, but it won't break apart. If you can send your grief—in tears, in rages, in laughter, or in total silence—into your shrine, you and your heart will become conduits through which the waters of life can flow. If you let the river flow through you, your bend in the river of all souls will be deepened and restored with healing fluidity. Your heart will not be emptied; it will be expanded, and you'll have more capacity to love, and more room to breathe. When you're done grieving, you won't need or want to erase the memory of your loss; instead, your loss will become a part of you, a part of your ancestral lineage, your strength, and your recognition of the fragility of life. You won't become bulletproof and grief-hardened; instead, you'll soften into the true strength that arises when you connect to grief and loss in sacred ways.

When your grieving process is done—when you have no more tears to send into the shrine and you feel that you've transported your dead into the next world—you (and anyone else involved in your grief ritual) should take some part of the shrine and wrap it or seal it in a way that signifies closure to you. Take this bundle and burn or bury it ceremonially, and dismantle your shrine completely (you can continue to display photos or items from the shrine, but you should remove them from the shrine area and place them in new configurations). It's important to bring closure to this mourning ceremony so that your soul, which loves ritual and feeds on imagery, will be able to mark the end of this formal grieving process. It's also healing to mark your closure with music and a food-based celebration of some kind. Music and food are healing, grounding, and welcoming to your body and your soul. After your funeral ritual is complete, remember to include your ancestors in your life—by talking or singing to them, by asking them questions, by praying to them, or by asking for their assistance and wisdom. Remember: death is undying; death is a window to the other world.

Remember, too, that grief is a natural bodily process. If you can stay in your body and honor the rituals of grief, you'll instinctively know what to do, without tremendous need for spiritual overviews or mental explanations. When you come up and out of the river of grief, your intellect and your spirit may be silent and prayerful for a while as they integrate everything they've witnessed in this profound, transformative process. Channeling grief—and honoring the reality of your body and your emotions—will help your intellect and your spirit to integrate and mature. Instead of hovering above the world in their often superior and disconnected way, your spirit and intellect will mature and experience wholeness in the deep and healing waters of grief.

WHAT TO DO IF YOUR GRIEF GETS STUCK

It's important to make a distinction between being caught in grief because you've fallen into the netherworld, and being caught in grief because your grieving process has not yet completed itself. Most of us are rushed through our public grief and left to do our real grieving on our own—without ritual, ceremony, or community. In many cases, trapped grief is just unfinished grief. If your grief is stuck simply because it is unfinished, walking yourself through the ritual practice for grief will help you complete your grieving process. Grieving takes its own time, and it won't leave you until you perform your sacred tasks. If your grief ritual isn't quite finished, you'll know it by the quality of connection you still have to your loss; you'll still feel a wrenching physical connection and a sense of unfinished business that requires more time to honor and process.

There is also a form of grief called "complicated grief" that seems to involve areas of the brain that are involved in addiction. In essence, you can become physically addicted to grief! If you're still actively grieving, crying, physically missing your loved one, and spiraling into anxieties and depressions more than six months after a death, please see your doctor or therapist and mention the possibility of complicated grief. Current data suggests that this form of grief can also affect your endocrine system, your sleep, and your hormonal balance, so don't ignore it!

You can also experience stuck grief when you're trapped in the netherworld of distraction and dissociation, as I was. In this situation, you may not be able to identify your emotional condition. You won't feel true grief because you won't actually be in the territory of grief. You'll be in the territory of running from grief, rationalizing grief, numbing grief, or making grief unreal. As a result, you may feel despondent, depressed, anxious, furious, panicky, or even suicidal. You may feel isolated from humanity and your own soul—cheated by the dead and betrayed by the living. You may also have trouble reaching out for help, companionship, or counseling. Reach out anyway. You're in the rapids, and you need human contact, counseling, and community in order to finally allow yourself to drop into the river and grieve.

HONORING GRIEF IN OTHERS

The first rule for creating sacred space for grief in others is not to rush in and pull them out of the river—not to sermonize or philosophize about death, the past, or the future. Grieving people need to be treated as sacred vessels through which the river of life is flowing in all its power and all its beauty, as souls who have one foot in this world and one foot in the next. Mourners are in deep ritual space, and your behavior should be reverent of the soul-work that is occurring. It is hard not to interfere with platitudes, homilies, and pep talks, but you must restrain yourself. This is the time for you to hold the world at bay and let the mourner fully experience his or her grief in words, in sobbing, in rages, in complete silence, in despair, in fits of laughter, in denial, or in whatever way the mourner chooses. If you can see yourself as an assistant *to* grief instead of a counselor, you'll be able to take your proper place in this ritual.

The second rule for creating sacred space for grief in others is to be separate enough from the death or loss (or to have grieved it fully enough yourself) to be able to act as a ritual keeper instead of a fellow mourner. If you haven't yet grieved the death or loss, you'll most likely drop into the river along with the mourner, leaving no one to hold the space on this side of the river. The analogy we made in the anger chapter about securing your own oxygen mask before helping others with theirs applies to this situation, too. There is no shame in being in the river of grief—it's a beautiful place to be—but the profound movements in grief take all your energy. If you're in mourning yourself, you won't have the capacity to create sacred space for another. You'll need to call in someone else to help you and the principal mourner.

You don't need to be emotionless and indifferent to be a good assistant—that's not the movement required at all. You just need to create and maintain clear boundaries between yourself and the mourner's deep process (setting your boundary on fire is an excellent idea). Your grounding and focusing abilities are also important because you've got to be able to move emotions through you as they arise. Grief travels (because it's a communal emotion as well as a private one), so even if you're focused, you may move into grief right along with the mourner. If you do, breathe deeply and relax your body consciously so that the grief can flow through your body and down into the ground (this is an incredible healing in itself). In this way, you can welcome and honor the grief while maintaining your position as an assistant.

If you can set up a grief shrine or area of mourning (with music, photos or sacred objects, candles, privacy, or anything that occurs to you or the mourner), you'll be able to establish sacred space for the mourner and yourself. When a ceremonial container exists, the mourner can pour his or her words and emotions into the shrine, instead of into you. Your task as an assistant is not to collect and process the mourner's grief in your own body, but to create a container and shrine that allows the mourner to release his or her emotions and the dearly departed safely into the next world.

When the grieving is finished, move yourself and the mourner away from the shrine (or the mourning area), and have something to eat or drink as a way to ground yourselves. Follow your instincts as to whether to break down the shrine. The mourner may want to preserve the shrine and continue grieving alone, now that there's a sacred space for grief. The mourner may also want to read through this grief chapter to gain input on how to proceed. Honor the mourner's wishes and close your session with thanks to the shrine. Check in with your grounding, your boundary definition, and your focus, and make sure to burn contracts or rejuvenate yourself (see pages 141–46, 151–53) when you have time alone for a few minutes. Working through grief (even as an assistant) changes you, and this change will alert your stasis tendencies. If you can rejuvenate yourself, you can integrate those changes and make your movements toward stasis as conscious as your movements toward change. Amen.

Remember to welcome your grief and let your body take charge of the process. Trust yourself and trust the process. If you enter the river with the help of the village inside you, you will come out the other side as a new person. Welcome and thank your grief.

22

Depression

Ingenious Stagnation

Focusing on Situational Depression

GIFTS
The brilliant stop sign of the soul

THE INTERNAL QUESTIONS
Where has my energy gone? Why was it sent away?

SIGNS OF OBSTRUCTION
Cycling despairs, angers, shames, anxieties, and manic elations
that disturb or halt your forward progress

PRACTICE
Listen closely. There is always good reason for energy and flow to vacate
your psyche, whether it's related to health, brain chemistry, injustice,
relationships, career, or old traumas. You should not attempt to move
forward until you understand the intelligence inherent in your depression.

DEPRESSION IS NOT A single emotion, but a constellation of emotions,
postures, decisions, and health issues that erect what I call the "brilliant
stop sign of the soul." Depression is an ingenious (albeit overwhelming)
movement in the psyche that takes you out of commission for crucial reasons. It's important to understand the difference between despair, which
arises when your natural sadness has become blocked or trapped—and

depression, which is a cyclical and unresolving movement through any number of blocked or overemphasized emotions (the emotional mix is different for each individual). Depression arises in response to exterior and interior conflicts that destabilize your psyche, and while it can be crushingly disruptive, depression has a vital healing purpose.

When people are suffering with depression, there are nearly always four or five deep and painful situations or health concerns transpiring at the same time. Though depression can and does spin out of control and destabilize bodily systems, emotions, mental functions, and visionary awareness, there is nearly always an inception point at which the depression arose in a very manageable way as a response to trouble or injustice that was already occurring. Treating the depression as a separate disease entity without addressing the very real situation it points to is an incomplete way to manage it, because depression is a natural protective response to disheartening or destabilizing stimuli. The practice for depression is not to launch yourself toward happiness for the sole (and ultimately joyless) sake of happiness, but to understand what has occurred—inside and outside of you—to disturb you. Your first task is not to erase your depression, but to focus yourself in the center of the village inside you so that you can view your depression not as a negative comment on your intrinsic value, but as a brilliant message about the specific (though obscured) issues you face.

If you're currently taking antidepressants (including St. John's wort or any other herb), you are welcome here. There is still plenty of work to do in the emotional realm when you're on antidepressants. In fact, you'll probably be better at working with emotions if you're on the right antidepressant. If you're on a suitable one, you won't be a zombie; you'll just be protected from falling into a bottomless pit. I empathize with the need for medication because I wrestled with my own horrific suicidal depressions for over three decades—and relief of any kind was a godsend. However, until recently, I was too brainwashed against conventional medicine to go near a real doctor, so I had no choice but to learn to deal with severe and debilitating depressions without medical help. This was excellent training for the work I did with people who would not or could not tolerate medications, but it did cost me a great deal.

Current research is showing that untreated depressions, especially major depressions, can teach the brain how to fall into depression more easily the next time. Untreated depressions can wear a path in the brain, just like other repetitive or poorly managed emotions can. Unfortunately, this pathway also affects the endocrine system, sleep patterns, memory, and even the DNA in your brain cells. You can damage your brain with untreated depressions, so they're nothing to fool around with. Get help! I did, finally, and not only am I now being protected from recurrent major depressive episodes, but I'm working my way back to proper sleep patterns and endocrine balance as well. There is also some preliminary data showing that antidepressants—specifically the SSRIs (selective serotonin reuptake inhibitors)—can reverse the damage that major depression wreaks on the DNA in brain cells. This is a relief!

Now, after I have advocated for medical intervention in cases of depression, it's important to understand which type of depression you have. I suffered from early-onset major depression (my first suicidal episode occurred when I was eleven), but I have no manic features or cycling anxieties. Depression that cycles with manic features is called bipolar depression, and it requires different treatment than major depression does. Bipolar is a tricky disease, and it's important to get it properly diagnosed and treated (treatments for major depression can actually make bipolar depression worse). Depression that cycles with anxiety, phobias, or OCD (obsessive-compulsive disorder) symptoms requires yet another form of treatment and is often helped with antianxiety medications and short-term cognitive-behavioral therapy. Low-grade chronic depression that lasts for two years or more is called dysthymic depression, and in some individuals, low light conditions can trigger seasonal affective depression. Additionally, women can suffer from hormone-related depressions, either as a part of their monthly cycle (premenstrual dysphoric disorder) or after the birth of a child (postpartum depression). These hormone-related depressions should be taken seriously; they can throw the entire body out of whack and train the brain to lean toward depression. Psychotic depression can look something like schizophrenia, with hallucinations or hearing voices, and atypical depression (which is currently being linked to either dysthymia or a mild form of bipolar depression called cyclothymia) involves heightened sensitivity, moodiness, increased appetite or weight gain, and oversleeping. Remember, too, from the chapters on anger, that cycling rages often mask an underlying depressive condition (especially in men). If you flare up with rage and righteous indignation a great deal of the time, please check in with your doctor or find an online depression questionnaire and take an honest self-assessment. Again, depression is nothing to fool around with.

In contrast to the above conditions, situational depression is the form of depression most of us are familiar with. It occurs when we feel down and sad, not just for specific reasons, but about everything. Situational depression is something that most of us have experienced: we feel continually down, unmotivated, isolated, teary, agoraphobic, or unable to sleep, eat, or function. Many people who suffer from situational depression swear by a certain drug, herb, meditation practice, exercise, dietary restriction, or just about anything else. As it turns out, they're not wrong. Situational depression is amazingly malleable and will respond to just about any change in routine. When mental health studies show that nondrug modalities such as therapy and meditation are just as effective as antidepressants in relieving symptoms, those studies are often being done on situational depression. Those of us with major depression, bipolar depression, hormone-related depression, and anger- or anxiety-linked depression disorders may require more intensive interventions. Bless yourself for moving through depression in whatever way you've been able to thus far, and know that proper diagnosis will protect your brain and your body.

The depression practice in this chapter works very well for situational depression, but it shouldn't be the only practice you use if you're experiencing the more serious forms of depression. The serious forms of depression are true illnesses, and you should treat them as illnesses and not as character defects. Love yourself, take care of yourself, and don't tough it out. Help is available.

THE MESSAGE IN SITUATIONAL DEPRESSION

Situational depression has become a rapids-level emotion in our culture, which values work over reflection, lords the intellect over the emotions, and treats the body and the spirit as absolute opposites. However, situational depression isn't truly a rapids-level emotion. The basic momentum behind situational depression is protective and self-respecting, and it arises at the behest of the village inside us. In a well-moderated psyche, depression acts as a kind of energetic tourniquet when some part (or all) of you is off-balance and headed for trouble; it is a conscious decision made by your central nature. The problem is this: most of us don't have any connection to the full village inside us. We think of ourselves in destabilizing terms: body over spirit (or vice versa), logic over empathy, spirit over emotion, or any number of unbalanced permutations. As a result, most of us have detached our elements and intelligences from one another, and thrown huge portions of our souls into the shadow, which leaves us with no functional awareness of why we initiate our depressions in the first place.

When we drop into situational depression, most of us understand on some level that we're somehow involved in disabling ourselves; unfortunately, we aren't taught to honor or celebrate our self-restriction as necessary and even sacred. Instead, we see (or are coerced into seeing) ourselves as disordered. Though depression actually exists to protect us *from* endangering movements and stances, our culturewide inability to live from the awakened center of our souls has instead led us to treat depression *as* the endangering movement. For decades, we've studied, tracked, analyzed, treated, drugged, and hunted down depression in an effort to expel it from our psyches. If any of these interventions worked on a more than symptomatic level, they certainly would have worked by now. But the bald truth is this: situational depression will return when it is required by the psyche because it is a logical and justified reaction to the internal, familial, social, financial, and political decay and injustice we face every day of our lives. I would even go so far as to say that if you look deeply into the condition of our culture—at our political system, at the way we treat our youth, our elders, the poor, the mentally ill, and those we incarcerate and war upon—and you're not depressed at all, then there's something truly wrong with you! Depression is not the problem; situational depression is a response to the problem, and it carries a gift for all of us.

If you have no empathic skills, you'll crumble in front of depression and lose your way. However, if you can focus and ground yourself and set your boundary, you can create the sacred space you need to engage your depression as a mentor instead of a tormentor. Emotions are your soul's deepest language; if you try to banish your depression (or any other emotional state), you'll essentially kill the messenger and leave your soul without a voice. If you can instead engage your depression honorably, you'll learn amazing things about yourself, your lifestyle, your relationships, your culture, and the world.

It took me twenty long years to engage my own depression in an honorable way, and when I finally worked up the courage to ask my depression what it wanted from me, I fully expected it to turn on me like a rabid dog. As I sat trembling inside my bright boundary, grounding and focusing myself with a kind of bleak desperation, I readied myself for the tirade I knew was coming. It never arrived. Instead, I was immediately overtaken by a startling vision of Londoners in World War II sending their children to relatives in the countryside. That was the introductory image; it told me that the depression was not attacking me, but sending parts of my soul away to safety while it held fast in a combat zone. This was a shock, and it had nothing whatever to do with anything I had been told about depression. There was a definite and palpable protective movement occurring inside me—not a disability or a lunacy, but a decisive and conscious maneuver made by a part of me I didn't know existed until that moment. Suddenly, with the help of that previously unrecognized aspect of myself, I was able to observe my emotions fighting to be heard over my internal din—struggling, gasping, and dying—as my depression worked desperately to save my life. I most especially felt the anger trapped beneath my depression, anger that wasn't able to protect me or restore my ravaged boundary, but was instead reduced to making agonizing, stopgap decisions in the face of tragedy.

I have since discovered the origin of the war my psyche was fighting so grimly, and why the children of my soul had to be sent away for their own safety. At the time, I was still running on the fumes of trauma, dissociation, emotional suppression, and massive internal clashes among each of my elements and intelligences. However, since I had learned (as most of us do) to gloss over and work around all my internal troubles, I no longer had clear awareness of them. In fact, I actually looked fairly good on the outside—pretty functional—except for my detestable, unrelenting

332

depression. In my opinion, depression was the only thing wrong with me; if it would just go away, I'd be happy and well. The vision my depression presented shook me out of my complacent, repressive trance because its depiction of a world at war was piercingly and inarguably accurate. When I was able to reframe my view of myself with the support of that vision, I marveled that I could feel anything *but* depression, because my psyche had become a full-scale battle zone. The crippling lack of energy, focus, peace, and happiness I experienced wasn't the problem, and it didn't arise by mistake or by accident; my energy was depleted because some part of me had sent it away on purpose—to keep it safe and alive until the end of my war. I have since observed this same situation in every case of depression I've encountered (though the components and intensity of each battle are unique to each person). Something sentient in the soul reacts to extreme internal or external instability by hiding energy in outlying areas until the center of the soul is habitable and capable of conscious action.

If you can take hold of this war analogy, it can help you remove the taint of pathology from your own movements into depression. Rather than seeing yourself as an incompetent or disabled person, you can bring compassion to your struggle and essentially roll up your sleeves and get to work—instead of being worked over. You can discover the logic behind your depression, which will help you see that no healthy forward movement can or should be undertaken from a position of strife and instability (you can't make coherent decisions or take effective actions if your own elements are trying to murder each other!). Instead of fighting a futile repressive battle that will only intensify your internal strife, you can honor your depression's inhibiting tactics; you can tune in to your depression and listen to its wisdom. Though this is a necessary healing step, it is a difficult step to take in a culture that urges you to soldier ever onward, instead of stopping to reflect upon the direction your life has taken.

Unfortunately, our culture does not value reflection, which means that the soul-rescuing essence of depression is not readily accessible. Instead, depression has been desecrated and pathologized, while our ability to address internal and external injustice has consequently deteriorated. If you agree to demonize depression, you won't be able to truly alleviate it, no matter what you do. You'll have no skills, no agility, and no true grasp of what is occurring in your psyche or the world. But if you can create sacred space and protect yourself from the deluded beliefs careening through our culture, you can perform the soul-honoring and lifesaving tasks your depression asks of you.

The honorable task of depression isn't to get happy, nor is it merely to restore your lost energy (or crank up your existing energy); these repressive and erasure-based approaches cannot in any way address the original imbalance that initiated your depression in the first place. Repressive techniques may erase your depression in the short run, but in the long run, where do they leave you? Do you have more skills or internal resources? Are you fully upright and emotionally competent? Or are you merely less depressed? Depression exists for a specific and protective reason, and it is not the enemy. It is not the creator of the war inside you, and it isn't even one of the combatants. Depression has the dreadful and thankless task of restricting your energy when an internal war has already started, and it grimly and deliberately impedes your ability to walk down the wrong path, doing the wrong thing with the wrong intention.

Your soulful task is not to erase your depression and keep walking; it's to understand your necessary movement into stagnation and to address your depression as a peer instead of a combatant. Your sacred task is to end the war between your elements, clear away the rubble, restore the flow in your internal kingdom, and make a home that the children of your soul would want to come back to.

The Practice for Depression

It's hard to ground or focus yourself during an unwelcomed depression because the depression sucks all your energy away, leaving you uninterested in effort of any kind. *This is a clue.* Depression is your psyche's way of alerting you to a serious disruption or imbalance. It acts almost in the way a circuit-breaker does when spikes of energy occur. Circuit-breakers will trip in response to electrical disruptions in order to protect the line behind the breaker from interruptions or surges. If you can grab on to this image, your depression will immediately seem less toxic; its existence will prove that you have a kind of protective circuit-breaker on your line.

The first movement in depression isn't an electrical engineering skill so much as it is a postural change. It's important to bow your head and listen closely to your depression (instead of collapsing before it or chasing wildly after your lost energy). In a depression, a brilliant and buried part of you is acting as your protector. Your proper response should be one of gratitude. Please remember to see your depression as a vital warning sign that your energy is spiking and leaking away while a war rages within your village. Your job is to honor the fall you've taken and use your depression's pinpoint focus to help you rise again with honor. When you do, your healthy vitality will return naturally.

The practice for depression, especially if you suffer from major, bipolar, hormone-related, or anger- or anxiety-linked depression, is a lifelong practice (which may include intensive therapy and antidepressants); it's not a set of tricks. Of course, all the skills in the raft-building chapter on pages 125–58 are necessary, but so is a study of the relationships between each of your elements and intelligences, focusing especially on your fiery vision and your airy logic. In most cases of depression, one or both of these will tend to dominate in your psyche (you'll be overly intellectual or massively transcendent, or both), which will throw your earthy body, your watery emotions, and the village inside you into disarray. This internal turmoil will then send you down a precarious path toward distractions, addictions, and dissociation—all of which will magnify your depressive tendencies and enter you into an uncomfortable feedback loop. When you're trapped in this loop, each of your elements and intelligences will spiral into confusion and infighting, so it's important to focus on the balancing practices on pages 58–61. When you can bring all parts of yourself to bear on the situation, you can take your rightful place at the center of your village and meet your depression honorably. In that sacred space, you'll be able to identify which parts of you are engaged in battle and which emotions are caught in the crossfire.

You can examine your grounding and focusing skills (or lack thereof) to discover how your body and your attention work (or don't work) together. You can also study the difficulties you may have had with any skill you've learned so far (there will always be some jarring discrepancy somewhere). Or you can simply ground yourself, light up your boundary, and ask the questions for depression: "Where has my energy gone?" and "Why was it sent away?" When you can bring all parts of yourself to bear on the serious issues your depression has been trying to alert you to, you'll completely understand the genius of sending your energy and the children of your psyche to the countryside. They're better off there. I think we should all go!

When you can ground and integrate yourself, you'll be able to stand inside your private sanctuary and differentiate between the many emotional states trapped inside your depression. You'll be able to feel the difference, for instance, between sadness and despair, between grief and world-weariness, between anxiety and healthy fear, and between apathy and an urge to suicide (see page 345). In each case, you'll be able to enter the practice for each emotion you feel and honor each of them in turn. Also, when you can ground the depressive stagnation out of your body, you'll be able to observe and address the physical, emotional, and mental habits that have built up around your depression, whether it's inactivity or hyperactivity, too much sleep or insomnia, over- or underexercising, repressing or exploding with certain emotions, massive mental activity or bouts of confusion, addiction, or dissociation, and so on. Then you'll be able to examine your contracts with your many reactive responses to depression, and destroy them as you ground yourself and clear all the clogs and spikes out of your system.

Of course, your rejuvenation practice (see pages 151–53) is vital. This practice fills you up, time and time again, with the energy you need to revitalize yourself. And in cases of depression, you really can't overdose on these healings. Some people healing from depression perform their rejuvenation practice twice a day for weeks on end. This is a wonderful way to restore yourself and maintain your skills if your depression tries to reanimate itself through sheer force of habit.

Conscious complaining (see pages 146–49) is another wonderful tool that can be considered an emergency first-aid kit for depression. Conscious complaining unlocks the chains that wrap themselves around your psyche, and it kick-starts your flow in a powerful way. This practice is so important for the healing of depression that I'd suggest creating a specific complaining shrine (with dark or annoying colors, pictures of bratty children and grumpy animals, and so forth) in order to sanctify and honor your depression. At first, your complaints will be pitiful and depressive, but if you persevere, they'll start to heat up nicely (which means your anger is returning with all its protective focus). Pay attention to these complaints; they point directly to the troubles that have dropped you into your current depression. Your practice then, when your resources and your village are restored, is to meet those troubles with your full-on, fully activated self, and to do what you can to bring balance to your life and justice to the world. Don't underestimate the power of a good complaining session. It can clear you out, restore your energy, and heal your soul!

PHYSICAL SUPPORT FOR DEPRESSION

Antidepressants work by restoring flow to some of the neurochemicals that become unbalanced by depression, but it's also helpful to restore your chemistry and bodily flow in other ways as well. Exercise and exertion, balanced with plenty of rest, help you move neurochemicals and hormones through your body more efficiently. Toning your muscles and raising your heart rate also places your body under a strain that is more manageable than the strain it experiences in an unchecked depression; exercise has an important healing and retraining function for a body suffering from depression. If your body can experience a safe form of strain—for instance, a twenty-minute run, a dance routine, or a period of weight-lifting—and is then allowed to rest and recuperate, you'll have a visceral experience of meeting strain and tension, managing it, and recovering from it. This is an excellent healing for your body, regardless of the form of movement or exercise you choose. What matters is that you exert yourself in a safe and conscious way and then allow enough time for your body to recover from your exertion. This recovery time is vital, because overexercising can throw you into depression just as surely as inactivity can. When you're dealing with depression, it's easy to force yourself into a grim exercise routine (or to cease all movement); unfortunately, both extremes are unhealthy. The key to coming back from depression is to treat activity and rest as equally important things.

If you're depressed and inactive, you should begin exercising gently and work your way slowly back to fitness; if you're an athlete dealing with depression, you should mix up your workouts so that you're not doing any specific activity more than once every other day (exerting yourself past fatigue and not allowing enough recovery time or enough sleep are surefire ways to make yourself physically and chemically depressed). Movement is essential for your health, but balance and flow are even more important.

It's also important to maintain flow in other areas of your life as well, particularly in your meditative practice. Make sure your practice is not primarily transcendent and dissociative, or it may actually intensify the internal struggles that provoke depression in the first place. If depression is a constant companion for you, please consider meditative practices that honor more than one element in your quaternity (good ones are dancing, yoga, tai chi, qigong, nature walks, art, reading, studying, and so on). Movement, flow, and quaternal balance are the keys to bringing yourself out of a depressive spiral.

Sleep is also imperative for your emotional and physical health, and many psychological and medical studies on the natural circadian rhythms of the body show that sleep disruptions (for instance, in night-shift or swing-shift workers) and sleep deprivation contribute greatly to depression and hormonal and chemical imbalances. As a species, we were meant to rise with the sun and sleep in the dark, but our modern lives have almost completely separated us from the natural cycles of the day and the seasons. This separation is certainly a result of our unbalanced focus on work and productivity to the exclusion of all else, and it has had consequences that we're only now beginning to comprehend. Our extreme productivity has created a population of overworked and overtired people who may be depressed (and unhealthy) simply because they are struggling under unreasonable sleep deficits.

Please be aware of your own sleep patterns if depression is an issue for you. If you require stimulants (coffee, tea, sugar, or herbal energy boosters) in the morning and depressants (alcohol, overeating, tobacco, or marijuana) at night, something is going on. All artificial stimulants and downers will disrupt your chemistry, your hormones, your circadian rhythms, your sleep cycles, and your energy. They may help you race through your day and collapse at night, but they'll only cement your depression. There is no replacement for good and sound sleep.

It's also important to look at your relationship with food and to observe your eating behaviors when your emotions or your depressive tendencies move forward. Do you slow down to feel your honest emotions, or do you race toward comfort foods (or extreme diets and regimens)? You can actually create food sensitivities by using food as a drug. If you treat your body as a thing and use food (or the lack of it) to lift yourself out of your depression, you'll disrupt your internal balance, which means you'll increase your depressive tendencies and spiral into ever more troublesome eating habits. When you're in a spiral like this, you don't have to swear off food forever; you just have to stand upright, shake yourself off, and treat food as food while you work with your emotions as emotions. If you like choco-late (or whatever), go ahead and eat it in moderation because it tastes good, but don't eat it because you're sad, anxious, depressed, or angry (and don't punish yourself for wanting it in any case). Again, it's all about balance and about respecting and honoring each element in your quaternity.

As a final dietary note, you may have heard that you should never eat when you're emotionally upset. While there is some truth to this admoni-tion, following it when you're depressed could mean that you don't eat for weeks! The balancing practice for eating in the presence of strong emo-tions is to name the emotion consciously and then name your hunger as itself. If your emotions and your hunger are improperly connected, you'll know it right away because your statements will tend toward emotional clutter: "I'm not really hungry, but I'm depressed and chocolate milk sounds soothing," or "Grilled cheese sandwiches mean love!" To bring consciousness to your eating, you can learn to say, "I'm depressed now, but I'm hungry for lunch," or "I'm really bummed about work, but I want some tomato juice." This simple awareness exercise will help you stop distracted and addictive eating in its tracks, because it will give a voice to both your watery emotions and your earthy hunger—and help you real-ize that they are (or should be) separate entities. When your emotions are trapped and troubled, they need to be honored and channeled, not fed!

BUT WHAT ABOUT HAPPINESS?

What about it? Depression isn't a happiness deficiency. It's a response to injustice and internal imbalance that diminishes your emotional agility and your ability to feel any emotion properly. Depressed people do experience happiness, but their souls are in so much turmoil that their happiness can't act upon them in truly healing ways. Then again, neither can their anger, their sadness, their fear, their shame, or anything else. If I could wave a magic wand and simply add more happiness to depressed people (without addressing any of their honest issues), they wouldn't be able to hold on to it. This new infusion of happiness would eventually leak away with every other emotion—and its loss would drop them into an even more depressive spiral. No, more happiness is not the answer.

When I tell people that depression is calling the soul to serious practice in response to a long-standing period of strife, they nearly always understand. But they also nearly always restate their original reason for seeking help, as if I haven't fully comprehended their situation. People struggling with depression usually remind me they want to go back to a time when they felt happy—when they had lots of energy, when the troubles of the world didn't bother them, and when they could do whatever they wanted without repercussions. And I always smile, because what I hear is that they want to go back to the lifestyle that dropped them into their depression in the first place, except this time they want to get away with it! They don't want to be impeded in any way; they want to be able to push their way through life no matter what is going on in their souls or in the culture. Well, bless their hearts—and bless mine and yours while we're at it—because I think that's what we all want: to be able to make it through life with no illness, no unhappiness, no death, no pain, no downtime, and no turmoil. We want to be invincible, endlessly happy, and wildly successful. We want to be the heroes of our autobiographies—always making the right choices. But we aren't always heroes, and we don't always make the right choices, and fortunately for us, our souls have a way to stop us when things get out of hand.

Depression is a wonderful teacher in its harsh way. It steps in when your intellect and your emotions are at each other's throats, when you fly over your emotions and batter them with logic, or run screaming from logic and follow only your transient desires. Depression jumps into the fray when your intellect begins to lose its ability to think coherently; when your body trammels toward meeting its needs for food, sex, and more stuff without any emotional, spiritual, or logical considerations; when your visionary spirit begins to lift away from your life; and when your emotions become dishonored, inflated, or ignored. Depression takes over after your sadness has asked you to release something, but you wouldn't; after your anger needed you to set a boundary, but you refused; after your shame asked you to amend your behaviors, but you kept right on misbehaving; and after your fear alerted you to certain danger, but you ignored your intuition and kept right on going, stumbling into one totally avoidable problem after another.

Depression doesn't arise when you're merely unhappy; it arises when you're fighting an exhausting battle that impedes your ability to act conscientiously. Though depression is often blamed for isolating people and making them socially and politically ineffective, depression actually stops you when you're *already* isolated and ineffective. If you were to simply add more happiness to your system, to power yourself up with joy and throw yourself back into the fray (see the topic of exhilaration on pages 373–76), your actions would be damaging to you and every person in your milieu, because your actions would spring from a psyche at war with itself (no matter how peppy you might feel). Happiness is a lovely and valuable emotion, but it is not a magic pill, nor is it the emotion you need when you're fighting a war. All of the happiness-based emotions arise naturally for their own reasons (not yours); they shouldn't be imprisoned, glorified, or lacquered over the top of true-but-unwanted emotions, or you'll throw yourself into a tailspin. Depression isn't a happiness deficiency; it's a rapids-level emotion in our culture. Therefore, the rapids-level mantra applies: the only way out is through.

THE INTERPLAY BETWEEN PERSONAL AND CULTURAL DEPRESSION

The practice for depression is full-bodied and complex because depression is a response to full-bodied and complex issues that arise not just from you, but from our culture itself. Therefore, when you're in a depression, it's important to approach the situation sociologically, and use your vision and all of your intelligences to help you identify which parts are personal and which parts come from cultural conditioning. For instance, trouble with eating and emotions has very little to do with you; it's a function of the way our brains associate sweets and fats with reward and comfort, and the way we've taught ourselves to eat over the top of our feelings. As such, nearly every modern person can be considered to have a moderate eating disorder. In this same vein, the fight you experience inside yourself (where your elements and intelligences are at war) is also not your personal pathology. We've all been trained to separate our elements and intelligences and repress each one in turn, which means we all suffer through the resulting tendencies toward distraction, addiction, dissociation, and depression. When you can bring all of yourself to bear on this damaging cultural conditioning and burn your contracts with it, you'll certainly alleviate your own depression, but more important, you'll begin to alleviate the trouble in our culture because there will be one less person carrying our cultural disease and one more awakened soul in our waiting world.

When you're in the awful throes of depression and quaternal infighting, it's hard to believe that such a world-changing thing is possible, which is precisely why your psyche has to inhibit you from making any focused or effective action! When your quaternity and your intelligences are at war, your psyche knows that you are part of the problem, and it will try to stop you from adding more unbalanced, depressive, powerless noise to the cacophony that is our modern world. Your task is not to fix the world so that you won't be depressed, nor to happy-peppy yourself up and erase your depression; it's to take your depression personally enough to get to work and clear the debris from your soul. When you're balanced, focused, and able to take an upright position in your own psyche, you'll spontaneously take an upright position in the world, and from that upright place, personal, social, and political justice will naturally begin to flow.

WHAT TO DO IF YOUR DEPRESSION GETS STUCK

It's important to distinguish between depression that is actually stuck, and depression that isn't quite through yet because you've still got imbalances to deal with. Please check into the balancing practices on pages 58–61, the addiction chapter on pages 77–89, and the raft-building chapter on pages 125–58. Please remember that relieving depression is only a first step. The journey is lifelong, and it involves constant awareness so you don't return to the powerful and culturally approved wholeness-trashing behaviors that lead inevitably to depression.

If you're meeting your depression in as many ways as you can (and you're getting restful sleep), but it just won't move at all, please see a doctor or therapist, and consider filling out a sleep questionnaire to see if you have any signs of a sleep disorder (snoring, high blood pressure, depression, and daytime sleepiness are warning signs of a possible sleep disorder). When you're dealing with recurrent depression, you'll need counseling and perhaps medical support before you can come back to balance again. Depression signals a serious situation. It is not a simple movement into sadness, anger, or fear; therefore, its practice can be quite involved. There is no shame in needing help, support, intervention, and camaraderie as you wrestle yourself back from imbalance into stability once again. Reach out!

HONORING DEPRESSION IN OTHERS

Honoring depression in people who have no emotional skills is a difficult task indeed, because they usually lack the capacity to identify or work with the many emotions and issues trapped beneath their depression. Sadly, attempting to create sacred space for depression in unskilled people can be somewhat hazardous to your own emotional health, due to the cyclical ingenuity of the depressive state. If you attempt to help depressed people heal this difficulty, set that boundary, or feel this feeling, you'll notice that as soon as they become functional in one area, another will fall into disorder—almost as if on schedule. In a very short period of time, you'll find yourself cycling along with them in a drama that has no resolution. There is an important reason for this: depression performs a vital protective function in the soul, and until people are upright again, their depression simply won't let them go.

Depression always points to a complex series of internal issues. The soul of a depressed person is being called to ritual, and that ritual will involve incredible changes. It's important for you to set your boundary strongly when you're around depressed people so you don't get roped into becoming a sort of overseeing high priest in their healing process. Though depressed people often need therapy, addiction counseling, or some sort of alleviating practice or substance, the true work of depression is always an inside job. Bless yourself for wanting to help, but know your limits. Help the depressed person find support and therapy. Depression can be a serious and life-threatening malady; as such, a depressed person may require far more help than a friend can provide.

Remember to welcome your depression as a signal of imbalance in your separate elements and intelligences, or of a fierce battle within the village inside you. Depression is *ingenious* stagnation; it stops you for a reason. Welcome and thank your depression.

23

Suicidal Urges

The Darkness Before Dawn

GIFTS
Certainty ~ Resolve ~ Liberty ~ Transformation ~ Rebirth

THE INTERNAL QUESTIONS
What idea or behavior must end now?
What can no longer be tolerated in my soul?

SIGNS OF OBSTRUCTION
Bleak, agonizing feelings that threaten your physical life
instead of offering transformation and reawakening

PRACTICE
Use your skills to burn your contracts and create a sacred ceremonial
death for that which torments you. If you honor and attend
to your suicidal urges in a grounded, empathic way, they will
stand up for your lost dreams and clear away everything inside
you that threatens them. Channeling your suicidal urges will, in
essence, give you a new life—it will give you your own life back.
However, if you're in crisis, please seek help immediately.

IF YOU'VE TURNED TO this chapter before reading anything else in this
book, and you're currently feeling suicidal, please stop right now and seek

help. Call your therapist, call your local suicide or crisis hotline, or in the United States, you can call the National Suicide Prevention Lifeline twenty-four hours a day free at 1-800-273-TALK (8255), or visit suicidepreventionlifeline.org. The pain and isolation you're feeling is real and valid, and this is a very serious situation, but you're not alone in any of it. Please reach out for the help that is all around you. We need you here—especially if you're a sensitive soul. We need you here with us on this side of the river. Please reach out for help, get your feet under you, and come back to this chapter when you're safe.

If you've turned to this chapter after gathering your skills in all of the emotions leading up to this one, welcome. This is where the rapids surge and roil with roaring intensity. In the territory of the suicidal urge, there is a great deal of obvious peril, but just as it is with every other rapids-level emotion, there is also an identical amount of healing power and radiant wisdom. Everything inside you has curative as well as destructive attributes. Each sorrow, joy, triumph, catastrophe, fear, or shame has its place in your wholeness. Each can move you toward enlightenment, just as each can throw you into desperate turmoil. Every part of you is a double-edged sword that can protect and heal you, or slice you to bits; suicidal urges are no exception.

In the territory of suicidal urges, you'll deal with crucial issues of life and death. If you don't have the support of close friends or a therapist, and don't yet have your skills under you—if you cannot ground and focus yourself, if you cannot create strong boundaries, and if you cannot channel your emotions (especially anger, rage, hatred, and shame)—you're not ready to enter this territory. Suicidal urges should only be approached when you're comfortable inside your vibrantly blazing boundary—inside your anger-supported sacred space—where their longing for death can be brought forward and channeled in sacred ceremonial ways. If you don't have access to each of the skills you need to create a sacred container for yourself (and access to therapeutic support), you cannot possibly move into practice yet. Please read the information on your boundary (see pages 134–41), as well as the chapters on anger, hatred, shame, and depression before you proceed. Attend to your soul and gather your skills and allies; these are the raging rapids.

THE MESSAGE INSIDE THE SUICIDAL URGE

Your empathic skills and your fully-resourced village of elements and intelligences are absolutely necessary in the territory of the suicidal urge, because suicidal urges move forward when the difference between who you are in your deepest self and who you've become in this world of distractions and trauma is so extreme that it can no longer be tolerated. Suicidal urges are an emergency message from lost parts of your psyche—parts that are in real danger of soul death in your current situation. Suicidal urges surge forward, sword in hand, shouting, "Give me liberty or give me death!" They are that serious about the issues they have come to address. However, your suicidal urges do not want to kill *you!* What they want is liberty from the life you're living, but they certainly don't want your physical life to end. That would be evolutionarily unproductive; all of your energies and all of your emotions exist to keep you alive and functional, alive and connected, alive and protected, and just plain alive. If you can understand that the primal intelligence inside you is and always will be dedicated to your survival and your wholeness, you'll be able to view your urge to suicide in a mythological and sacred way instead of treating it as a literal wish for physical death. I've been present at enough natural deaths to be able to state unequivocally that the atmosphere and emotions that arise when death occurs naturally feel nothing whatever like the atmosphere that surrounds a suicidal urge.

Suicidal urges aren't literal death-wishes; they are actually the last resort of a soul in torment. They arise when your brain chemistry or your untreated sleep disorders have thoroughly destabilized you. Suicidal urges arise after your fears have been overwhelmed, and you've fallen into one endangering situation after another; after your angers have been crushed and your boundaries have been trampled; after you've been separated from your sadness and your grief and have fallen into unrelenting despair; and after your shame has become so besieged that you're no longer capable of moderating your own behavior. Suicidal urges arise after severe traumas have thrown you back and forth between the first two stages of traumatic initiation so many times that you've become exhausted by loss; after years of dissociation, distraction, avoidance, and addiction; and after shocks so profound that you can barely remember what normal life feels like.

Suicidal urges come forward with all their intensity and all their ferocity when your situation is so unbearable that you require an intense infusion of energy, *but they do not come to kill you.* Your suicidal urges arise when you need enough energy to wrench yourself bodily, emotionally, psychologically, and spiritually out of a situation that is killing you already.

Suicidal urges are your last defense, which is why they carry such intensity. The only other emotion that comes close in intensity is panic, which arises to give you the energy you need to shoot forward to the triumphant third stage of initiation. If we only think with one or two parts of ourselves (and can't work with our emotions), panic attacks and suicidal urges will throw us into complete chaos, and we may not survive them. However, if we have empathic skills and can understand what role these emotions play in our healing, we'll be able to take full advantage of the incredible brilliance locked inside both of these states.

Panic appears to be powerless and severely disordered (and seems to be about cowardice), yet when you can dive into it with all your skills, you'll discover incredible power and limitless courage inside it. The same is true of the suicidal urge. If you have no skills and only one or two elements are awake in your soul, you'll see only madness and death in the suicidal urge; but if you can enter its sacred territory with clear intentions and empathic agility, your suicidal urge will help you rediscover your sanity, your soul's true path, and your devout and death-defying love of life.

Trying to talk a suicidal urge away with beautiful tales of the inherent meaning of life does not in any way address its reality. All the sweetness and light in the world are a total lie to the suicidal urge, and they only serve to degrade and ignore its message. Suicidal urges don't want to be lulled to sleep with pretty songs. Suicidal urges are filled with rage and grief and every other thing, and they only come forward when your issues have become so serious and soul-endangering that only a fierce and warriorlike stance can address them. This is no time for lullabies; suicidal urges require a ceremonial end to the situations that are tormenting and endangering you. When you can engage with your suicidal urges from within your grounded and well-defined sanctuary, you can create a sacred ceremonial death for the soul-killing ideas, attachments, attitudes, and behaviors that have taken you so achingly far from your true path.

When you ask prayerfully, "What must end now?" and "What can no longer be tolerated in my soul?" the force inside your suicidal urge will help you perform some of the deepest soul-work you'll ever experience. The answers it gives you will always point to one or more (usually more) situations that are destroying your harmony, your functionality, and your ability to live and breathe freely. When you approach your suicidal urge prayerfully and ceremonially, it will give you clear answers about what must end: "This behavior, that addiction, this idea, this unfinished trauma, these relationships, this endless depression, this job, these excuses, this total lack of art and music, this poverty, these feelings of worthlessness, these flashbacks . . . " If you can welcome it in a grounded and ceremonial manner, your suicidal urge will identify your deepest troubling issues with pinpoint accuracy, and it will contribute the precise energy you need to rescue yourself and save your own life. If you can take hold of the fierce intensity it brings, you can set your boundary on fire, ground yourself fiercely, torch your painful contracts in huge conflagrations and infernos, and set yourself free. In this empathic way, and in this sacred space, your suicidal urge will have its kill, and then it will abate as it is meant to. If you can work with suicidal urges in this grounded ceremonial way, they will create a vibrant new boundary, place you strongly in the center of your village, and give you the focus you need to restore yourself to wholeness, agility, and resourcefulness once again.

Suicidal urges will not endanger you if you know how to channel them honorably. In fact, in some cases suicidal feelings can even comfort you with thoughts of escaping the cruelties of this world, ending your drama, and falling into a never-ending sleep. However, while the idea of suicide can be strangely comforting, the reality of suicide is a complete disaster. The people left behind are often shattered almost beyond recognition, the grieving continues for years on end, and their world is torn apart. When people come to me in the throes of a suicidal urge, I always try to help them understand that their problems are indeed horrific, but that they themselves are necessary, wanted, and needed on this side of the river to deal with those problems in their own unique way. I try to help them see themselves not as broken and meaningless people, but as sacred shrines through which the deepest troubles of the world are trying to be made conscious in order to be healed. When people can carry their suicidal urges in this sacred way, and can understand that no one else in the world can match or even approximate the specific brilliance they bring to their deepest issues, the feeling shifts, and they become what their suicidal urge always meant for them to be: soul warriors. Yes, the information inside suicidal urges is deep, powerful, and intense, but so are we, which means we can bring our power and intensity to these urges and channel them into transformation and healing.

Please be aware that suicidal urges contain huge amounts of anger. If you don't know how to work with anger (see pages 177–79), you may repress it and spiral into dissociative turmoil (and the "soft" suicides of addictions). However, if you can learn to channel your angers and rages, you can rely upon their intensity to help you destroy your excruciatingly unworkable contracts with any behaviors, mindsets, beliefs, or attitudes that have thrown you into torment. Your fierce angers can give you axes and mauls and flamethrowers to use against the destructive and soul-killing situations that brought them forward in the first place. When you can channel your angers, you can use their intensity not to hurt yourself, but to bring your soul back from hell. Remember that suicidal urges arise when situations in your life have spiraled so dangerously out of control that a ceremonial death is necessary. If you can work with your suicidal urges and the angers they contain in sacred, ceremonial, and empathic ways, they can offer you the imaginal experience of death without hurting you in any way.

The Practice for Suicidal Urges

These are the rapids, and you shouldn't enter them without preparation. You've got to be quite a river runner if you want to keep your head above water during a suicidal urge. It's usual for a first channeling session to be a combination of a roller-coaster ride, the Russian Revolution, and your first day at a new job. But after that, they get easier (if you tend toward suicidal urges, you'll probably continue to experience them in varying degrees, which is not a problem if you know how to channel them). Please remind yourself that this practice can't erase your suicidal urges, because nothing can or ever should erase your emotions. Suicidal urges are extremely important emotional states that arise when you're in serious trouble. You need them! If you learn to channel and honor them, and they return because your life has gotten away from you again for whatever reason, welcome them! They're your allies, and they'll lighten up considerably when you treat them as such. Let me show you what I mean.

I'll share a run-through of a channeling session I did for a suicidal urge I had in response to having been onstage as a lecturer and healer (where audience members brought huge amounts of unconscious needs, wishes, and demands that I picked up and tried to address while I was performing, teaching, and watching the clock at the same time), so you can see what it looks like to shoot these rapids. If you were running a real river, you'd watch the other rafters to see how they made it through the rough spots before you ever got in your own raft.

First, I sat down and focused myself, set my boundary on fire (suicidal urges contain massive amounts of anger, so it's important to create a really strong boundary before you channel them), and grounded myself strongly. Then I put a large, scroll-sized contract in front of me (inside my boundary), and dropped into the feelings I had been avoiding for so long. I say *feelings* because this trouble about being onstage certainly didn't start out as a suicidal urge. It started with fear, which I ignored, then dropped to anxiety, which I also ignored, then to shame, depression, physical illness, and finally to a suicidal urge (which I had been ignoring for about a month by that time). This spiral could easily have been averted if I had listened to my original fear in the first place, but I was so obscenely busy and overwhelmed that I didn't make any time for myself. Bad empath!

I asked my suicidal urge to come forward, but I didn't feel its fierce, furious intensity right away. Instead, I felt some darkness, some depression, and some sadness. I projected dark colors, a watery blue sadness, and a gray depressed feeling into my personal space so these emotions would know they were welcome and acknowledged. I didn't fill my personal space with Mr. Bunnies because this wasn't a Mr. Bunny situation. I filled my personal space with the actual emotions I felt at that moment. Then I asked my personal question for the suicidal urge: "What must end now; what must be killed?" Suddenly I saw on that imaginary contract a vision of myself onstage, complete with all the emotional debris that image held for me at the time. As I saw myself, dressed up, nervous inside but projecting warmth and humor to everyone else, and masquerading as a fiery extrovert when I'm really introverted and sensitive, I felt a tremendous sadness that came all the way from childhood, so I poured that on the contract and cried a bit. Within seconds, I began to feel light and giggly, simply because I had finally seen myself and felt my feelings. I then moved to conscious complaining, and complained aloud about not being able to be myself onstage. I used a lot of "can't" phrases (I can't be myself; I can't sing to set the feeling tone in the room without it seeming like a performance; I can't be everything to everyone; I can't figure this out), and those powerless, whiny statements brought my suicidal urge surging forward, mace in hand! In response, I hurled all the "can'ts" onto the contract, rolled it up very tightly, and threw it violently out of my boundary. My suicidal urge helped me focus an intense stream of fire onto that contract and burn it to a crisp.

As I moved through the material trapped under my suicidal urge, I discovered fears that were trying to help me prepare myself for the very difficult stage-work I was doing, angers and shames that were trying to help me set boundaries and behave in honorable and self-honoring ways, contentments that had been trying for months to tell me when I had done something right (I couldn't hear them, because I was so busy ignoring all of my feelings), enviousness that was trying to help me learn better social skills from performers who intimidated me, griefs about the private life I had lost, and every other feeling. When I completed the session (it took about ten minutes), I knew that I was absolutely forbidden to return to the stage in that same way, and that I had to do some intense research, self-study, boundary-setting, and rejuvenation practices before I could ever appear in public again. However, even though I had a big job ahead of me, I felt hopeful, empowered, happy, and grounded because each of the emotions trapped under my urge to suicide revitalized me. They helped me understand the specific (and completely overwhelming) issues I faced, and they contributed the precise information and intensity I needed to heal myself. My stage work and my stage persona were dishonoring my soul, the souls of the people in my audiences (because I couldn't be authentic), my writing career, and my livelihood. That stage persona needed to die before it destroyed my life. Channeling my suicidal urge helped me kill it off so that I could be reborn to my true needs. In the ensuing months, I worked diligently to understand the physical, emotional, intellectual, and spiritual supports I required to feel comfortable onstage, and now I can go onstage as an empathic, irreverent, singing, sensitive person who doesn't have a stage persona as much as a stage presence. And I can live with that.

CHANNELING YOUR OWN SUICIDAL URGE (IF YOU'RE READY)

When you're ready to work with your own suicidal urges, it's important to fire up your boundary and intensify your grounding, because this emotion brings intense energies with it. It also travels alongside many trapped emotions and traumatic memories, so it's equally important that you know your way around your entire emotional realm. Suicidal urges arise at the end of a long struggle. They are truly the darkness before the dawn, which means you should prepare yourself for their intensity by becoming proficient in each of your empathic skills, and comfortable with each of your elements and intelligences. It's important to have a balanced and honored body, a healthy and resourced intellect, a good connection to your visionary spirit, and a strong sense of your emotions so that your central nature will be agile, resourced, and fully able to work with the many flows you'll encounter when you ask your suicidal urge why it has come forward. You should also know your way around a conscious complaining session (see pages 146–49), because it acts as a safety release valve for any intense or trapped feelings (including suicidal urges). If you can complain out loud like there's no tomorrow and burn contracts while you do so, you'll reduce the drag on your soul, restore your focus, and break through any feedback loops that may entrap you. Then, if your suicidal urge is still active, you can go in and deal with its deep-seated issues quickly, instead of having to slog through a morass of clogged emotions. Conscious complaining heals!

When you're ready to work with your own suicidal urge, you may want to have a therapist with you. Follow your intuition, listen to any concerns you have, and gather all the support you need. Then, when you're ready, please create an incendiary "flame on!" boundary, and focus and ground yourself firmly in your body. Breathe deeply and soothe your body by patting your knees or rubbing your belly gently if you feel nauseated or fired up. Suicidal urges can really terrify your body, so you should comfort yourself and let your body know that you won't hurt it.

If any fear comes up for you, please move it into your protected personal space and continue grounding (this will help to calm your body). If you want to turn your entire boundary into a frightened color, do it. Welcome your fear and let it know you're awake to it, but don't let it destabilize your body. Do the same for any other emotions you may feel. Bring them out into your personal space and let them know you recognize and welcome them. If you feel overwhelmed, increase your grounding, soothe your body, and burn any number of contracts with whatever emotions come forward. Support the flow if you can. If you can't tolerate the flow right now, you can stop this channeling session.

To do so, bend over and touch your hands to the floor, then get up and shake your body all over, and move in any way that feels right. If you have any comfort foods, it's helpful to eat some slowly and carefully. In any case, please eat or drink something to ground yourself, and then go do something fun, or watch a funny show or video—nothing intense, scary, or dramatic. You need lightness!

If you're ready to continue, please place a large contract in front of you, and ask "What needs to end now?" or "What can no longer be tolerated in my soul?" An alternate question that may work for you, if you're comfortable with it, is "What must be killed?" If that question is too jarring, use the first two, whichever you like best. Then simply wait to see what appears on your contract. Remember that you don't have to "see" anything. You can hear, feel, sense, or just use your imagination to identify whatever your psyche decides to place onto your contract. You may sense pictures and sounds, one or more emotions, written or spoken words, hazy memories, or entire videologues. Your psyche works in its own way, and however you experience this process is the right way. Work with what is presented to you.

If you see or sense an image of yourself, know that this is not a literal wish for the end of your physical life. You're in a ceremonial ritual space now, where death is not literal, but figurative and imaginal. Observe the image that has been presented to you, and notice what you're wearing, what age you are, what you're doing or feeling, or what your body image or posture says about you (as I did with my stage persona). Something in this image is endangering you, and your sacred task is to identify the trouble you sense, and separate yourself from its destructive influence.

When you have a full sense of whatever images, ideas, or feelings came forward for you, roll up this contract, throw it out of your boundary, and burn it with whatever level of intensity you feel. When a suicidal urge is active, you may have a great deal of aggression available to you; don't repress it—use it to destroy your contract. Slice your contract in two with a guillotine, shoot at it with a cannon, torch it with a flamethrower, or crush it with a Sherman tank. Be honest and true to this emotional state, and it will help you obliterate the entrapping and soul-killing situations, behaviors, postures, health issues, and mindsets that forced it to come forward in the first place. Let your suicidal urge have its kill in this sacred space, and it will move through you and move on as all emotions should do. Know that you aren't hurting yourself or anyone else, no matter how ferocious your contract-destruction methods become. You're grounded and protected, you're working with your own emotional energy in your own sacred territory, and you're setting yourself free with the help of this intense emotion. In fact, the intensity with which you destroy these contracts will correlate directly to the level of release you'll achieve. When a suicidal urge arises, it brings you the ferocity you need to rescue your soul from hell; this is no time for pretty songs and fluffy kittens. Let this emotion perform its sacred task!

When you've destroyed this first contract, watch for shifts and changes inside yourself. If a new emotion comes forward, welcome it, create a new contract for it, and keep working. If your body brings discomfort forward, pat and soothe it, increase your grounding, or place yet another new contract in front of the distressed area and see if your body wants to move the distress out onto it. If it does, roll up this new contract tightly, throw it away from you, and burn it with whatever emotional intensity you feel. If thoughts and ideas spring forward, welcome them and write them down if you want to. If the thoughts are distressing, place them onto a contract as well, and watch your emotions as they react to these thoughts.

Roll this contract up, throw it out of your boundary, and burn it (or blow it up!) with whatever level of intensity you feel. Keep working in this way, always using your suicidal urge (or whichever emotion you're feeling at the moment) to destroy your contracts. Welcome and channel the emotions that present themselves. Welcome each thought, emotion, sensation, and vision as it comes, place all of them onto any number of contracts, and let them go completely! Set yourself free.

You can end this channeling session any time you feel done, either because you're finished with this issue for now, or because you feel tired or overwhelmed. Bend over and touch the floor; then stand up and move your body in any way you like. Have a glass of water or a small snack to ground yourself, and then finish this session with your rejuvenation practice. This process moves so much energy through you that you can essentially consider yourself a new being. It's important to rejuvenate yourself so you can welcome yourself fully back into life.

After channeling a suicidal urge, you'll be in a very different place, and you may have a new soul assignment as well. The channeling of this urge always reconnects you to your dreams and your innate intelligences. With its blessing, you'll have new information about which of your elements or intelligences needs to be revitalized and integrated, which skills you need to focus upon, which direction you need to take in your life and your career, which relationships you need to amend or restore, and which parts of your heart and soul were abandoned. You'll most likely have quite a bit of work ahead of you, but this work will now be about your soul's truest vision and your heart's truest path. That's good work if you can get it!

Bless your suicidal urge and welcome it into your emotional realm; it only arises when your soul is in absolute peril. If you can work with it in sacred space, it will give you the precise amount of energy you need to revitalize your exhausted spirit, heal your suffering body, soothe your tormented intellect, clear your clogged emotions, and save your indispensable life.

WHAT TO DO IF YOUR SUICIDAL URGES GET STUCK

If you feel a constant wish to end your life, and that wish does not respond to channeling, please seek immediate help from a therapist or call your local crisis hotline (look in the Yellow Pages under "Crisis Services"), the National Suicide Prevention Lifeline at 1-800-273-TALK (8255), or visit suicidepreventionlifeline.org. Reach out for help. We need you here on the planet, alive and kicking, alive and complaining, alive and struggling, alive and laughing, but most important, alive. Please reach out!

HONORING SUICIDAL URGES IN OTHERS

Listen carefully for threats of suicide and treat them as actual emergencies. When people threaten to kill themselves, they're almost never kidding. Even if they don't actually go through with their plans, the fact that they put those plans into words means they're in a world of pain. This is a rapids-level situation, and it requires the assistance of a therapist or a suicide hotline (see above).

You can, however, create sacred space for a friend who is feeling suicidal simply by being available to talk about it. When I felt suicidal, the sense that I couldn't share my feelings with others—because they'd be afraid or offended, or because I might drag them down with me—made my suicidal urges much worse. If you can just say outright, "How are you feeling about death right now?" or "Did the counselor help you explore your suicidal feelings?" you can bring the suicidal urge out of the shadows. Secrets and repression are not at all helpful at a time like this, and if you can clearly state the obvious and provide a listening and supportive ear, your friend will probably breathe a big sigh of relief. Suicidal urges are intensely isolating, and it's important to step in and make a welcoming space in *this* world for people who are feeling a strong pull toward death. You'll be astonished at how this simple act will help your suicidal friend. This kind of welcome is also extremely valuable if your friend needs medication, because it can sometimes take a while to find the right one; you don't want people to feel as if they're only going to be valuable when they're "normal" again.

If you encounter "soft" suicidal urges, such as those exhibited by addicts and people trapped in endangering replays of their unhealed traumas, please understand that they are in a kind of separate reality that doesn't completely mesh with this one. Addictions and post-traumatic disorders essentially spiral people into the raging rapids, not just in the emotional realm, but in the physical, mental, and spiritual realms as well. These turbulent states can be necessary steps in their journeys to soul-making (if they survive), but while this turbulence is in full swing, it essentially shuts down people's capacity to relate to anyone or anything but the addiction or the trauma. As a friend, you've got to understand that healing from this sort of turmoil is often a very involved process that requires physical, intellectual, emotional, psychological, and medical intervention.

However, the first and most important healing influence is your friend's sincere desire to become well. If he or she wants to become well, you can find competent help, and support him or her with your love and companionship as the healing proceeds. If your friend doesn't want to be well, then it's important that you protect yourself. Call out for help and support for yourself, and do what you can to alert professionals that your friend is in serious trouble and needs more help than you alone can provide.

Remember to welcome your suicidal urges, not as literal wishes for death, but as signs that something inside you is already threatening your life. Suicidal urges are the darkness before dawn. Let them have their kill in a sacred, empathic way, and you'll be reborn into this life. Welcome and thank your suicidal urges.

24

Happiness

Amusement and Anticipation

GIFTS
Merriment ~ Gaiety ~ Hope ~ Delight ~ Wonder
~ Playfulness ~ Invigoration

THE INTERNAL STATEMENT
Thank you for this lively celebration!

SIGNS OF OBSTRUCTION
Lack of belief in possibilities or the future;
the unwillingness to play; or the inability to release happiness
and feel your deeper emotions

PRACTICE
Celebrate your happiness and let it go; it can only flow
freely when you allow *all* of your emotions to flow.

THE *Tao Te Ching* calls happiness the most dangerous emotion, not in and of itself, but because of the way we behave in relation to it. We chase after it, sell our souls for it, and try to cement ourselves into its territory, no matter what else is going on in our lives. This exploitation of happiness jeopardizes us, because when we refuse to honor any emotion except happiness, our emotional landscapes become stagnant and unbalanced, which makes us chase even more furiously after happiness. Consequently, we spiral into emotional suffering, mental confusion, physical imbalance, and spiritual malaise. By chasing after happiness, we create the most joyless lives imaginable.

Recent research has also shown that we're absolutely terrible at predicting what will make us happy or unhappy. In his 2006 book, *Happiness: The Science Behind Your Smile,* psychologist Daniel Nettle explores numerous studies that show humans to be truly clueless about happiness. For instance, most of us are certain that money will make us happy, but studies of lottery winners show that sudden riches are, in fact, very shocking and tend not to impact winners' baseline happiness levels in positive ways. Also, while being poor is certainly detrimental to health and well-being, only those people who reach a comfortable level of income can be said to be truly happier than the poverty-stricken. The fact is that after a modest level of financial comfort is reached, at, say, an annual family income of fifty to sixty thousand in 2007 U.S. dollars, there is no correlation whatsoever between more money and more happiness.

It's interesting to note that many people use the word "unhappy" to describe any troubling emotion, as if happiness were the expected and required state, while anything else merely equaled its opposite. "Unhappy" is a cheap and lazy word, though: does it mean you're sad, angry, anxious, apathetic, fearful, depressed, despondent, ashamed, or what? It's important to know, because happiness is not the opposite of any emotion (though we've certainly been told otherwise!). Happiness is not the opposite of anger, because happiness doesn't strip you of honor or boundaries. It's also not the opposite of sadness, because happiness doesn't strip you of your ability to ground, let go, or rejuvenate yourself. Happiness is not the opposite of fear either, because it doesn't strip you of your instincts or your ability to take action. No, happiness doesn't exist in a divergent emotional universe; it carries its own unique emotional energy that blends and dances beautifully with all your other emotional energies. Happiness performs a specific function in your soul, but only if it is treated with respect and allowed to arise in its own way and in its own time.

Happiness seems to be a difficult emotion for many of us to grasp because it is so often paired with the word "idiot" in some form or fashion (happy fool, blissful ignorance, slaphappy—that sort of thing). But happiness isn't ignorance or foolishness; happiness holds our sense of wonder and anticipation of good things, and it looks forward to the future. It is in many ways a child's emotion in our culture, because growing up nearly always requires the growing away from happiness and ease. We all have to become serious and choose our careers with IRAs and 401(k)s and dental plans in mind, and we're inundated with any number of admonitions: "Sure, music makes you happy, but will it pay the rent? Art and dancing aren't honest work! We can't be happy all the time; some of us have to provide for our families!" In response to this crackdown on happiness, we're surrounded by many books and seminars that tell us how to play, how to find work we love, how to bring money to ourselves in fun ways, and so forth. Though these books often sell, their messages seem to remain on the margins because there's a powerful belief that only children are happy, while adults are serious and hardworking.

The only flaw in our society-wide argument against happiness is this: children are actually very serious and hardworking, in addition to being happy and playful! If you've ever built a fort with a group of eight-year-olds or helped a child with a particularly daunting homework assignment, you'll have seen a work ethic that far exceeds any adult's. Children have an exquisite ability to focus themselves on huge problems and projects, yet not feel crushed, and I think that's because they have the permission to be happy and to play. Being allowed to laugh, clown, fool around, and play allows children to flow into and out of struggles and to continually replenish and resource themselves by moving fluidly between work and play. Play, comedy, and happiness contribute fluidity and agility to the soul. As such, they should not be relegated to the world of childhood. We all require a great deal of play and silliness to balance our intensity and seriousness if we want to accomplish anything worthwhile.

If you've been convinced that happiness is the wrong emotion to feel in the dire atmosphere of the present day, just sit with that idea for a moment and ask yourself if our current epidemic of familial decay, social upheaval, emotional disorders, and political impotence could have anything whatever to do with the fact that adults are expected to work like draft horses, yet aren't allowed to be silly and hopeful and happy. If you look to the future, do you see grim death, disaster, and global warming—about which you can do precisely nothing? Well, that's very adult of you. But can you get into a playful state where you imagine us turning this giant behemoth of a society around so that it serves us, instead of us serving it? Can you see it in your wildest dreams? Because you used to, every day—remember?

You came into this world trailing, as Robert Bly wrote in *A Little Book on the Human Shadow*, "spontaneities wonderfully preserved from our 150,000 years of tree life, angers well preserved from our 5,000 years of tribal life—in short, with our 360-degree radiance." I remember, as a child, looking at world hunger and creating hundreds of solutions for it. Sending my lima beans to China was just one facet of a multi-tiered plan of action. Do you remember your own world-saving plans? Each of us came into this life with all the vitality and brilliance we need to save the world; we've just forgotten how to access it.

I notice that truly successful people (who really live their dreams and save the world one heart at a time) give themselves permission to be happy, even slaphappy, while allowing equal time for the adult view, the depression, and the truth of the degradation all around us. Truly successful people find an intense problem and then throw themselves at it full-on—like it's a game of Red Rover—with their entire emotional arsenal. In unsuccessful people, I see a pathetic scrabbling after happiness without the balance of serious introspection and hard work, or I see a constant press toward endless work without the balancing influence of play, laughter, or a willingness to look ridiculously hopeful while working for a different future. Such unsuccessful people can't get out of their own way, which means they aren't particularly effective as workers, dreamers, or agents of change. Successful people, on the other hand, allow themselves to flow and moderate between work and play, between seriousness and goofiness, and between honest hope and honest despair, which means they can bring their full-bodied selves to any task they choose. Their happiness arises not because they repress all their other emotions, but because they live whole and resourced 360-degree lives.

Here's a fun fact about happiness: a 2008 study by Harvard medical sociologist Nicholas Christakis and political scientist James Fowler showed that happiness is actually contagious in social networks, and that it seems to travel more effectively than unhappiness (yes, "unhappiness" is an emotionally incoherent term, but we know what they mean).[12] Basically, if you have a happy friend, or even a friend of a friend, your chances of feeling happy increase; therefore, it's important to be aware of the emotions you share with others. Smiling, laughing, goofing, and friendliness are behaviors we can share when we feel them, and in so doing, we'll increase the health and happiness of others. Keep one caveat in mind when you use humor, however. Watch out for sarcasm. As we've all learned online and through misunderstood e-mails, sarcasm can look and feel exactly like anger (which is usually what it is).

If you want more happiness in your life, look closely at the stories you tell yourself. Whether you glorify happiness or shun it as frivolous, you can heal yourself by bringing your relationship with happiness out in the open, placing it on a contract, and releasing yourself and your happiness from any unhappy stories you've created. Let your happiness flow as but one of your emotions, and trust it to arise naturally (and playfully) as it helps you restore your flow.

The Practice for Happiness

Your task, when happiness arises naturally, is to laugh, goof, smile, and dream ("Thank you for this lively celebration!") and then flow into your next task or your next emotion. If you try to imprison your happiness, you'll spiral into a forced kind of gaiety (that's exhilaration—see pages 373–76) that will deaden your entire emotional realm and increase your tendency toward depression. The key to working with happiness healthfully is to see it as a momentary passage and not a final destination. Interestingly, if you give your happiness complete freedom and welcome whichever emotions you feel before and after it arises, your happiness will tend to arise more and more often and in response to more and different stimuli. The trick then, when happiness flows more freely, is to continue to let it flow instead of showcasing it as proof of your emotional agility. Flow is the key!

Remember to welcome your happiness on *its* timetable—not yours. Learn to recognize happiness in all its forms instead of grasping at it gracelessly. Welcome, honor, and thank your happiness. Then let it go.

25

Contentment

Appreciation and Recognition

GIFTS
Enjoyment ~ Satisfaction ~ Self-esteem ~ Renewal ~ Fulfillment

THE INTERNAL STATEMENT
Thank you for renewing my faith in myself!

SIGNS OF OBSTRUCTION
Inability to feel satisfied with yourself, or the unwillingness
to challenge yourself and risk failure

PRACTICE
Celebrate your excellent fortune and skills; then move on to your
next challenge. Real contentment follows real accomplishments.

HAPPINESS TENDS TO ANTICIPATE a bright future, while contentment tends to arise after an inner achievement. Contentment arises when you're living up to your own expectations and your internal moral code, and when you've accomplished an important goal or done your work well and properly. Contentment comes forward in response to tangible actions and the mastery of clear-cut challenges. Contentment also arises when you've successfully navigated through your difficult emotions—especially your angers, hatreds, and shames. When you've restored your boundary, honored the boundaries of others, and corrected your actions or made amends, your contentment will come forward to confirm and validate your excellent behavior. Authentic contentment arises reliably when you respect yourself and others, and when you respect your emotions and allow them to guide your behavior.

Social structures often interfere with your authentic contentment by trying to replace or usurp your natural internal confirmations with prizes and praise that come from outside. While it's nice to receive gold stars, awards, extra privileges, and special attention, these fabricated confirmations can actually short-circuit your own ability to feel honest pride or self-worth unless someone throws a party every time you accomplish something. External praise also contains a troublesome aspect that is not a part of internal contentment—and that's competition. All external praise and awards come with built-in comparisons that place you in competition with others. Though the awards and praise may have value, they tend to isolate you from your peers and identify you as a competitor or a pleaser, which will often bring your natural shame forward to question the "fun" of winning. In natural contentment, there is no shame, because your achievements aren't about doing better than others, but about honoring your own good judgment and your own values.

If you can't connect with your natural contentment, you may have a short circuit that was created by authoritarian, scholastic, or parental structures. This short circuit may lead you to seek praise and awards instead of your own internal confirmations. This often means you'll tend toward pleasing and perfectionism instead of wholeness and emotional agility. You'll tend toward following this rule, chasing that award, and constantly measuring yourself against external expectations, instead of allowing your honest emotional reactions to guide you. Luckily, you know what to do with externally applied expectations and behavioral control: burn your contracts and reanimate your authentic contentment once again! Then, when you're connected to your own internal wisdom, you can guide, correct, and validate yourself in self-respecting ways rather than relying on external validation.

The Practice for Contentment

The practice for all of the happiness-based emotions is extremely simple and infinitely hard (at first): you acknowledge them, thank them, and then let them go completely. If you force your contentment (or any other form of happiness) to be your leading emotional state, you'll lose your way in a split second. Real, honest contentment arises naturally when you work with all of your emotions in healing and honorable ways. Welcome your contentment with open arms when it arises, thank it, and congratulate yourself ("Thank you for renewing my faith in myself!"), and then let it go and trust it to come back the next time you honor yourself and behave in ways that make you feel proud.

Remember to welcome and honor your contentment: it arises when you've done an excellent job. Good on you! Thank your contentment.

26

Joy

Affinity and Communion

Includes Exhilaration and Honoring Happiness in Others

GIFTS
Expansion ~ Communion ~ Inspiration ~ Splendor
~ Radiance ~ Bliss

THE INTERNAL STATEMENT
Thank you for this radiant moment!

SIGNS OF OBSTRUCTION
Inability to feel connected to humanity or the world, or
unwillingness to release joy and feel your other emotions

PRACTICE
Celebrate your joyousness and let it flow naturally.
Joy will seek you out if you let it move in its own time
and in its own way—not in yours.

JOY IS DIFFERENT FROM happiness in that it is deeper and larger somehow.
It is closer in its essence to contentment, but instead of coming forth after
an achievement, joy seems to come forth during moments of communion
with nature, love, and beauty—when you feel as if you're one with everything. If you can recall the expansive, light-filled, and powerfully calm
feelings you have when you're in your favorite natural setting at the most

beautiful time of day, or when you're with a person or animal you love and trust utterly, you'll be able to identify joy.

Joy is possibly the trickiest and most dangerous of all the happiness-based emotions, not in and of itself, but because of the way we treat it. Joy is considered the queen of all emotions—the one we're supposed to stay in at all times and in all situations. It's treated almost as an orgasmic emotional state—as a peak experience—which means that people spend a lot of time working toward it as a goal instead of living consciously and appropriately in relation to it. Joy has even become a central goal of many fire-only spiritual practices, where an amazing amount of time and energy is spent in the single-minded pursuit of the expansive and communal sensations inside joy. If you don't look at it empathically, joy seems to offer freedom from the body, the mind, the "difficult" emotions, and the bonds of this world. However, true joy arises naturally and spontaneously only during times of full-bodied wholeness, when you experience your favorite nature scene, your brilliant vision, or your dearest love with your body, your multiple intelligences, your emotions, your visionary spirit, and the fully resourced village inside you. The wonderful sensations of joy arise not because you shut down element after element, but because all parts of you are awake enough to be touched and permeated by radiance and bliss.

Joy usually arises after you've come to the end of a long and arduous path; for instance, you often have to travel a long way to get to your favorite natural setting, just as you often have to struggle through many painful relationships before you find your heart's true companion. For this reason, joy and contentment are more connected to each other than to happiness—because both joy and contentment arise in response to honest work and triumphs inside you, whereas happiness usually arises to give you a quick vacation from all the work you need to do before you can truly feel contentment or joy. This special relationship between joy and hard work is not universally understood, because most people are surprised by joy and see it as a mysterious gift from the cosmos rather than a natural human emotion. The most likely explanation for this confusion is that while we all work very hard, we tend to work in ways that deny our wholeness, which means we don't have the full-bodied capacity to truly experience joy on a regular basis. As a result, most of us separate joy from its brother and sister emotions and treat it as some sort of magical visitation. But joy is not magic—it's an emotion. In fact, it's the emotion you access when you perform your rejuvenation practice. Surprise! Notice, however, that we use this flowing form of joy after hard work, after intense change, and in relation to the wholeness we're trying to create and nurture. We're not just jacking ourselves up. We're using joy appropriately, just as we use our free-flowing sadness, fear, and anger appropriately in our grounding, focusing, and boundary-definition practices.

Joy ebbs and flows reliably, not only in response to hard work and contentment, but to grief as well. Joy often follows or travels alongside grief in a healthy psyche, which may seem puzzling to you if you don't understand the opportunity for communion that lives inside both joy and grief. These two emotions are deeply connected; if you enter into the beautiful work that awaits you in the deep river of grief, you'll become one with the continuum of spirits—one with the births and deaths of all souls. That's communion, which places you immediately into the territory of joy, both while you're in the river performing your sacred grief-work and after you come up and out of the water to rejoin life on this side of the river again.

When we as a culture severed our bodies from our visionary spirits (and our emotions from our intellects) and ran screaming from death, we impeded our ability to feel honest joy. For thousands of years, we've chased after, grasped at, and tried to imprison joy in any number of excruciatingly doomed ways. As it turns out, joy has been seeking us our whole lives, and if we can stop running after it and start to feel all our honest emotions, joy will inexorably find us. Whole people feel real, natural joy—without artificial stimulants, avoidance behaviors, the denial of death, arduous meditative practices, or any other forced techniques. Whole people understand that joy is not a goal in and of itself, but that joy only arises in a life that's resourced with honest hardships, triumphs, ordeals, loss, hard work, love, laughter, grief, and wholeness.

The Practice for Joy

We already have a practice for the free-flowing form of joy, so I sort of tricked you into freeing up this area of your emotional realm by teaching you to use joy to rejuvenate yourself. I wanted to get you used to joy, which arises naturally when you've done honest and strenuous work to arrive at a place of communion with all parts of yourself and the world. Your grounding and integrating task when joy arises is to remind yourself that the hard work is just as beautiful, and just as meaningful, as the joy. Now that you can connect the seemingly otherworldly presence in joy to the very worldly and full-bodied work you did to bring your joy forward, you'll have an easy time celebrating and then releasing your joy naturally ("Thank you for this radiant moment!"). Afterward, you can get back to your real work, which will lead you naturally and inevitably—again and again—back to your real joy.

HONORING HAPPINESS, CONTENTMENT, AND JOY IN OTHERS

When people around you are imbued with happiness, contentment, or joy, there is very little for you to do but enjoy them. However, this can be a difficult task if your own relationship with any of these emotions is skewed. In order to truly honor an emotion in another person, you've got to understand it in yourself first. In the territory of happiness, this means knowing how to celebrate and release the happiness-based emotions instead of holding on to them for dear life, or dismissing them as signs of childishness or idiocy.

Let me prepare you right now for a fall, because you'll almost certainly make mistakes in this emotional territory. You may unknowingly disparage the giddy happiness in other people or overpraise or inhibit others instead of helping them create sacred space for their own natural contentment. You may also try to hook yourself into another's joy and convince him or her to imprison it so you can experience it vicariously. We've all had so much bizarre socialization in regard to the happiness-based emotions that we behave strangely around them. Therefore, be gentle with yourself and know you'll awaken if you can fall and rise again, make amends, and burn your own contracts with the truly odd ideas we all have about happiness.

WHEN CONTENTMENT, HAPPINESS, AND
JOY GET STUCK: EXHILARATION

We've looked at the three healthy forms of happiness: contentment, which is like a deep and healing breath that follows a sense of inner achievement; the giddier state of happiness, which bubbles up, takes your hand, and skips with you into the bright future; and joy, which arises when you've worked hard and honorably to arrive at a place of beauty and full-bodied communion. However, there's also a trapped and frantic emotional state that arises when you try to cement yourself into the territory of happiness: it's called exhilaration.

In exhilaration, you become not happy and silly, but skittery, delirious, and ungrounded. Natural contentment and joy tend to be grounding, and though happiness adds a lightness and frivolity to your soul, it doesn't pull your grounding out of the earth. Whereas happiness makes you feel like a hopeful kid again, exhilaration makes you feel hyperactive and nearly fraught, as if your happiness will disappear if you take your eyes off it for one second. Exhilaration prompts you to keep moving from one "happy" thing to the next—from one bite of comfort food to a whole cake in one sitting; from one pleasant idea to the next; or from one stimulating love affair or ecstatic purchase to the next, without ever stopping to feel any grief or remorse about your erratic behavior. Exhilaration throws you into addictions and distractions of every kind, and it's a crystal-clear sign of a rupture between your spirit and your body (hence your ungroundedness) and a conflict between your emotions and your logical intellect (hence your refusal to feel any other emotion and your inability to think clearly). Exhilaration can feel gorgeous and empowering, but it is associated with neurochemical imbalances, so you have to be very careful in this emotional territory.

Though endless happiness is celebrated the world over, unending exhilaration brings just as much trouble as unending depression, anger, fear, or despair. All emotions are damaging if you imprison them, just as all emotions are healing when you channel them honorably. Exhilaration, though, is especially damaging because it helps people seduce and imprison their happiness and joy in order to see only the bright, upbeat, and happy side of life. Exhilaration addicts usually ignore their sadness, explain away their fear, chase away their anger, and repress their grief so completely that they become incapable of relating in any useful capacity. In essence, their exhilaration is used as a hallucinogen or a stimulant—as a total distraction from real life.

Imbalances in any emotion bring about turmoil, but the dramas of exhilaration addicts are often deeply unsettling. If the exhilaration is part of a manic or bipolar depressive cycle, it can spin people into extreme levels of activity; they may become chaotic and self-destructive, or wildly and unrelentingly industrious (this latter condition is considered less hazardous than the former, but both lead inexorably back into the depths of depression).

In some cases, exhilarated people may gather many followers (think cults) because they live an overwhelmingly seductive lie that says one can be joyful at all times, as if that one emotion were enough. Unfortunately, when difficulties inevitably arise and personalities clash, these exhilaration addicts often cannibalize one another because they have no idea how to work with any emotion except exhilaration. In these cultic, high-control groups, anger tends to decay into passive-aggressive rage; normal fears disintegrate into anxiety and paranoia; and honest sadness becomes unmanageable depressions, sleep disorders, and suicidal urges.

True happiness, contentment, and joy bring delight into your conscious awareness—but only if you treat each one honorably. If you try to paste a haunted smile onto your face and throw yourself into a nightmare of never-ending exhilaration, you'll destabilize every part of yourself. Healthy joy, happiness, and contentment are meant to be as fleeting as healthy anger, grief, fear, or any other emotional state. They were never meant to be held hostage or used to gain prestige in an emotionally stunted world.

The Practice for Exhilaration

Focus and ground yourself right now! Can you? If you've been trying to stay in exhilaration, joy, bliss, or whatever they're calling it this year, don't be surprised if you're completely unable to focus yourself. Also, don't be surprised if your life is in an uproar. I've noticed that groups of exhilaration addicts try to convince each other that their uproar is a gauge of their exhilaration maintenance abilities (as if the god of exhilaration is testing their mettle), but don't fall for that scam! Exhilaration-caused uproar is a natural reaction to emotional imbalance, and it will occur whenever any emotion is imprisoned. If you're being knocked about by exhilaration, bring your excellent judgment forward and take a close look at people trapped in despair, hatred, depression, or any other single emotion. Their imbalance will throw their lives into an uproar very similar to yours. There's nothing particularly brilliant about an exhilaration-caused uproar.

Your healing practice in this territory is the same as the practice for people trapped in depression, because both exhilaration and depression spring from quaternal imbalance, emotional suppression, and avoidance behaviors. You should start at the beginning of the book again, because you'll need to review the elements and intelligences to discover where your village is unbalanced; you'll need to move from there to the chapter on addictions and distractions; you'll need to understand trauma and its connection to emotional suppression; and you'll need to review the entire chapter on the empathic practices so that you can integrate your body and your visionary spirit, create sacred space and distinction for yourself, utilize your free-flowing emotions honorably, and connect to the earth once again. Then, as your trance lifts and all of your other trampled emotions begin to emerge again, you can work with each of them in turn. Remember that no emotion is bad or good; they are all natural and necessary reactions and sensibilities that should flow freely. Enjoy your happiness, your contentment, your joy, and your bliss—and then move on as you're meant to. You have more work to do, more emotions to feel, and more life to live.

HONORING EXHILARATION IN OTHERS

Exhilaration is an addictive and dissociative state; as such, it can't truly be honored or supported in safe ways until the exhilarated person is ready to come back to earth. If you're involved with generally healthy people, you can simply wait until they come off their high, and then help them connect to whatever true feelings they've been running from. If you're involved with a person who's struggling with a manic or bipolar disorder, please help him or her find a competent therapist or doctor; this is a situation that requires more help than a friend can provide. Stay close to your friend and offer your help, support, love, and prayers, but know that severe cyclical bipolar disorder requires expert medical, emotional, and psychological intervention.

If you're involved with people who adhere devoutly to exhilarated fire-only practices, you may have to protect yourself from them for your own health and well-being. Though it is wrenching to write this, the fact is that exhilaration addicts usually have to burn themselves to a crisp before they can come out of their trance states. If they're involved in cultic groups, they may have to lose everything and deconstruct completely before they can truly see what is occurring in their lives, because they're often strictly controlled and trapped. Send these people your love, and let them know you'll be there when they awaken, but know your limits. Exhilaration addiction and cult membership is an endangering state that requires far more help than a friend can provide (see Further Resources for brilliant books by sociologist and cult expert Janja Lalich).

Remember to welcome your joy in its free-flowing state every time you rejuvenate yourself, and make room for its mood state by doing your work in the inner and outer worlds with compassion, humor, intensity, and love. Thank your joy, but also remember to thank yourself. Your real work brings your real joy forward.

27

Stress and Resistance

Understanding Emotional Physics

IMAGINE THIS SCENARIO: You wake up on a Saturday morning, bleary-eyed and disoriented, to find your alarm clock dark and silent. The electricity in your house is off, and you don't know what time it is. You leap out of bed, search for your cell phone, and discover that it's 9:15—and your parents' anniversary party, which you're hosting, starts at noon. You focus yourself intently, prioritize your schedule, and rush to get ready. You jump in the shower, but the hot water runs out because your water heater is electric. Then you realize with a sickening thud that your blow-dryer is electric as well—as are all your kitchen appliances, which means you can't cook any of the food you bought for the party. Okay, you can still save the day; you can go to the deli and get a cheese and vegetable tray—not perfect, but it will do. You throw your clothes on, grab an apple for breakfast, run out to the garage by 9:30, your hair still wet, and start your car before remembering that your garage-door opener is electric as well. You get out of your car and try to disengage the garage-door mechanism, but it's completely jammed. You find a wrench and really lean into the job, realizing one moment too late that the "leaning" side of your body is now covered with garage-door grime—and the mechanism still won't disengage. Now you're not only late, but you're hungry, wet, dirty, and trapped in your garage. How do you feel? If you're like most people, you'll answer "stressed-out."

My empathic question to you, and I hope your own empathic question to yourself, is, "What does 'stressed-out' actually mean?" What do you feel when you enter into the state you identify as stress? Are you angry? Are you ashamed of yourself? Are you anxious? Confused? Panicky? Furious? Depressed? All seven at once? Do you feel like crying? What do you feel when events conspire to thwart your every movement? What do you feel when you're late? What do you feel when you make mistakes or when you look uncoordinated or incompetent? What do you feel when your appliances, tools, cars, and utility companies fail you? What do you feel when scheduling conflicts and demands pile one on top of another until you're overwhelmed? And what do you feel when you're not in control of your life?

"Stressed-out" is not an acceptable answer to any of these questions, because stress is not a emotion. The word "stress" doesn't even come from the world of emotions; it's a term from the world of physics and engineering, where it is defined as a pressure, pull, or force exerted on one thing by another, or the internal resistance of a thing to the external forces applied to it. Interestingly, this word that refers to things—to inanimate objects—has found its way into our emotional vocabulary. And our emotional definition of stress nearly equals the definition given to us by engineers; it has helped us view ourselves as objects being acted upon by forces, instead of living, agile, and resourceful organisms. The word "stress" has become a universal catchall for emotions in a culture that doesn't have a functional emotional vocabulary. Now if we're sad, furious, frightened, exhilarated, exhausted, despondent, ashamed, mournful, panicky, or even suicidally depressed, we can use the word "stress" to describe our condition. This is not a sign of empathic awareness or emotional fluency.

What would a person with a functional emotional vocabulary do in the stressful scenario above? The steps would be different for each of us, but what about alerting all the guests by phone and asking for cooking help or alternative party locations? What about taking some time to cry and feel the loss of the wonderful party experience that might have been so that you can restore yourself and prepare for the party that will be? What about calling the electric company and finding out when your service will be back on? What about complaining out loud to your garage door and really reading it the riot act (and perhaps pounding on it with the wrench a few times) so you can clear the decks and restore your resilience and your sense of humor? What about rescheduling? What about moving the party to a restaurant or a park? What about asking a neighbor to help you with the garage door or take you to the deli? What about sitting with the fear that people will think you're a failure? What about sitting with the shame you feel when you let other people down? What about being honest about your emotions?

If you can meet a stressful situation as a living, breathing, and emotive being, you can respond to it in a hundred different ways. You can perform many different experiments in emotional physics and navigate through your troubles, traumas, and stresses in ways that will increase your awareness, your resources, your integrity, and your ability to access your deepest issues (stressful situations always expose your deepest issues). Your task is not to create a stress-free and perfect existence (perfectionism is absolute proof that you've lost your flow), but to learn to respond resourcefully when stressors appear.

Stress is a relationship between your living organism and the forces of the world; your responses to these forces (not the forces themselves) determine your outcome. Painful stressed-out responses aren't a necessity in every stressful situation; there are dozens of ways to react. This thing called "stress"—this increase in adrenaline, this sense of pressure, this physical tenseness—is simply a fear-based readiness response that tries to activate and prepare you for change and unpredictability. It's a normal and healthy reaction. Trouble arises not from your stress response or even from the change or upset that triggered it; trouble arises when you lose your agility, your flow, your resourcefulness, and your liveliness, and become an inanimate object.

When your flow and agility are gone, the actual stressor almost becomes unimportant; in fact, you can be just as stressed-out by falling in love as you can by losing your job. Falling in love asks you to drop your boundaries, which often forces you to deal with your deepest issues of trust and intimacy—while losing your job disrupts your social and financial security, which may force you to question and even completely redesign your career and your life. If you can ground and focus yourself and honor the emotions that move forward during such challenges, you'll be able to meet them in agile and resourceful ways. But if you don't have emotional skills, both of these challenges may knock you flat. In fact, if you don't have skills, you can be knocked flat by just about anything—a missed appointment, a sideways look from a co-worker, or a lost set of keys. The size of the stressor doesn't matter; your capacity to respond to it does.

If you don't have the capacity to respond resourcefully to the many disappointments, sudden changes, pressures, and shocks life brings you, you may hide behind stress. We all do it. We all hide our real emotions and tell people we're stressed-out, which means we don't have to explain tense behavior that covers up our angers, anxieties, or suppressed tears. We don't have to question our stress-relieving buying sprees that cover up our depressions or despairs. We don't have to address our stress-based addictions and distractions that cover up our panics, furies, or traumatic memories. We don't have to change our stressful eating and health-care habits that cover up our emotional distress, our intellectual confusion, our physical exhaustion, or our spiritual malaise. When we hide behind the term "stressed-out," we don't have to explain ourselves or question our behaviors, and most important, we don't have to slow down to feel anything. When we're stressed-out, we're no longer responsible for ourselves; we become slates upon which the troubles of the world are written; we become things—not vibrant and questing organisms, but mere victims of schedules, utility companies, finances, personality clashes, illnesses, the weather, traumas, and life itself.

When you feel stressed-out, please understand that you're disconnected from your grounding, your flow, your agility, your sense of humor, your instincts, your ability to set a boundary, and your interior village. Stress-relieving practices like deep breathing and relaxation are lovely (though crying is often more relaxing than either of them), but if you don't go in and ask yourself what you're feeling, you'll continue to experience the imbalances that lead inevitably to stressful suffering. If you can learn to respond to stressors by grounding and setting a safe boundary around yourself, you can bring your full-bodied insight to the stressful situation.

For instance, if you experience a gnawing stomachache, a sore neck, tight or clumsy muscles, powerful food cravings, or any other physical sensations, you can ask your body what these sensations mean for you; you can work with your body instead of running from your discomfort. You can also connect with your emotions. If you're afraid, you can ask yourself what you sense, and what actions you need to take. If you're angry and too many things are getting under your skin, you can fire up your boundary and complain (consciously) like there's no tomorrow. If you feel like crying, you can cry! If you're full of amorphous anxieties and confusions, you can question your intentions and relieve your ambiguity. If you're crushed by unmoving despair, you can ask, "What must be released?" so that you can be rejuvenated. If you're depressed, you can ask where your energy has gone. If you're exhausted, you can take a hot bath and get some sleep. No matter what you feel, you can use your skills to work through the deep and often painful issues that stressful situations always uncover.

You can also observe your thoughts. If your mind is spiraling into disorder or is hyperactivated, trying to plot a way out of your troubles, you can reconnect with your fear-based intuition and instincts, and bring order and focus to your inner chaos. You can also connect meaningfully with your eagle nature (rather than abuse its visionary capabilities to merely escape from your current situation) and ask it for direction. You can pay attention to your dreams and your visions, and you can stop yourself in the middle of a stressful situation and observe your situation from an eagle's-eye view. For instance, if you always feel powerfully ashamed when you let people down, or if you're consistently unwilling to ask for help, perhaps you can see that something in this electrical outage is giving you the opportunity to finally face these issues head-on. When you can observe life with the help of your visionary spirit, you'll understand that the flow of each day isn't so much about schedules, work, or parties as it is about stretching and challenging yourself so that you can live more fully. If you can bring your fiery eagle nature into play, you may find that this electrical outage was not a personal affront to you or your plans, but might just be an opportunity for you to meet and work with your neighbors, to rely upon your siblings and friends, to connect with your parents in a new way, or even to make plans to alter your relationship with the utility company and get yourself a solar array. You really can't know why events unfold as they do, or what each day has in store for you—just as you can't be certain that the things you perceive as mistakes, hindrances, and stressors really are.

We can't control the flows of the world, but we can prepare ourselves for just about any eventuality by nurturing flow and balance within our own psyches and by becoming conduits through which the currents of honesty, ingenuity, vision, insight, and emotions can flow in response to any stimuli (stressful or otherwise).

Stress in itself is not the problem; stress is a necessary and even sacred part of life. Without it, you would be untested, undifferentiated, unchallenged, and insufficiently resourced. Even the word "stress" tells us this: an alternate definition for stress is to underscore, accentuate, or emphasize something. When you feel stressed-out, you are in many ways slowing yourself down to notice, emphasize, and underscore (albeit unconsciously) the important issues that arise within you. Your key task during stressful times is not to strive for a stress-free life or an impenetrable psyche, but to work with your stress responses in honest and soul-honoring ways. Stressors always uncover important issues; therefore, if you can wade into your stress responses with all of your skills and resources, you can wend your way into the deepest regions of your soul. If you try to avoid stress or repress your stress responses (or express your stressed-out behaviors in incompetent ways), you won't gain the agility you need to engage with the often stressful flows of life in all their power and unpredictability.

If you're physically grounded and supple, your flexibility will help you meet your changing (and often unstable) environment in resourceful ways. If you're mentally alert and adaptable, your intelligences and focus will help you think, plan, and plot your way through any opportunity or adversity. If you're emotionally awake and agile, your watery genius will help you bring a wealth of emotional energies to bear on any difficulty or delight you encounter. If you're spiritually aware and open to visions, dreams, and daydreams, your fiery strength will help you bring your far-ranging vision to every part of your life—from moments of great joy or sorrow to the most mundane of annoyances. And if you nurture balance between each of your elements and intelligences, your interior village will be resourced with all of your wisdom plus hundreds of thousands of years of ancestral wisdom, which means you'll have access to more strength, more intelligence, more emotional brilliance, and more vision than you'll ever need. When you're fully resourced and balanced, you won't have to run from stress, whether it's "bad stress" or "good stress." In fact, when you have skills, you may learn to embrace your stress responses as some of your most insightful teachers.

Maintaining your consciousness in this way may seem like a lot of work, but it actually takes less energy (and less money!) to live a conscious life than it does to run screaming from stress into avoidance, addictions, behavioral turmoil, dissociation, or stress-relieving distractions of every kind. Consciousness finds beauty and solace in what is, while distractions always need more and bigger and newer and different.

UNEARTHING THE INGENUITY OF
STRESS AND RESISTANCE

Stressed-out responses occur when we resist the flow of the moment. Though we've all learned to pathologize resistance (and run from stress), there's a deeper story flowing underneath these situations. I want to go back to the dictionary for a moment to look at the definition of the word "resistance," which also comes from the world of physics (and chemistry). Resistance is the ability to oppose, withstand, or strive against an action or a thing. For instance, a resistor in an electrical circuit interferes with and opposes the flow of electricity in order to turn it into heat or power, while a chemical resistor opposes the action of a corrosive agent (such as an acid) and protects substances from erosion or disintegration. In physics and chemistry, a resistor can create change, or it can act as a protection against change. Resistors have an almost alchemical ability to use their oppositional capacities to transform one thing into another.

This same quality exists in emotional resistance. In the chapter on addictions, I introduced the Buddhist saying, "Suffering is discomfort multiplied by resistance." This maxim has been used as a warning against resistance, and while examining your own resistance is a necessary step in your journey toward awareness, there's a deeper story at work here as well. If the act of resistance can take a simple discomfort and turn it into full-blown suffering, it means that resistance has a magical and alchemical ability to take an ordinary annoyance, an unsettling situation, or a change in plans, and use it to drop you into the very core of your issues. If you've learned to pathologize your resistance, or if your practice or your attitude asks you to omit resistance (and avoid suffering) in any of its forms, you may mistakenly miss out on your chance to become a true empathic genius. In your enforced and artificial calmness, you may actually lose your capacity to react and change, to access your intuition, to challenge yourself, and to uncover your deepest issues.

Baruch Spinoza's excellent adage, "Suffering ceases to be suffering as soon as we've formed a clear and precise picture of it," tells us that suffering is relieved only by staying *with* the suffering until insight is achieved. If you understand that resistance can magically drop you into suffering—and that this suffering, if honorably held, will lead directly to insight and healing (and the blessed third stage of initiation), then perhaps you'll learn to treat your resistance as a sacred movement that can transform even the most mundane situation or occurrence into a brilliant and soul-expanding opportunity for awakening and enlightenment.

Resistance is not the problem; it's actually a gift of emotional alchemy. If you can honor your resistance and turn consciously toward your suffering (and your stress responses), you'll become tremendously resourceful and useful in ways unimagined by those who strive for calm and unaffectedness at all costs. Your task is not to erase resistance, but to embrace it, to notice what you're resisting and why, to notice what you're stressing over (and unconsciously emphasizing) and why, and to understand why you've brought your soul to a dead stop and dropped yourself into the sacred territory of suffering. True awakening cannot come from slipcovering your soul and pathologizing your emotions or your emotional resistance; true awakening can only occur when you allow emotions, resistance, and suffering to touch, inform, and even seriously disrupt you. The only way out is through.

Your internal ability to embrace and work with the alchemical force of resistance will certainly increase your awareness, but it will also increase your capacity to bring healing to our culture. In the larger world, there are many things that *need* to be resisted and suffered consciously if we're going to gain the insight we need to survive as a species: racism, warmongering, brutality, ignorance, sexism, ageism, commercialism, the exploitation of the natural world and the third-world populace, the glorification of greed, the deterioration of the environment, the loss of childhood and elderhood, the separation of the sexes and the classes, and the empowerment of corporate structures at the expense of all living things. If you have the capacity to work with the alchemical magic of resistance, you can become not just a soul warrior in the depths of your own psyche but also a soul warrior and a conduit through which transformational human awareness, social justice, and societal healing can be made manifest in our waiting world.

28

Emotions Are Your Native Language

The Fine Art of a Life Well Lived

CURRENT UNDERSTANDING OF HUMAN evolution places the first appearance of modern humans at about 195,000 years ago, and while there is much argument about the beginnings of our acquisition of spoken language, current estimates trace it to somewhere between 40,000 and 50,000 years ago. During this time, humans evolved separately from other primates and created languages through which they could share their ideas about past, present, and future, and even the purely imaginal. We became able to pass on our knowledge, our training, our experience, our ideas, our dreams, and our fantasies—and our linguistic intelligence created the foundation for all human cultures that followed.

If you do the math on the estimates above, you'll notice that our pre-lingual period is three times longer than our current linguistic era. This doesn't mean that we spent 145,000 years as dimwits. If you spend any time with animals, you'll know that we clearly *communicated* before we had formal language; we just did it by expressing information through touch, gesture, stance, eye contact, playacting, vocalization, humor, and emotion.

We still do.

Humans are an incredibly empathic species, and for most of us, our reliance upon our nonverbal and preverbal skills far outweighs our reliance upon the spoken or written word. Our love of the tactile, visual, and musical arts, our love of nature and sensuality, our love of physical humor, our love of animals and babies—all of these access our empathic and prelingual communication skills. We were empaths first, and throughout our evolutionary history we used our empathic skills three times longer than we used language. It helps to remember this as you embark upon your own empathic journey. Emotions are your first language, they're your native language, and they carry with them as much brilliance and power (perhaps more?) as the human languages that sprang from them.

You *are* an empath, and as an empath, you're able to engage with emotions because you have the capacity to identify and welcome them as distinct and specific entities. This means that you have endless amounts of information at your disposal. You may get knocked down by some of your emotions, because the realm of water is an extremely lively and frequently turbulent place. But the glory is not in never falling; it's in using the vitality your emotions give you to rise every time you fall. Your empathic skills can't make you infallible, but they can make you more capable and resourceful, more able to work in the depths, and more able to live a brilliant, vigorous, and meaningful life. They'll give you the capacity to flow and meander; to stop in strange and unusual places; to experience peculiar, startling, or even troubling things; and to fully engage, in an open and questing way, with whatever you encounter.

When you have the resources you need to fully engage with your emotions, they may seem to intensify, but what's really happening is that your capacity for working with and identifying them is increasing—in the same way that your ability to identify and locate previously ignored bodily sensations will increase when you undertake a good exercise program. When you have more skills, your emotions may become more noticeable, and your emotional realm may become less clear. If so, congratulate yourself. This is a sign of a healthy water element!

If you've ever studied the ecology of real bodies of water, you'll recall that healthy lakes, streams, and oceans are never completely clear. Healthy lakes, for instance, should contain plenty of organic material (which can make them quite murky). There is even a name for this kind of lake: it's called a *eutrophic* or "good foods" lake. If a lake is crystal-clear, it may look nice, but it doesn't contain enough food to sustain life (clear lakes are called *oligotrophic* or "few foods" lakes). The healthiest lakes contain both eutrophic areas and oligotrophic areas, because too much organic matter (and not enough flow) can eventually choke out a lake, while crystal clarity is a sign of impending lake death. This same principle holds true in the waterways of your soul.

Your emotional realm should contain plenty of material (even murky material): your anger and fear should come forward when they need to; your sadness, grief, and depression should know that they are welcome; your jealousy and envy should be able to flow through you; your hatred, shame, joy, and contentment should have open access to your life; and all of your internal flows should be nurtured and encouraged. Consider again a healthy eutrophic lake: sometimes the lake is clear in areas; sometimes it has algal blooms to feed the fish and insects that in turn feed the lake; and sometimes (usually in the spring and fall) the lake will experience an upwelling, where the murk on the lake bottom will cycle upward and infuse the entire lake with food and organic material. When you nurture your internal waterways, this same lively cycling will occur inside you, because your emotions are vibrant entities that have their own reasons for arising, their own timetables for upwelling and clarity, and their own wisdom. This wisdom is hundreds of thousands of years old, and you'll never be able to capture all of it; however, as an empath, you can work with whatever your psyche presents to you.

When you work as an empath, you won't become superior or invincible; you'll simply become more able to work with your emotions, your body, your multiple intelligences, your eagle nature, and your interior village than the average person. Revel in this; it will actually make you more valuable to the world as it is. Your innate empathic skills will help you engage with deep questions, deep suffering, deep adventures, and deep connections to all living things.

EXPANDING SACRED SPACE: UNDERSTANDING EMOTION SHRINES

In each emotional territory, you learned to create sacred space by honoring emotions in yourself and others. As you continue in your empathic work, you may become more aware of the suffering around you and more involved in the often harrowing journeys of the people in your life. This is an important transition because it means that you're making the world around you safer for emotions and emotional awareness. However, it also means that your own emotional agility will be called upon more often, because some of the people you know may experience emotional turmoil that is unaddressable for any number of reasons (neurological imbalances, addiction, isolation, dissociation, traumatic residues, unwillingness to be well, attachment to unbalanced practices, and so forth). It can be very hard to stand by and watch someone repeat an emotional or traumatic feedback loop over and over again, and to know that there is currently nothing you can do to help them.

When people are heavily involved in trauma and turmoil (and don't want any help), they may seem to be trapped, but in many ways, they're performing heroic tasks in some of the deepest and darkest regions of the soul. If you can expand your concept of sacred space and see them as living shrines to those dark regions—as soul warriors still fighting in the trenches of resistance and suffering—you can sanctify their journeys and reframe your attitude toward them. If you can shift your perspective and honor the strength and courage of someone in turmoil, you can shift your behavior and your demeanor so that you don't add insult to injury by fretting over them or treating them as broken and disordered victims. If you can see them as living shrines and honor them as soul warriors, you'll lighten their load and contribute to their eventual healing. You can support yourself in this task by identifying their leading emotion in order to understand the gifts and challenges they carry and to discover what sort of shrine they are.

For instance, anger shrines, or people who struggle with persistent anger, rage, fury, apathy, shame, and hatred, carry the gifts and challenges of boundary-setting, honor, self-protection, and social justice. Sadness shrines, or people dealing with unmoving sadness and despair, carry the gifts and challenges of release, rejuvenation, and the honoring of loss. Grief shrines carry the sacred gifts and challenges of deep and transformative loss and the rituals of mourning. Fear shrines, or people dealing with persistent cycles of fear, anxiety, worry, confusion, panic, or terror, carry the gifts and challenges of instincts, intuition, action, and the journey to the blessed third stage of initiation. Envy and jealousy shrines carry the gifts and challenges of piercing sociological awareness, loyalty, and security.

Depression shrines carry the gifts and challenges of ingenious stagnation and the retrieval of the authentic self. And suicide shrines carry the sacred gifts and challenges of profound transformation, liberty, and rebirth. Each struggle, each trauma, each emotion, and each area of suffering holds gifts as well as challenges.

If you can treat people in turmoil as shrines and warriors on a quest for redemption in the depths of the soul, you can envision their struggle as sacred, rather than dropping yourself into despair about them. Though you may mean well, your concern about them (and your wish for an end to their suffering) could be misplaced because these people may be working in precisely the way they need to work right now. Remember that suffering can only cease when it has been fully experienced and understood. When you know this, your hopes for suffering people can become more precise—and more useful. Instead of praying for an end to their suffering (which is a vital part of any whole life), you can honor their struggle and pray for an increase in their clarity, strength, agility, and capacity to work in the depths. You can also model your own empathic skills for them if they are at all open for input.

You can't really know why people remain in their suffering or when they'll gain a clear and liberating understanding of it, but you can trust their innate capacity for change and healing by bowing to them silently and thanking them for holding their difficulties with such focus, and for being living shrines through which the troubles of the world can be revealed, comprehended, and resolved.

TENDING YOUR OWN SHRINE

You are also a living shrine—to consciousness, empathy, and flow. You should tend to yourself as a shrine and support your balance and agility with activities that bring all parts of you into play. Make time for art and music, feeling and thinking, relaxing and daydreaming, reading and study, exercise and dance, sensuality and comfort, rest and sound sleep, work and intensity, and plenty of laughter and play. Honor your multiple intelligences, your physical sensations, your spiritual visions, your emotional realities (and your need to complain!), and the village inside you. You are an irreplaceable living shrine through which emotions, thoughts, sensations, visions, dreams, and genius can flow into this world; you're an empath, a soul warrior, and a treasure.

Thank you for making this journey with me and for bringing your heart and soul to this work. Thank you for the honor of your presence and for making our world safer for empathy, emotions, and emotional people. My usual farewell phrase is "blessings and peace," but by now, you can handle more material than that, so I'll end with this: Blessings and anger, blessings and fear, blessings and contentment, blessings and deep sorrow, blessings and slaphappiness, blessings and envy, blessings and soaring joy, blessings and powerful grief, blessings and appropriate shame, blessings and ingenious depression, blessings and meaningful suffering, blessings and laughter that makes milk come shooting right out of your nose. Blessings and wholeness to you.

Acknowledgments

IT SEEMS THAT THERE'S an accepted flow to book acknowledgments, where spouses and families are last (but not least) to be thanked. That's silly.

My writing career couldn't have flourished without the support of Tino Plank, my husband, partner, editor, fellow survivor, fellow monkey, and best friend. Tino saw the talent and intensity in me when I was a single mom struggling in poverty, and he gave me the support and encouragement to write the books that were stacked up inside me. He introduced me to the men's movement, to Malidoma and Sobonfu Somé of the Dagara tribe, to the work of Robert Bly and James Hillman, and to Michael Meade. We read and wrote poetry together, studied Jung and the shadow, healed our childhood traumas, created my publishing and teaching careers, became soul warriors together, and left the New Age together. Tino has loved me through several unrelentingly dark nights of the soul and several gorgeous dawns; he is why I know for certain that love is not an emotion.

When I left my New Age career in 2003, I stepped off a cliff. The people (besides Tino) who carried me aloft and valued me even though I was a lapsed avatar are: my intense, loving, and fall-down funny son, Eli McLaren; my fierce friend and singing partner, Nancy Feehan; my sociology professor and writing partner, Tony Waters; sociologist, cult expert, and writing partner Janja Lalich; the original Tree of Laughing Tree, the late, great Pennie Austin-Wilson; lapsed yogi Mick Goodman; skeptic

Robert Carroll; skeptic Terry Sandbek and his wife, Sharon Billings; and my siblings, parents, and extended family.

In terms of the writing of this book, I thank Tami Simon of Sounds True, who knew even back in 1999 that I didn't belong in the New Age. It took me a while to catch on, but thanks go to Tami for being right and for giving me back my career. Thanks also to the love of Tami's life, Julie Kramer, who helped me articulate my calling as a teacher and as a social scientist.

Haven Iverson took on this gigantic manuscript and edited it so devotedly, so intricately, and with such clarity that she made me bring up my game and focus on the book with new eyes. At Sounds True, Buddhist geek Vince Horn produced the audio workshop for this book, and we had a great time. At Sounds True, I also thank Kelly Notaras, Jaime Schwalb, Aron Arnold (*excellent* swear words), Matt Licata, Anna Frick, Marjorie Woodall, Allegra Huston, and Shelly Rosen for all their support and humor.

I'm also grateful for the screamingly funny people who sing with me every week in our group, St. Pink's Infirmary: Judy, Judith, Linda, Eden, Shayne, Nancy, Mary, Sandy, Danielle, Candace, Nefera, and sometimes Eli. I'm happy to call you my friends.

And of course, I thank *you* for reading this book. Writing is a relationship and a conversation; I'm honored that you've taken the time to listen, to reflect, and to feel your way through this book. Thank you!

Notes

1. There is also some preliminary evidence suggesting that people on the autism spectrum may have deficient mirror neurons, which could mean that they have difficulties reading the thoughts and emotions of others and, therefore, have a hard time becoming normatively socialized.

   However, in 2007, I had the great good fortune to work with a group of autistic college students, and while I assumed that my excessive reliance upon my mirror neurons placed me at the opposite end of the autism spectrum, I actually found that the autistics and I shared the feeling that humans were a chaotic and confusing species. I also found that the way I liked to behave when I was alone—quiet, calm, and extremely honest about the foibles of myself and others—was also the preferred way of being among many of my autistic friends. Although many people believe that autistics are blind to human behaviors, my hypothesis is that many people on the autism spectrum may sense those behaviors too acutely and in too many different ways and are therefore dealing with painfully disorganized sensory overload.

2. The chronicle of my six-year transition away from my New Age career and metaphysical thinking, *Missing the Solstice ~ and ~ Discovering the World*, is available through my website: karlamclaren.com.

3. K. Christoff, et al., "Experience Sampling During fMRI Reveals Default Network and Executive System Contributions to Mind Wandering," *Proceedings of the National Academy of Sciences* 106, no. 21 (2009): 8719-8724.

4. Actually, Spinoza wrote that "Emotion, which is suffering, ceases to be suffering as soon as we form a clear and precise picture of it." But emotion isn't suffering. So he was half right.

5. Though I am touting tribal initiations as positive things in the context of this discussion, I don't mean to glibly ignore the fact that some tribes perform ritual male and female circumcision and other horrors. Humans are primates, and all primates are violent and altruistic, delightful and terrible; it's not as if tribal humans are somehow better than modern humans. We're all just humans; every one of us embodies all of the glory and all of the horror inherent to our species. What we chose to do with our glory and our horror is up to each one of us.

6. *Your One-Year Old; Your Two-Year Old;* etc. Louise Bates Ames and Frances Ilg wrote a series of books about the developmental stages of children between the ages of one and fourteen. These books can help survivors of childhood trauma understand what was occurring developmentally during their trauma so that they can begin to understand their traumatic behaviors in the present day and separate from them in healthy ways.

7. If you're concerned about grounding seemingly unpleasant emotions into the earth, consider this: ours is a planet built by volcanic eruptions, ice ages, deluges, hurricanes, lighting strikes, and continent-splitting earthquakes. Your crankiness, your fear, your grief, your anger—even your homicidal or suicidal feelings—are nothing compared to the primordial forces that shape our planet. You are an earthling; nothing you feel is alien or unwanted, and nothing you feel is unwelcome on our living planet.

8. No one had questioned the efficacy of positive affirmations until psychologist Joanne Wood at the University of Waterloo and her colleagues put the idea to the test. What they found and reported (in the July 2009 issue of *Psychological Science*) is that positive affirmations made people with low self-esteem feel worse about themselves and that affirmations had only a moderate positive effect on people who already had high self-esteem. The researchers also found that subjects who were allowed to think good and bad thoughts about themselves felt better than ones who were told to enforce positive thoughts at all times. As a social scientist and an empath, I say: *Hah!*

9. See Dr. Jill Bolte Taylor's account of the left-hemisphere stroke that activated in her a feeling of spiritual oneness in her book, *My Stroke of Insight* (New York: Viking, 2007).

10. E. A. Holmes, et al., "Can Playing the Computer Game 'Tetris' Reduce the Build-up of Flashbacks for Trauma? A Proposal from Cognitive Science," *PLoS ONE* 4, no. 1 (2009).

11. The linguistic history of panic and terror are interesting. Panic comes from the Greek god Pan, who was a shepherd, among other things. When sheep would startle at nothing and scatter for the hills, the early Greeks thought Pan was scaring them for fun. These scatterings were called "Panic terrors." As it is with people who use the word "guilt" when they're feeling shame, it's fascinating that "terror" moved out of our lexicon and was replaced by "panic." The emotional state is terror, but we prefer to hang out in the fiery realm of the gods (with Pan) when terror comes forward!

12. J. H. Fowler and N. A. Christakis, "The Dynamic Spread of Happiness in a Large Social Network: Longitudinal Analysis over 20 Years in the Framingham Heart Study," *British Medical Journal* 337 (December 2008): 12338.

Further Resources

EMOTIONS AND EMPATHY

Animals in Translation: Using the Mysteries of Autism to Decode Animal Behavior. (2005). Temple Grandin. New York: Scribner.

Descartes' Error: Emotion, Reason, and the Human Brain. (1995). Antonio Damasio. New York: Picador.

Emotion: The Science of Sentiment. (2002). Dylan Evans. New York: Oxford University Press.

Emotional Intelligence: Why It Can Matter More Than IQ. (2006 10th Anniversary Edition). Daniel Goleman.

Happiness: The Science behind Your Smile. (2006). Daniel Nettle. New York: Oxford University Press.

Mirroring People: The New Science of How We Connect with Others. (2008). Marco Iacoboni. New York: Farrar, Straus, and Giroux.

Obedience to Authority: The Unique Experiment That Challenged Human Nature (1974). Stanley Milgram. New York: Harper & Row.

Stigma: Notes on the Management of Spoiled Identity. (1963). Erving Goffman. New York: Simon & Schuster.

Suicide: A Study in Sociology. (1951). Emile Durkheim. New York: Free Press.

The Dangerous Passion: Why Jealousy is as Necessary as Love and Sex. (2000).
David M. Buss. New York: The Free Press.

The Lucifer Effect: Understanding How Good People Turn Evil. (2007). Philip
Zimbardo. New York: Random House.

The Managed Heart: Commercialization of Human Feeling. (2003). Arlie
Hochschild. Berkeley, CA: University of California Press.

Wishcraft: How to Get What You Really Want. (2003). Barbara Sher and
Annie Gottleib. New York: Ballantine.

TRAUMA HEALING

Healing Trauma. (1999). Peter Levine. Audiotapes. Boulder, CO: Sounds
True.

It Won't Hurt Forever: Guiding Your Child Through Trauma. (2001). Peter
Levine. Audiotapes. Boulder, CO: Sounds True.

Take Back Your Life: Recovering from Cults and Abusive Relationships. (2006).
Janja Lalich & Madeleine Tobias. Berkeley, CA: Bay Tree Publishing.

The Gift of Fear: Survival Signals that Protect Us from Violence. (1999). Gavin
de Becker. New York: Dell.

Waking the Tiger: Healing Trauma. (1997). Peter Levine. Berkeley, CA:
North Atlantic.

UNDERSTANDING THE SOCIAL WORLD

Bounded Choice: True Believers and Charismatic Cults. (2004). Janja Lalich.
Berkeley, CA: University of California Press.

Context Is Everything: The Nature of Memory. (2000). Susan Engel. New
York: W.H. Freeman.

*Family: The Making of an Idea, and Institution, and a Controversy in
American Culture.* (1999). Betty Farrell. Boulder, CO: Westview Press.

Inside Social Life: Readings in Sociological Psychology and Microsociology.
(2004). Spencer Cahill, Ed. Los Angeles, CA: Roxbury.

Opinions and Social Pressure. (1955). Solomon Asch. New York: Freeman

Outliers: The Story of Success. (2008). Malcolm Gladwell. New York: Little,
Brown & Company

The Cultural Study of Work. (2003). Edited by Douglas Harper and Helene Lawson. Lanham, MD: Rowman & Littlefield.

The Spirit Catches You and You Fall Down: A Hmong Child, Her American Doctors, and the Collision of Two Cultures. (1997). Anne Fadiman. New York: Farrar, Straus and Giroux.

THE BRAIN AND NEUROSCIENCE

Descartes' Error: Emotion, Reason, and the Human Brain. (1995). Antonio Damasio. New York: Picador.

How We Decide. (2009). Jonah Lehrer. New York: Houghton Mifflin.

How We Know What Isn't So: The Fallibility of Human Reason in Everyday Life. (1993). Thomas Gilovich. New York: Free Press

Kluge: The Haphazard Construction of the Human Mind. (2008). Gary Marcus. New York: Houghton Mifflin.

Mistakes Were Made (But Not by Me): Why We Justify Foolish Beliefs, Bad Decisions, and Hurtful Acts. (2008). Carol Tavris and Elliot Aronson. New York: Harcourt.

My Stroke of Insight: A Brain Scientist's Personal Journey. (2008). Jill Bolte Taylor. New York: Viking.

On Being Certain: Believing You Are Right Even When You're Not. (2008). Robert Burton. New York: St. Martin's Press.

Phantoms in the Brain: Probing the Mysteries of the Human Mind (1998). V.I. Ramachandran and Sandra Blakeslee. New York: Quill William Morrow.

Predictably Irrational: The Hidden Forces That Shape Our Decisions. (2008). Dan Ariely. New York: HarperCollins.

The Body Has a Mind of Its Own. (2008). Sandra Blakeslee and Matthew Blakeslee. New York: Random House.

Why We Believe What We Believe: Uncovering Our Biological Need for Meaning, Spirituality, and Truth. (2006). Andrew Newberg. New York: Free Press.

SHADOW WORK, MYTHOLOGY, AND TRIBAL WISDOM

A Little Book on the Human Shadow. (1988). Robert Bly. SanFrancisco: HarperSanFrancisco.

Meeting Your Shadow: The Hidden Power of the Dark Side of Human Nature. (1991). Edited by Connie Zweig and Jeremiah Abrams. New York: Tarcher/Putnam.

Owning Your Own Shadow. (1993). Robert Johnson. San Francisco: HarperSanFrancisco.

Ritual: Power, Healing, and Community. (1993). Malidoma Somé. Portland, OR: Swan Raven.

The Essential Jung. (1983). Edited by Anthony Storr. New York: MJF Books.

The Essential Rumi. (1995). Coleman Barks. San Francisco: HarperSanFrancisco.

The Healing Wisdom of Africa. (1999). Malidoma Somé. New York: Viking.

The Rag and Bone Shop of the Heart: Poems for Men. (1992). Edited by Robert Bly, James Hillman, and Michale Meade. New York: HarperCollins.

The Soul's Code: In Search of Character and Calling. (1996). James Hillman: New York: Random House.

The Water of Life: Initiation and Tempering of the Soul. (2006). Michael Meade. Seattle: GreenFire Press.

Welcoming Spirit Home. (1999). Sobonfu Somé. Novato, CA: New World Library.

ADVENTURES FOR YOUR MULTIPLE INTELLIGENCES

Bonk: The Curious Coupling of Science and Sex (2009). Mary Roach. New York: W.W. Norton.

Faith, Madness, and Spontaneous Human Combustion: What Immunology Can Teach Us About Self-Perception. (2003). Gerald Callahan. New York: Berkley Books.

How We Die: Reflections on Life's Final Chapter. (1995). Sherwin Nuland. New York: Vintage.

Take a Nap! Change Your Life. (2006). Sara Mednick. New York: Workman.

The Man Who Loved Only Numbers: The Story of Paul Erdös and the Search for Mathematical Truth. (1999). Paul Hoffman. New York: Hyperion.

The Promise of Sleep: A Pioneer in Sleep Medicine Explores the Vital Connection Between Health, Happiness, and a Good Night's Sleep. (2000). William Dement. New York: Dell.

Your Inner Fish: A Journey into the 3.5-Billion-Year History of the Human Body. (2009). Neil Shubin. New York: Pantheon.

Index

405

About the Author

KARLA MCLAREN is an award-winning author and empath whose ground-breaking approach to the emotions has taken her through the healing of her own childhood trauma into an empathic healing career, and now into the study of sociology, neurology, and cognitive and social psychology.

Karla has taught thousands of people through her four books and five audio-learning sets, and at such venues as the Omega Institute, Naropa University, and the Institute of Noetic Sciences. Additionally, as a prison arts educator with the William James Foundation, she has utilized singing, drumming, and drama to help men in maximum security prisons explore and heal long-held emotional traumas.

In her academic career in sociology and social science, Karla served as a researcher and editor on the books *When Killing Is a Crime* and *Take Back Your Life: Recovering from Cults and Abusive Relationships*. She has recently completed an academic study on the stigmatization of GLBT (gay, lesbian, bisexual, and transgender) youth in fundamentalist religions.

Karla lives in California with her husband and son, and is choral director and comic relief for St. Pink's Infirmary. Her website is karlamclaren.com.

About Sounds True

Sounds True was founded in 1985 with a clear vision: to disseminate spiritual wisdom. Located in Boulder, Colorado, Sounds True publishes teaching programs that are designed to educate, uplift, and inspire. We work with many of the leading spiritual teachers, thinkers, healers, and visionary artists of our time.

To receive a free catalog of tools and teachings for personal and spiritual transformation, please visit soundstrue.com, call toll-free 800-333-9185, or write to us at the address below.

PO Box 8010
Boulder, CO 80306